THE MOUNTAIN MEN
and the Fur Trade of the Far West
IX

OTHER PUBLICATIONS BY LEROY R. HAFEN –

1926 – *The Overland Mail, 1849-1869*
1927 – editor, *History of Colorado*, 3 volumes
1931 – *Broken Hand: the Life of Thomas Fitzpatrick* (with W. J. Ghent)
1932 – editor, *Villard's Past and Present of the Pike's Peak Region*
1933 – *Colorado, the Story of a Western Commonwealth*
1938 – *Fort Laramie and the Pageant of the West* (with F. M. Young)
1941 – *Western America* (with C. C. Rister) ; revised, 1950, 1970
1941-1942 – editor, *Southwest Historical Series*, volumes IX, X, XI
1943 – *Colorado: a Story of the State and its People* (with Ann W. Hafen)
1948 – *Colorado and its People*, 2 volumes
1950 – editor, *Ruxton of the Rockies*
1951 – editor, *Ruxton's Life in the Far West*
1953 – *The Colorado Story* (with Ann W. Hafen)
1924-1954 – editor, *The Colorado Magazine*
1954 – *The Old Spanish Trail* (with Ann W. Hafen)
1954-1962 – editor, *The Far West and Rockies Series*, 15 volumes (with Ann W. Hafen)
1960 – *Handcarts to Zion* (with Ann W. Hafen)
1962 – compiler and editor, *The Hafen Families of Utah*
1965-1972 – *Mountain Men and Fur Trade of the Far West*, vols. 1-9
1966 – *Our State: Colorado – A History of Progress* (with Ann W. Hafen)

Also contributions to numerous other publications and journals. For further detail see *LeRoy R. and Ann W. Hafen, their writings and their notable collection of Americana given to Brigham Young University Library* (1962, 109 pages)

"Trapping Beaver" from a Painting by Alfred Jacob Miller
Courtesy of The Walters Art Gallery, Baltimore, Maryland.

THE MOUNTAIN MEN
and the Fur Trade
of the Far West

biographical sketches of the participants
by scholars of the subject
and with introductions by the editor

under the editorial supervision of

LeRoy R. Hafen

State Historian of Colorado, Emeritus
Professor of History, Brigham Young University

Volume IX

THE ARTHUR H. CLARK COMPANY
Glendale, California
1972

To the Memory of
my Beloved Wife and Collaborator

ANN WOODBURY HAFEN

Contents

Illustrations

For the map of the "Fur Country of the Far West,"
see the first volume of this series, at page 20.

Editor's Note and Acknowledgment

Since this Mountain Men Series was launched at the Western History Association Conference at Denver, nine years have produced nine volumes of biographical sketches. Lists of contributors and of biographees will be given in volume ten, preceding the extensive general index for the Series.

It has been a remarkable cooperative effort with eighty-four contributors writing 292 sketches. The work is not definitive; in fact it could hardly be, for the list might be extended almost indefinitely. Noticeably missing are some men on whom material is readily available in other published volumes – such men as Zenas Leonard, Pauline Weaver, John J. Astor, Alexander Henry, J. C. Luttig, and others. Nevertheless, the sketches, collectively, constitute a reference work of enduring value.

Composed by so many persons, the articles vary greatly in style and quality, but this, with original approaches and treatments, has largely eliminated monotony. The two most prolific contributors are Dr. Harvey L. Carter and Mrs. Janet Lecompte, both of Colorado Springs – each with over thirty sketches. These two generous friends match the quantity of their writing with the highest quality.

The publishers have been most thoughtful and cooperative. They have assembled most of the 126 portraits and 45 other illustrations, and have done various other tasks that have helped to make the editor's work enjoyable.

Through this project I have come in contact with numerous persons, both scholars and history buffs, who are keenly interested in Mountain Men and their period. These persons have cooperated willingly and to the enrichment of the project; and my own life has been greatly enriched through acquaintance with each of these engaging personalities. I appreciate these fine friends — old-time acquaintances and the newly found.

My thanks to all!

LeRoy R. Hafen

Provo, Utah

Publisher's Preface

In this, the ninth volume of the Mountain Men Series, will be found forty-one articles containing biographical sketches of forty-three more of the men engaged in the trans-Mississippi fur trade of the first half of the nineteenth century.

The sketches in this volume, as in the first eight, are arranged alphabetically under the surname of the subject person. This same format has been used in all volumes of the Series.

With this the ninth volume the text material of the Series comes to a conclusion. The tenth and final volume of the set will provide a guide to the biographies, authors and illustrations, and a complete index to the text material of the biographical sketches and the introductory monograph. With this index the student of the Fur Trade period will be provided an indispensable reference tool for his research.

The reader is referred to the summary history of the fur trade, presented in the first section of volume I, for the general background history and the contribution of the fur men in advancing the frontier. Likewise, for the area concerned, the large map which appears at page 20 of volume I, will be of value in connection with the text of all volumes.

Again we express sincere thanks to the scholars of the fur trade era, for their cooperation in contributing the valuable biographies presented in this work.

Gratitude is also extended to all those who have assisted in furnishing copy for the portraits and illustrations. These persons include the authors of the articles, the personnel of several historical societies and other archives of Western materials, and others as indicated in the captions.

AUGUSTE PIERRE CHOUTEAU
From Thomas James, *Three Years among
the Indians and Mexicans,* 1916.

PIERRE CHOUTEAU, JUNIOR
From J. Thomas Scharf, *History
of St. Louis,* 1883.

RAMSAY CROOKS
From H. M. Chittenden, *American Fur Trade*, 1935.

EDWARD DE MORIN
Courtesy of Nebraska State
Historical Society, Lincoln.

JOHN B. DIDIER
Courtesy of Nebraska State
Historical Society, Lincoln.

JAMES DOUGLAS
Courtesy of the Provincial Archives,
Victoria, British Columbia.

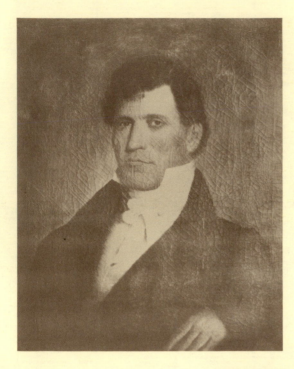

RUSSEL FARNHAM
Courtesy of Missouri Historical
Society, St. Louis.

RICHARD GRANT
Courtesy of Idaho State
Historical Society, Boise.

WILLIAM T. HAMILTON
Courtesy of Montana
    Historical Society, Helena.

ROBERT MELDRUM
Courtesy of Montana Historical
Society, Helena, from a photo by
Cheney's Art Gallery, Oregon City.

DAVID MERIWETHER
Courtesy of the Museum of
New Mexico, Santa Fe.

PIERRE DIDIER PAPIN
Courtesy of South Dakota State
Historical Society, Pierre.

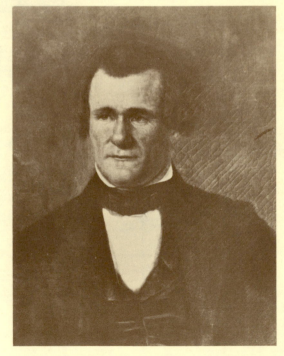

SIMON PLAMONDON
Courtesy of Harriet D. Munnick,
West Linn, Oregon.

JOHN F. A. SANFORD
Courtesy of South Dakota State Historical
Society, Pierre. From its *Collections* vol. 9.

ROBERT STUART
A daguerreotype. From P. A. Rollins
Discovery of the Oregon Trail, 1935.
Courtesy of Edward Eberstadt & Sons.

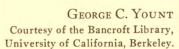

GEORGE C. YOUNT
Courtesy of the Bancroft Library,
University of California, Berkeley.

The Mountain Men

Joseph Bissonet, dit Bijou

by LeRoy R. Hafen
Brigham Young University

Joseph Bissonet, son of Louis Bissonet and Genevieve (Routier) Bissonet, was born in St. Louis, June 15, 1778.[1] His father died and his mother re-married, the stepfather being named Bijou. Joseph and his older brother Louis thereafter frequently used the name Bijou.[2]

Joseph appears in the Pierre Chouteau Sr. ledger accounts from July 26, 1806, to December 28, 1807, for goods, provisions, doctor's fees, merchandise in small amounts (apparently for personal use) totaling $185.77½ (p. 133). He is charged for sundry merchandise bought between January 1808 and May 1811 in amounts totaling $544.44; and paid for in part *"par un compte d'ouvrage fourni"* and paid in full by July 1811 (p. 141).[3]

In the Manuel Lisa fur trade venture up the Missouri River in the spring of 1812, Joseph Bissonet and his brother Louis were both listed as members of the expedition.[4] Louis is referred to several times in Luttig's journal – pages 34, 54, 56, 79, 104, 105, 109 – but the younger brother, Joseph, is not mentioned individually, except for his enlistment.

---

1 Collet's Cathedral Records Index (data kindly supplied by Mrs. Janet Lecompte).

2 In the Edwin James account of the Major Long Expedition of 1820 this explanation is given: "Joseph Bijeau [Bijou] (or Bessonet, which is his hereditary name, the former having been derived from a second marriage of his mother) had performed in a very adequate and faithful manner the service of guide. . ." Reuben G. Thwaites, *Early Western Travels* (Cleveland, 1905), XVI, p. 58. See also John C. Luttig, *Journal of a Fur Trading Expedition on the Upper Missouri in 1812-1813,* edited by Stella M. Drumm (New York, 1964), 148-49, 158.

3 These accounts were found at the Missouri Historical Society, St. Louis, by Mrs. Lecompte in December 1970, and generously copied out for me. The name in this account is listed as Joseph Lacroix Bissonette.   4 Luttig, *op. cit.,* 158.

In 1815 Joseph joined the well-known trapping and trading venture of A. P. Chouteau and Jules DeMun into the Southwest. The adventures and misfortunes of the expedition have been adequately recounted in other biographical sketches in this present Series and need not be repeated here. The party was captured on the Arkansas River and taken to Santa Fe, where the members were imprisoned for forty-eight days. Following their release and return to Missouri some members made a "Statement and Proof in the Case of Chouteau and Demun of their loss and treatment by the Spaniards." It was signed before the Justice of the Peace in the County of St. Louis, Territory of Missouri, Sept. 25, 1817, by Joseph Bissonet, Etienne Provost, and nine others, each signing by an "x".[5]

During the two years of trapping and trading the members of the party ranged widely, as is indicated by the information given by Bissonet to members of the Major Long Expedition of 1820. In fact, this service with Chouteau and DeMun was only part of the time Bissonet had spent on the upper waters of the Arkansas and Platte rivers. While serving Major Long in 1820 he gave a full account of the Chouteau-DeMun adventures of 1815-17. In describing Bissonet's service to the Long Party, Dr. Edwin James, botanist of the expedition, wrote of him:

> He had formerly been resident in the western wilds in the capacity of hunter and trapper during the greater part of six years.
> He had traversed the country lying between the north fork of the Platte and the Arkansas in almost every direction. His pursuits often led him within the Rocky Mountains, where the beaver are particularly abundant. He appears possessed not only of considerable acuteness of observation but of a degree of candour and veracity which gives credibility to his accounts and descriptions.[6]

Major Long's exploring party set out from Engineer

---

[5] Found in *Annals of Congress,* 15 Cong., 1 sess., vol. 2, pp. 1957-58.
[6] James account of the Long Expedition, in *Early Western Travels,* XVI, pp. 58-59.

Cantonment, near Council Bluffs on the Missouri River, June 6, 1820, with twenty men. A week later at the Pawnee Republic village on the Loupe Fork of the Platte River, the Major tried to employ a guide and interpreter to accompany the party on the farther journey.

> It was with great difficulty [writes Captain John R. Bell, official journalist of the expedition], the Commanding Officer could engage two Frenchmen, traders residing with the Indians, to accompany our party as far as the Arkansas river – liberal offers of reward had no effect and it was not until he threatened to report them to the government and have them removed from the Villages, that they agreed to go. Mr. Bijeau [Bijou, or Bissonet] was hired as Indian interpreter and Guide and Mr. Ladeau [Abraham Ledoux – see his sketch in volume III] as Pawnee interpreter.[7]
>
> Each was paid one dollar per day.[8]

Dr. Edwin James, of the expedition, wrote:

> Both were Frenchmen, residing permanently among the Pawnees, and had been repeatedly on the headwaters of the Platte and Arkansa, for the purpose of hunting and trapping beaver. Bijeau [Bissonet] was partially acquainted with several Indian languages; in particular that of the Crow nation, which is extensively understood by the Western tribes, and, by frequent intercourse with the savages he had gained a complete knowledge of the language of signs, universally current among them.[9]

Bissonet was to guide Major Long up the Platte to the mountains, south to the Arkansas, and down that river eastward. Enroute he gave the major information regarding geography of the region, Indian signs, customs, etc.

Having arrived at the forks of the Platte River, Bissonet described to Major Long the source of the North Platte, which was in a "circumscribed valley within the mountains called the Bull-pen."[10] This was the beautiful mountain-

---

[7] *The Journal of Captain John R. Bell, Official Journalist of the Stephen H. Long Expedition to the Rocky Mountains, 1820,* ed. by Harlin M. Fuller and LeRoy R. Hafen (Glendale, Calif., 1957), 122-23.   [8] *Ibid.,* 104.

[9] *Early Western Travels,* XV, p. 220. See also Bell's *Journal,* 212.

[10] *Early Western Travels,* XV, p. 235.

encircled North Park, Colorado, farther west than the Long party was to penetrate.

On June 28th the party came to an Indian fortified camp on the South Platte near the site of present Sterling, Colorado. Captain Bell writes:

> On examining the Indian fortified camp last evening, there was found three small sticks each about 6 feet long, peeled of the bark, on each of them was fastened three leather thongs at the distance of 6 inches apart commencing from the small ends of the sticks. There was also found 16 buffalo skulls, fifteen of them arranged forming the circumference of a circle, the other was placed in the centre, on which was painted 30 black stripes & a small half circle. These were explained to us by our Guide & interpreter, Bijeau as follows – The stripes and marks on the buffalo skull, and the arrangement of them, signify that the place was last occupied by a war party of the Pawnee Loups returning from the Spanish frontier – the sticks, that they had taken 3 scalps.[11]

Bissonet told the party of the boiling springs – *Fontaine qui Bouille* – and guided some of the men to them. Captain Bell wrote:

> It is a custom with the wandering bands of Indians, that travell this region of country, when passing these springs, to make offerings to the Great Spirit, by casting ornaments of beads, shells, etc. into them, attended with a sort of ceremony or religious form. Some of these articles of sacrifice was obtained by Lieut. Swift from the springs & brought in. Bijeau informs us that french traders when in this country, examine these springs & take from them articles thus religiously deposited by the nations and trade them off to the same people again for skins. Dr. Say employed in obtaining from the interpreters information relative to the Indian manners, habits, & customs.[12]

South of Pike's Peak Bissonet pointed out the spot where he and others of the Chouteau-DeMun party had been captured by the Spaniards from New Mexico in 1817.[13]

When Long divided his party on the Arkansas River, Bissonet and Ledoux accompanied the detachment under

---

[11] Bell, *op. cit.*, 136-37.   [12] *Ibid.*, 166.   [13] *Early Western Travels*, XV, p. 308.

Captain Bell. They had completed their assignment as guides and interpreters and were eager to cross country and return to their trading at the Pawnee villages. Bell records:

> We sepparated from these men with feelings of regret, being truly sensible of the important services they had rendered as guides and interpreters. In our interviews with the savages Bijeau was all important, from having spent the greater part of his life with Indians, he was well acquainted with their general disposition, and the best pollicy to be pursued with them — faithful as our interpreter, and I believe of the strictest truth and veracity. May they have a safe and pleasant journey to their friends and residence of their choice, and success in trade & avocations.[14]

Dr. Say also had high praise: "We cannot take leave of them without expressing our entire approbation of their conduct and deportment, during our arduous journey; Bijeau, particularly, was faithful, active, etc."[15] Before leaving the Bell party, Bissonet drew a map to guide them on the farther journey.[16]

Of the subsequent career of Joseph Bissonet little is known. In the Pierre Chouteau ledgers in the Missouri Historical Society Library, St. Louis, a few fugitive entries are found. In December 1822, he purchased merchandise for trade amounting to $205 (page 8 of Ledger D). On November 10, 1827, he is listed among hopeless debtors as owing $7.50 (Ledger O, p. 330). On March 20, 1828, Joseph's wife is charged with $2 in cash and $8 in merchandise, and on June 9, 1828, he is credited "for made up work," $10. On May 8, 1828, this entry: "paid Julia [presumably his wife] for you $5." Some other petty items are also listed in Ledger P on January 28, March 19, and May 5, 1829. Similar petty items are recorded in Ledger R from May 28, 1830, through November, 1831, including listing of "Mrs. Joseph Bissonnet," "Brazille Bissonet," and "J. Bissonet Jr."[17]

---

14 Bell's *Journal*, 217.   15 *Early Western Travels*, XVI, p. 226.   16 *Ibid.*, 255.
17 These items were found and graciously supplied by Mrs. Lecompte.

Accounts in Ledgers EE and HH record larger transactions with "J. Bissonette" in 1841, 1842, and 1846. The item in Ledger EE, page 193, is: "1841, May 9 Paid P. D. Papin's dft to J. Bissonette $580"; and the one in Ledger HH, p. 226, is: "April 18, 1846, U M O 1845 J. Bissonette for balance of wages, $374.75." These undoubtedly refer to the Joseph Bissonette, prominent trader at Fort Laramie whose biography appears in volume IV, pp. 49-60, of this Series, and who was a nephew of Joseph Bissonet *dit* Bijou, the subject of the present sketch.

In Stella Drumm's biographical account of Louis Bissonet *dit* Bijou she writes that, when Louis died in 1836, one of his heirs was his brother Joseph Bissonet, then living in Mexico (probably New Mexico).[18] Whether or not Joseph Bissonet *dit* Bijou returned to Missouri has not been determined, nor have we found the date or place of his death.

18 Luttig, *op. cit.*, 149.

Lemuel Carpenter

by Iris Higbie Wilson
University of San Diego

The record of Lemuel Carpenter's activities as a Mountain Man is slight. Indeed there is only one instance of his known participation in a fur-trading expedition. Nevertheless, his story deserves telling for several reasons. First, he followed a typical Mountain Man pattern – a native of Kentucky, a sometime resident of Missouri, and a "foreigner" in Santa Fe. Second, he arrived in California with other fur traders from New Mexico, having traveled the Gila Route in 1831-1832.[1] Third, upon settling in the Los Angeles area, he became one of the unique, well-respected "yanqui rancheros" who narrowed the gap separating Anglo Americans and native Californios.[2] Lastly, although following the same path as a number of ex-Mountain Men who achieved notable success in California,[3] Lemuel Carpenter ended his life on a totally different note – he failed. Ironically, the one enduring memory of him lies in a coldly statistical California Supreme Court case entitled *Nieto vs. Carpenter,*[4] a landmark decision finally handed down in favor of defendant Carpenter. It was a hollow victory, though, since just a few days earlier financial pressures had driven him to put a bullet through his head.[5]

---

[1] J. J. Warner, "Reminiscences of Early California, 1831 to 1846," in Historical Society of Southern California *Annual Publications,* VII (1908), 190; Hubert Howe Bancroft, *History of California,* III (San Francisco, 1886), 388; Robert Glass Cleland, *Cattle on a Thousand Hills* (San Marino, 1951), 113.

[2] Major Horace Bell, *On the Old West Coast,* ed. by Lanier Bartlett (New York, 1930), 10-12; Cleland, *op. cit.,* 113.

[3] For example William Wolfskill, Isaac Williams, John Rowland, William Workman, and Benjamin D. Wilson.

[4] 7 Cal. 527 (1857); 21 Cal. 455 (1863). I am grateful to my husband, Paul D. Engstrand, for briefing these lengthy decisions.

Lemuel Carpenter is something of an enigma. No diary or personal letters are available for glimpses into his thoughts or feelings. Although one contemporary characterizes him as "of the most honorable standing, respected by all who knew him," [6] further descriptions are lacking.[7] Some facts, however, provide a thread of continuity. He was born in Shelby County, Kentucky, in 1807 and moved with his father to Clay County, Missouri, in 1815.[8] Like so many young men of the period, Carpenter accompanied a trading caravan to Santa Fe – the second one of the year 1831 – and reached the New Mexican capital in early summer.[9] He may have joined one of the trapping expeditions working out of the area in 1831-1832 or possibly tried his luck in one of the regional mines. Whatever the result of his experience in the Southwest, Carpenter took out a passport on October 6, 1832, to go to the "Internal States," [10] which could have

[5] Carpenter's obituary in the *Southern Vineyard,* November 19, 1859, explained that "expenses and difficulties brought upon him by this suit, augmented by his unaptness to manage the intricacies of the law and absorption of principal by interest, reduced him to a condition that prompted him to raise his hand against himself."

[6] Bell, *op. cit.,* 10.

[7] The few references to Carpenter are divided almost equally between "Lemuel" and "Samuel." His signature caused his name to be picked up by others as Samuel and apparently he was even called Samuel by some. His claim to Rancho Santa Gertrudes (*Samuel Carpenter, Claimant, vs. The United States, Defendant,* Case No. 339 [194 Southern District], The Bancroft Library, Berkeley, California) contains the declaration by Abel Stearns that "Lemuel Carpenter and Samuel Carpenter are the same person."

[8] *Southern Vineyard,* Nov. 19, 1859. The California Census of 1852, III, p. 72 (typescript copied under the direction of the Genealogical Records Committee Daughters of the American Revolution of California, 1934, California State Library, Sacramento), gives Carpenter's age as 44, whereas the Los Angeles Census of 1836 (J. Gregg Layne, "The First Census of the Los Angeles District, *Historical Society of Southern California Quarterly,* XVIII [June, 1936], 99ff), lists him as 24, or presumably born in 1812. Bancroft, in his Pioneer Register and Index (*History of California,* II, p. 742), has Carpenter as 22 in 1836 and 28 in 1840.

[9] J. Albert Wilson, *History of Los Angeles County* (Oakland, 1880), 35; Harris Newmark, *Sixty Years in Southern California,* ed. by Maurice H. and Marco R. Newmark (Boston, 1930), 180.

[10] Passport no. 102 issued October 6, 1832, to Lemuel Carpenter in book of passports issued in Santa Fe, 1828-1836, Ritch Papers, no. 108, Huntington Library, San Marino, California. Others receiving passports at the same time were "José Paulding, Guillermo Cord, Cyues Alejandro. Guillermo Fesh, Daniel Sell, Gesardr Hope."

meant Sonora, Chihuahua, or the Californias.

Traveling the Gila River route in the company of Cyrus Alexander, William Chard, Joseph Paulding, Daniel Sill, and perhaps others, Carpenter entered southern California in January, 1833. Information about this trip is sketchy at best,[11] although one reminiscent account indicates that the "group may have trapped their way to the Colorado and then lost their furs while crossing."[12] Another says only that they "came by way of Sonora."[13] Except for Alexander, who later participated in the sea otter trade, none of these men continued in the fur business after reaching the Pacific Coast.[14]

Soon after his arrival in California, Lemuel Carpenter turned to a pursuit which for a time lent him a note of distinction in early annals. In 1834 he established a soap factory known as "La Jabonería" on the west bank of the San Gabriel River near present-day El Monte.[15] Using refuse tallow and, according to J. J. Warner, "the native natron, or soap weed, of which large quantities effloresced in some parts of the country near Los Angeles, as an alkali for the making of hard soap,"[16] Carpenter supplied local residents

[11] Bancroft, *California,* III, p. 388, summed up the trip: "In the winter of 1832-3 another party arrived from New Mexico, under circumstances nowhere recorded, so far as I have been able to learn. This party, the exact date of arrival is not known, included Joseph Paulding, Samuel Carpenter, William Chard, and Daniel Sill."

[12] Donald C. Cutter and David J. Weber, "Cyrus Alexander," this *Series,* v, p. 29.

[13] Wilson, *op. cit.,* 35.

[14] According to Warner, "Reminiscences," 190, William Chard continued his occupation as a butcher, planted a vineyard with Carpenter, and later moved to the Sacramento Valley; Joseph Paulding remained in Los Angeles as a cabinet maker, built his own lathe, and made the first two billiard tables in California out of mahogany brought from San Blas. Daniel Sill was described by Benito Díaz in *Sill vs. Reese* (ms. in the Bancroft Library) as "an armourer, blacksmith, and carpenter by profession, who worked in Yerba Buena in the year 1842 or '43."

[15] Wilson, *op. cit.,* 35 and 69; Newmark, *op. cit.,* 180; Bell, *op. cit.,* 309, note 1; Layne, *op. cit.,* 91.

[16] Warner, "Reminiscences," 190. Natron is hydrated sodium carbonate sometimes called native soda or nitre; Warner's "soap weed" may have been soap plant (*Chlorogalum pomeridianum* of the *Liliaceae* family) or the soapwort, an herbaceous plant belonging to the genus *Saponaria,* which yields a soap-like substance. Cur-

and made enough money to acquire a small vineyard.[17] Shortly thereafter he married María de los Angeles Domínguez, a native Californian, and began to raise a family.[18]

By 1843 Carpenter had prospered sufficiently in the soap business to purchase Rancho Santa Gertrudes, a 24,000 acre tract of rich land "than whose soil (watered, as it is by the San Gabriel River) none more fertile can be found in the world."[19] He paid its owner Josefa Cota de Nieto $4,000 "which was at the time considered a high price for the land."[20] During the next few years, Carpenter spent another $5,000 for improvements [21] and eventually owned "thousands of head of horned cattle and a corresponding number of horses. He had a good ranch house, a vineyard, corn fields, barley fields, springs, streams and lakes."[22] "El Carpintero," as his friends affectionately called him, became a true "son of the country," pursuing his commercial and agricultural interests, participating in pueblo activities, and joining his neighbors in local petitions.[23]

iously, Cyrus Alexander, as recalled by nephew Charles in 1876, also engaged in soap making since the soil "in the vicinity of San Diego was impregnated with alkali so strongly that by shoveling it into hoppers, and draining water through it, the lye would be strong enough for soap manufacturing purposes." See Charles Alexander, "The Life and Times of Cyrus Alexander," ms. in the Bancroft Library.

17 Records of the Ayuntamiento of Los Angeles, vol. II, p. 1005, Los Angeles City Archives, Los Angeles, California.

18 Cleland, op. cit., 113; Marion Parks, "In Pursuit of Vanished Days," Historical Society of Southern California Annual Publications, XIV (1929), 172. The California Census of 1852 lists Carpenter's children as Susana, Jose, L., Refugio, Francisco, and H., ranging from 16 years to 6 months.

19 Newmark, op. cit., 180.

20 "Deposition of Abel Stearns," Samuel Carpenter vs. The United States, Case no. 339, Bancroft Library.

21 Nieto vs. Carpenter, 7 Cal. 529.

22 Bell, op. cit., 10. Within the five square leagues of Rancho Santa Gertrudes, confirmed to Carpenter in 1854, lie the present towns of Santa Fe Springs (where oil was discovered in the 1920s), Downey, Rivera, and Los Nietos. See also W. W. Robinson, Ranchos Become Cities (Pasadena, 1939), 64-65.

23 A few of Carpenter's business receipts can be found in the Stearns Papers, Box 71, Huntington Library. Records of the Ayuntamiento of Los Angeles, vol. II, show that in 1836 he served on a vigilante committee and that in 1846 he complained, with twenty-six others, about the need for stricter supervision of Indians.

Late in 1844, Carpenter and other southern Californians offered their services to Pío Pico in opposition to Mexican-appointed Governor Manuel Micheltorena. In February 1845, he fought "in defense of Los Angeles" at the Battle of Cahuenga, a minor skirmish which led to Micheltorena's departure from California.[24] During the Mexican War, Carpenter took up the American cause and served in a small company of men organized under Benjamin D. Wilson. Through a breakdown in communications, the group was captured at El Chino ranch and held prisoner until weakness in the Mexican position led Andrés Pico to release them on January 6, 1847.[25] Carpenter returned to his family at Santa Gertrudes.

The American take-over of California somehow brought an unwelcome change in the fortune of Lemuel Carpenter. He spent one year in the gold mines but did not do well.[26] It then seemed that his "business sense had become numbed by that easy faith in his fellow man which characterized the Californians when they negotiated one with another over financial matters."[27] Major Horace Bell recalled that at Christmas time in 1853, Carpenter borrowed fifty dollars from the local "boticario" (druggist) only to find a year later that the note bore interest "at the rate of 12½ per cent a day compounded daily."[28] By December, 1854, it had turned into five thousand dollars and the druggist issued a note for the total amount at 5 per cent a month compounded monthly. Another year's interest required the issuance of a new note for $9,154 again at 5 per cent per month.[29] Bell may have exaggerated the facts, although Robert Glass

---

[24] Bancroft, *California,* IV, pp. 495-511.

[25] Michael C. White, *California All the Way Back to 1828* (Los Angeles, 1956), 56. See also Joseph Wood, "Isaac Williams," this *Series,* VII, pp. 375-76.

[26] "Deposition of Lemuel Carpenter," *Julian Workman, et al vs. The United States,* Case no. 574, Bancroft Library. Parks (*op. cit.,* 171) describes Carpenter as a man "who prospered under Mexico but failed under the United States."

[27] Bell, *op. cit.,* 10.   [28] *Ibid.,* 11.   [29] *Ibid.*

Cleland termed it "a trivial debt, swollen to huge proportions by chicanery and outrageous interest rates."[30] In any event, the amount increased until Carpenter became so heavily indebted to John G. Downey (the druggist) and his business partner James B. McFarland, that Carpenter and his wife were forced to mortgage Rancho Santa Gertrudes to them in 1856.[31] In October 1858, Downey and McFarland commenced proceedings to foreclose on the property since Carpenter was unable to pay his bloated debt. On December 16, 1858, the case of Lemuel Carpenter "an Insolvent Debtor" was heard in Los Angeles; the sheriff's sale was held in November 1859.[32]

At the same time that Carpenter faced his financial crisis with Downey, another effort was being made to evict him from his home and rancho at Santa Gertrudes. In January 1853, heirs of Manuel Nieto – the six children of then deceased Josefa Cota – claimed that their mother could not have alienated the property under the "declaration of ownership" given to her by Governor José Figueroa in 1834.[33] The court reviewed the facts and found that Manuel Nieto's four children, successors in interest of Manuel's immense Spanish grant of 1784, had applied for and received in 1833 a partition of the original tract.[34] Josefa Cota, widow of son Antonio María Nieto, retained the land known as Santa Gertrudes and, having judicial possession, lived there with her children until 1843. In December of that year, finding herself in "indigent circumstances," Josefa conveyed the property "for valuable consideration" to defendant Car-

---

[30] Cleland, *op. cit.,* 113.

[31] "Deposition of John G. Downey," *The United States vs. F. J. Carpenter, Administrator,* ms. in the Bancroft Library.

[32] Los Angeles *Star,* January 15, 1859; Cleland, *op. cit.,* 113; Parks, *op. cit.,* 171.

[33] *Nieto vs. Carpenter,* 21 Cal., 466-69.

[34] *Nieto vs. Carpenter,* 7 Cal., 528. Nieto's land was "bounded on the south by the ocean, on the east by the river Santa Ana, on the north by the old road leading from San Diego to Monterey, and on the west by the river San Gabriel, containing thirty-three leagues."

penter after securing the approval of Governor Manuel
Micheltorena. Carpenter thereupon occupied the land, mak-
ing it his residence until his death in November 1859. Josefa
Cota died in 1847.

The California Supreme Court, six years after the 1853
action was filed, rendered its decision, the significance of
which would be felt by all those having purchased property
within former Spanish and Mexican land grants. Chief
Justice Stephen Field, writing the opinion in 1863,[35] outlined the reasons why plaintiffs – the grandchildren of Nieto
– were *not* entitled to recover the land. Essentially, the grant
made by Governor Figueroa to Josefa Cota on May 21,
1834, was not a confirmation of the title existing in Manuel
Nieto's heirs since 1784, but a concession made and ap-
proved by the authority of the Mexican government under
the colonization law of 1824 and regulations of 1828.[36] That
even though paragraph one of Figueroa's grant advised
Josefa Cota that "neither she, nor her heirs, shall have
power to divide or sell the same," [37] the subsequent approval
of the sale given by Governor Micheltorena in December
1843, altered the circumstances. Therefore, since "[T]he
Governor had authority to remove the restraint upon the
alienation of the premises contained in the first condition of
the grant . . . the subsequent sale of the grantee to the
defendant passed the title to him absolutely." [38]

This decision might have been timely for Lemuel Carpenter had it not been for some unfortunate delays accompanied by mounting legal costs. The Supreme Court first
upheld the trial court's approval of Carpenter's rights by a

---

[35] Although decided in 1859, "the pressure of other business" did not permit the
justices to prepare the opinion at that time (21 Cal., 459).

[36] 21 Cal., 494.   [37] 7 Cal., 532.

[38] 21 Cal., 494. Carpenter's attorneys, James A. McDougall and Solomon A. Sharp,
described Micheltorena as "a man of learning and ability" and commented that
"[T]he Nietos never dreamed that they had been defrauded until it was discovered
after the introduction of our government, people, language, laws, and lawyers"
(*Ibid.,* 472).

decision in October 1856. It granted a rehearing, however, and by a decision rendered in April 1857, reversed itself and returned the case to the trial court.[39] At the new trial plaintiffs were successful and won their claim to the former Nieto land; but on appeal the Supreme Court reversed the trial court and this time judgment was entered for Carpenter in July 1858. Nevertheless, another rehearing was granted and the case re-argued at the October term, 1859.[40]

By this time, however, Carpenter did not care whether or not he won, since for him there could be no victory. Clearance of title to his magnificent rancho meant only one thing – that the sheriff's sale of the property to McFarland and Downey could proceed.[41] Shortly before the court handed down its final decision – upholding once and for all Carpenter's ownership of Santa Gertrudes,[42]– the emotional and financial strain upon the defendant had become unbearable. On November 5, 1859, the combination of tragic circumstances forced Lemuel Carpenter to take his own life.[43] Francis J. Carpenter, administrator of his father's estate, listed assets of "personal property only," and made no claim for any part of Santa Gertrudes.[44]

---

[39] *Ibid.*, 459.   [40] *Ibid.*

[41] According to the deposition of John G. Downey (*The United States vs. F. J. Carpenter,* Bancroft Library), he and McFarland "became the purchasers of the whole of said premises so described in said mortgage for the sum of sixty thousand dollars" the previous April – but this was before the court decision could have allowed its transfer. Parks (*op. cit.,* 171) places the date of sale as November 14, 1859, on the $60,000 bid of Downey and McFarland; although Cleland (*op. cit.,* 113) says that on November 9, 1859, the property "was sold by the sheriff to James P. McFarland and John G. Downey for $2,200!" The latter figure no doubt represented the amount of actual cash involved.

[42] Chief Justice Field wrote the opinion of the court at pages 483-94.

[43] *Southern Vineyard,* Nov. 19, 1859.

[44] "Letters of Administration," *Estate of Samuel Carpenter,* ms. in the Bancroft Library. Carpenter was survived by his widow and five children.

Eustache Carriere

by LeRoy R. Hafen
Brigham Young University

Eustache Carriere was born in La Rivière du Chene, Canada, the son of Baptiste and Marie (Lajeunesse) Carriere.[1] Although we do not have the date of his birth, it was probably some time before 1795, for he enlisted with Manuel Lisa's expedition which ascended the Missouri River in 1812 to trade with the Indians in the upper country.[2]

John Luttig, clerk of the Lisa Expedition, reported that on November 30, 1812, Carriere and two companions, while trapping at the Big Bend of the Missouri River were killed by the Sioux Indians,[3] but this proved to be a false report.

A Michael Carrier was with the notable Chouteau-DeMun trading expedition of 1815-17 in the Southwest,[4] but this person was probably not Eustache, though he may well have been a relative.

By January 1820, Eustache Carriere was back in Missouri, for on the third of that month at Florissant, Missouri, he married Josette Therese Jusseaume, daughter of the prominent fur trader and Indian interpreter René Jusseaume.[5]

Of the trapping career of Eustache almost nothing is known, but he was reputed to have found gold in 1835 in the Rocky Mountains while trapping in that region.[6] Some

---

[1] Editorial note by Stella M. Drumm in John C. Luttig, *Journal of a Fur Trading Expedition on the Upper Missouri, 1812-1813,* ed. by Stella M. Drumm (New York, 1964), 77.

[2] He appears in the list as "Ustache Carier," *ibid.,* 157.   [3] *Ibid.,* 98.

[4] Michael Carriere signed a statement that he was employed by Chouteau and DeMun, 1815-17, and for the two years received $200. The Chouteau-DeMun Claim, recorded in *Annals of Congress,* 15 Cong., 1 sess., vol. 2, p. 1959.

[5] Note by Stella Drumm in Luttig, *op. cit.,* 77.

[6] Reported in the Kansas City *Journal of Commerce,* September 15, 1858.

substantiation of his whereabouts and activity at the time is found in the American Fur Company records located at the Missouri Historical Society Library, St. Louis, where this entry is found:

> Sioux Outfit 1836. July 19. To cash paid Ustache Cariere $56.06 [7]

When gold in paying quantities was definitely found and the Pike's Peak gold rush occurred in 1858-59, Eustache Carriere came forward with his gold discovery story and suddenly gained national notoriety. His statement was published and re-published in the newspapers and gold rush guidebooks of the period and he was suddenly lionized.[8]

The first and perhaps the fullest account of his story appeared in the Kansas City *Journal of Commerce* on September 15, 1858:

> For many years the traders from this city to the mountains have believed in the existence of gold in the head streams of the Arkansas and South Platte. As long ago as 1835, Eustache Carriere, a French trapper now living, superannuated, with the Chouteau family in this city, was lost from his party in that region, and wandered for several weeks through the country, during which time he collected in his shot pouch numerous specimens, which he carried with him to New Mexico. They proved to be gold, and a party was there formed and returned with M. Carriere to search for the locality. He was unable to find the streams where he had collected his specimens, and was tied up and severely whipped by the Mexicans, under the supposition that he did not wish to disclose their location. This was the first discovery that we have been able to learn. The Catholic missionaries have frequently found specimens in possession of the Kansas Indians and others, who annually visit the country for hunting.

His story was widely used to promote the gold rush, but how long he survived his short-lived fame we cannot say.

---

[7] Volume X, p. 460. In volume II, p. 349, is an entry for Eustache Carriere, but no further information is given on the page.

[8] See repetitions of this story as reported in LeRoy R. Hafen, ed., *Pike's Peak Gold Rush Guidebooks of 1859* (Glendale, 1941), 30-31, 194, 242, 262, 279, 288.

Alexander Carson

by RUTH STOLLER
Dayton, Oregon

About half-way between the Yamhill County (Oregon) town of Carlton and Yamhill, and just west of the main highway that extends between them, lies a hill known as Alec's Butte. It was named for an early day fur trapper, Alexander Carson, who met his death there at the hands of the Indians he thought were his friends. The hill is situated in country that Alec knew and loved. On and off through many years he had hunted and trapped this North Yamhill country and to him it was home.

Alexander Carson was born about 1775, possibly in Mississippi. His father, Alexander Carson, Sr., had settled there in 1760. Alec's grandparents were William and Eleanor (McDuff) Carson, who brought their family to Pennsylvania in about 1755 and to Iredell County, North Carolina in 1760.[1]

Thomas J. Hubbard,[2] who came to the Oregon Country with Wyeth's 1834 expedition and knew Carson well during the last year or two of his life, said that Carson had come out to the mountains with Lewis and Clark and, after returning to the States, engaged with Hunt for the overland Astoria party. If Alec had been with Lewis and Clark, it would have been as one of the engages who accompanied the party as far as the Mandan Villages, and after wintering there, sooner or later returned to St. Louis.[3]

Another claim of Hubbard's was that Alexander Carson

---

[1] Charles G. Clarke, *Men of the Lewis and Clark Expedition* (Glendale, Calif., 1970), 68.

[2] Letter of Thomas Hubbard to James Nesmith written in 1858; copy in Oregon Historical Society Library, Portland.   [3] Clarke, *op. cit.*, 26-30.

was a cousin of William Canning (or Cannon) who also came with the overland Astorians. Whether or not there was a blood relationship between the two is not proven, but they most certainly were good friends and were often together, not only as Willamette freemen, but on Hudson's Bay Company fur trapping expeditions.

After Alec's return from his trip to the upper Missouri with the Lewis and Clark party, he spent several years hunting and trapping with various expeditions that went out from St. Louis. So it is not surprising to find him and a friend, on May 22, 1811, floating nonchalantly down the Missouri River in a canoe, two lone men, miles from civilization, passing through a country infested with hostile Indians.[4] They had just spent two years trapping and hunting near the head waters of the Missouri and were now on their way back to St. Louis. On this particular day they were destined to meet Wilson Price Hunt and his overland Astorians. Hunt and his party were on their way up the river and had come to a region where the Indians were considered dangerous. They were naturally apprehensive when they first sighted Alec's canoe coming toward them, but their apprehension turned to amazement when they found it held not Indians but two white men. Carson and Ben Jones, his companion, were easily persuaded to abandon their St. Louis trip and join Hunt's party. Hunt was delighted to have picked up a couple of seasoned trappers for his journey to the Pacific, especially since several of his men had deserted.

The group struggled on up the river and by June 7 had arrived in the Arikara country where Carson and Jones had spent the preceding winter. Carson was anxious to repay the Indian who had fed him during that time, and bought sev-

4 Washington Irving, *Astoria, or Anecdotes of an Enterprise beyond the Rocky Mountains,* ed. by Edgeley W. Todd (Univ. of Okla. Press, 1964), 170; and *Bradbury's Travels,* in R. G. Thwaites, ed., *Early Western Travels* (Cleveland, 1905), V, p. 93.

eral things from Hunt's supplies as gifts. When he took them to the Indian, they were refused, the Indian giving as a reason that Carson was poorer than he.[5]

In September the Hunt party reached present day Idaho and here Alec Carson and three other trappers were detached from the group to trap in Snake River country for the winter. They were outfitted with traps, arms, and horses. When they had gathered a sufficient amount of furs they were to load them on their horses and either get them to the mouth of the Columbia or to any trading post that might be established by the company.[6]

By the following spring, Carson and the three men had finished their trapping and had started for the Missouri River, when they were attacked by the Crow Indians. One of the party, Pierre Detaye, was killed and the rest were robbed of all they had. The three survivors turned back toward the Snake River and, finally, were fortunate enough to meet several others of the Astor party. The whole group proceeded to Donald McKenzie's newly established trading post (near the site of Orofino, Idaho) on the Lewis River. There they remained until McKenzie brought his men to Astoria on January 16, 1813.

Alec did not remain long at Fort Astoria, which was the name given to the newly established headquarters of the Pacific Fur Company on the west coast. Hunting was poor in the area and provisions were short, so by the end of January, he was one of the men sent to Wallace House on the Willamette. The post had been established just north of present day Salem in November of 1812 by William Wallace and J. C. Halsey.[7] Here game was plentiful and meat, both dried and fresh, was sent to Fort Astoria. Trade was

[5] Thwaites, *op. cit.,* v, pp. 178-79.

[6] Robert Stuart, *Discovery of the Oregon Trail,* ed. by Philip Ashton Rollins (New York, 1935), 178-79.

[7] Gabriel Franchere, *Adventure at Astoria 1810-1814,* ed. Hoyt C. Franchere (Norman, 1967), 73.

carried on with the valley Indians and the free trappers trapped the streams nearby.

This would have been Carson's first visit to his beloved Willamette Valley and after this, though he might leave it for a time, he would always return. He was one of the free-men who trapped the tributaries of the Willamette River that winter and spring. He must have thoroughly explored this section of the Willamette, including the valley of the Yamhill River, because records of the Astorians show that among the furs received from the Willamette before June 1, 1813, were 154 beaver skins from Carson and Delaunay.[8]

That fall the Pacific Fur Company changed hands and the new owners, the North West Fur Company, established a new post on the Willamette, several miles downstream from the Wallace House. The Wallace House was all but abandoned and apparently was only used occasionally by the trappers as a place to stay while they were trapping in the area.

While all this was going on, Alec continued to hunt on the Willamette. In the spring of 1814 the trappers from the Willamette were called to Fort Astoria, which had now been rechristened, Fort George. On March 20, 1814, Alexander Henry noted in his journal: "The last of the free Americans, John Day, Carson, and Canning arrived from the Willamette." A few days later Carson made arrangements with the North West Company to hunt for halves on "Spanish River." Then on April 4, 1814, he left in the brigade for the interior as a passenger in canoe no. 6.[9]

How long Alexander Carson hunted in the interior is not known, but probably it wasn't long until he found his way back to the Willamette Valley. In a letter that Donald McKenzie wrote to Wilson Price Hunt from Fort Nez

---

8 J. A. Hussey, *Champoeg: Place of Transition* (Portland, 1967), 26.
9 Elliott Coues, *New Light on the Early History of the Northwest* (Minneapolis, 1965), 856-57, 861, 875.

Perces (Walla Walla) in April 1821, he says: "Some of the former hands are in the country still. For instance St. Amand – Carson – Cannon – Lucier – Gervais are trapping in the river Walamet as usual." [10]

With the merger of the Hudson's Bay Company and the North West Fur Company in 1821, the new company, under the name of the Hudson's Bay Company, endeavored to put the Willamette freemen to work. As a result Alexander Carson was with Peter Skene Ogden on his first Snake River Expedition in 1824-25. This was the expedition that was to become such a nightmare to Ogden. The freemen and the Iroquois of the party were negligent about keeping watch over their horses and a good many horses were stolen by the Indians. Then several of the freemen and Iroquois deserted to the Americans. Alec was among the deserters, but he was one of the very few who paid his debts before he left. To make up for it, he took a horse which did not belong to him. As soon as Ogden found the horse missing, he sent one of his men after it. Carson put up no defense, although one of the Iroquois wanted to, and the man and stolen horse were soon back in Ogden's camp.

That night, because Ogden had refused to sell them tobacco, some of the defectors planned an attack on Ogden's outfit. As far as Alec was concerned, this was carrying the whole nasty business too far. As soon as he could, he stole over to the other camp and warned Ogden about the proposed attack, and then left again. Ogden immediately set up the necessary defenses and put on an extra guard. When the deserters showed up, Ogden was so well organized that nothing came of the affair.[11]

Carson remained with the Americans, at least until after

---

[10] *Oregon Historical Quarterly,* Mar. 1942, p. 12.

[11] In order to get the whole story of this episode, it is necessary to refer to Hudson's Bay Record Society *Publication,* vol. XIII, *Ogden's Snake Country Journals, 1824-26* (London, 1951), 52-53, 234-35; and *Oregon Historical Quarterly,* XXXV, p. 111.

Ashley's trapper rendezvous in July 1825. There he turned in fifty-one beaver and two otter skins.[12] Sooner or later, he found his way back to the Willamette Valley and in the summer of 1829 was preparing to go with Ogden on the latter's last Snake River Expedition. On August 12, 1829, Carson dictated a will to Dr. John McLoughlin at Fort Vancouver. "As I am on the Eve of starting for the Snake Country I have requested in case of any accident happening to me that you will please pay to Mr. William Canning on Order any Sum or Sums of Money which may be due to me by the Hudson's Bay Co. and also give him all and whatever Effects you may have in your possession appertaining to me." Carson signed with a cross and the document was witnessed by P. S. Ogden, J. E. Harriott and George Barnston.[13]

This Snake River Expedition left from Walla Walla in the fall of 1829 and went south to the Humboldt and Colorado rivers. Ogden followed the Colorado almost to its mouth and then turned north and crossed over into the San Joaquin Valley and descended that river to the bay of San Francisco. He then went up the Sacramento to its headwaters and back to Walla Walla where he arrived on June 30, 1830. The outfit returned to Fort Vancouver and on August 4 set out again with Ogden for Fort Walla Walla. Here Ogden transferred his charge to John Work.[14] When Work started on his first Snake River Expedition, Carson was with him. This time Alec was to have some responsibility of his own. He was to have charge of five men who were to hunt for the winter in the vicinity of the Boise River in southwestern Idaho. They would meet the main party in the spring at a prearranged place and proceed with them back to headquarters.

---

12 Dale L. Morgan, *The West of William H. Ashley* (Denver, 1964), 121.

13 Hudson's Bay Record Society *Publication,* vol. VI, *Leters of Dr. John McLoughlin to the Governor and Committee, Second Series, 1839-44* (London, 1943), 12.

14 Burt Brown Barker, ed., *Letters of Dr. John McLoughlin* (Portland, 1948), 137-38.

But Alexander Carson was not destined to be a leader of men – he was too easy-going for that. His years of experience in the wilderness should have taught him something, and this was what his superiors were depending on.

Alec and his men were detached from the main expedition, as planned, on September 7, 1830. There were six men, four women, and thirty horses in the party. Work records the discouraging ending to the venture in his journal entry for July 19, 1831. "The different parties who separated from camp have arrived. The party whom I left in September had the misfortune to lose the whole of the horses, nearly 30 in number early in the spring. They imprudently allowed them to stray a short distance from camp where there were a few Indians in the evening about sunset. The loss was the result of a great degree of negligence on the part of the men. They also put what few skins they had with other articles in caches, which the Indians found and carried off, from a pack to a pack and a half of the few beaver they had." [15]

After this episode Carson went back to his life as a Williamette freeman. But not for long. In the spring of 1832, Dr. McLoughlin gave Michel Laframboise a list of freemen that he wanted him to enlist for his southern expedition and Carson's name was on it.[16] The expedition, with Carson along, was on its way by May 1.

The party traveled through the Willamette Valley to the Umpqua and on into California. There, in January 1833, they met John Work's California expedition, which had left Walla Walla in September 1832. An American trapping party under the leadership of Ewing Young was in the same area.[17]

The presence of the Americans was a constant source of

---

[15] "Journal of John Work," in *Oregon Historical Quarterly,* XIII, p. 366, and XIV, pp. 313-14.   [16] Barker, *op. cit.,* 267.

[17] Alice Bay Maloney, ed., *Fur Brigade to the Buenaventura* (San Francisco, 1945), 36.

worry to John Work. He tried to keep track of them by sending out spying parties. On March 18 he wrote: "Sent off the party after the Americans, 20 men & 11 Indians with their traps and two horses each. A. Carson is at the head of the party. I wished to send Michel but was obliged to detain him to go to the Mission." On March 27: "Did not raise camp in order that Michel might get ready to go after the men who started on the 18th Inst. and ascertain where they are and what they are doing, & to point out a rendezvous where the two parties are to meet." [18]

On the 31st Michel returned with all the men. They had not accomplished their purpose and again John Work was unhappy with Alexander Carson.

> I am much dissatisfied with these men's conduct particularly in turning back before they had come up with the Americans.   .   .   The men lay the fault of not fulfilling their object on each other. Indeed the old man (A. Carson) who was at their head and who appeared the fittest person among them, is too easy, tho' sufficiently experienced for the task and listens too much to babling among the people.[19]

The two parties separated again on May 13 and Michel with his group returned to Fort Vancouver by way of the coast, arriving on July 13.

This was Alec's last fur trapping expedition. He now became a settler of the valley he loved so much, but in a different way than his friends who were taking up land and becoming farmers under the eagle eye of the Hudson's Bay Company. Alec remained a trapper, spending most of his time in the Yamhill Country – away from the others in the solitude that he seemed to prefer.[20] In his employ was a Tualatin Indian named Boney, who had a wife and son.[21]

Sometime in the spring of 1836 Carson spent two or three

---

[18] *Ibid.*, 38.   [19] *Ibid.*, 39.

[20] "Reminiscences of Louis LaBonte," in *Oregon Historical Quarterly,* I, p. 175.

[21] This and the subsequent story of Carson's murder are taken from Thomas Hubbard's letter to James Nesmith, written in 1858. A copy is in the Oregon Historical Society Library, Portland.

weeks at the home of Thomas Hubbard. He was sick during this time and when he thought he was able to travel, he left Hubbard's accompanied by Boney and his family. The first night they camped on the hill that became known as Alec's Butte. According to Hubbard, the whole Tualatin tribe was also camped there. During the night, while Carson was asleep in his tent, Boney forced his son, a boy of twelve or fourteen years, to shoot Carson in the head. Boney's son later confessed the crime and went with Hubbard and a group of men to show where Carson's things had been cached by the Indians. What could be found of Carson's property was turned over to William Canning.

After Carson's murder the will he had made in 1829 was sent into the Hudson's Bay Company headquarters in England so that whatever money was due him could be turned over to Canning. The Board of Governors sent back a letter saying that since Carson had come back safely from the expedition on which he had gone in 1829, the will was null and void. The letter came while Dr. McLoughlin was on a leave of absence, so it was up to James Douglas to answer it. He minced no words.

I regret that technical inaccuracy or inattention to legal forms, should have invalidated Alexander Carson's Will. His compact with Canning is a circumstance well known to many persons here, and it is certain that he intended to dispose of his property according to the provisions of that deed. The parties are from the United States, and joined the Fur Trade upwards of 20 years ago. They have since maintained no correspondence with their families, and I believe are not known to a relative on earth, so that in the absence of a Will there is no prospect of the money being ever claimed. I forward a certificate No. 2 which may remove or greatly modify the objections taken to the Will and I really wish that it may enable your Honors, without incurring liability, to pay the funds over to the legattee, a singularly obstinate and suspicious old man, who will not readily admit the force of legal distinctions.[22]

22 Hudson's Bay Record Society, *Publication,* vol. IV, *Letters of McLoughlin, First Series, 1825-38* (London, 1943), 237.

Certificate no. 2 was a statement signed by Pierre Bellique and William Johnson stating that Carson had often said that at his death all his property was to go to William Canning and that his will was deposited in the Hudson's Bay Company's establishment at Fort Vancouver. The Company decided to comply with Carson's wishes and McLoughlin was authorized to transfer Carson's balance to Canning's account. Carson's account was finally closed in favor of Canning on January 21, 1842.[23]

There were not many men as widely connected with the fur trade as was Alexander Carson. He had trapped in almost every fur-bearing region west of the Mississippi and, at one time or another, had worked for nearly every large fur company. But with all his experience in the fur trade, he never rose above the status of a trapper. It took a firm hand and rigid discipline to be a leader among the Mountain Men and Alec simply could not bring himself to be the necessary tyrant. Every time he was given the responsibility of leading a special group, the mission met with disaster. The final evaluation was always the same – A. Carson was too careless and too easy on his men. Nevertheless, he deserves a place among the fur trade immortals, if only as the embodiment of the easy-going, independent freeman of that era.

---

[23] *Ibid.,* 13.

Toussaint Charbonneau

by LeRoy R. Hafen
Brigham Young University

Toussaint Charbonneau, who accompanied the Lewis and Clark Expedition, 1805-1806, was born in Canada about 1759.[1] He early entered the fur trade, was employed by the North West Company at Pine Fort on the Assiniboine River in 1793-94,[2] and was a trader in the region for two years.[3] He appears to have been something of a Lothario, as reported in the John MacDonell Journal.[4]

According to Maximilian, Prince of Wied, Charbonneau was with the Minnetarees on the Knife River branch of the Missouri in present North Dakota as early as 1796, and lived with them for the next thirty-seven years,[5] apparently not continuously, however. He was known, says Maximilian, by five names: "Chief of the little village," "The man who possesses many gourds," "The great horse from abroad,"

[1] John C. Luttig, *Journal of a Fur Trading Expedition on the Upper Missouri, 1812-13,* ed. by Stella M. Drumm and A. P. Nasatir (New York, 1964), 136.

[2] Elliott Coues, ed., *The Manuscript Journals of Alexander Henry and of David Thompson, 1799-1814,* 3 vols. (New York, 1897), I, p. 50.

[3] In the *Journal of John MacDonell, 1793-1795,* he is mentioned on the following dates as a trader and employee: Nov. 6, 1793, and Feb. 2, Nov. 10, Nov. 12, Dec. 17, Dec. 23, and Dec. 31, 1794; and on Jan. 6, March 3, and March 9, 1795. Portions of this journal are reproduced in Annie H. Abel, ed., *Chardon's Journal at Fort Clark, 1834-1839* (Pierre, S.D., 1932), 270-71.

[4] *Ibid.* [On March 4, 1795]. "St. Denis, Charbonneau, and St. Pierre set out for Mont a la Basse to court the Foutreau's daughter a great beauty"; [and May 30, 1795] "Tousst. Charbonneau was stabbed at the Manitou-a-banc end of the P.I.P. [Portage la Prairie] in the act of committing a Rape upon her Daughter by an old Saultier woman with a Canoe Awl – a fate he highly deserved for his brutality – It was with difficulty he could walk back over the portage."

[5] *Travels in the Interior of North America by Maximilian, Prince of Wied,* in R. G. Thwaites, ed., *Early Western Travels,* XXII (Cleveland, 1905), 345.

"The forest bear," and a fifth which "is not very refined" –
hence not given.[6]

Charbonneau obtained from his friends the Minnetarees a
Shoshone girl, Sacajawea, whom they had captured about
1800, when she was near ten years of age. Charbonneau subsequently married her. He also had two other Indian wives
in 1804.[7]

While Lewis and Clark were wintering at the Mandan
village, 1804-05, Charbonneau contacted them and asked for
employment as an interpreter.[8] Perhaps a decisive factor in
his favor was the fact that his wife, Sacajawea, was of the
Shoshone tribe, which Lewis and Clark intended to meet on
their farther journey. Indeed her presence with the explorers was to be very important in establishing friendly
relations with the Shoshones and in procuring horses and
information for the journey ahead.

During the stay of the exploring party at Fort Mandan,
Sacajawea gave birth to a baby boy on February 11, 1805,
Meriwether Lewis acting as midwife.[9] The child, Jean Bap-
tiste, was to be carried by his mother on the long trip to the
Pacific and back. See the account of him in volume I of this
Series, pages 205-224.

The general character and usefulness of Charbonneau on
the journey was not notable. Lewis in listing and appraising
the members of the expedition, says of Charbonneau: "A
man of no peculiar merit; was useful as an interpreter only,
in which capacity he discharged his duties with good faith,

[6] *Ibid.,* XXIII, p. 221. See also references to Charbonneau in XXII, pp. 351, 352, 357,
363; XXIII, pp. 218-22, 227, 254; and XXIV, pp. 44, 50, 65.

[7] R. G. Thwaites, ed., *Original Journals of the Lewis and Clark Expedition* (New
York, 1904). See these entries: I, p. 219 (Nov. 11, 1804), "two Squars [squaws] of
the Rock mountains purchased from the Indians by a frenchman Chaboneau came
down"; and I, p. 240 (Christmas Day, 1804) [The day was spent in dancing], "no
women were present save Charbonneau's three wives, who were only spectators"
[Thwaites note].

[8] *Ibid.,* I, pp. 217, 274-75. On page 287 Clark, in listing the personnel of the trip,
writes: "Shabonah and his Indian Squar to act as Interpreter & interpretress for the
snake Indians."   [9] *Ibid.,* I, pp. 257-58.

from the moment of our departure from the Mandans, on the 7th of April, 1805, until our return to that place in August last, and received, as a compensation 25 dollars per month, while in service." [10]

Apparently Captain Clark had a higher regard for Charbonneau — as will soon be apparent — than did Lewis, although this is noted in Lewis' journal on August 14, 1805: "this evening Charbono struck his indian Woman for which Capt. C. gave him a severe reprimand." [11]

Charbonneau and his wife remained with the Minnetarees when the exploring expedition descended the river. Upon leaving Charbonneau on August 17, 1806, Clark wrote in his journal:

> we offered to convey him down to the Illinois if he chose to go, he declined proceeding on at present, observing that he had no acquaintance or prospects of makeing a liveing below, and must continue to live in the way that he had done. I offered to take his little son a butifull promising child who is 19 months old to which they both himself & wife wer willing provided the child had been weened. they observed that in one year the boy would be sufficiently old to leave his mother & he would then take him to me if I would be so freindly as to rais the child for him in such a manner as I thought proper, to which I agreed, &c. [12]

Three days later, while floating down the river, Clark wrote a letter to Charbonneau:

> Sir: Your present Situation with the Indians givs me Some concern — I wish now I had advised you to come on with me to the Illinois where it most probably would be in my power to put you in Some way to do Something for your Self . . .   You have been a long time with me and have conducted your Self in Such a manner as to gain my friendship, your woman who accompanied you that long dangerous and fa-

---

[10] *Ibid.*, VII, pp. 360-61. Privates on the expedition were given but $5 per month. Charbonneau was paid for 16 months and 11 days, making $409.16 2/3. In addition he was given $91.16 2/3 for a horse and a lodge. Later he received a bounty land grant of 320 acres, the same as given to privates who served on the expedition. Luttig *Journal,* 39.

[11] Thwaites, *Original Journals,* II, p. 348.   [12] *Ibid.,* V, p. 344.

tigueing rout to the Pacific Ocean and back, diserved a greater reward for her attention and Services on that rout than we had in our power to give her at the Mandans. As to your little Son (my boy *Pomp*) you well know my fondness for him and my anxiety to take and raise him as my own child. I once more tell you if you will bring your son Baptiest to me I will educate him and treat him as my own child – I do not forget the promis which I made to you and Shall now repeet them that you may be certain – Charbono, if you wish to live with the white people, and will come to me I will give you a piece of land and furnish you with horses Cows & hogs – If you wish to visit your friends in *Montreall* I will let you have a horse, and your family Shall be taken care of untill your return – if you wish to return as an Interpreter for the Menetarras when the troops come up to form that establishment, you will be with me ready and I will procure you the place – or if you wish to return to, trade with the indians and will leave your little *Son Pomp* with me, I will assist you with merchendize for that purpose and become my self conserned with you in trade on a Small scale that is to say not exceeding a perogue load at a time –. If you are desposed to accept either of my offers to you and will bring down your *Son* your famn Janey had best come along with you to take care of the boy untill I get him – let me advise you to keep your Bill of Exchange and what furs and pelteries you have in possession, and get as much mor as you can –, and get as many robes, and big horn and Cabbra Skins as you can collect in the course of this winter. and take them down to St. Louis as early as possible in the Spring – When you get to St. Louis enquire of the Governor of that place for a letter which I shall leave with with him for you – in the letter which I shall leave with the governer I shall inform you what you had best do with your firs pelterees and robes &c and derect you where to find me – If you should meet with any misfortune on the river &c. when you get to St. Louis write a letter to me by the post and let me know your Situation. . . I shall be found either in St. Louis or in Clarksville at the Falls of the Ohio.

Wishing you and your family great suckcess & with anxious expectations of seeing my little dancing boy Baptiest I shall remain your friend William Clark [13]

Charbonneau, his wife and son subsequently came down to St. Louis, and apparently remained in the region for several years, but we have found no record of the Frenchman's

[13] *Ibid.*, VII, pp. 329-30.

detailed activity. According to Henry Brackenridge they tired of "civilized life," and welcomed an opportunity to return to the upper Missouri country. They left their son, Jean Baptiste, in the charge of William Clark, who placed him in school in St. Louis.

In 1811 Charbonneau was hired by the prominent fur trader, Manuel Lisa, to serve as interpreter and trader, at a salary of $250 per year.[14] The Lisa party set out from St. Charles on April 2, 1811. Brackenridge, who accompanied the expedition and gives much valuable information on the venture, writes:

> We had on board a Frenchman named Charboneau, with his wife, an Indian woman of the Snake nation, both of whom had accompanied Lewis and Clark to the Pacific, and were of great service. The woman, a good creature, of a mild and gentle disposition, greatly attached to the whites, whose manners and dress she tries to imitiate, but she had become sickly, and longed to revisit her native country; her husband, also, who had spent many years among the Indians, had become weary of a civilized life.[15]

John Jacob Astor's Wilson Price Hunt expedition also ascended the river in 1811, and had set out ahead of Lisa. Although competitors, the two needed a united front to face hostile Indians on the upper river. Accordingly, when Lisa reached the Omaha villages he sent Charbonneau and an Indian guide ahead on May 19th to catch up with Hunt and ask him to wait for Lisa's party. On May 26th Charbonneau returned with the message that Hunt had promised to wait at the Ponca village.[16] Charbonneau presumably stayed in the upper country trading for the company for two or more years.

Lisa returned down river with the company's furs in the fall of 1811. He helped reorganize the Missouri Fur Com-

---

[14] "Fur Trade Papers, 1812," Missouri Historical Society, St. Louis.

[15] *Brackenridge Journal,* in R. G. Thwaites, ed., *Early Western Travels,* VI, p. 32.

[16] R. E. Oglesby, *Manuel Lisa and the Opening of the Missouri Fur Trade* (Norman, Okla., 1963), 111, 112.

pany and in May 1812, again set out from St. Louis heading the company's trading venture.[17] For an account of these activities we have the detailed diary of John C. Luttig, who accompanied Lisa as clerk.

Luttig first mentions Charbonneau on September 17, 1812, when the latter rides into camp with news of Indian danger. Thereafter Charbonneau appears frequently in Luttig's journal – especially going to trade with the Gros Ventres. Luttig once accuses Charbonneau of stirring up the Indians and says he should be hung for his perfidy.[18] Lisa's company founded Fort Lisa on the Missouri River near the present boundary between North and South Dakota, on November 19, 1812, and this post became headquarters for Charbonneau and the other traders. Here Luttig recorded on December 20, 1812: "this Evening the wife of Charbonneau a Snake Squaw, died of a putrid fever she was a good and the best Women in the fort, aged abt 25 years. She left a fine infant girl." [19] This was almost certainly the wife Sacajawea.

Edward Rose, a mulatto of generally ill repute, and known as "Five Scalps," told Captain Reuben Holmes that Charbonneau suggested a plan of going out to the Snake Indians near the Rocky Mountains and there purchase Arapaho women and girl prisoners and bring them to the trading posts on the upper Missouri for sale to traders for wives. According to Rose, who supplied much questionable detail, the two carried out the plan successfully.[20] This appears to have been done about 1814.

In July 1816, Charbonneau was back in Missouri, where he was employed by Julius DeMun for a trading venture to

---

17 *Ibid.*, 126.

18 Luttig, *op. cit.*, 84. For other references to him, see pp. 78, 79, 83, 84, 86, 89, 92, 93, 97, 106, 109, 121, 124, 128, covering dates to March 3, 1813. Charbonneau was paid $250 per year by Lisa in 1812 and 1813, as recorded in "Fur Trade Papers," 1812, Missouri Historical Society, St. Louis.   19 Luttig, *op. cit.*, 106.

20 Capt. Reuben Holmes, "Five Scalps," in Missouri Historical Society, *Glimpses of the Past*, v, nos. 1-3 (Jan.-March, 1938), 19-22.

the upper Arkansas River. A. P. Chouteau and DeMun had assembled a party of trappers in St. Louis the year before and had gone to the southern Rockies and had entered Spanish territory. The next spring DeMun returned to Missouri for additional men and supplies. Among his new recruits was Toussaint Charbonneau, who worked for DeMun and Chouteau the ensuing year. Presumably Charbonneau was with the party when it was taken to Santa Fe and there imprisoned by the Spaniards, who confiscated their goods. Finally the Americans were released and returned home.[21]

In the statement of claims of Chouteau and DeMun is the sworn statement of Toussaint Charbonneau that he was engaged with Julius DeMun from July 1816 to July 1817 to trade with the Indians on the upper Arkansas and Platte, and that he was paid $200 for the service. In the general statement was an affidavit signed by eleven men who had served two years, 1815-1817, and now recounted their experiences, including this: "We remained in prison (some of us in irons) forty-eight days."[22] Presumably, Charbonneau was one of those so imprisoned.

Not long after his return Charbonneau was employed by the United States Indian Department as interpreter at the Upper Missouri sub-agency. A long series of vouchers for his pay are preserved in the records of the Bureau of Indian Affairs. They extend from 1819 to 1838. The first noted is for his service from April 1, 1819, to June 30, 1819, at the rate of $400 per year.[23] Charbonneau's appointment as interpreter was doubtless due, at least in part, to the friendship

---

[21] "The Journals of Jules DeMun," transl. by Nettie H. Beauregard and ed. by Thomas H. Marshall, in Missouri Historical Society *Collections,* v, nos. 2 and 3 (1928).

[22] "Statement and Proof in Case of Chouteau and DeMun, of their Loss and Treatment by the Spaniards," in *15 Cong., 1 sess.,* vol. 2, pp. 1957-59.

[23] Vouchers for 1819, 1820, 1825, 1827, 1828, 1829, 1830, 1831, 1835, and 1838 are reproduced by Annie Heloise Abel, in her edition of *Chardon's Journal at Fort Clark, 1834-1849* (Pierre, S.C., 1932), 278-82.

and sponsorship of William Clark, Superintendent of Indian Affairs at St. Louis.[24]

Miss Stella M. Drumm, in a biographical sketch of Charbonneau in her edition of *Luttig's Journal,* p. 137, writes: "Charbonneau had many friends among the traders, Indian agents, and travellers of the West. In letterbooks and manuscripts to be found among the archives of travellers, are many favorable references to him. . . Francois Antoine Lacrocque of the Northwest Company speaks very favorably of him." [25] General Henry Atkinson and Major Stephen W. Kearny mentioned in their journals that they saw Charbonneau at a Mandan village in 1825.[26] Maximilian, Prince of Wied, during his sojourn on the upper Missouri River in 1833, found Charbonneau of great service to him as an interpreter and otherwise.[27]

While he was interpreter for the government, Charbonneau also carried on extensive trade with the Indians, for himself or for fur trading companies. An excellent sampling of this activity is recorded in the *Fort Clark Journal, 1834-39,* edited by Abel.[28] Francis A. Chardon, clerk at Fort Clark, especially enjoyed Charbonneau's cooking on occasion. On Christmas Day, 1834, Chardon writes: "last Night at ½ past 10 O'Clock we partook of a fine supper Prepared by Old Charboneau, consisting of Meat pies, bread, fricassied pheasants Boiled tongues, roast beef – and Coffee." [29]

---

24 See Clark's letter of September 27, 1833, to the acting Commissioner of Indian Affairs, D. Kurtz, Wash., D.C., explaining "the necessity for the continuance of Charbonneau," etc. Records of the Bureau of Indian Affairs, Letters Received, 1833, Mandan; photostat copy of this and related documents, 1832-35, in possession of LeRoy R. Hafen.   25 Luttig, *op. cit.,* 137.   26 Stella Drumm's notes in *ibid.,* 138.

27 R. G. Thwaites, ed., *Early Western Travels,* XXII, pp. 16, 345, 351, 352, 363, and elsewhere; see index.

28 Abel, *op. cit.* Trading trips to the Gros Ventres are recorded on pages 51, 53, 54, 56, 61, 62, 121, 126, 129, 132, 135, 138, 150, 155, 161, 162. Typical are these two entries: [June 25, 1837]: "Sent Charboneau to the Little Mandan Village to distribute a few twists of tobacco to the heads of Departments" (p. 119). [Feb. 11, 1838]: "Charboneau arrived from the Gros Ventres with two horses loaded with Tongues" (pp. 149-50).

Chardon gives a detailed record of the smallpox epidemic of 1837 that decimated Indian tribes on the upper Missouri. On August 31st he records: "The Number of Deaths up to the Present is very near five hundred – The Mandans are all cut off, except 23 young and Old Men."[30] Charbonneau apparently did not take the disease, but his squaw died of it on September 6, 1837.[31]

The next year Charbonneau married again. Chardon writes in his journal on October 27, 1838:

> Old Charboneau, an old Man of 80, took to himself and *others* a young Wife, a young Assinneboine of 14, a Prisoner that was taken in the fight of this summer, and bought by me of the Rees, the young Men of the Fort, and two *rees,* gave to the Old Man a splendid *Chariveree,* the Drums, pans, Kittles &c Beating; guns fireing &c. The Old gentleman gave a feast to the Men, and a glass of grog – and went to bed with his young wife, with the intention of doing his best.[32]

Charles Larpenteur, after a brush with Indians on the upper Missouri in 1838, writes: "When our fears were at the highest pitch we perceived an individual with pants and a red flannel shirt on, looking very much like a white man. To our surprise and joy, we found that it was old Mr. Charbonneau, who had been 40 years among the Missouri Indians."[33]

In the summer of 1839 Charbonneau voyaged down the Missouri to St. Louis. Joshua Pilcher, who had succeeded William Clark as Superintendent of Indian Affairs at St.

---

[29] *Ibid.,* 18. Chardon continues with an intriguing description of the guests and their conduct:

"the brilliant assembly consisted of Indns Half Breeds, Canadians, Squaws and children, to have taken a Birds eyes view, of the whole group, seated at the festive board, would of astonished any, but those who are accustomed to such sights, to of seen in what little time, the Contents of the table was dispatched, some as much as seven to nine cups of coffee, and the rest in like proportion."

Other special dinners prepared by Charbonneau for the Fourth of July and other holidays are described by Chardon on pages 80, 89, 93, 120, 121, etc.

[30] *Ibid.,* 133. [31] *Ibid.,* 135. [32] *Ibid.,* 173.

[33] Elliott Coues, ed., *Forty Years a Fur Trader on the Upper Missouri: the personal narrative of Charles Larpenteur, 1833-1872* (New York, 1899), I, p. 141.

Louis, wrote to the Commissioner of Indian Affairs at Washington on August 26, 1839:

> On the 21st inst. Toussaint Charbonneau, the late Mandan Interpreter, arrived here from the Mandan villages, a distance of 1600 miles, and came into the office, tottering under the infirmities of 80 winters, without a dollar to suport him, to ask what appeared to me to be nothing more than just, and I accordingly have paid his salary as Interpreter for the Mandan sub-agency, for the 1st & 2d quarters of this year, with the understanding that his services are no longer required. This man has been a faithful servant of the Government — though in a humble capacity. He figured conspicuously in the expedition of Lewis and Clark to the Pacific and rendered much service. For the last fifteen years, he has been employed as the Government interpreter at the Mandans, and never received notice of the intention of the Department to dispense with his services, until some time in July, in consequence of the remote situation of the post. Under these circumstances I thought, and still think it but right that he should be paid, and believe it will meet your sanction, to be charged, (as there has been no allotment for that sub-agency), to the contingent account of the District." [34]

Where he spent his last days and where he died have not been determined.[35] But among the Sublette Papers in the Missouri Historical Society's collections at St. Louis is evidence that he was dead by 1843. Witness this document:

> I promise to pay J. B. Charbonno the Sum of Three hundred and twenty dollars, as soon as I dospose of land Claimed by him said Chabonno from the estate of his deceased Father. St. Louis Augt 14, 1843
>
> Francis Pinsoneau (seal)
>
> [On back] August 17th 1843   To be paid W. A. Sublette
>
> J. B. Charbonno [36]

---

[34] Reprinted in Drumm, *op. cit.*, 140-41.

[35] A letter from the Director of the Missouri Historical Society of Aug. 7, 1970, states that the Society has been unable to find the time or place of Charbonneau's death.

[36] Sublette Papers, Missouri Historical Society, St. Louis.

No portrait of Charbonneau is known to exist. However, it is possible that Carl Bodmer, while accompanying the Maximilian expedition, may have represented Charbonneau in some of his paintings of groups, though none of the men is specifically identified as Charbonneau.

Auguste Pierre Chouteau

by JANET LECOMPTE
Colorado Springs, Colorado

Despite his shortcomings, Auguste Pierre Chouteau was a man of unusual mental, moral and physical stature. Tall and well-built, like most frontiersmen he was ruddy-faced from years in the sun and wind, yet he had the ease and grace of a high-born Frenchman, and his conversation sparkled with wit and anecdote. His one-time competitor in the Indian trade called him honorable, frank and independent, which was ultimate praise coming from a rival trader. A man who knew his family called him the most gifted and brilliant of all the Chouteaus.[1] But to his friends and relatives in St. Louis who expected much of him, his life was a disappointment. He neglected his family; he was improvident and often incompetent in business. His debts mounted up beyond hope of repayment – both those he owed and those owed him – and he died crushed under obligations.

Although debt was the hub of his existence for many years, A. P. Chouteau will be remembered not as a financial failure but as one of the best-known and best-loved of all the Indian traders. He lived with the Indians, had Indian wives and children, and his influence with many tribes was enormous. On a dangerous frontier where territory was disputed with bloodshed, his patience and wisdom helped to keep peace. He was a good trader and a good man.

---

[1] John Francis McDermott, *The Western Journals of Washington Irving* (Norman, 1944), 110; William Waldo, "Recollections of a Septuagenarian," in *Glimpses of the Past*, Missouri Historical Society, v, nos. 4-6 (April-June 1938), 81; John Campbell to the Secretary of War, Western Creek Agency, Aug. 19, 1831, in Letters Received at the Office of Indian Affairs from the Creek Agency West, 1826-36, National Archives Microfilm Publication (hereafter cited as N.A.M.P.), M 234, R 236.

A portrait of Auguste Pierre Chouteau appears herein at page 17.

He was born on May 9, 1786 in St. Louis, eldest son of Pierre Chouteau, a leading fur trader in a village of fur traders, and his wife Pelagie Kiersereau Chouteau. His mother died when he was seven, leaving four children: himself, Pierre, Jr., Paul Liguest and Pelagie. His father remarried and sired five more sons: Francis Gesseau, Cyprian, Louis Pharamond, Charles and Frederick.[2] As the eldest son, Auguste was probably taken as a child to visit the Osage Indians at Fort Carondelet where his father enjoyed exclusive trade privileges from 1794 to 1800. When Auguste was nearly eighteen, Meriwether Lewis secured his appointment and that of his cousin Charles Gratiot to the Military Academy at West Point. In the summer of 1804, the boys went as far as Washington with Auguste's father, who, as first United States Indian Agent of Louisiana Territory, was taking fourteen Osages to visit the president.[3]

The young men went on to West Point where they studied for two years, taking their vacations with families selected by Auguste's ambitious father for the purpose of introducing them into society and procuring them suitable friends.[4] They graduated in June 1806, Auguste ranking fourth and Charles sixth in a class of fifteen. Gratiot stayed in the army, becoming a general in 1828, but A. P. Chouteau's military career was brief. He was commissioned ensign in the Second Infantry, served as aide-de-camp for General Wilkinson at Natchitoches and elsewhere for a little over six months, then resigned on January 13, 1807, to enter the fur trade. In spite of his short service, he was ever after called "Colonel."[5]

His first assignment in the fur trade was to establish a post

[2] Frederic L. Billon, *Annals of St. Louis in Its Territorial Days* (St. Louis, 1888), 168-69.

[3] Donald Jackson, ed., *Letters of the Lewis and Clark Expedition, with Related Documents* (Urbana, 1962), 171-72, 189n, 199.

[4] Letter of Pierre Chouteau to Samuel McKer, St. Louis, Dec. 7, 1804, Pierre Chouteau Letter Book, Chouteau Collection, Missouri Historical Society, St. Louis.

[5] Francis B. Heitman, *Historical Register and Dictionary of the United States Army* (Washington, 1903), I, pp. 300, 470; Louis Houck, *History of Missouri* (Chicago, 1908), II, p. 381.

for his father among the Mandan Indians. By May 1807, he
had assembled a boat and pirogue (large dug-out canoe)
and thirty-two men. Joining him on his journey upriver
were two other parties: Ensign Nathaniel Pryor and fourteen soldiers escorting the Mandan chief She-ha-ka back to
his village after a visit east; and a trading company of ten
men bound for the Sioux. They all left in the latter part of
May and arrived at the Arikara villages on September 9, to
face six hundred and fifty menacing Indians gathered on the
beach. The Indians seized the rope of Chouteau's boat containing merchandise and waved the soldiers to go on. Chouteau begged the soldiers not to abandon him, whereupon
Ensign Pryor yelled at him to offer the Indians something.
Chouteau offered them half his goods and a man to trade
them, but it was not enough. The Indians demanded all his
arms and ammunition, and then began firing at his boat,
which was stuck on a sand bar. His men shoved the boat free,
but four of them were killed or mortally wounded before
all the boats were floating downstream beyond the Indians'
fire, headed back to St. Louis.[6] The campaign was an ex-
pensive failure, but William Clark reported to the Secretary of War that "young Mr. Choteau behaved verry well." [7]
In the summer of 1808, Chouteau again went to the Upper
Missouri to trade with the Sioux, returning in the fall.[8]

On February 15, 1809, Auguste married his first cousin,
Marie Anne Sophie Labbadie, daughter of the prominent
St. Louis merchant, Silvestre Labbadie and his wife Pelagie
Chouteau.[9] Auguste and Sophie had ten children, but the

---

[6] Letter of Nathaniel Pryor to William Clark, St. Louis, Oct. 16, 1807, in Jackson,
Lewis and Clark, 432-37; letter of William Clark to Henry Dearborn, St. Louis, June
1, 1807, in Clarence Edwin Carter, *The Territorial Papers of the United States,* XIV
(Washington, 1949), 126.

[7] Letter of William Clark to Henry Dearborn, Oct. 24, 1807, William Clark
Papers, Mo. Hist. Soc.

[8] License dated May 25, 1808 in T. M. Marshall, ed., *The Life and Papers of
Frederick Bates* (St. Louis, 1926), I, p. 31.

[9] Marriage contract, Mo. Hist. Soc. W. J. Ghent says in his sketch of A. P. Chouteau in the *Dictionary of American Biography* (N.Y., 1929), II, p. 92, that they were
married in the church Aug. 13, 1814, a civil ceremony having preceded.

marriage cannot have been a very good one after 1822 when
Auguste left St. Louis to live among the Osage. There is no
indication that his wife ever visited him in the Osage country, and his visits to St. Louis were limited to a few days
once or twice a year. Nor do his letters to relatives in St.
Louis ever mention his wife, who outlived him by twenty-
seven years.[10]

During the winter of 1808-09, the St. Louis Missouri Fur
Company was organized with A. P. Chouteau, then twenty-
two, as a partner standing in for his father who as Indian
Agent for the Osage was not supposed to engage in trade.[11]
In February 1809, the company contracted with the government to return the still-homeless Mandan chief She-ha-ka to
his village for a $7000 fee. Pierre Chouteau headed the ex-
pedition as far as the Mandan villages, leaving in May,
delivering the chief and returning to St. Louis in November.
Auguste accompanied his father to the Mandans, then went
farther up the river to trade with other Indians, remaining
on the Upper Missouri until May, 1810. He never again
traded on that river, although he seems to have been a
member of the St. Louis Missouri Fur Company until it
dissolved in September, 1813.[12]

---

[10] Their children were a son, Augustine, born 1812; Emilie Sophie, born Sept. 14,
1813, married Nicola de Menil in 1836; Susanne, born 1815, married Louis R. Cor-
tambert; Marie Antoinette (Manette) born 1816, married Ringrose J. Watson; Pierre
Sylvestre, born 1819, married Louisa Alvarez, died 1870 of consumption; Virginia,
born 1826, married John G. Priest; and four others who died either unmarried or
young: Pelagie, Marie E., Louis and Aimee [Billon, op. cit., 170; Paul Beckwith,
Creoles of St. Louis (St. Louis, 1893), 50; #1439 (Auguste P. Chouteau), Probate
Court Records, St. Louis County, Mo; letter of Jeanne Blyth to writer, St. Louis,
Dec. 6, 1970]. Sophie died in 1862. In 1863 her daughter Marie Antoinette made for
her sister Virginia a hair wreath of their mother's hair which is in the Missouri
Historical Society, St. Louis [Mrs. Stewart McCormack, "Elegant Accomplishments," in Bulletin, Mo. Hist. Soc., XXI, no. 3 (April 1965), 213]. Mrs. McCormack
assumes, incorrectly I believe, that "M. Ate." who signed her name thus on the back
of the wreath was "Marie Augustine."

[11] Letter of Pierre Chouteau Jr. to the Secretary of War, St. Louis, Sept. 1, 1809,
in Carter, op. cit., XIV, pp. 312-19.

[12] Richard Edward Oglesby, Manuel Lisa and the Opening of the Missouri Fur
Trade (Norman, 1963), 103, 137, 142, 208. I say "seems" because, although he signed

Perhaps as early as the spring of 1812, A. P. Chouteau became a trader with the Osage Indians.[13] By 1815 he had become father of his eldest half-Osage son, Augustus Clermont, by the Osage woman Masina, but by this time he may well have sired female children by other Osage women (who were described by Jules DeMun as "brazenly licentious").[14] During the War of 1812, it was decided to use Osage warriors to protect white settlements from hostile Indians. In the spring of 1813, A. P. Chouteau gathered two hundred sixty Osage youths and marched with them towards St. Louis. At the mouth of the Osage River, three hundred sixty miles from their village, Auguste received an order from Governor Howard disbanding the little army. The capabilities of Auguste were recognized in an endorsement on Governor Howard's order stating, "if we make use of the Osage in War the appointment of young Chotou is adviseable."[15]

---

the Company's "Articles of Agreement" on March 7, 1809 as "A. P. Chouteau" and voted on December 7, 1812 as "A. P. Chouteau," other references in this company's papers are to "Auguste Chouteau, Jr.," the name under which he had entered the Military Academy but also the name by which his uncle, Auguste Chouteau, was sometimes known. See, for instance, Auguste Chouteau Jr.'s commission as St. Louis Militia Commander, dated July 15, 1807, which he accepted by letter the same day, at a time when A. P. Chouteau was on the Upper Missouri. (Marshall, *Bates*, I, pp. 157-58, 161.)

[13] A letter of Gov. Howard to the Secretary of War dated July 15, 1812, encloses the account of "A. Chouteau Junr." against the Osages for depredations (Carter, *op. cit.*, XIV, p. 577). Again, this could be A. P. Chouteau, or his uncle, or even his cousin Auguste Aristide Chouteau, Auguste Chouteau's son who lived at the La Saline post in the 1820s and died at the Verdigris post in 1834 (Billon, *op. cit.*, 166).

[14] "The Journal of Jules DeMun," in *Collections,* Mo. Hist. Soc., v, no. 2 (Feb. 1928), 196. Augustus Chouteau, described as a French-Osage, was admitted to the Harmony Mission School on Jan. 28, 1824, at age 9. James Chouteau, another French-Osage and probably the son of Liguest Chouteau, was admitted Oct., 1823, at age 10 [William W. Graves, *The First Protestant Osage Missions, 1820-1837* (Oswego, Kan., 1949), 171]; Liguest Chouteau also had a son Augustus born in 1815 of his white wife Constance Dubreuil, and Auguste Aristide Chouteau had a son Augustus born 1811 (Billon, *op. cit.*, 166, 171). So one must take care in identifying an Auguste or Augustus Chouteau.

[15] Letter of Pierre Chouteau to the Secretary of War, May 20, 1813, in Carter, *op. cit.*, XIV, pp. 271-75.

In January 1813, Pierre Chouteau asked William Clark to help obtain the Osage sub-agency for his son Auguste. The appointment was not made until August 1814, and in the meantime Auguste traded with the Osages, proposing in the fall of 1813 to sell all his deerskins at 30¢ per pound to John Jacob Astor through Astor's agent, Charles Gratiot.[16] Even after his appointment, Auguste continued to trade illegally with the Indians.[17] It was the last time he would jeopardize his Indian trade to accept the abysmal pay of a regular Indian agent or sub-agent, but he continued all his life to aid the government in its Indian relations, usually without any pay at all.

In the summer of 1815, Auguste returned to St. Louis and made plans with Jules DeMun for an expedition to the Rocky Mountains and beyond. They bought goods and equipment from Auguste's brother Pierre Chouteau, Jr., and their mutual brother-in-law Bartholomew Berthold, proprietors of the dry goods firm of Berthold & Chouteau, who also became equal partners in the venture. On September 10, 1815, Chouteau and DeMun left St. Louis with forty-six men, arriving two months later at the headwaters

---

[16] Letter of P. Chouteau to Gen. Wm. Clark, St. Louis, Jan. 28, 1813, Pierre Chouteau Letterbook, Chouteau Coll.; letter of Wm. Clark to the Secretary of War, St. Louis, Aug. 20, 1814, in Carter, *op. cit.*, XIV, pp. 786-87; letter of Charles Gratiot to John Jacob Astor, St. Louis, Sept. 7, 1813, Gratiot letterbook, 160-161, Mo. Hist. Soc.

[17] "Young Aug^te P. Chouteau had only 50 packs of deer skin in his wintering ground on the Osage river . . ." wrote Charles Gratiot to J. J. Astor on March 20, 1815 (Gratiot Papers, Mo. Hist. Soc.). The Chouteaus were notorious for breaking the law in this respect, probably because during the Spanish regime they had been rewarded for acting as agents of the government among the Indians with whom they traded. A. P. Chouteau's father was severely criticized not only for trading while serving as Indian agent but for making his charges accept their annuities in goods on which he profited instead of in specie which was stipulated in the treaty. See Carter, *op. cit.*, XV, pp. 98-9, XIII, p. 510; Donald Jackson, ed. *The Journals of Zebulon Montgomery Pike* (Norman, 1966), I, pp. 209, 251; Marshall, *Bates*, 45-47, 86-92. Liguest Chouteau also combined his sub-agency with his Indian trade; see Wm. Clark to the Secretary of War, St. Louis, March 26, 1825, and A. McNair to Wm. Clark, St. Louis, March 20, 1825, in Letters Received, Office of Indian Affairs from St. Louis Superintendency, 1824-1826, N.A.M.P., M 234, R 747.

of the Arkansas. While DeMun went to Santa Fe to request permission of the Spanish governor to trap on the Rio Grande del Norte, Chouteau and his men made camp on the Huerfano River south of the Arkansas in land claimed by Spain. DeMun's mission was a failure, but Chouteau and his trappers had made a good hunt. In February 1816, DeMun set out for St. Louis to obtain more goods, and Chouteau and his men went north to the waters of the South Platte near present Denver and traded with a large camp of Kiowas, Arapahos, Kiowa-Apaches and Cheyennes. With forty-four packs of furs, Chouteau returned to the Arkansas and descended it, planning to meet DeMun at the mouth of the Kansas River. In what is now western Kansas, his party was attacked by 150 to 200 Pawnees. Chouteau quickly retired to an island in the Arkansas (afterwards called "Chouteau's Island") where he piled up his baggage to make a fort, and his men shot it out with the Indians, killing seven. Chouteau lost one man dead and three wounded.[18]

At the mouth of the Kansas, Chouteau and DeMun loaded their furs on barges bound for St. Louis and returned with their men to the Upper Arkansas.[19] Chouteau again camped on the upper waters of the Huerfano while DeMun went to see the governor at Santa Fe. This time the governor's stern warning was to stay out of Spanish territory. DeMun returned and they moved camp lower down the Huerfano to wait for the end of winter. In March 1817, DeMun again went to New Mexico where he was arrested and brought back to the Arkansas by two hundred soldiers investigating a report of an American fort. Finding no fort, the soldiers ordered the Americans to return to St. Louis.

---

[18] Janet Lecompte, "Jules and Isabelle DeMun," in *Bulletin*, Mo. Hist. Soc., XXVI, no. 1 (Oct. 1969), 30-31.

[19] Chouteau was again appointed sub-agent to the Osages in 1816 "for special purposes," which probably meant delivering presents or messages at the Osage village as he passed through on his way to the mountains. *American State Papers: Indian Affairs*, II, p. 76.

Instead, Chouteau and DeMun camped south of the Arkansas once more, where in May they were finally arrested, taken to Santa Fe and imprisoned for forty-eight days. During his imprisonment, as William Waldo tells the story, Chouteau was taken before the governor:

> His superior powers of conversation and his courtly address so captivated the Spanish Governor, that he would frequently have the Colonel carried from the prison to his house, to amuse and entertain him. On one of these occasions, when the Governor had favored his visitor with a long catalogue of his numerous generosities and benefactions on his behalf, he paused, and with great earnestness demanded what more he would have. The Colonel quietly replied, *"Mi libertad, Senor Gobernador."* This so incensed the boastful magistrate, that the prisoner was quickly ordered back to his vile cell.[20]

When they arrived at St. Louis early in September 1817, in rags and on one poor horse apiece, they filed claim with the United States for over $30,000 worth of goods confiscated by the Spaniards. The claim was not allowed until thirty-four years later, when both Chouteau and DeMun were dead.[21]

A. P. Chouteau never again went to the mountains. In 1826, William Ashley offered him $100 a month or a third share of the profits if he would lead a trapping expedition, but Auguste declined, saying that he knew there were gains to be made in the mountains, but that in spite of all his ambition, he had no desire to see that country again.[22] He ex-

---

[20] Waldo, "Recollections," 81-82.

[21] A document in the Chouteau Collection dated June 17, 1818, signed by A. P. Chouteau, P. Chouteau Jr., Jules DeMun and Bartholomew Berthold, asks the government to pay A. P. Chouteau the sum of $30,380.74. The claim was rejected by the Board of Commissioners under the Florida Treaty of 1819, then turned over to attorney Thomas H. Benton, who was to receive 10% of the amount he could recover. After the Mexican War, the U.S. paid claims of its citizens against Mexico, and in June 1851, the heirs of Chouteau and DeMun were awarded their claim plus interest, amounting to $81,772, of which 10% went to Benton and the remainder after fees and expenses to Pierre Chouteau Jr. and to the heirs of A. P. Chouteau, DeMun and Berthold ("Account of Money received from the United States Government for Claim against the Mexican Gov^t," Chouteau Coll.).

plained his feeling more fully in a letter to the Secretary of War in 1831:

> Shortly after the war, I went upon a trading expedition to the head of the Arkansas, and was taken by the Spaniards. When I was near Santa Fe, I was invited by them to visit that place. Convinced of my own innocence, and believing the invitation to be an act of hospitality, I unhesitatingly accepted what I believed was intended as a mark of respect. Immediately upon my arrival in town, I was arrested, thrown into prison, charged with revolutionary designs, my property confiscated; and, after having undergone an examination in which my life was endangered, I was discharged, without any compensation for my property which had been taken by violence. Upon my return home, I determined to abandon a trade that was attended with so much risk.[23]

The Chouteau-DeMun expedition ended in great loss, but A. P. Chouteau's next venture was an even worse disaster, for it had a baleful effect on his career and family relationships for the rest of his life. Late in 1817 he borrowed money from Berthold & Chouteau and with Jules DeMun opened a mercantile business in St. Louis known as A. P. Chouteau, DeMun & Co., or Chouteau, DeMun & Sarpy. On September 14, 1818, DeMun dropped out and young John B. Sarpy and Chouteau continued business in a new brick store and dwelling built by Chouteau in the winter of 1819-20 at 94 North Main. Auguste also built himself a two-story frame dwelling at 54 North Main, perhaps indicating his serious purpose of remaining in St. Louis as a merchant.[24]

---

[22] Letter of Ashley to P. Chouteau Jr., Feb. 2, 1827, and of A. P. Chouteau to B. Pratte & Co., Dec. 17, 1826, both quoted in Dale L. Morgan, *The West of William H. Ashley* (Denver, 1964), 159-60, 308. Nevertheless he was eager to profit by such an expedition and offered his brother Liguest and cousin Melicourt Papin as leaders and his sickly half-brother Pharamond as clerk, but nothing came of it (Letter of A. P. Chouteau to B. Pratte & Co., Vers de Gris, 17 Dec., 1826 (in French), Chouteau Coll.).

[23] Letter of A. P. Chouteau to Lewis Cass, Western Creek Agency, Nov. 12, 1831, in "Fur Trade, and Inland Trade to Mexico," *Sen. Doc. 90, 22 Cong., 1 sess.* (Ser. 213), 60.

[24] J. Thomas Scharf, *History of Saint Louis City and County* (Phila., 1883), I, pp. 150, 153, 198, 582-83; "Dissolution of Partnership with Julius DeMun and J. B.

The business failed. By 1821 Auguste's frame house and brick store were occupied by others.[25] His debt to Berthold & Chouteau, amounting with interest to $66,000 fifteen years later, was a veritable fortune requiring a lifetime of work or a windfall of good luck to repay. Auguste was a failure unprecedented among the vigorous and ambitious Chouteaus. What family arguments and agonies of group decision were suffered in determining Auguste's future do not appear in the family records, but in 1822 Auguste left St. Louis, his wife and children, his immense debt, and moved to the Osage country once and for all.

On July 15, 1822, Auguste and his brother Liguest took out a two-year license at St. Louis to trade with the Osages and Kickapoos on the Arkansas.[26] The timing was good. Government stores or factories at Fort Osage (Fort Clark) and Marais des Cygnes (Osage River) had just been abandoned, and the Indians were ready to move from their old village to a better hunting ground. So the Chouteau brothers bought $14,851.19 worth of merchandise and had it shipped via the Mississippi and Arkansas rivers to the mouth of the Neosho River.[27] Auguste set out immediately for the Grand Osage village on the Osage River to persuade the chief, White Hair (Pahuska) and his people to follow him south to the vicinity of Three Forks, the junction of the Verdigris, Neosho (Grand) and Arkansas rivers, a beautiful country whose ample water, grass and salt attracted hordes of fur-

Sarpy, under firm of Chouteau, DeMun & Co., dissolved on the 14th September, 1818. Henceforth to be carried on by Chouteau and Sarpy." *Missouri Gazette,* Oct. 2, 1818; "Appraisal of Isaac H. Griffith for carpenter work done on A. P. Chouteau's new store on Main Street, Sept. 9, 1819," Chouteau Coll.

[25] Scharf, *op. cit.,* I, pp. 150, 153.

[26] "Abstract of Licenses," in Letters Received, Office of Secretary of War Relating to Indian Affairs, 1800-1823, N.A.M.P., M 271, R 4. Liguest had been trading and living with the Osages since 1814. In 1819 he was their sub-agent, and in 1820 he took a delegation of them to Washington (*American State Papers: Indian Affairs,* II, pp. 289-98).

[27] "Abstract of Licenses," *loc. cit.;* Grant Foreman, *Indians and Pioneers* (New Haven, 1930), 142.

bearing animals. The country was not new to these Indians; in 1802 Auguste's father had led the Grand Osages to Three Forks to hunt and trade, but White Hair's people had later returned to their old village, leaving the larger portion of the band ("Les Cheniers" they were called) on the oak-covered banks of the Verdigris under Chief Clermont.[28]

At "La Saline," a big salt spring about thirty-five miles up the Neosho from its mouth, A. P. Chouteau settled down in a house built the year before by the half-Osage Joseph Rivar (Revoir) just before he was murdered by Cherokees.[29] For nearly a year White Hair and his Indians hung about La Saline accepting Chouteau's abundant food and hospitality and making up their minds whether to move there. Finally, after a council in August 1823, the Indians decided against it, and made a new village on the Neosho some fifty miles farther up the river from La Saline.[30] By this time Auguste's

[28] Foreman, *Indians and Pioneers,* 19-24.

[29] Most Oklahoma historians err in crediting A. P. Chouteau with establishing this post in 1817, in partnership with Rivar. The trading firm of Chouteau & Rivar was indeed licensed on August 23, 1817, to trade with the Osages, but the Chouteau involved was Auguste's brother Liguest, as is shown by a receipt in the Missouri Historical Society dated St. Louis, Sept. 16, 1818, made out by "Chouteau DeMun & Co." to "P. L. Chouteau, Rivar & Co.," and by the fact that A. P. Chouteau was on his way home from the mountains in August 1817. There is insufficient evidence for dating the post's establishment 1817 anyway, especially since the Union Mission Journal of June 24, 1821, plainly states that Rivar "had just formed a settlement at [La Saline]" when he was murdered. (Foreman, *Indians and Pioneers,* 117). For other Oklahoma blunders, see Vinson Lackey, *The Chouteaus and the Founding of Salina, Oklahoma's First White Settlement, 1796* (Tulsa, 1939); for its refutation see *Chronicles of Oklahoma,* XXIV, no. 4 (Winter 1946-47), 483-91.

[30] Rev. Pixley's Journal and Union Mission Journal, quoted by W. Graves, *op. cit.,* 179-82. In the Ayer Collection, Newberry Library, Chicago, there is an invoice of merchandise taken by A. P. Chouteau to trade on the Osage and Arkansas rivers in 1823. Goods totalled $25,509.56, as certified by B. Pratte & Co. on July 24, 1823. Chouteau therein lists his clerks as Melicour Papin, A. Frances Chardon, Theodore Papin, A. A. Chouteau, Christopher Sanguinet and Ant.e Dehaitre. His hands were Pierre Larivière, Charles Mongin, Bat.e Jeanette, Benj.n Dejardin, Francois Tayon, Julien Perras, Joseph Gina, Francois Mascan, Etienne (mulatto man), Jack (negro man), J. Giraud, J.h Tremblé, Francois Tremblé, Bat.e Pacquet, Bat.e Chaurette, Benj.n Lagoterie, Bat.e Delorme, Francois A. Simoneau, Jean Marie Courville, Benj.n Toin, Antoine Martel, Bat.e Lalie, Joseph Bisson, Joseph Gervais, Boismenou.

cousin Pierre Melicourt Papin had arrived to take over
trading operations at La Saline, which, after the departure
of White Hair's band, were meager indeed. By the fall of
1825, Melicourt and his clerk Michel Giraud had established another post on the Neosho near White Hair's new
village, where they continued to live and trade for many
years to come.[31]

Chouteau kept his Osage family at La Saline and doubtless considered it his home, but his business was centered
thirty-five miles southwest on the Verdigris. Within two
months after he had taken up La Saline in September 1822,
Chouteau bought Brand's and Barbour's settlement, consisting of ten or twelve log houses, thirty acres of land
cleared for farming, and a ferry, located on the east side of
the Verdigris half a mile below its rapids and four miles
from its mouth.[32] Here were Chouteau's office, warehouse,
store and boat landing, as well as fields producing forty-five
to fifty bushels of corn and eighteen to twenty of wheat per
acre, described as "a very large farming establishment."[33]
At his Verdigris post he traded with all who needed his
merchandise – emigrating Creeks, Cherokees and Choc-
taws; Clermont's Osages who lived in huts strung along the
Verdigris fifty to sixty miles from its mouth and at "La
Grosse Cote" even farther up (but within walking distance
for the agile Osages) ; and white settlers pushing the frontier
west from Arkansas.

Here also Chouteau worked to reduce conflict between

---

[31] License of A. P. Chouteau, Sept. 16, 1826 (in Letters Received, OIA from St.
Louis Superintendency) gives the location of Melicourt's new post. See also Ledger
X, Chouteau Coll. Chouteau's letters to Melicourt in the Chouteau Collection cease
in April 1824, when it appears that Melicourt moved and Auguste Aristide Chouteau came to live and farm at or near La Saline.

[32] Union Mission Journal, Dec. 10, 1822, quoted in Graves, op. cit., 60; Grant
Foreman, Pioneer Days in the Early Southwest (Cleveland, 1926), 75.

[33] Letter of A. P. Chouteau to Senator Thomas H. Benton, quoted in Grant Foreman, The Five Civilized Tribes (Norman, 1934), 148; Thomas Forsyth to the Secretary of War, St. Louis, Oct. 24, 1831, Sen. Doc. 90, loc. cit., 75.

bands and tribes, races and individuals, all vying for the fruitful land and its profitable crop of animals. In November 1823, a band of Clermont's Osages killed a party of white hunters trespassing on Indian lands on the Blue River. The survivors reported the massacre at Fort Smith, and a detachment of soldiers was sent to A. P. Chouteau's post to force the Osages to give up the murderers. Osages and army officers were to meet for a conference at the Falls of the Verdigris above Chouteau's in March 1824, but only Clermont showed up, for the rest of the Indians were either hunting or at war. The murderers later surrendered and were acquitted.[34]

In the summer of 1824, soldiers from Fort Smith came to establish Fort Gibson on the east side of the Neosho about three miles from its mouth, and Chouteau traded with them for provisions and silverware. Later he accepted "all sorts of kindnesses" from officers of the post, and frequent invitations to parties there. At a Fourth of July observance in 1826, it was recorded that thirteen toasts were drunk and speeches made by, among others, A. P. Chouteau.[35]

Auguste bought his goods from and sold his furs to Bernard Pratte & Co. of St. Louis, successors to Berthold & Chouteau, of which his brother Pierre, Jr. was still a principal partner. Auguste's territory, known as the "Osage Outfit," included four trading posts in 1825: at the Little Osage village or old factory at Marias des Cygnes, kept that year by his half-brothers Francis Guesseau and Cyprian; at La Saline, kept by his cousin Auguste Aristide Chouteau; on the Neosho ten miles below White Hair's village, kept by his cousin Melicourt Papin; and at the Verdigris post where his young half-brother Louis Pharamond Chouteau was

---

[34] Foreman, *Indians and Pioneers,* 159-201.

[35] Foreman, *Pioneer Days,* 167; letter of Auguste P. Chouteau to Auguste Chouteau, Verdigris, [August] 14, 1828; letter of A. P. Chouteau to B. Pratte & Co., Grand Saline, Neosho, Aug. 30, 1824, Chouteau Coll.

clerk. In 1825 these four posts handled about thirty thousand dollars worth of goods, brought by keelboats from St. Louis up the Missouri and Osage rivers to the Osage River post, or in steamboats down the Mississippi and up the Arkansas to the mouth of White River, thence in Chouteau's barges or those of a contractor to the mouth of the Neosho. In late spring and late fall, after the Indians made their hunts, the peltry was floated down to New Orleans on barges, then shipped to New York and abroad. Chouteau often accompanied his shipments to New Orleans in the spring, and after 1830 he often went to New York to oversee the sale of his furs.[36]

In 1825 business was good at Three Forks and prospects even better. A treaty with the Osages made at St. Louis on June 2, 1825, had exchanged the Indians' lands in Missouri and Arkansas for lands in present Kansas and Oklahoma, with an added annuity of $7000, which with any luck would end up in the pockets of the principal trader. The treaty also set aside eight sections of the new Osage reserve including the big salt spring and Joseph Rivar's house, for Chouteau's children, his half-breed wife Rosalie and her brother An-

---

[36] Trading license of A. P. Chouteau in "Abstract of Licenses," 1825, Letters Received, OIA from St. Louis Superintendency; Thomas Forsyth to the Secretary of War, Oct. 24, 1831, *Sen. Doc. 90, loc. cit.,* 71. In 1823 the Chouteau brothers shipped 372 packs of red deerskins weighing 38,659#, along with four more packs of gray deerskins, three of red deerskins and five of bearskins, worth altogether $15,705.10 (Journal D under "April, 1823," Chouteau Coll.). In 1824 they shipped 363 packs of deerskins weighing 38,757#. After freight and insurance charges from the Neosho to New Orleans to New York, deductions for damaged skins and commission charges of J. J. Astor & Sons, the brothers had a balance of $1778.98, or $889.49 apiece (Journal D under "August, 1824," Chouteau Coll., and letter of A. P. Chouteau, April 4, 1824, cited by Foreman, *Pioneer Days,* 83). In 1825 the Osage Outfit produced (Ledger M, p. 81, Chouteau Coll.):

50,000 pounds deerskin	@ .30	$15,000.00
400 pounds beaver	@3.25	1,300.00
177 pounds otter		575.25
2019 raccoon and wolf	@ .25	504.75
60 bearskins	@2.00	120.00
		$17,500.00

thony. Only two of Chouteau's children, James and Henry, were by Rosalie; two other sons, Augustus Clermont and Paul, were by Rosalie's sister Masina, who formed part of the household. In addition, Chouteau had two daughters, both named Amelia, by two other Osage women – one the beautiful Mihanga (My-han-gah; Mo-Hon-Go) who was exhibited in Europe in 1829, and the other Chimihanga, who had also borne Liguest Chouteau a child.[37]

Suddenly in 1826 the fur business at Three Forks became so bad that Auguste doubted B. Pratte & Co. would continue to outfit him. An increase in human population had driven away the game; "deerskins," wrote Chouteau, "which have been the principal business, are entirely finished."[38] His best hope now lay in selling his merchandise to white settlers, to Cherokees and to Creek Indian emigrants forced by the United States to leave their homes east of the Mississippi and move to Three Forks after a treaty promising them, as Chouteau understood, $200,000 in annuities.[39] In the fall of 1826 the Creek Indian agent bought "improvement rights" (Chouteau could not sell the land, only the improvements) to some of Chouteau's buildings on the Verdigris for use as the Western Creek Agency, for which feeble Pharamond Chouteau became sub-agent until his death in 1831. By February 1828, the Creeks began arriving, a hundred or so at a time. In 1829 there were twelve hundred of these civilized farming people in continuous little homesteads along the

[37] Charles J. Kappler, *Indian Affairs: Laws and Treaties* (Washington, 1904), II, pp. 217-21; Foreman, *Pioneer Days,* 258; Grant Foreman, "Our Indian Ambassadors to Europe," in *Collections,* Mo. Hist. Soc., v, no. 2 (Feb., 1928). Chimihanga's child by Liguest was Pelagie, born 1824 (Osage Baptismal Records, 1820-1843, from the St. Paul and Kansas Osage Missions, originals at St. Mary's, Kansas, copies among the Indian Papers, Mo. Hist. Soc.).

[38] Letter of A. P. Chouteau to B. Pratte & Co., Vers de Gris, Dec., 1826 (in French), Chouteau Coll.

[39] The treaty of January 24, 1826, promised $217,600 to individual Creek chiefs and a "perpetual annuity" to the whole nation of $20,000 (Kappler, *op. cit.,* II, pp. 264-68).

Verdigris and Arkansas, huddled together for fear of the warlike Osage, Delaware, Shawnee and Kickapoo around them.[40]

Instead of being rich, as Chouteau had expected, the Creeks were destitute. In the treaty, the United States had promised them food, clothing and money, as well as guns, ammunition and traps with which to support themselves by hunting. But it gave them nothing, not then nor for years to come. So Chouteau outfitted them, fed them, clothed them, and charged the cost of $5,201.93¾ to their annuities, for which the government did not reimburse him during his lifetime.[41]

Chouteau's trade continued to be poor in 1828, for his Indian customers were kept impoverished by errors of the United States government and its agents.[42] In that year, through a blunder of the Secretary of War, a treaty with the Cherokees ceding their country in Arkansas, gave them a reserve instead on the Verdigris and Neosho, on lands already claimed and settled by Creeks and Clermont's Osages, who would now be forced to move again.[43] Clermont's people were further distressed when in June 1829, United States agent J. F. Hamtramck's distribution of Osage annuities flagrantly favored White Hair's band over that of Clermont. On Chouteau's advice, Clermont had refused to accept the unfair distribution, and Chouteau supplied his Indians with their necessities, assuming the risk that the government would not repay him.[44]

---

[40] Foreman, *Indians and Pioneers*, 294-300.

[41] He cashed the Creeks' bounty money in the amount of $1186.43¾, and furnished them spinning wheels and corn worth $332.75; the "improvement rights" to buildings on the Verdigris made up the balance.

[42] In August, 1828, Chouteau wrote, "for two years my business has been bad . . ." (A. P. Chouteau to A[uguste] Chouteau, Verdigris [Aug.] 14, 1828, Chouteau Coll.   [43] Kappler, *op. cit.*, 288-92.

[44] Letters of J. F. Hamtramck to General Wm. Clark, Aug. 29, 1829, and A. P. Chouteau to John H. Eaton, May 29, 1830, and others in Letters Received, OIA from Osage Agency, 1824-41, N.A.M.P., M 234, R 631; also letter of A. P. Chouteau to Pierre Chouteau Jr., Grand Saline, July 6, 1829 (in French), Chouteau Coll.

Agent Hamtramck's shabby proceedings had been witnessed not only by A. P. Chouteau but by Sam Houston, the big ex-governor of Tennessee whose notorious shattered marriage had sent him in bitterness and rage to live with his old friends the Cherokees, now on the Arkansas. Furious at the injustice to the Indians, Houston embarked on a six-hundred-mile trip through the Indian country gathering evidence against corrupt Indian agents, which he presented in person to President Jackson in the spring of 1830. As a result, Agent Hamtramck was dismissed, as were some of his superiors in the Indian Department. On Houston's recommendation, Paul Liguest Chouteau was made Osage agent, and A. P. Chouteau received the money he had advanced Clermont's band the summer before.[45]

On Houston's return from Washington, he and Chouteau were appointed commissioners to make peace between the Osage and Delaware, which they accomplished by paying the Osage $800 for eight members of their tribe killed by Delawares.[46] Houston and Chouteau became fast friends. Houston settled down on Cherokee lands near Chouteau's Verdigris post in a log trading house he called "Wigwam Neosho" with a pretty Cherokee girl. There he traded for a time without a United States license on grounds that the Cherokees had adopted him into the tribe long ago in Tennessee. He began to drink heavily – the Osage name for him was "Big Drunk" – and he lost an election for a seat on the Cherokee council in the spring of 1831, which enraged him.[47]

Sam Houston was anything but a hero at this period of his life, but he was always a leader, except for one occasion

---

[45] M. K. Wisehart, *Sam Houston, American Giant* (Washington, 1962), 62-72; Jack Gregory and Rannard Strickland, *Sam Houston with the Cherokees, 1829-1833* (Austin, 1967), 62-66.

[46] Letter of Col. Matthew Arbuckle to Maj. Gen. Alex Macomb, Cantonment Gibson, May 31, 1830, and letter of A. P. Chouteau to John M. Eaton, Western Creek Agency, May 29, 1830, Letters Received, OIA from Osage Agency.

[47] Wisehart, *op. cit.,* 62-72; Gregory and Strickland, *op. cit.,* 62-66.

when he appears to have been led by A. P. Chouteau, by most accounts an honest and straight-forward man, into some questionable dealings in Osage half-breed reserves. It probably started innocently enough in August 1830, when Chouteau was appointed by the Osages to assess the value of their improvements within the Cherokee reservation. On September 1, 1830, Chouteau, having done some assessing of his own improvements, sold Houston and his fellow-traders, David Thompson and John Drennan, two of the eight sections granted Chouteau's wife and children in the Osage treaty of 1825, for which Chouteau was trustee.

White men, as all parties to this transaction well knew, could not own land in the Indian country. Nevertheless, Houston and his friends paid Chouteau $3000 in cash and merchandise for the land, including the valuable Grand Saline which, on the strength of Houston's Cherokee allegiance, they meant to work. But by 1832, the validity of Houston's Cherokee citizenship was denied, and Houston, Thompson and Drennan could not use their land. Chouteau apparently offered to return their money should the government buy out the Osage half-breeds for a good price; at any rate Chouteau joined Houston and some Cherokee leaders in Washington in the spring of 1832 to urge the government to remove the Osages from Cherokee lands. The government hedged; the plot failed; and Chouteau, for the time being, was $3000 ahead. But after his death, Drennan seized six of Chouteau's valuable slaves in payment of the debt, and Chouteau's heirs were the losers.[48]

Neither Houston nor Chouteau were in Washington solely on the business of the Osage reserves in the spring of 1832.

<hr>

[48] Letter of Gov. Montfort Stokes to Commissioner of Indian Affairs, March 19, 1839, quoted in Foreman, *Pioneer Days*, 260-61; Wisehart, *op. cit.*, 62-79; Gregory and Strickland, *op. cit.*, 129; assessment made by A. P. Chouteau and P. L. Chouteau, Saline, Sept. 20, 1830, in Letters Received, OIA from Osage Agency; George Vashon, Cherokee Agent, to the Secretary of War, Jan. 4, 1832, quoted in Foreman, *Pioneer Days*, 194-95.

Houston had to defend himself against charges of fraud in contracts for supplying Indian rations the year before, and Chouteau was a witness for him. Acquitted of the charges, Houston returned to the Cherokees in September 1832, and departed soon after for Texas, leaving Wigwam Neosho to his Cherokee wife and the Saline he never really owned to his partners, who, being unable to make use of it, gave or sold it to the Cherokee John Rogers to work.[49]

Chouteau's principal purpose at Washington that spring was to wrest from a recalcitrant government the money it owed him for supplying the Creeks and the money it had owed the Creeks since 1826, for which Chouteau presented a power of attorney from the Creek chiefs. He was unsuccessful.[50]

While in Washington pressing his claims, Chouteau was asked by the Secretary of War to give his aid to a commission appointed to examine the country set apart for emigrating Indians west of the Mississippi. Accordingly, at Independence Chouteau met the commissioners, Henry L. Ellsworth, Governor Montfort Stokes of North Carolina, and John F. Schermerhorn, along with three distinguished gentlemen who came along for sheer adventure – Washington Irving, Charles Joseph Latrobe and the young Count de Pourtales. Chouteau escorted the visitors to his trading house, making their trip memorable with hunting lessons and camping craft.[51]

---

[49] Gregory and Strickland, *op. cit.,* 129.

[50] Power of attorney from the head chiefs of the Western Creek nation to A. P. Chouteau, March 1, 1832; letter of John Campbell to Lewis Cass; Letters Received, OIA from Creek Agency West, 1826-36. The guns, traps, etc. were shipped in 1834 but the boat sank below Fort Smith in December and only part of the goods were retrieved (Foreman, *Five Civilized Tribes,* 147-49).

[51] Letter of A. P. Chouteau to Lewis Cass, Washington, July 14, 1832, Letters Received, OIA from Osage Agency; Henry L. Ellsworth, *Washington Irving on the Prairie or a Narrative of a Tour of the Southwest in the year 1832* (N.Y., 1937); McDermott, *Western Journals of Irving* (Norman, Okla., 1944); Charles Joseph Latrobe, *The Rambler in North America, 1832-1833* (London, 1836).

The house at La Saline that the commissioners saw in 1832 was perhaps the same that Joseph Rivar had built in 1821, but much improved. In the spring of 1831, Chouteau had engaged twenty to thirty men who worked all summer on the place, putting up new buildings and remodeling old ones, probably intending to sell them for a high price to the government.[52] In the spring of 1832, Washington Irving spent a night in Chouteau's establishment and left in his journal a lively description of it:

Come in sight of Col's house – white log house with Piazza, surrounded by trees. Come to beautiful, clear river, group of Indian nymphs half naked on banks – with horses near – arrival at house – old negro runs to open gate – mouth from ear to ear – group of Indians round tree in court yard – roasting venison – horses tethered near – negroes run to shake hand and take horses – some have handkerchief across head – half breeds – squaws – negro girls running & giggling – dogs of all kinds – hens flying & cackling – wild turkeys, tamed geese – Piazza with Buffalo skin thrown over railing – room with guns – rifles.

Supper, venison stakes, roast beef, bread, cakes, coffee – waited on by half breed – sister of Mr. Choteau's concubine – adjourn to another room – pass thro open hall in which Indians are seated on floor. They come into the room – two bring in chairs – the other seats himself on the floor with his knees to his chin – another Indian glares in at the window. House formed of logs – a room at each end – an open hall with staircase in the centre – other rooms above – in the two rooms on ground floor two beds in each room with curtains – white washed log walls – tables of various kinds – Indian ornaments &c.

Half breeds loitering about the house – dogs & cats of all kinds strolling about the hall or sleeping among harness at one end of the piazza. . . A quarter mile from the Col's house is his race course on a beautiful little level Prarie. He has a great number of horses which the blacks drive by the house in a drove. . .[53]

---

[52] Letter of John Campbell, Western Creek Agent, to the Secretary of War, Aug. 19, 1831, Letters Received, OIA from Creek Agency West; letter of A. P. Chouteau to Hon. Lewis Cass, Washington, July 14, 1832, Letters Received, OIA from Osage Agency.

[53] McDermott, *Western Journals of Irving*, 108-12.

For an Indian trader, Chouteau lived well; too well, perhaps, for the ever-precarious state of his finances.

The commissioners had experienced A. P. Chouteau's hospitality, and they were now to feel his power. In March 1833, they met with eight hundred Osages at Fort Gibson, with P. L. Chouteau as Osage Agent, A. A. Chouteau as interpreter and A. P. Chouteau furnishing rations. For three weeks the commissioners tried to make Clermont's Osages accept an inferior reservation to the north, but their object was defeated by Clermont and A. P. Chouteau, who demanded larger annuities and what was termed an "inadmissable" amount of land. The conference was a failure and the commissioners blamed Chouteau and his brothers: "Col. [A.P.] Chouteau has long been the great friend and counselor of the Osage nation, and [such is] the unlimited influence the Chouteaus seem to possess over the nation . . . that it would be difficult if not impracticable to make a treaty against their opinions." [54]

The treaty prevented Chouteau from going to Washington that spring, but in the summer of 1833 he went as far as St. Louis, where he wrote the Secretary of War and Commissioner of Indian Affairs about the Osage reserves and his claims against the government.[55] The payment of Chouteau's claims became very important to him in 1833 and for all the years ahead, for suddenly his debt to his brother Pierre and associates was becoming too big to be ignored. In June 1833, a flood washed away all his buildings on the Verdigris, along with the Creek Agency buildings and most of the nearby

[54] Letter of Montfort Stokes, Henry L. Ellsworth and J. F. Schermerhorn to Lewis Cass, Fort Gibson, April 2, 1833, Letters Received, OIA from Osage Agency. A. P. Chouteau was known as "Colonel"; his brother P. L. Chouteau as "Major," the common title for Indian agents.

[55] Letter of A. P. Chouteau to Elbert Herring, St. Louis, Aug. 11, 1833, Letters Received, OIA from Creek Agency West; Foreman, *Pioneer Days,* 214.

Creek village, thereby reducing his customers to paupers.[56] His own losses were well over $10,000.[57] In the spring of 1834, he went to Washington and New York, to buy goods and sell furs, but to his further distress, a large proportion of his deerskins arrived damaged. His family still had confidence in him, however, for it was he and Pierre Menard who represented the family company in the sale of the American Fur Company's Western Department to Pratte, Chouteau & Co. in New York in May 1834.[58] At Washington he again pressed his claims against the government and at least had the satisfaction of seeing Congress allow the Creek claims – but it was a hollow victory, for no money was appropriated to pay them during his lifetime.[59]

Nor could he recover the money the Osages owed him. On January 5, 1835, another treaty council with the Osages was held at Fort Gibson, at which the treaty commissioner refused to insert a clause paying the Indians' debts to their traders, a common practice in treaties of that period. It was to A. P. Chouteau's credit, as the commissioner acknowledged, that Chouteau told the Indians not to let their debt to him of $3404 prevent them from making a good treaty.[60] After the treaty was signed, Chouteau left immediately for Washington to urge payment of the Osage annuity as stipulated in the treaty, but the treaty was not ratified.[61]

Chouteau had other errands in the East in the spring of

---

[56] Foreman, *Five Civilized Tribes,* 23; various letters and documents in the Letters Received, OIA from Creek Agency West.

[57] In September 1833, his account with the American Fur Company which only three months earlier had shown a credit of over $5000, was reduced to a debit of $13,725.98 (Ledger H, Chouteau Coll.).

[58] Letter of A. P. Chouteau to Pierre Chouteau Jr., Philadelphia, May 30, 1834 (in French) and letter of Ramsay Crooks to Pratte Chouteau & Co., New York, May 31, 1834, both in the Chouteau Coll.

[59] Letter of A. P. Chouteau to Pierre Chouteau Jr., Philadelphia, May 30, 1834, (in French), Chouteau Coll.

[60] Letter of F. S. Armstrong to Elbert Herring, Fort Gibson, Jan. 6, 1835, Letters Received, OIA from Osage Agency.

[61] Letter of A. P. Chouteau to Elbert Herring, Washington, Feb. 29 [sic], 1835, Letters Received, OIA from Osage Agency.

1835. In St. Louis he formed a partnership with Robert Payne for trade with the Cherokees, who were the only Indians at Three Forks rich enough to buy his goods. Then he went to Philadelphia and purchased merchandise from various firms, mostly from Siter, Price & Co. who sold him $30,000 worth of goods on credit and loaned him $10,000.[62] He also enrolled his son Pierre Sylvestre in Mr. A. Bolmar's Institution for Boys at West Chester, Pennsylvania – and then, whether from indifference or some other cause, left him there for three years with never a word to Mr. Bolmar, letting his brother Pierre pay the bills.[63] By August he had returned to the Verdigris and was awaiting his partner Robert Payne when he discovered that the Cherokee agent would not allow him to rent a store on the Cherokee reserve. His letters to the Commissioner of Indian Affairs and entreaties to the sub-agent were to no avail; by August of 1836 he and his partner had still not sold their goods and were unable to make payments to Siter, Price & Co.[64]

In the meantime Chouteau had found a new market for his goods, and had built a new trading post. In August 1835, a treaty of "perpetual peace and friendship" was made between the civilized Indians on the Arkansas and the wild Indians of the plains. A. P. Chouteau was not present, but Augustine A. Chouteau, presumably his eldest son, was a witness at the council, which was held at Camp Holmes (also called Camp Mason) on the left bank of the Canadian

[62] So Siter, Price & Co. claimed in its suit brought in January 1838 (Chouteau Coll.). A. P. Chouteau's account with P. Chouteau Jr. & Co. shows that on December 29, 1838, he owed $22,356.18 in drafts drawn on Ramsay Crooks in favor of Siter, Price & Co., no doubt representing the amount after credits and set offs (Pierre Chouteau Jr. Ledger, 1836-55, Chouteau Coll.).

[63] Letter of Ramsay Crooks to A. P. Chouteau, New York, June 13, 1835; letter of Crooks to Bolmar, Oct. 7, 1837; Bolmar to A. P. Chouteau, West Chester, Oct. 15, 1838; Bolmar to Crooks, Feb. 26, 1838, in *Calendar of the American Fur Company's Papers,* American Historical Association, *Annual Report, 1944* (Washington, 1945), nos. 579, 3270, 5105, 4042.

[64] Letter of A. P. Chouteau to Elbert Herring, Western Creek Nation, Aug. 16, 1835, Letters Received, OIA from Creek Agency West.

a hundred miles west of Fort Gibson at present Lexington, Oklahoma. At the site of the camp and shortly after the treaty council, Chouteau built a stockade fort on a creek henceforth known as Chouteau Creek, to trade with the Comanches, Wichitas and other Indians. In 1835 and 1836 Chouteau was at this trading post only sporadically, and the business was handled by his clerks. In July 1837, Liguest Chouteau resigned as Osage agent, bought goods in partnership with Auguste and went to trade at the post at Camp Holmes, whence a large number of Osage were expected to follow him.[65]

In the summer of 1837, Chouteau established another trading post for the Kiowas, who had not signed the treaty at Camp Holmes in August, 1835. Liguest Chouteau had been commissioned to find the Kiowas and offer them a treaty, and had joined A. P. Chouteau in providing $5000 worth of presents, for which, as usual, the government delayed reimbursement. A. P. Chouteau and Montfort Stokes were United States commissioners for the treaty, which was signed at Fort Gibson on May 26, 1837 by the Kiowas, Ka-ta-ka (Kiowa Apaches) and Ta-wa-ka-ro (Tawakoni), and the chiefs of the Comanche, Wichita, Cherokee, Creek, Choctaw, Osage, Seneca and Quapaw nations. Afterwards, A. P. Chouteau built a little fort on the west bank of Cache Creek about three miles below present Fort Sill. A trader the Kiowas called "Tome-te" traded there for the short time the post was in operation.[66]

---

[65] Kappler, *op. cit.*, II, pp. 435-39; Gregg, *Commerce of the Prairies,* Thwaites edition, xx, p. 107; letter of William Armstrong, acting Choctaw agent, to C. A. Harris, Dec. 27, 1837, and letter of P. L. Chouteau to Wm. Armstrong, Saline, July 1, 1837, in Letters Received, OIA from Osage Agency. Letters from A. P. Chouteau in the *Calendar, A.F.C. Papers* and in the Chouteau Collection, all dated from the Verdigris post, suggest that he spent no extended periods of time at Camp Holmes. They are dated Jan. 4, 1836, Jan. 24, 1836, April 17, 1836, April 25, 1836, June 10, 1836, Aug. 15, 1836, Dec. 13, 1836, Jan. 24, 1837, April 17, 1837.

[66] Kappler, *op. cit.,* II, pp. 480-91; James Mooney, "Calendar History of the Kiowa Indians," in Bureau of American Ethnology, *17th Annual Report* (Washington, 1898), 171-72.

In spite of the recent treaties of "perpetual peace," by the summer of 1837 the Indians of the southwest were in a dangerous mood, for during the Texan revolution both Texan and Mexican agents had attempted to convert the Indians to their respective causes, and the result was a threat of general Indian warfare. In this emergency, A. P. Chouteau was commissioned on July 27, 1837, as special agent to the Comanches and other tribes to prevent hostilities. His duties were to travel among the Indians, make peace and invite the Comanches and Kiowas to send a delegation to Washington in the spring of 1838.[67] In November, Chouteau arrived at his Camp Holmes post with an escort of dragoons and sufficient provision and animals for him to spend the winter there and gather up his Indians. But during the winter he reported that because all the Indians were at war, he could not get them together until the spring.[68]

In May, Chouteau was visited by twenty-two principal chiefs of eight different prairie tribes, whom Chouteau named as the "Pa-do-ka, Ky-o-wah, Ka-ta-ka, Yam-pa-rhe-ka or Comanche, Sho-sho-nee, Hoish, Co-che-te-kah and Wee-che-tah." To the Indians' disappointment, Chouteau refused to take them to visit the President in Washington, because, as he wrote the Commissioner of Indian Affairs in June, their people were too widely scattered and all at war. Instead he gave them presents, urged them to keep peace, and told them he would return to Fort Gibson for the rest of the summer and meet them again at Camp Holmes in October.[69]

There were very strong personal reasons why Chouteau did not wish to take the Indians to Washington that summer. One was an injury to his thigh so severe that he could not

[67] Foreman, *Pioneer Days,* 230n; Report from the Office of Indian Affairs, Dec. 1, 1837, *H. Doc. 3,* 25 Cong., 2 sess. (Ser. 321), 567, 597-99.

[68] Foreman, *Pioneer Days,* 234-37, quotes from two interesting letters about the Indians written by Chouteau in December and from another written in June at Camp Holmes.   [69] *Ibid.,* 234-39.

ride a horse. The other was the monstrous debt he had accumulated which suddenly broke open and rained disgrace and ruin on him. In January 1838, Siter, Price & Co. brought suit for $40,000 against Chouteau & Payne.[70] Forced by Siter, Price & Co's suit to take action of his own for a much larger and longer-standing debt, on March 21, 1838, Pierre Chouteau Jr. sued A. P. Chouteau for $500,000. The just debt, as J. B. Sarpy made affidavit the same day, was $66,000 after allowance for credits, and such was the amount of the judgment rendered. On March 22, A. P. Chouteau's property in St. Louis was attached – a house and lot in Block 29 between Main and Second streets, two domestic slaves worth $1000, furniture worth $696.75. The whole was sold at public auction for $26,844.40, and Chouteau's wife and children were put out of the house with nothing more than the clothes on their backs.[71]

A. P. Chouteau's account with the Osage Outfit of Pratte, Chouteau & Co. was promptly closed, and Antoine Janis and Toiniche Dehetre were immediately despatched to the Arkansas country to fetch the unfortunate delinquent back to civilization to meet his creditors. But he would not come; no matter how urgent his financial problems, his commitment to the Indians could not be put aside. On May 23, 1838, he made out a power of attorney to the St. Louis lawyers Lewis V. Bogy and Joseph J. Spalding, which Janis took back to St. Louis, and then Chouteau returned to Camp Holmes.[72]

---

[70] By arrangement with Pierre Chouteau, Jr., judgment was not rendered against the defendants until 1840, when they were ordered to pay $12,509.92. Chouteau Coll.

[71] #1439 (A. P. Chouteau), Probate Court Records, St. Louis County, Mo.; suit for trespass brought by Siter, Price & Co. vs A. P. Chouteau, Chouteau Coll.; two executions, both dated July 18, 1838, against A. P. Chouteau, one by Pierre Chouteau, Jr., surviving partner of Berthold & Chouteau claiming $66,000, the other by Pierre Chouteau, Jr., John P. Cabanné, John B. Sarpy, Bernard Pratte, J. F. A. Sanford, Pierre Menard and Felix Vallé, surviving partners of Pratte Chouteau & Co., for $4,139. Chouteau Coll.

[72] #1439 (A. P. Chouteau), Probate Court Records, St. Louis.

Because of illness, Chouteau was not able to meet the Indians at Camp Holmes in October 1838, as he had planned. During that month he was reported ill at Fort Smith and not expected to recover. By December he had managed to return to Fort Gibson where, on Christmas Day, 1838, he died. He was given a military funeral with all the honors by his officer friends, and was buried in the Fort Gibson cemetery.[73]

Perhaps he died of an injured thigh or its complications, perhaps of despair over his financial ruin. He died as he lived, in debt, and his unfortunate family inherited nothing. In the treaty of 1835 with the Cherokees, Chouteau's half-breed wife and children had been awarded $15,000 for their eight sections of land, with which Chouteau, acting as trustee, bought thirty-two valuable slaves. After his death, most of the slaves returned to their former owners, the Creek Indians, who refused to give them up. Rosalie and her children were left destitute, living at La Saline which now belonged to the Cherokee nation. Rosalie tried to become a Cherokee citizen, but until she married a Cherokee, her claim to citizenship was invalid.[74] Chouteau's property at La Saline and the Verdigris post was dissipated soon after his death, local creditors making off with slaves, livestock, goods and wagons. Antoine Janis was again sent from St. Louis to collect what was left of Chouteau's estate at Three Forks and, with the help of Captain Robert E. Lee of Fort Gibson, found some merchandise, wagons, forges and other equipment, along with seventy-odd head of horses and mules which were taken to St. Louis and sold. After his assets

[73] Foreman, *Pioneer Days*, 239. William Waldo says he died alone among the prairie Indians and his negro servant brought his body to his nephew, Capt. Paul at Fort Gibson, for burial ("Recollections," 82). His obituary in the *Missouri Republican* of Jan. 18, 1839, says he died "at his plantation, the Grand Saline." Another letter says he died near Fort Gibson (*Calendar, A.F.C. Papers, loc. cit.*, Jan. 16, 1839, #5490); and Gregg says he died at Fort Gibson (*Commerce of the Prairies*, Thwaites ed., xx, pp. 107-08.)

[74] Foreman, *Pioneer Days*, 257-61, 289-91.

were counted, Chouteau's estate still owed creditors nearly $25,000.[75]

A. P. Chouteau's failure in the world of white men did not diminish his reputation among the Indians, who valued a man differently. In the spring of 1839, Santa Fe trader Josiah Gregg and his party took shelter in Chouteau's Fort, the little abandoned log stockade post at Camp Holmes. They had not been there long before a party of Comanches came up and warmly welcomed them, thinking it was Chouteau returning to the fort with fresh supplies of merchandise. Gregg writes: "Great was their grief when we informed them that their favorite trader had died at Fort Gibson, the previous winter."[76] The Comanches' grief is a fitting eulogy for one of the best of the Indian traders.

[75] Account of A. P. Chouteau in the Pierre Chouteau Jr. Ledger (1836-1855), and Ledger cc, Chouteau Coll; Foreman, *Pioneer Days,* 255-61.

[76] Gregg, *op. cit.,* Thwaites ed., xx, p. 108. The Kiowas were also devoted to Chouteau. Says James Mooney ("Calendar History," *loc. cit.,* 172): "Under the name of *Soto,* Chouteau is still held in affectionate remembrance by the Kiowa."

Pierre Chouteau, Junior

by JANET LECOMPTE
Colorado Springs, Colorado

Pierre Chouteau, Junior, was born January 19, 1789, at St. Louis, the second son of Pierre Chouteau and the grandson of the founder of St. Louis, Pierre Laclède Liguest. For at least a century the Chouteaus were the leading family of St. Louis – a clan whose many intermarriages produced a tight core of social and business eminence. If one wished to make a name or a fortune in St. Louis, it was best to be born a Chouteau, and to marry another, as did Pierre Chouteau, Junior.

Young Pierre's mother was Pelagie Kiersereau, an orphan and only child reared by her grandfather, Joseph Taillon. She married Pierre Chouteau on July 26, 1783, and died ten years later, leaving four children, Auguste Pierre, Pierre Junior, Paul Liguest and a daughter Pelagie. A year after his wife's death in 1793, her widower married Brigitte Saucier who presented him with five more sons, François Gesseau, Cyprian, Louis Pharamond, Charles and Frederick.[1] Most of them became fur traders, which is not surprising for at that time the fur trade was the town's only business.

Of Pierre Chouteau's eight sons, it was young Pierre who inherited his father's name as well as his nickname "Cadet," referring to a second-born son. He also inherited his father's shrewdness and diligence, and his lust for wealth and

[1] Frederic L. Billon, *Annals of St. Louis in Its Territorial Days* (St. Louis, 1888), 168-69.

power.[2] But the son's ambition came not altogether from the father, nor in any part from the placid, frivolous creole society of his heredity. It came from the new materialism of the nineteenth century, and from its first behemoth exponent, John Jacob Astor. The interest in Chouteau's character lies in the conflict between the gentle, home-loving creole he was, and the grasping American tycoon he became.

Educational advantages in the village of St. Louis were meager, but young Cadet managed to learn whatever mathematics were necessary for a fur trader, and to write a handsome and legible hand. He also learned to read and speak English, but he so much preferred his native French that he stubbornly wrote all his letters in that language, to the annoyance of his non-Gallic correspondents. At maturity he looked and acted the aristocrat he was – tall, erect, black-eyed and black-haired. In repose he was often grave and contemplative, but in conversation, animated and cheerful. His personality was well-integrated. Seldom does his correspondence reveal a flash of temper or a sough of self-pity. His manner was unfailingly gracious, easy and affable with everyone, from the political leaders of the country to the lowliest boatman, yet he was resolute and, when necessary, politely ruthless. He commanded deference from all who knew him and a well-founded fear from those who opposed him.[3]

At about the age of fifteen, or since "earliest manhood" as he says in his Last Will and Testament, young Cadet en-

[2] For contemporary estimates of the senior Chouteau's character, see James Wilkinson's letter of Nov. 26, 1805, and Albert Gallatin's of Aug. 20, 1804, in Donald Jackson, *The Journals of Zebulon Montgomery Pike* (Norman, 1966), I, pp. 209, 251; and other letters in *The Life and Papers of Frederick Bates,* ed. Thomas Maitland Marshall (St. Louis, 1926), I, pp. 45-47, 86-92.

[3] Biographical sketch of Pierre Chouteau, Junior, by Pierre Chouteau, ms., Chouteau Collection, Missouri Historical Society, St. Louis; William Hyde and Howard L. Conard, eds., *Encyclopedia of the History of St. Louis* (New York, 1899), I, pp. 363-64; "Address of Hon. Elihu B. Washburne . . .", Jefferson City, 1881, Missouri Hist. Soc. A portrait of Pierre Chouteau, Jr. appears herein at page 17.

gaged in the fur trade, first as a clerk in his uncle Auguste's office[4] and then as a trader to the Osage Indians, among whom his father had traded since youth and made a small fortune. Cadet was at the Little Osage village as early as September 1806, when he sold Zebulon Pike a horse. As "Peter Chouteau jr" he was issued a license on September 26, 1807, to trade with the Great and Little Osage and went up the Missouri and Osage rivers with two boatloads of merchandise to spend the winter with these Indians. In the spring he returned, his trade no great success.[5]

While Cadet was thus engaged, his father and elder brother Auguste accompanied an expedition up the Missouri to return to his village the Mandan Chief Shehaka, brought east by Lewis and Clark. The expedition was turned back by hostile Arikaras and the project abandoned until 1809, when a successful attempt to return the chief was again led by Cadet's brother and father. In their absence, Cadet was left in charge of his father's business, which he handled with great seriousness. He even presumed to write the Secretary of War a respectful but firm letter defending his father from charges of dereliction of duty as Osage Indian Agent in undertaking the mission up the Missouri.[6]

In early spring 1810, Cadet left St. Louis to go five hundred miles up the Mississippi to the present site of Dubuque, Iowa. There Julien Dubuque had bought land from the Fox Indians in 1788 and mined lead with their labor. The Span-

---

[4] J. Thomas Scharf, *History of Saint Louis City and County* (Phila., 1883), I, p. 183; but H. M. Chittenden, *The American Fur Trade of the Far West* (N.Y., 1902), I, p. 382, says he started out in his father's office.

[5] Jackson, *Z. M. Pike*, I, p. 312n; *Life of Bates*, I, pp. 202-03; Richard Edwards and M. Hopewell, M.D., *Edwards's Great West and her Commercial Metropolis* (St. Louis, 1860), 537.

[6] Letter of Pierre Chouteau *fils* to the Secretary of War, Sept. 1, 1809, in Clarence Edwin Carter, ed., *The Territorial Papers of the United States*, XIV (Wash., D.C., 1949), 312-19. See Nathaniel Pryor to William Clark, St. Louis, Oct. 16, 1807, in Donald Jackson, ed., *Letters of the Lewis and Clark Expedition . . .* (Urbana, 1962), 432-37, for evidence that Pierre Jr. was not on the first expedition up the Missouri, as several historians have assumed.

ish government had granted Dubuque the land in 1796 and Auguste Chouteau had bought half of it, or 72,324 acres, in 1804, with the provision that on Dubuque's death all the property would revert to Chouteau and his heirs. Cadet, intending to manage his uncle's share of the business, found on arrival in April that Dubuque had died three weeks earlier. He was greeted with respect and affection by the Indians, and continued to live there off and on until the start of the War of 1812, when he returned to St. Louis. He retained an interest in the lead mines and the acreage around them until the United States courts denied his claim to them in 1845 and an appeal ended unfavorably in 1854.[7]

In 1813, at the age of twenty-four, Cadet opened a store in St. Louis with Bartholomew Berthold, a highly-educated gentleman from the Italian Tyrol who had come to the United States as a merchant in 1798 and had kept a store in St. Louis from 1809 until 1812. On May 1, 1813, Berthold & Chouteau began selling crockery, hardware, dry goods and groceries purchased at Baltimore and Philadelphia, in a two-story building at 11 North Main (St. Louis's first brick building).[8] It was no coincidence that Cadet's partner was his brother-in-law (Berthold had married Pelagie Chouteau in 1811), for creole St. Louisans regarded their relatives with the greatest loyalty and affection and kept their businesses closely held within the family. Not until Cadet

7 "Petition to the Senate and House of Representatives of the U.S. setting forth rights of claimants to tract of land known as Dubuque Mines," Jan. 10, 1837, Chouteau Coll.; Carter, *op. cit.,* XIV, pp. 73-75; "Dubuque Claim. Memorial to the Hon. the Senate and House of Representatives of the United States of America . . . Praying for the confirmation of the title to a tract of land granted to Julien Dubuque by the Baron de Carondelet . . . on the 10th of November, 1796. St. Louis, 1845," Chouteau Coll.; Richard Herrmann, *Julien Dubuque, His Life and Adventures* (Dubuque, 1922), 47, 56. Scharf and Chittenden place Cadet at the lead mines in 1806-1808; Stella Drumm, in 1808, (in her sketch of "Pierre Chouteau," *Dictionary of American Biography,* IV (1929), pp. 93-4) ; and Charles P. Chouteau's obituary, in 1806, (*St. Louis Globe-Democrat,* Jan. 6, 1901).

8 Billon, *op. cit.,* 127, 129, 234; Scharf, *op. cit.,* 150, 196; Carter, *op. cit.,* XIV, p. 791, and XV (1950), p. 85.

had been in business for many years and suffered many disappointments did he choose business associates outside his family.

Nor was there any need for Cadet, in a family with as many connections as the Chouteaus, to seek a wife of another lineage; and he chose his first cousin. On June 15, 1813, six weeks after the opening of the new store, he married Emilie Anne Gratiot, twenty-year-old daughter of Charles Gratiot and Victoire Chouteau,[9] and in so doing strengthened his relationships with useful men on his wife's side of the family – her sister Julie's husband, Jean P. Cabanné, who was to be Cadet's partner for many years, and Emilie's brother Charles who was to be a general in the United States Army and of great value to Cadet during his lobbying years in Washington.

Unfortunately we have no portrait of Emilie Gratiot Chouteau. She may have been beautiful like her sister Isabelle DeMun, or she may have been elegant and charming like her sister Julia Cabanné. Even if she were neither beautiful nor stylish, Emilie was a delightful woman. Bouncy and good-natured, she was blooming with health and seldom affected by the constant illnesses that attacked nearly everyone else in that era, and particularly her husband. Friends and family were her exclusive concern, and they kept her busy. Wrote her son-in-law Sanford in 1838 with affectionate amusement: "Mother is now occupied in arranging her new carpets – all Bustle and if it was not that, it would be something else *equally pressing*. Occupation. Occupation. Action! Action! I cannot imagine what would become of her without it."[10] Above all, Emilie was the soul of kindness and her family adored her. "Go often to kind Emilie's,"

9 Billon, *op. cit.,* 170. Stella Drumm in the *Dictionary of American Biography* sketch says they were married in the church on Aug. 13, 1814, the earlier marriage being a civil one.

10 John F. A. Sanford to P. Chouteau Jr., Jan. 12, 1838, Chouteau Coll.

wrote Jules DeMun to Isabelle in 1816,[11] and in a letter addressing Emilie as "My Dearest Mother," Sanford thanks her for her "unvarying kindness to me & mine." [12] To Cadet she was "my beloved wife and companion" for nearly fifty years of marriage.[13] They had five children born in the family home at Main and Vine, three of whom survived infancy: Emilie, born February 3, 1814; Julia, born February 18, 1816; Pierre Charles born December 25, 1817, died 1818; Charles Pierre, born December 2, 1819; and Benjamin Wilson, born August 17, 1822 and died soon after.[14]

The little firm of Berthold & Chouteau was the foundation of the great fur company that dominated the west for half a century. For the first year or so, it was merely a store on the main street of St. Louis. Then, inevitably, it slipped into the fur trade. In 1814 the company sent traders to the Otoes, Pawnee Loups and Pawnees on the Platte and Missouri rivers,[15] and in 1815 it outfitted Cadet's older brother Auguste Pierre and brother-in-law Jules DeMun for an expedition to the Rocky Mountains at the sources of the Platte and Arkansas rivers, to trade with the Arapahos, Comanches and other Indians. The expedition ended in such financial misery that Cadet never again trusted the mountain part of the fur trade.[16]

A. P. Chouteau and Jules DeMun returned to St. Louis in September 1817, and established the firm of Chouteau, DeMun & Sarpy, the latter being John B. Sarpy, nineteen-year-old cousin of the Chouteaus. By September 1818, DeMun had dropped out and Chouteau had borrowed a

---

11 *Bulletin,* Mo. Hist. Soc., XXVI, no. 1 (Oct. 1969), 29.

12 Sanford to Emilie Chouteau, Feb. 22, 1839, Chouteau Coll.

13 Last Will and Testament of Pierre Chouteau, Jr., 17 August 1865, copy in Mo. Hist. Soc.

14 Oscar W. Collet, *Index to St. Louis Cathedral and Carondelet Church Baptisms* (St. Louis, 1918) ; Billon, *op. cit.,* 171.

15 Carter, *op. cit.,* XIV, p. 791.

16 See sketch of "Jules DeMun," this *Series* vol. VIII.

large sum of money from Berthold & Chouteau to continue business as Chouteau & Sarpy in Berthold & Chouteau's new brick building. Chouteau & Sarpy was dissolved in 1821, but A. P. Chouteau never paid his debt to Berthold & Chouteau. In 1838 Cadet sued his brother for everything he owned, and won.[17] What bitterness and disillusionment surrounded this break in family relations will probably never be known, for if there were family letters about it, they seem to have disappeared.

In the early years, Berthold & Chouteau's principal opponent in the St. Louis mercantile business was Jean P. Cabanné & Co., whose senior partner was related to the partners of Berthold & Chouteau. Family gatherings in this era must have been carefully controlled affairs to maintain peace among the guests. When Bernard Pratte, grandson of Cadet's aunt Pelagie joined Cabanné in 1816, a family merger would seem to have been indicated, but it was six years in coming. On January 30, 1819, a newspaper advertisement announcing the dissolution of Cabanné & Co. was signed by "Pr. Chouteau Jr.",[18] but Cabanné did not immediately join Berthold & Chouteau, except for one brief, dismal venture. In 1819 a large expedition led by Manuel Lisa was financed by Berthold & Chouteau and by Cabanné, among others. The expedition returned before reaching the mountains because its leader was afraid his partners were doing him out of his just profits in his absence. Berthold & Chouteau had put in $22,286.45 and Cabanné $14,929, most of which was lost, and the joint venture came to an abrupt end.[19]

After that, competition in the fur trade based at St. Louis

[17] Notice of dissolution of partnership, Sept. 14, 1818, in *Missouri Gazette*, Oct. 2, 1818; Billon, *op. cit.*, 129, 143, 152; Scharf, *op. cit.*, I, pp. 582-83; #1439 (Auguste P. Chouteau), Probate Court, St. Louis County, Mo.

[18] "Reminiscences of General Bernard Pratte, Jr.," *Bulletin*, Mo. Hist. Soc., VI, no. 1 (Oct. 1949), 59-61; newspaper advertisement, Lisa Papers, Mo. Hist. Soc.

[19] Richard Edward Oglesby, *Manuel Lisa and the Opening of the Missouri Fur Trade* (Norman, 1963), 168-71.

grew like weeds in a vacant lot. The vacuum created by the demise of Cabanné & Co. was quickly filled by the Missouri Fur Company whose principals, all intelligent and forceful men, were Lisa, Joshua Pilcher, Lucien Fontenelle, Andrew Drips, William Vanderburgh and Charles Bent. This company was highly successful at charging up the Missouri and establishing trading posts.[20] Berthold & Chouteau, rising timidly to the challenge, sent Joseph Brazeau ("Cayowa") to establish a post near Cedar Island in present South Dakota, but the rest of its posts in 1819 were far closer to home: François Chouteau's near the mouth of the Kansas River, Paul Liguest Chouteau's at the Osage village, Robidoux's and Papin's at the Nishnabotna, Sylvestre Pratte's and Baronet Vasquez's near the Omaha village.[21] By 1823 the company had other little posts on the Missouri besides Fort Cayowa – at the Poncas (under Pascal Cerré), at the Arikaras (under Citoleux) and among the various Sioux divisions, the Saones (under Sire and Brazeau), Oglallas (under Gratiot), Yanktons (under Pescay) and Santee (under Defont) – which altogether that winter turned out 877 packs of buffalo robes and 1355 pounds of beaver.[22]

Opposition continued to mount. In 1822 William Ashley began sending his annual company of trappers to the Rocky Mountains with increasing success, and by 1824 high-priced beaver brought in traders' wagons from Santa Fe began reaching the St. Louis market. But worst of all – or best, as it turned out for Cadet, was the competition of John Jacob Astor. Since 1816, Astor's agents had bought a few furs from Cabanné & Co. and from Berthold & Chouteau, but it was not until 1822 that Astor's American Fur Company

---

20 For information about the Missouri Fur Company and other fur trade matters of general knowledge and interest not hereafter footnoted, see H. M. Chittenden's *American Fur Trade,* published in 1902 but still the best treatment, and LeRoy Hafen's useful summary in vol. I, this *Series.*

21 "Trade and Intercourse," *American State Papers,* Indian Affairs, vol. II, p. 202.

22 "Tableaux ou l'on expose la quantité de peleteries que chacque post a traite dans l'hiver 1823 au 1824," Chouteau Coll.

established a strong Western Department in St. Louis, which meant to sell all the goods and buy all the furs in the west.[23]

Thus it happened that Cadet began his lessons in cut-throat competition from one of its all-time masters, John Jacob Astor. On February 9, 1822, Bernard Pratte, now a partner in the reorganized firm of Berthold, Chouteau & Pratte, signed an agreement with Ramsay Crooks to sell to the American Fur Company buffalo robes at $2.75 apiece and deerskins at 33½¢ per pound, and to buy goods from it for a period of one year.[24] The arrangement was highly profitable for Cadet. On December 7, 1822, he received a book profit of $25,097.76, of which $16,053.65 was his third share of profits earned by Berthold, Chouteau & Pratte.[25]

From this time forward, year by year, Cadet and his associates would learn Astor's techniques: upon dissolution of a rival company, Cadet would take over its posts and men, territories and trade, allowing no fragment of the defunct company to attach to other rivals; opposing local suppliers would be confronted with vicious price wars; competition that could not be smashed, such as William Ashley's unique ventures, would be supplied with either goods or backing and the profits shared; political influence would be fully exploited, and liquor shamelessly sold to the Indians when necessary; traders would work on shares, so that the company would profit both from selling them goods and buying their furs, and their territories would be carefully divided. These were the principles behind successful fur trade management, and Cadet violated them only at his peril.[26]

By May 1823, J. P. Cabanné had joined Berthold & Chouteau, and the name of it was henceforth Bernard Pratte & Co. Cabanné took over the post at Council Bluffs as man-

---

[23] R. Crooks Letter Book, 1816-1820, Chouteau Coll; Kenneth Wiggins Porter, *John Jacob Astor, Business Man* (Cambridge, 1931), II, pp. 692-93, 717-18.

[24] Agreement in the Chouteau Coll.   [25] Journal D, Chouteau Coll.

[26] Some of these principles are elucidated in Porter, *Astor*, 815-38; others become evident in the present sketch.

ager of the lower Missouri trade; Berthold ascended the river in the fall of 1824 to take charge of upper Missouri posts; Bernard Pratte handled the external affairs of the company; and John B. Sarpy settled down in the counting house where he handled the St. Louis books and correspondence for the rest of his life. But over them all as general superintendent, his growing ability the crown and glory of the firm, was Pierre Chouteau, Junior.[27]

In the fall of 1824, Cadet and Emilie left their children in St. Louis and went to New York in their carriage with Bernard Pratte, undoubtedly to explore the possibility of a closer association with Astor's firm. After a three-week trip over foul and dangerous roads, Emilie found New York and its people very pleasant, and she would often accompany her husband there in the future. In the city they spent much time with Ramsay Crooks, who was soon to marry Bernard Pratte's daughter, Emilie, thereby earning the right to address Cadet as "mon cher cousin" in a warm and affectionate correspondence that lasted twenty years. Cadet and Emilie also went to Niagara Falls, which, if not entirely for business purposes, was apparently the last vacation Chouteau allowed himself. But no arrangement with the American Fur Company resulted from this journey.[28]

Astor would not have benefitted from an association with B. Pratte & Co. at this time. The St. Louis firm had still not mastered the mechanics of competition, and its traders were always lagging behind. The ineffective Cayowa had been replaced by Berthold as head of the upper Missouri operations, but Berthold was a weak and gentle person who was ignored by his clerks. Cabanné on the lower Missouri was neither cool enough nor quick enough to outguess the bright competition leaders. Only the traders among the Osages —

27 B. Pratte & Co. to O. N. Bostwick, St. Louis, May 26, 1823, and Cabanné to Chouteau, May 26, 1823, both in Chouteau Coll.

28 Crooks to P. Chouteau, Jr., Nov. 1, 1824 and Dec. 6, 1824, and Pierre Chouteau to P. Chouteau, Jr., Dec. 14, 1824, in the Chouteau Coll.

Cadet's brothers A. P. Chouteau and Paul Liguest Chouteau, and his cousin Pierre Melicourt Papin – were without serious competition, and only because fine peltry was scarce in their territory. Elsewhere the company was short of men with nerve and experience. To make profits it was forced to share ventures with other traders – with the Missouri Fur Company and with slippery old Joseph Robidoux, who, in the sheep's clothing of a B. Pratte & Co. employee, made his own expeditions in direct or indirect competition.[29]

B. Pratte & Co.'s worst mistake was its "Taos Adventure." In the fall of 1824, the company bought 1500 pounds of beaver trapped in the southwest, a pale fur that to their surprise sold better than the dark northern variety. Excited but cautious, the partners bought a one-third interest in Ceran St. Vrain's small outfit for trading with trappers in New Mexico in 1825, which earned them little. The following summer the company sent Sylvestre S. Pratte, Bernard's son, to Taos to take charge of nearly 120 free trappers who spread out in different parties hunting for two years from the Rio Grande to the Gila and as far north as the Platte River and Lake Utah. The business was a calamity, one of the parties under Michel Robidoux being massacred and the others bringing in few furs. Young Pratte died in the mountains in October 1827, but not before he had signed what Cadet disconsolately referred to as "these inexhaustible fur-drafts" which the company was forced to honor.[30] Historian H. M. Chittenden's judgement that Chouteau turned to profit everything he touched was far from true, especially in these early years.[31]

But his time was coming. In June 1826, Ramsay Crooks

---

[29] See correspondence of J. P. Cabanné, Chouteau Coll; sketch of "A. P. Chouteau," this volume; Dale L. Morgan, *The West of William H. Ashley* . . . (Denver, 1964), 154, 156-67; J. Robidoux to P. Chouteau, Jr., March 15, 1825, Chouteau Coll.

[30] W. B. Astor to O. N. Bostwick, Nov. 11, 1824, Chouteau Coll; David J. Weber, "Sylvestre S. Pratte," this *Series*, vol. VI.   [31] *American Fur Trade*, I, p. 383.

was again in St. Louis proposing to all the partners of B.
Pratte & Co. – Pratte, Cabanné, Berthold and Chouteau – a
merger with the American Fur Company. They also dis-
cussed means of eradicating their most persistent competition, the Columbia Fur Company, a band of energetic
Britishers including Kenneth McKenzie, William Laidlaw,
Daniel Lamont and James Kipp, with an American named
Tilton as front man. In 1822 this company began trading at
St. Peters and by 1826 had worked westward to the Mandans, threatening the American Fur Company on the upper
Mississippi and B. Pratte & Co. on the upper Missouri. The
combined power of the two companies would be needed to
stop the intruders.[32]

In the fall of 1826 Chouteau, after buying goods in Philadelphia and selling furs in New York, signed an agreement
dated December 20, 1826, with John Jacob Astor, making
B. Pratte & Co. the sole western agent of the American Fur
Company. They agreed to make a joint concern of their two
St. Louis fur companies, sharing equally in profit and loss.
The American Fur Company would furnish all supplies,
collecting 7% interest on all disbursements and 5% commission on all goods imported from England, and on all
charges, including transportation and insurance and the
60% duty charged on woolen goods. No commission was to
be charged on American goods. B. Pratte & Co. would offer
its whole collection of furs to the American Fur Company.
If Astor did not choose to buy them, they would be sold by
Astor at a commission of 2½%. If not sold by September 25
of each year, they would be offered at public sales held in
October or at reduced prices in April. Pierre Chouteau,
Junior, was to be agent of the American Fur Company, general superintendent of the business and director of affairs in
the Indian country at an annual salary of $2000 and travel-

---

[32] Porter, *Astor*, 745-53.

ing expenses. Bernard Pratte was to act in his stead in case of illness (Cadet was frequently and severely ill during this period) or absence from St. Louis. Berthold and Cabanné were to remain in charge of the Sioux country and Council Bluffs respectively at a salary of $1200 apiece. The new company would begin on July 1, 1827, or with the outfit for that year, and continue for four years, or until the returns of 1831.[33]

Now the little family company of Berthold & Chouteau, a French creole organization of limited imagination and effectiveness, was backed by the country's biggest monopoly. The power and wealth of Pierre Chouteau, Junior, may be said to have begun in 1827, even though he had already been in the fur business for twenty years.

The immediate advantage of Chouteau's 1826 association with the American Fur Company was the acquisition of strong and capable men to lead his enterprises. In the summer of 1827 the Columbia Fur Company succumbed, even though their traders had out-maneuvered B. Pratte & Co. traders all along the river that spring. The American Fur Company took it over intact with its men and trading posts; henceforth it was called the Upper Missouri Outfit ("U.M.O."), and operated from the mouth of the Big Sioux River to the mountains. Kenneth McKenzie was paid $2000 a year as its head. William Laidlaw, James Kipp and Daniel Lamont each managed a trading post and its trading parties, and they were all excellent men. In September 1828, the Missouri Fur Company fell apart. Joshua Pilcher remained in the mountains; Charles Bent soon afterward abandoned the upper Missouri for the Arkansas; but Lucien Fontenelle, Andrew Drips and William Vanderburgh signed up with the American Fur Company and became partisans or bri-

---

[33] Articles of agreement, with letter of P. Chouteau, Jr., New York, Dec. 21, 1826, to B. Pratte & Co., Chouteau Coll.

gade leaders of trappers in the mountains, and they, too, were all excellent men.[34]

There was still William Ashley who, as Chouteau wrote, "is always in my way."[35] In 1826 Ashley had brought more beaver out of the Rocky Mountains than anyone knew existed. When Ashley made Chouteau a proposition for the summer of 1827 to furnish goods and buy furs for Ashley's successors, Smith, Jackson & Sublette, Chouteau accepted. The expedition was highly profitable and Chouteau, for a time, forgot his distrust of trapping and was eager to send a party like Ashley's to the mountains under Kenneth McKenzie. But prudence or fear prevailed, and McKenzie remained on the Missouri to build a post (later called Fort Union) at the mouth of the Yellowstone as a base of operations and a headquarters for his outfit.[36] During the 1830s there were many hundreds of American Fur Company men divided into outfits – at Fort Union, Fort Clark, Fort Pierre; among the Oglalla, Huncpapa, Saone, Yancton, Yanctonnais and Brulé divisions of the Sioux; at the Sacs, Iowas, Osages, Kansas, Poncas, Otoes and Rees; at White River, Cherry River, Bois Blanc, Platte and Vermillion.[37] And there were traveling salesmen who sold goods to free trappers in the mountains. In the summer of 1829 McKenzie sent Etienne Provost to gather in trappers at a predetermined rendezvous to trade their furs for goods with William Vanderburgh. Thus began ten years of such "mountain business" which Cadet thought was a waste of men and money from beginning to end. The company never arrived on time at the rendezvous with its goods, thereby losing most of the trade, and some of its finest men, including

---

[34] Chittenden, *op. cit.,* I, p. 330n; Cabanné to Chouteau, Oct. 14, 1828, Chouteau Coll.

[35] P. Chouteau, Jr., New York, Dec. 21, 1826, to B. Pratte & Co., St. Louis, Chouteau Coll.

[36] P. Chouteau, Jr., to McKenzie, Sept. 28, 1827, and Crooks to Chouteau, July 2, 1828, Chouteau Coll.   [37] Journal v, Chouteau Coll.

Vanderburgh, were killed by Indians. These expeditions, as Chouteau wrote Astor in 1833, were an annual financial loss, but they were continued until 1839, for the company could not afford to abandon the mountains to its rivals.[38]

The concomitant of a healthy business is rivals, and Cadet's company always had its share. One was Joseph Robidoux, whom Cabanné bought out in 1828, paying him $1000 a year to stay in St. Louis for two years.[39] A shaky little organization known as Papin & Co., or the French Fur Co., was bought out in October 1830, for the sum of $21,000. To keep its leaders from forming another company, two of them – Pascal Cerré and Honoré Picotte – were hired for $1000 a year, a generous salary for men whose fidelity the company had no reason to trust.[40] The most dangerous competition of these years was Smith, Jackson & Sublette (after 1830 the Rocky Mountain Fur Co.) whose experienced partisans were followed by Drips, Fontenelle and Vanderburgh to their secret sources of beaver, or sometimes to a nest of murderous Blackfeet, as when Vanderburgh was killed.

As general superintendent of the company, Chouteau had other matters to deal with as well. One was his own frequent illness, which in late 1827 was so debilitating that he asked Crooks to replace him as St. Louis agent of the company. Crooks could not leave New York, and by February 1828, Chouteau was feeling well enough to face other problems of the year, such as Bartholomew Berthold. In the fall of 1827, Berthold had lied to the customs people about some imported beads. Because of this and Chouteau's illness, the other partners briefly considered dissolving the company.

---

[38] Chittenden, *op. cit.*, I, pp. 365-66.

[39] Cabanné to P. Chouteau, Jr., Oct. 14, 1828, Chouteau Coll.

[40] Theodore Papin to P. M. Papin, Feb. 24, 1831, Chouteau Coll. Crooks warned Chouteau of the "endless number of spies you have around you – there are perhaps more Papins and Picottes in your service than you are aware of. . ." (Crooks to Chouteau, Feb. 23, 1834, Chouteau Coll.).

There were other worries – the settlement with the Columbia Fur Company which dragged on because the appraisal of their upper Missouri inventory had been too high, and the company's new retail store in St. Louis which was built cockeyed – the architect miscalculated the ground level.[41]

Along with the burdens of a growing business, Chouteau occasionally garnered his share of glory. In 1830 the inventive Kenneth McKenzie proposed a steamboat to haul goods to and from the upper Missouri (one was already making the run between St. Louis and Fort Leavenworth). Chouteau adopted the idea with alacrity, bought a boat in Pittsburgh for $7000 or $8000 and boarded it, all enthusiasm, when it left St. Louis for the upper Missouri on April 16, 1831. Although the boat was optimistically named the "Yellow Stone," low water kept it for days at the Ponca post and it went no farther up the river than Fort Tecumseh. Undismayed, Chouteau again boarded it next spring in company with his future son-in-law John F. A. Sanford, then upper Missouri Indian Agent, and the painter George Catlin. The boat left St. Louis on March 26, 1832, reaching the condemned Fort Tecumseh two months later, at which time Chouteau christened its successor "Fort Pierre." The boat went on to Fort Union at the mouth of the Yellowstone, finally justifying its name, and returned to St. Louis by July 7, doing a hundred miles a day. It was proclaimed a stunning achievement by the press and Chouteau was widely congratulated. Next season another boat, the "Assiniboine," went up the river and from then on there were always steamboats on the upper Missouri, until the railroads did the job more cheaply.[42]

---

[41] Letters from Ramsay Crooks to P. Chouteau, Jr., dated Feb. 15, 1828, Feb. 29, 1828, April 6, 1828, July 2, 1828, all in the Chouteau Coll.

[42] Chittenden, *op. cit.*, I, pp. 339-41; P. Chouteau, Jr., to William Renshaw, Pittsburgh, Nov. 25, 1831; P. Chouteau, Jr. to Gen. B. Pratte, Poncas River, May 31, 1831; J. J. Astor to P. Chouteau, Jr., Sept. 28, 1832; all in the Chouteau Coll., George Catlin, *Letters and Notes on the Manners, Customs, and Condition of the North American Indians* (London, 1841), I, p. 14.

Company steamboats gratuitously carried many scientists, artists and European adventurers to the upper Missouri region – Prince Maximilian of Weid-Neuweid in 1833 and 1834, J. J. Audubon in 1843, the Swiss artist Rudolph Friederich Kurz in 1850 and others, all of whom praised the generosity of the company in newspaper interviews and published reports. It was as good public relations as Chouteau could have hoped for in that era.

In the fall of 1831, Cadet and his wife went east not only to buy a steamboat and goods for the trade but also to see their daughter Emilie, who was ill at her convent school in Georgetown. The trip was miserable; Chouteau wrote home that he had caught a cold in Philadelphia and was homesick and worried about his daughter. When young Emilie was well enough to travel, they returned in a new coach and horses bought in Washington, arriving home in February. By November Emilie had recovered sufficiently to marry John F. A. Sanford. Two years later Sanford resigned as Indian Agent, and went to work for his father-in-law, who soon came to value the young man's loyalty and tactful handling of delicate affairs and angry opponents. Emilie died April 27, 1836, leaving a son, Ben, who became Cadet's favorite and badly-spoiled grandchild. John F. A. Sanford remained Cadet's right hand until Sanford's death twenty years later.[43]

Like all fur traders, the American Fur Company sold liquor to Indians, sparingly on the Missouri below the Mandans, abundantly above, to compete with the Hudson's Bay Company. William Clark, the sympathetic Superintendent of Indian Affairs at St. Louis, regularly issued the company

---

[43] P. Chouteau, Jr., to William Renshaw, Philadelphia, Jan. 6, 1832; P. Chouteau, Jr., to J. B. Sarpy, Washington, Feb. 6, 1832; Crooks to P. Chouteau, Jr., New York, Jan. 3, 1832, and Feb. 10, 1832; and P. M. Papin to P. Chouteau, Jr., Nov. 12, 1832; all in the Chouteau Coll. Marriage announcement in the *Missouri Republican,* Nov. 27, 1832; John F. A. Sanford to the Commissioner of Indian Affairs, Feb. 4, 1834, in Letters Received by the Office of Indian Affairs from the St. Louis Superintendency, National Archives; Emilie's obituary in the *Missouri Republican,* April 28, 1836.

permits for ample supplies of liquor "for the use of the boatmen." Then in July 1832, a bill passed Congress excluding spirituous liquors from the Indian country, whether intended for boatmen or Indians. In August 1832, government agents at Fort Leavenworth ignored William Clark's permit and destroyed over a thousand gallons of whiskey on board the "Yellow Stone." At the same time a rival trader named Leclerc passed Fort Leavenworth in his boat and was not thoroughly searched. Furious at this inequity, Cabanné sent his own men after Leclerc, who stopped the trader and seized his liquor. Leclerc returned to St. Louis to report the illegal arrest and seizure and sue the company. Chouteau finally settled with Leclerc for $9200, and Cabanné was banned from the Indian country for a year.[44]

In 1833 there was no liquor to be had on the Missouri. In desperation, McKenzie set up a distillery at Fort Union and made his own. Rival traders passing Fort Union on their way to St. Louis reported the distillery, and by the end of 1833, Chouteau was in Washington trying to explain to Indian Commissioner Elbert Herring that McKenzie had been making wine from the wild pears and berries of the region – an innocent botanical experiment and nothing more. Nobody was fooled, but such was the power of the company that the affair was dropped, after Chouteau promised he would conform to the law, as he had no intention of doing.[45] As he explained later, "it could not be expected that the traders should be very observant of the law, when the officers appointed to enforce [it] neglected to do so." [46]

In the spring of 1834, discouraged by ill health, John

---

44 John Dougherty to William Clark, Nov. 10, 1831, in Letters Received, OIA from St. Louis Superintendency, which contains many documents describing this affair.

45 Crooks to P. Chouteau, Jr., Feb. 23, 1834; Kenneth McKenzie to Crooks, Dec. 10, 1833, Fort Union Letter Book and other letters in the Chouteau Coll.; P. Chouteau, Jr. to William Clark, Nov. 23, 1833 and other letters in Letters Received, OIA from St. Louis Superintendency.

46 P. Chouteau Jr. & Co. to Messrs. T. H. Harvey and T. G. Gantt, Jan. 12, 1842, in Letters Received, OIA from St. Louis Superintendency.

Jacob Astor retired from the American Fur Company, of which he owned 90% of the stock (Crooks and Robert Stuart owned 5% each). Crooks bought the Northern Department and called it the American Fur Company. B. Pratte & Co. bought the Western Department and called it Pratte, Chouteau & Co. The name change was long due. Berthold had died in 1831; Cabanné, though still a partner, had lost his status after the Leclerc debacle; Bernard Pratte was eastern agent for the company until he died in 1836; but it was plainly Pierre Chouteau, Junior, as the new St. Louis manager, who deserved to have his name on the door. The terms of the agreement were proposed by Ramsay Crooks in September and accepted by the middle of December:

> The American Fur Company will import from Europe, and purchase in the United States, all the supplies you require for your trade, the former at 12 months and the latter at the usual credit, for which we will charge you a commission of 2½ percent. We will sell all the Furs, skins and other property you may send to New York, or we will ship the same for sale abroad, for either of which modes of disposing of your goods, we will charge you a commission of 2½ percent. We will accept your Bills to such an amount as your business may require, and will charge you a commission of one percent on such part as you do not provide funds to meet. If you wish the sales of your goods guaranteed, we will do so, at the established customary rates. You will understand that the present proposition is provisional on the expectation of doing all your business . . . a limited portion of your affairs I would not engage to transact on these terms.[47]

So Astor bowed out, and without his guidance Cadet began making mistakes that would cost the company dearly. When Cadet was in New York in February 1834, he bought out the Missouri River forts and equipment of Sublette & Campbell, a company which had been organized in December 1832, with unlimited credit from William Ashley and Robert Campbell for both the Missouri River and moun-

[47] Crooks to Pratte, Chouteau & Co., Sept. 6, 1834 and December 20, 1834, American Fur Company papers in the New York Historical Society.

tain trade. After one unprofitable season on the Missouri, Campbell offered to sell out to McKenzie at Fort Union, if McKenzie would stay out of the mountains for a year. McKenzie refused, certain of his ability to drive Sublette & Campbell off the field, but when Sublette went to New York in February 1834, Chouteau accepted his offer. Chouteau promised Sublette to retire from the mountains for a year, which made it impossible for his company to supply Drips and Fontenelle, their mountain leaders. Cabanné was not quick enough with his offer of other employment, and at that year's rendezvous, Drips and Fontenelle joined with James Bridger, Thomas Fitzpatrick and Milton Sublette in Fontenelle, Fitzpatrick & Co., a formidable opposition. Chouteau's company was forced to buy them out at the 1836 rendezvous, after which the joint company became the Rocky Mountain Outfit which lost money for Pratte, Chouteau & Co. every year until it was dissolved in 1839.[48]

In 1835, Chouteau reorganized the business, and not to everyone's satisfaction. Out of the Upper Missouri Outfit territory he created a Sioux Outfit headed by Honoré Picotte, and he notified William Laidlaw at Fort Pierre not to send an outfit to the Platte, which now was in Sioux Outfit territory. Outraged at having his territory curtailed, Laidlaw quit and sold his share of the Upper Missouri Outfit to Jacob Halsey. Daniel Lamont also quit the company, sold his share to D. D. Mitchell in 1835, and then went into business with Peter and Joseph Powell as Powell, Lamont & Co., buying robes and beaver from the upper Arkansas River and Santa Fe, and providing stiff competition for Chouteau in those areas. Laidlaw also joined Powell, Lamont & Co., but sometime after Lamont's death in 1837 he

<hr>

[48] J. C. Cabanné to Fontenelle, April 9, 1834, Drips papers, Mo. Hist. Soc.; Dale L. Morgan and Eleanor Towles Harris, eds., *The Rocky Mountain Journals of William Marshall Anderson* . . . (San Marino, 1967), 309-10.

returned to work for Chouteau.[49] Because of these and other
signs of disaffection, Chouteau's administration was reported in 1836 to be "highly unpopular with the principal
persons in the interior." Benjamin Clapp in the New York
office attempted to analyze the difficulty: "I am inclined to
believe that Mr. Chouteau has allowed his fears to be operated on by his opponents, that he has temporized, & under-
taken to conciliate until he has gotten himself into pretty
much of a snarl."[50]

Part of the trouble may have been Chouteau's preoccupa-
tion with Indian treaties, which caused him to spend much
of his time away from St. Louis and from the direct management of his business. In the 1830s the government was
eager to move Indians west of the Mississippi and give their
lands to settlers, which it accomplished by treaties promising the Indians an annuity in cash or goods for their lands,
and payment of their debts to traders. Since the debts to
traders were those which fur companies had long ago written off as uncollectable, payment of them was like a donation
from public funds, and well worth Chouteau's time and
energy. He made a trip to the upper Mississippi to be witness on September 28, 1836, to a treaty with the Sacs and
Foxes which allowed his company payment of a debt of over
$20,000. This was the only treaty at which Chouteau was
present, but some member of his firm attended all other
treaties with Indians owing the company money, and their
efforts eventually bore rich fruit. The Sioux treaty of 1837
allowed $90,000 for payment of all the traders' debts, and
the Winnebago treaty of 1837 allowed $200,000. But actual
payment of the debts was often years away from the signing

---

[49] Laidlaw to P. Chouteau, Jr., March (or May) 14, 1836 and Jacob Halsey to P.
Chouteau, Jr., June 16, 1836, Chouteau Coll.; Annie Heloise Abel, ed., *Chardon's
Journal at Fort Clark, 1834-1839* (Pierre, 1932), 219, n.67.

[50] Benjamin Clapp to Ramsay Crooks, Sept. 28, 1836, American Fur Company
papers in the New York Hist. Soc.

of the treaty, and that was where Chouteau's work began.[51]

Directly after returning from the Sac and Fox treaty conference in September 1836, Cadet went east. In Pittsburgh he bought a new steamboat replacing the "Assiniboine" which had burned in 1835; in Philadelphia he bought goods; in Washington he petitioned for confirmation of title to the Dubuque claim.[52] He also lobbied for Senate confirmation of the Sac and Fox treaty – but in vain. In March 1837, he returned home. Scarcely a month later he was called east again to meet a crisis. In April 1837, the country was suffering a financial panic. Drafts were called in, companies failed, banks suspended specie payments. As a result, the Commissioner of Indian Affairs was threatening to pay Sac and Fox annuities not in specie as the treaty of 1832 specified, but in bank notes or merchandise. Chouteau objected with all his strength and voice. When he advised the Indians to accept nothing from the government but hard money, the government retaliated by threatening to legislate against traders' rights to advise Indians. Chouteau and Crooks talked in Washington with Indian Commissioner Harris in June, but they could not alter his intentions. On June 14, Chouteau started home again, to tell the Sac and Fox chiefs waiting in St. Louis that they would not receive their annuities in cash that year. Nor did the company receive payment of its Indian debts, either that year or until 1842, when a new Sac and Fox treaty allowed the company $112,109.47 for traders' debts.[53]

[51] Charles J. Kappler, *Indian Affairs: Laws and Treaties* (Washington, 1904), II, pp. 476-78, 493-94, 498-500, 549.

[52] J. Throckmorton to P. Chouteau, Jr., Pittsburgh, April 20, 1837, and "Petition to Senate and House of Representatives . . . setting forth rights of claimants to . . . Dubuque Mines," Jan. 10, 1837, Chouteau Coll.; John B. Whetten, New York, to Pierre Chouteau, Jr., Philadelphia, Mar. 9, 1837 (#2437); *Calendar of the American Fur Company's Papers,* American Historical Association, *Annual Report, 1944* (Washington, 1945), II, p. 276.

[53] Pratte, Chouteau & Co. to American Fur Co., May 22, 1837 (#2605); Pratte, Chouteau & Co. to American Fur Co., May 29, 1837 (#2641); Henry H. Sibley to

On November 21, 1837, Chouteau left St. Louis for the third time that year, to spend four months lobbying in Washington for payment of debts owed the company by Sioux and Winnebagos, as provided for in treaties now awaiting Senate confirmation.[54] But it was years before the treaty money was appropriated and paid, and in the meantime Chouteau made many uncomfortable journeys in rocking, jolting coaches, and spent many months of many years in Washington and New York, talking endlessly to friends and enemies of the treaties and using every means, fair or foul, to achieve his ends. One of his friends whom he used shrewdly was Missouri Senator Thomas H. Benton. In March 1843, Senator Benton, who had strongly opposed the Sioux treaty confirmation, suddenly relaxed his opposition and voted for it – after talking to Chouteau and borrowing $1000 from him on favorable terms.[55] Benton served Chouteau in other ways, and not without profit. In 1851 he succeeded in obtaining payment of the claim of A. P. Chouteau and Jules DeMun against the Mexican government for $30,000 worth of goods confiscated in 1817. For Chouteau, who was beneficiary of the claim by this time, Benton got $81,772; for himself, 10% of that amount.[56]

The firm of Pratte, Chouteau & Co. terminated by limitation with the peltry returns of 1839. When Bernard Pratte

American Fur Co., Oct. 7, 1837 (#3277); American Fur. Co. to Joseph Rolette, June 9, 1837 (#2674); American Fur Co. to Pratte, Chouteau & Co., June 17, 1837 (#2701); Pratte, Chouteau & Co. to American Fur Co., June 30, 1837 (#2768); all in *Calendar, A.F.C. Papers,* II, pp. 293, 297, 301, 304, 312, 360; Kappler, *Indian Affairs,* II, pp. 546-49.

[54] Pratte, Chouteau & Co. to American Fur Co., Nov. 24, 1837 (#3560); American Fur Co. to Charles H. Gratiot, Dec. 30, 1937 (#3754); P. Chouteau, Jr., to Ramsay Crooks, Feb. 22, 1838 (#4022); *Calendar, A.F.C. Papers,* II, pp. 387, 403, 427.

[55] William Nisbet Chambers, *Old Bullion Benton, Senator from the New West* (Boston, 1956), 263. Chouteau was in the east from May to July, 1839, from spring through the summer of 1841, and from November 1842, to March 1843. Chouteau Coll.

[56] "Account of Money Received from the United States Government for Claim against the Mexican Govt. St. Louis June 12, 1851." Chouteau Coll.

died on April 1, 1836, Chouteau assumed full management of the company. Bernard Pratte, Junior, kept his father's interest until 1838, when he left the company to serve in the Missouri legislature. By 1838, other partners were John P. Cabanné, John B. Sarpy, J. F. A. Sanford, Pierre Menard and Felix Vallé. The new company, organized in May 1839, was known as P. Chouteau Jr. & Co. until it was sold in 1865. It was capitalized at $500,000, of which Cadet and his father (who lived until 1849) owned a little more than half. Other partners were, for once, of Chouteau's own choosing – Joseph A. Sire, John F. A. Sanford and John B. Sarpy, who each owned stock worth $80,000. Sire, long a steamboat captain on the upper Missouri, continued to manage that part of the business. Sanford was company lobbyist in Washington from 1837 to 1840 and manager of the New York office when it opened in 1841. Sarpy remained in St. Louis, in charge of accounts. In 1842 Kenneth McKenzie and Benjamin Clapp also became partners, but both had withdrawn by 1853.[57]

The organization of P. Chouteau Jr. & Co. in 1839 marked the end of the closely-held family business. Jean P. Cabanné withdrew from the company and applied that fall to Crooks in New York for goods to pursue the Indian trade in partnership with Bernard Pratte, Junior, in opposition to P. Chouteau Jr. & Co. His plans did not mature and he died in 1841 at odds with Chouteau's firm, but with good Emilie Chouteau at his bedside. Shortly after his death, his son John Charles Cabanné formed a company with Bernard Pratte, Junior, which opposed P. Chouteau Jr. & Co. on the Missouri and North Platte until 1845.[58]

---

[57] Pratte Chouteau & Co. to Crooks, July 9, 1839 (#6519), *Calendar, A.F.C. Papers*, II, p. 664; John E. Sunder, *The Fur Trade on the Upper Missouri, 1840-1865* (Norman, 1965), 5-6, 69. At the time of Sire's death in 1854 and Sarpy's in 1857, each owned 26% of the stock of the company (Sanford had retired from the firm in 1853) *ibid.*, 161. Just as Chittenden's work is my general source for the fur trade up to 1840, Sunder's book is my source for these later years.

The biggest change Cadet made in the company's operations was in finally terminating the mountain business with the returns of 1839. No longer could his trappers compete with those of the Hudson's Bay Company who ranged from the Pacific Ocean to within fifteen days' travel of St. Louis trading duty-free goods that were cheaper and better than American goods. And beaver, the principal crop of the mountains, was not only scarce but in small demand, as nutria and silk had all but replaced beaver in the tall hats then in fashion.[59]

The company's business henceforth was mainly in buffalo robes. Besides the upper Missouri, centers of that trade were the North and South Platte and the Arkansas, where Bent, St. Vrain & Co. traders had dominated since 1834. In 1836, P. Chouteau Jr. & Co. got a foothold on the North Platte by acquiring Sublette & Campbell's Fort Laramie (Fort William; Fort John) and in 1838 made a friendly pact with Bent, St. Vrain & Co. to stay off the South Platte if the other company would stay off the North Platte. Before long Bent, St. Vrain & Co. was buying its supplies, selling its furs and paying its employes at the St. Louis store of P. Chouteau Jr. & Co. Much of the company's income depended upon this independent subsidiary which regularly produced quantities of buffalo robes and a little Santa Fe beaver through the lean 1840s.[60]

The full force of the panic of 1837 hit the west in 1841. In June, Chouteau's London agent wrote desperately, "the

---

[58] Bernard Pratte, Jr. to Crooks, Oct. 7, 1839 (#6898), and Geo. Ehninger to Bernard Pratte, Jr., Oct. 28, 1839 (#6990), *Calendar, A.F.C. Papers,* 698, 707; Sanford to P. Chouteau, Jr., & Co., June 28, 1841, Chouteau Coll.

[59] Advertisement in the *Missouri Republican,* May 10, 1839, announcing termination of the mountain business; *Niles National Register,* Oct. 3, 1840, p. 68, c. 1.

[60] Agreement between H. Picotte of Pratte, Chouteau & Co., and Ceran St. Vrain of Bent, St. Vrain & Co., July 27, 1838, Chouteau Coll.; ledgers CC, Z and DD all have records of goods bought by Bent, St. Vrain & Co. in 1838 and 1839, and ledger AA has a list of Bent men paid at P. Chouteau Jr. & Co. in St. Louis, as do subsequent ledgers.

fur trade is dead," [61] for small-pox had ravaged the Indians, fur markets abroad were closing, prices had plummeted, money was tight, credit non-existent. Suddenly everybody wanted out of the business. From New York, Crooks wrote that his health demanded a change of occupation. From Prairie du Chien, Hercules Dousman wrote that he and his partners Joseph Rolette and Henry H. Sibley would like to sell their Western Outfit to Chouteau on agreeable terms. From St. Louis, Chouteau wrote that he wished to withdraw his personal supervision from the company, leaving it in younger hands. [62]

Crooks achieved his change of occupation the hard way. On September 10, 1842, the American Fur Company suspended payment under pressure of bad times and bad debts, and the great monopoly was no more. Dousman and Sibley (Rolette had died) solved their problem by selling their Western Outfit to Chouteau on July 18, 1842, in New York. [63] But Cadet's own wish took longer to fulfill, for the "younger hands" he had in mind were still a bit too young. Chouteau was certain, however, that his boy Charles would indeed take over the business in time.

Educated by the Jesuits at Florissant as a child, Charles was sent to the Peugnet School in New York City in 1834, at the age of fourteen, along with some Berthold and Cabanné boys and Crooks' three little girls. Crooks and his wife entertained the boys once a fortnight, lecturing them on the value of education. At eighteen, Charles' formal education ended, and in the summer of 1838 he left New York with Crooks to visit the company's posts at St. Peters and Prairie du Chien. When the arduous journey was finished,

[61] C. M. Lampson to American Fur Co., June 16, 1841, (#11,044), *Calendar, A.F.C. Papers,* III, p. 1076.

[62] Crooks to P. Chouteau Jr. & Co., Jan. 27, 1841, Chouteau Coll.; Hercules L. Dousman to American Fur Co., Jan. 20, 1841 (#10,137), *Calendar, A.F.C. Papers,* III, p. 993; Crooks to Chouteau, Jan. 27, 1841, Chouteau Coll.

[63] *Niles National Register,* Oct. 1, 1842, p. 80, c. 1; American Fur Company to Charles W. Borup, July 18, 1842 (#12,973), *Calendar, A.F.C. Papers,* III, p. 1247.

Crooks pronounced Charles "an excellent young man." Back in St. Louis, Charles began four years of training in the firm of Chouteau & McKenzie, a wholesale mercantile house started in May, 1838, by his father and Kenneth McKenzie (who had sold out of the Upper Missouri Outfit, apparently to F. A. Chardon). Then Charles worked for a year in his father's New York office and two years in London and on the continent. He returned to St. Louis in 1845 and married his cousin Julia Gratiot, daughter of General Charles Gratiot. By 1845 Charles was twenty-five years old, but it was another five years before he took over P. Chouteau Jr. & Co., and freed his father from direct supervision of the business.[64]

Chouteau's focus for the next four years, when he was not doing business in New York or Philadelphia, or lobbying in Washington, was the elimination of liquor in the fur trade. Although the fur market hit its depths during the winter of 1841-1842, opposition traders swarmed over the upper Missouri, North and South Platte country. Their liquor, principal weapon in the war for furs, was dissolving the Indians' family and tribal relationships and (far more alarming to Chouteau) their ability to hunt buffalo and make robes. In 1841, Chouteau decided to dry up the competition by enforcing the long-ignored law prohibiting liquor in the Indian country. With the cooperation of the Indian Department, Chouteau worked out a plan to send an agent with a supporting company of dragoons to tour the Indian country, destroying liquor and arresting vendors.[65]

All sorts of things went wrong. The agent chosen was

---

[64] Hyde and Conard, *Encyclopedia of History of St. Louis,* I, pp. 361-62; B. Pratte to P. Chouteau Jr., Oct. 11, 1834; Crooks to P. Chouteau Jr., Jan. 24, 1836; Crooks to P. Chouteau, Oct. 17, 1838, all in the Chouteau Coll.; obituary of Charles P. Chouteau, *St. Louis Globe-Democrat,* Jan. 6, 1901. Chouteau sold his share of Chouteau & McKenzie to McKenzie in the spring of 1840. Another short-lived mercantile partnership of Chouteau's was started in late 1838 with J. C. Barlow, a merchant of Louisville married to Chouteau's niece, Virginia, daughter of A. A. Chouteau.

[65] John F. A. Sanford to Andrew Drips, July 10, 1842, Drips Papers, Mo. Hist. Soc.; D. D. Mitchell to T. Hartley Crawford, Oct. 25, 1841, Letters Received, OIA from St. Louis Superintendency.

Chouteau's faithful partisan, Andrew Drips, who could not
have escaped the charge of partiality for his old employers
even if he had been more scrupulous than he was. The company of dragoons was not allowed, and Drips' only deputy
was recalled after a season, so that for over two years Drips'
finger was the only plug in the dike. But the Sioux cooperated in keeping liquor out of their country and Chouteau's
traders were sternly denied liquor. By 1845 Drips was able
to say – and agonized cries from the upper Missouri traders
bore him out – that "illicit whiskey has entirely disappeared
from the Upper Missouri country." The competition also
disappeared. In 1845 both Pratte & Cabanné and the Union
Fur Co. gave up. Drips had done his work well – too well,
in fact, for in the fall of 1845 Chouteau's company wrote its
associate Henry H. Sibley in Minnesota asking if liquor
desperately needed for the Assiniboine and Blackfeet could
be smuggled in from the north (Sibley said no). Drips was
removed in the spring of 1846 and next season all was back
to normal – opposition traders everywhere and the Indian
country awash in alcohol.[66]

Chouteau had been successful in drying up the competition if only temporarily, but the sins of his own traders were
not forgiven. In 1846, spurred on by accusations of an opposition trader and former employe, seven separate suits
amounting to $25,000 were instituted in the St. Louis Dis-
trict Court against P. Chouteau Jr. & Co. for selling liquor
to Indians. After two years of delays, disappearing witnesses

---

[66] D. D. Mitchell to T. Hartley Crawford, Feb. 27, 1843, and endorsements, Letters
Received, OIA from St. Louis Superintendency; H. Picotte to P. Chouteau Jr. & Co.,
Jan. 4, 1844, Chouteau Coll.; Jos. V. Hamilton to D. D. Mitchell, March 7, 1844,
Letters Received, OIA from Upper Missouri Agency, National Archives; Thomas H.
Harvey to T. Hartley Crawford, July 9, 1844, and Andrew Drips to Thomas H.
Harvey, June 1, 1845, *ibid.*; H. H. Sibley to P. Chouteau Jr. & Co., Feb. 23, 1846,
Chouteau Coll.; Picotte to P. Chouteau Jr. & Co., March 10, 1846, Fort Pierre Letter
Book, Chouteau Coll.; Report of T. P. Moore, Sept. 21, 1846, *H. Exec. Doc. 4,* 29
Cong., 2 sess. (Ser. 497), 288-96. Both Sunder (*op. cit.,* 47-84) and Abel (*op. cit.,*
259) have a far more sinister viewpoint of Chouteau's motives.

and conflicting testimony, the court accepted a compromise suggested by the company that it forfeit $5000 and costs. In a letter summing up the trial, the company admitted that its subordinates had sold liquor to Indians every year they had operated, but only in violation of company instructions and positively without the knowledge of partners in the firm, a pious deceit. In 1848, the letter stated, "the liquor trade has now no existence in the Indian country" – but the company knew as it wrote those words that as long as there was competition in the fur trade, there was liquor also.[67]

In 1846 the Mexican War broke out, and by the time it was over in 1848, Bent, St. Vrain & Co. were ruined, along with the fur business of the southwest. The Santa Fe Trail was jammed with soldiers, teamsters and emigrants, all with their guns pointed at whatever moved in the brush, be it rabbit or friendly Indian. Soon there were no more friendly Indians. The South Platte business which had been Bent, St. Vrain & Co. territory was abandoned, and the North Platte fell victim to more soldiers and emigrants. Fort Laramie was sold to the Army in 1849, and from then on P. Chouteau Jr. & Co., managed by Charles Chouteau, operated only on the upper Missouri, where it held undisputed sway for another fifteen years, although declining year by year. The company was sold in 1865 to J. B. Hubbell of Mankato, Minnesota, who styled his business "The Northwest Fur Company" and carried it on to extinction.[68]

Though his company was finally in "younger hands" from 1849 on, Pierre Chouteau, Junior, was a decade away from retirement. As long ago as 1835, Chouteau had attended a meeting to discuss the possibility of a railroad from St. Louis to Fayette, and to the iron and lead mines in the

[67] P. Chouteau Jr. & Co. to William Medill, Dec. 5, 1848, and P. Chouteau Jr. & Co. to T. H. Harvey and T. G. Gantt, Jan. 12, 1849, both in Letters Received, OIA from St. Louis Superintendency. See also Sunder, *op. cit.*, 113-16.

[68] See Sunder, *op. cit.*, for a detailed account of these last years.

southern part of Missouri. Railroads were to be the play-
things of his old age. In 1849 he established in New York
the firm of Chouteau, Merle & Co. in partnership with a
New Orleans merchant with whom the company had done
business since the 1830s. Later Chouteau's son-in-law joined
the company which then became Chouteau, Merle & Sanford, and was engaged in selling railroad iron.[69]

In 1849, Chouteau became a partner with François Vallé
and James Harrison in the American Iron Mountain Co.,
dedicated to mining Iron Mountain and developing 25,000
acres around it. The mine was forty miles over hills and
hollows from Ste. Genevieve, and had been unproductive
because of difficulty in transporting ore. In 1851, the company built a twelve-foot wide plank road – the wonder of its
day – between Iron Mountain and Ste. Genevieve. Seven
years later a branch of the Illinois Central, established by
Chouteau and others and named the Iron Mountain and
Southern Railroad, put the plank road out of business, but
greatly increased the value of the Iron Mountain property.
In 1858, Chouteau, Harrison & Vallé took over a blast fur-
nace built in 1853, and later another at Irondale, twelve
miles north. Two thousand men were employed at Iron
Mountain in its heyday, and millions of dollars worth of ore
was extracted from it, mostly after Chouteau's death. Chouteau, Harrison & Vallé tried to develop the place as a summer colony, as well. From New York in 1858, Chouteau
wrote Dr. Maffitt, Julie's husband, urging him to see that
"Mama" visited "our Saratoga or Newport" during the
summer. The company also established the Laclede Rolling
Mill within the city limits of St. Louis.[70]

[69] Scharf, op. cit., I, p. 181; advertisement for sale of railroad iron by Chouteau,
Merle & Co., Sept. 3, 1850, Chouteau Coll.; John F. A. Sanford to Charles P. Chouteau, April 2, 1852, Chouteau Coll.; Edwards and Hopewell, op. cit., 356.

[70] Last Will and Testament of Pierre Chouteau, Jr., Aug. 17, 1865; "The Passing
of Iron Mountain," St. Louis, July 29, 1906, clipping in Missouri Historical Society;
"Reopening of Iron Mountain Workings. . .", St. Louis Star, Aug. 31, 1923; P.
Chouteau, Jr. to Dr. William Maffitt, Aug. 9, 1858, Chouteau Coll.

Chouteau, Merle & Sanford reorganized in 1852, becoming Pierre Chouteau Jr., Sanford & Co. Sanford had become ever more important to Chouteau through the years. Their relationship was very close; Chouteau allowed Sanford and Ben $5000 a year in addition to the large income Sanford had from his share of P. Chouteau Jr. & Co. and Pierre Chouteau Jr., Sanford & Co. When Sanford, a widower for sixteen years, married again in 1852, Chouteau, in the gracious family tradition, took the lady to his heart and made the Sanford home his headquarters in New York when Emilie was not with him. When "Mama" was in New York, she too went to dine with Belle Sanford and her two little children twice or three times a week. Sanford withdrew from P. Chouteau Jr. & Co. in 1853 to manage Chouteau's growing interests in other fields, such as the Ohio and Mississippi Railroad which Chouteau had helped incorporate in 1851, and the branches of the Illinois Central Railroad which he was developing.[71]

After 1850, Chouteau reluctantly spent more time in New York than in St. Louis, but whatever the press of business, his love and need for his family back in St. Louis was apparent in his letters. He worried over Julie's expected confinement; he shopped for Emilie's furs and corsets, and expressed his serious concern that her new teeth fit no better than the last set.[72] Sanford was probably correct in stating to Charles that the family should have made its home in New York years earlier, where there was a better field for business.[73] But Pierre Chouteau, Junior, was very much a product of the creole village of St. Louis, now grown to a metropolis but still the little pond where he was a big fish.

---

[71] John H. Thompson to Dr. Maffitt, July 11, 1859, and July 29, 1859; John F. A. Sanford to Charles Chouteau, April 2, 1852; P. Chouteau, Jr. to Emilie Chouteau, July 25, 1854; all in Chouteau Coll.; Scharf, *op. cit.*, II, p. 1180; agreement between Chouteau, Sarpy and Sire, Aug. 30, 1853, Chouteau Coll.

[72] Letters of P. Chouteau, Jr. to his wife and Julie dated Sept. 8, 1854, Nov. 27, 1854, and Oct. 4, 1856, Chouteau Coll.

[73] John F. A. Sanford to Charles P. Chouteau, April 2, 1852, Chouteau Coll.

And he was perplexed. A letter to Julie in 1852 reveals a lifetime of doubts about his purposes and ideals:

> As to business, I, who would like to withdraw from it, find myself drawn in deeper than ever. Rail Road Iron, Bonds of the state, of the town, of the Railroad, i.e., Central Railroad of Illinois, coal mines; so you see, my dear Julie, that I do just the contrary of what I would like. . . As long as I have been in business I have never been as sanguine of clearing so much in so few years. You will doubtless ask, why all these speculations, why risk the substance already won, when we have enough on which to be happy if we know how to enjoy it. This question on your part would be perfectly just and reasonable if a man has enough moderation, enough judgement to comprehend it, but whether it be ambition or advantage or even perhaps a little vanity, he lets himself be subjugated. He does not like to be stationary when everything around him seems to go forward.[74]

The year 1857 was the beginning of the end, a time when Chouteau had to be stationary and watch everything around him go forward, or backward. In April when he was in New York, he heard of the death in St. Louis of John B. Sarpy and was greatly upset. He was hardly less so when his son-in-law, Dr. Maffitt, refused to accept an interest in the fur business and take over Sarpy's job.[75] A worse blow came in May when John F. A. Sanford died.[76] In 1858, Maffitt was struck with a paralysis which did not finish him off until 1862. Later in 1858 Chouteau himself became ill and spent much time at Hot Springs for an ailment that affected his sight. Early in 1859 he became incurably blind, and was doomed to spend the last six years of his life in total darkness.[77] His beloved Emilie died on August 24, 1862, and was

---

[74] Pierre Chouteau, Jr. to Julie, July 8, 1852, Chouteau Coll., translated by Mrs. Max Myer.

[75] P. Chouteau, Jr. to Dr. William Maffitt, April 6, 1857, and April 24, 1857.

[76] He died on May 5, 1857, supposedly driven insane by his involvement in the Dred Scott case. See biography of John F. A. Sanford in this volume.

[77] Many letters in the Chouteau Collection trace the progress of Pierre Chouteau, Jr.'s blindness and Dr. Maffitt's paralysis.

buried in Calvary Cemetery. He died three years later on September 6, 1865, aged 76, and was buried beside her.[78]

What Chouteau's estate amounted to can only be estimated; one historian has guessed "several millions."[79] He left over four hundred thousand dollars in railroad bonds alone;[80] he had very large interests in the Indian country; a third of the Laclede Rolling Mill and the Iron Mountain property of Chouteau, Harrison & Vallé; valuable real estate in the towns of St. Paul, St. Anthony and Hastings, Minnesota, and even more valuable lots in downtown St. Louis.[81] He died rich but not universally beloved. His detractors, then and now, have with some justification called him a master of fraud, debaucher of Indians, corrupter of government officials, abuser of public funds. He was, indeed, one of the great manipulators in the history of United States commerce.

But in the memories of his family and the depths of his being he remained to the end a simple French creole.

---

[78] Last Will and Testament of Pierre Chouteau, Jr.; obituary of P. Chouteau, Jr. in the *St. Louis Republican,* Thursday, Sept. 7, 1865.

[79] Stella Drumm, "Pierre Chouteau," *Dictionary of American Biography,* IV, p. 94. Chouteau left $5000 in his will for the Catholic orphans of St. Louis, the only bequest to other than his heirs, which illustrates a facet of his life: he was ever openhanded with his family, but to no one and nothing else would he give either time or money. His civic achievements were paltry. I have found only that he served as delegate to the Missouri Constitutional Convention in May, 1820, and as commissioner to locate a site for the St. Louis courthouse in 1822 (Scharf, *Saint Louis,* I, pp. 571, 728).

[80] #7159 (Pierre Chouteau, Jr.), Probate Court, St. Louis County, Mo.

[81] Last Will and Testament of Pierre Chouteau, Jr.

Ramsay Crooks

by HARVEY L. CARTER
Colorado College

Right hand man of John Jacob Astor for many years and his successor in the fur business, Ramsay Crooks, qualifies as a Mountain Man by reason of his having been one of the overland Astorians, both going to and returning from the Pacific Coast.

The parish register of Middle Greenock, northwest of Glasgow, Scotland, recorded his birth in these words, "Ramsay, lawful daughter to William Crooks, Shoemaker and Margaret Ramsay, born 2nd and baptised 7th January, 1787."[1] His widowed mother migrated to Montreal, Canada, with her four children, April 25, 1803.[2]

There are various statements concerning the activities of young Ramsay Crooks for the years 1803 to 1807, which are somewhat contradictory and have not been resolved. He is reported to have been a clerk for a mercantile establishment in Montreal, to have gone with fur traders from Montreal to Niagara, to have been a clerk for the fur trader, Robert Dickson, at Michilimackinac for a year, and to have been employed in the fur trade by George Gillespie, about

---

[1] Philip Ashton Rollins, *The Discovery of the Oregon Trail* (New York, 1935), lxxxii, cxxxv. Rollins attributes the error to the fact that Ramsay was a name used in Scotland for persons of either sex. My own discovery, at the age of 38, that my birth had been recorded as that of "Infant Carter," without further specification, was a sufficient circumstance for me to grow the beard, which I have since retained, despite increasing competition in recent years.

[2] *Ibid;* see also J. Ward Ruckman, "Ramsay Crooks and the Fur Trade of the Northwest," in *Minnesota History,* VII (March 1926), 19. There is no biography of Ramsay Crooks, but he is the central character in a detailed survey of the fur trade, in David Lavender, *The Fist in the Wilderness* (New York, 1964). See page 1 of that work where Lavender indicates that two elder brothers may have preceded the arrival of Ramsay Crooks in Canada, with his mother and sister.

1805, which employment brought him to St. Louis.[3] It is even possible that all these reports are true. What is certain is that the sixteen year old Crooks found work at once and that most of it was in the fur trade and that he was in St. Louis at least as early as the spring of 1807, with sufficient funds to form a partnership with Robert McClellan, for the purpose of trading with the Indians up the Missouri River.[4]

The partners, outfitted by Labbadie and Chouteau, ascended the Missouri into present South Dakota in the fall of 1807, but were forced by the hostility of the Sioux and the Arikarees to drop back to Council Bluffs, where they erected a trading post and which they operated with moderate success. In the summer of 1809, they attempted to follow Manuel Lisa's Missouri Fur Company outfit to the upper Missouri waters but were importuned by the Sioux to remain in their country. They tricked the Sioux into going out to scour for furs and again dropped back to Council Bluffs. They attributed the actions of the Sioux to the machinations of Lisa.[5]

Crooks and McClellan dissolved their partnership in 1810 and Crooks went to Michilimackinac in June of that year. Meeting there with Wilson Price Hunt and his overland Astorians, en route from Montreal to St. Louis, he joined as a partner in the Pacific Fur Company, with an allotment of five shares. Leaving Michilimackinac on August 12, they traveled by way of Green Bay, up the Fox River, down the Wisconsin River to the Mississippi and thence down the river to St. Louis, arriving on September 3, 1810.[6] They left St. Louis on October 21, after Crooks had recruited Joseph Miller as a partner, and went by boat up

---

[3] Lavender, *op. cit.*, 57-59, 71, 78-79; also Ruckman, *op. cit.*

[4] Stella M. Drumm, "More about Astorians," in *Oregon Historical Society Quarterly* (December, 1923), XXIV, p. 347.   [5] *Ibid.*

[6] Kenneth W. Porter, *John Jacob Astor: Business Man* (Cambridge, 1931), I, pp. 182-84. Lavender, *op. cit.*, 88-120, summarizes the business relationship of Crooks and McClellan and their business connection with the Astorian enterprise.

the Missouri to the mouth of the Nodaway where winter camp was established. McClellan, descending the Nodaway, was also persuaded by Crooks to become a partner in the enterprise. Camp was broken on April 21, 1811, and the heroic but ill-fated expedition was on its way to the Pacific.[7]

Crooks was in very bad health during much of the journey. When they procured horses at the Arikaree villages and struck westward guided by those wilderness wanderers Hoback, Reznor, and Robinson (whom they had met and persuaded to turn back), Crooks was so ill he was forced to travel in a travois for about two weeks in late July and early August. He survived a canoe accident on October 28 when Antoine Clappine was drowned in the Snake River. After this, Crooks headed a party to go back for the horses which they had abandoned at Henry's Fort but he was forced to give up the idea and return after three days.[8]

On November 9, when the party divided into small groups near present Milner, Idaho, Crooks headed a group of nineteen that proceeded down the left bank of the Snake River for about three weeks, when they reached present Homestead, Oregon. Here on December 6, they made contact with Hunt's party on the right bank of the stream and Crooks crossed the stream to confer with Hunt but was unable to return. For some days, Crooks was so ill that he delayed the progress of the party. He attempted to ferry meat across to his former companions but was too weak to succeed and it was accomplished by others who had at first refused. John Day, a particular friend of Crooks, was brought over to the right bank, in even worse condition than Crooks himself. Crooks now persuaded Hunt to leave him behind with Day and Dubreuil. They were later joined by three other Frenchmen who lagged behind Hunt's party.

[7] Washington Irving, *Astoria,* ed. by Edgeley W. Todd (Norman, 1964), 134-35, 137-39, 151-52, 155.

[8] *Ibid.,* 218, 223, 276. Crooks was alert to the danger of striking the rock at Caldron Linn but his warning went unheeded or was not heard by Clappine.

Crooks and Day alone finally reached the Columbia and began making their way down it, but they were forced to stop among friendly Indians and were finally rescued by Robert Stuart's command as it returned from the Okanagon. Thus, Crooks did not reach Astoria until May 11, 1812, and two days later he gave up his partnership in the venture.[9]

He and McClellan joined the small group of returning Astorians led by Robert Stuart, which left Astoria on June 29, 1812. Crooks was also in poor health during the return trip, especially during the period that McClellan disassociated himself from the rest of the party. Crooks was not a very robust man and the privations endured on these journeys were so great that much stronger men than he were affected. Crooks could and did look back on his experiences with pride, if not with pleasure. In later years, he contended that the returning party had crossed the continental divide at South Pass and this, although long contested, is now generally accepted.[10]

Crooks reached St. Louis in April 1813, and received word from Astor that he regretted his severance of relations with the Pacific Fur Company. By the fall of that year, Astor, who seems to have formed a high opinion of Crooks' abilities, had worked out a plan whereby Crooks would go to Michilimackinac to recover furs stored there belonging to Astor. However, the island was in the hands of the British and Crooks refused to go. Astor worked out arrangements with both the American and Canadian governments which enabled Crooks to accomplish his mission in 1814, after which he sold muskrat pelts to hatters along the Ohio River, and bought ginseng for Astor until the War of 1812 ended.[11]

---

9 *Ibid.,* 280-82, 294-304, 345-47. Throughout his book, Irving supplies details concerning Crooks that could only have been learned orally from him, since they do not occur in the journals of Hunt and Stuart.

10 The letter of Ramsay Crooks, originally published in the *Detroit Free Press,* July 1, 1856, is reproduced in Rollins, *op. cit.,* cxxxv-cxxxvi. In this letter, Crooks enumerates and names the seven returning Astorians who crossed South Pass, of whom he was then the sole survivor.

Crooks continued to act as Astor's agent in the years 1815-1817, although on what terms is not definitely known. Much of his time was spent in Michilimackinac or in that vicinity, although he seems to have made a trip to St. Louis in 1816.[12] He also formed a connection with a half-breed Chippewa woman during this period which resulted in the birth of a daughter, Hester Crooks, born on Drummond Island, May 30, 1817. Crooks assumed responsibility and she was educated at the Mackinac Mission School. She was married in 1834 to a missionary, William Thurston Boutwell. Crooks took an affectionate interest in his daughter and her family and visited them in later years.[13]

On March 17, 1817, Astor offered Crooks a one-twentieth interest in the American Fur Company and a salary of $2,000 per year to be his agent at Montreal, New York, and Michilimackinac, and Crooks accepted the offer.[14] The arrangement ran for three years and was later extended for one year. During this period, 1817-1821, Crooks was not only engaged in the fur business itself but he was the spearhead of an active political campaign to secure the abolition of the United States government's factory system, which all private traders viewed as inimical to their interests. He secured the powerful support of Senator Thomas Hart Benton of Missouri, and of Governor Lewis Cass of Michigan Territory. The efforts of the American Fur Company were successful in 1822 when, on May 22, Congress passed an act to abolish the "United States Trading Establishments with the Indian Tribes."[15]

On March 27, 1821, Crooks and Stuart renewed their

11 Porter, op. cit., I, pp. 267-73.   12 Ibid., II, pp. 693-97.

13 Grace Lee Nute, "Wilderness Marthas," in Minnesota History (September, 1927), VIII, pp. 248-52.

14 Porter, op. cit., II, p. 700. Robert Stuart was employed on the same terms simultaneously, except that his salary was $1,500 per year.

15 Ibid., II, pp. 709-18. See also Paul C. Phillips, The Fur Trade (Norman, 1961), 88-95. Lavender, op. cit., 284-313, graphically describes the work of Crooks in obtaining the abolition of the government factory system.

agreement with Astor for a period of five years, with the difference that Crooks was given a one-fifth interest in the American Fur Company, while Stuart's interest remained one-twentieth.[16] The fact that Crooks had gone to Paris in 1821 to discuss policies with Astor may have had a bearing on his preferred status. During the period 1821-1826, Crooks spent more time in New York but made an annual trip to Michilimackinac and usually to St. Louis as well.[17]

On October 1, 1826, Stuart renewed his agreement with Astor for five years at a salary of $2,500 per year and fifteen per cent of the net profits. The terms offered by Astor to Crooks at this time are not known but, whatever they were, Crooks deemed them unsatisfactory and held out for a more favorable offer. Presumably his demands were met for he also renewed for five years, but again the precise terms are unknown.[18] Crooks had married, on March 10, 1825, Emilie Pratte, youngest daughter of Bernard Pratte, prominent St. Louis fur merchant and this undoubtedly worked to his advantage.[19] Besides he had become virtually indispensable to Astor, and both of them knew it.

Crooks had urged upon Astor the establishment of a Western Department of the American Fur Company and beginning in 1822, this was done through Bernard Pratte and Company, of St. Louis, although it was not until 1826 that the American Fur Company began a more active role in the Far West. The big company met with considerable competition, as is well known, but was eventually to emerge in the dominant position. Not always able to crush opposition, it was forced to buy out its more active opponents and absorb them.[20]

In 1834, when Astor decided to get out of the fur busi-

[16] Porter, *op. cit.*, II, p. 715.

[17] W. J. Ghent, "Ramsay Crooks," in *Dictionary of American Biography* (New York, 1930), IV, p. 565.   [18] Porter, *op. cit.*, II, p. 743.

[19] Ghent, *loc. cit.*   [20] Porter, *op. cit.*, II, pp. 734-71.

ness, the Western Department was purchased by Pratte, Chouteau and Company and the Northern Department by Ramsay Crooks and certain associates.[21] Crooks soon moved the headquarters of the American Fur Company, which designation he was allowed by the terms of his purchase to retain, from Mackinac Island to La Pointe, on one of the Apostle Islands in Lake Superior. The company was hard hit by the business depression of 1837 but managed to survive until 1842, when it was finally forced into the hands of receivers.[22] Crooks, however, continued as a buyer and seller of furs in New York City until his death, which occurred on June 6, 1859.[23]

By his marriage to Emilie Pratte he had nine children, of whom only three daughters seem to have survived him. His business in later years was quite profitable and he continued to use the old name of the American Fur Company. For a man whose health was always frail and uncertain Crooks was amazingly active. He usually traveled by canoe, even on the Great Lakes. He was thoroughly acquainted with all details of the fur business. His relations with both Indians and whites were smoothly conducted. He was urbane and affable in his social relations and tough-minded and incisive in business, but possessed a great reputation for honesty. His residence in New York City was at 14 St. Marks Place and he was buried in Greenwood Cemetery in Brooklyn.[24]

---

[21] *Ibid.*, II, p. 779.

[22] Ruckman, *op. cit.*, 26-31. Lavender, *op. cit.*, 418, ascribes the bankruptcy of the American Fur Company more to the ruinous competition of the Ewing Brothers of Fort Wayne, Indiana, than to the business depression.

[23] Ghent, *loc. cit.*

[24] Stuart, *op. cit.*, xc-xci; Ruckman, *op. cit.*, 30-31; Lavender, *op. cit.*, 418-19.
A portrait of Crooks appears herein at page 18.

Edward de Morin

by PAUL D. RILEY
Nebraska State Historical Society

Edward de Morin (commonly spelled and pronounced Moran) was born in Montreal, Canada, September 28, 1818, the son of a *voyageur* and trader on the St. Lawrence. In 1834, Morin began trapping on the Illinois River near Fort Dearborn, and with others took his furs by boat to New Orleans in 1836. He returned to St. Louis that same year and was employed by the American Fur Company. He spent the winter of 1836-37 among the Ponca at the mouth of the Niobrara River. After five years with the company, he spent six years each trading for Rabbit & Cottin, and Harvey, Primeau & Co. In 1844 Morin wintered in California, near Sutter's Fort.[1]

Morin was married in 1848 to Valentine Peters of St. Louis, probably the daughter of Thomas and Victoria Peters. The 1850 census for St. Louis shows Edward "Morein," wife and daughter living with L. Roy, along with members of the Peters family. Morin was enumerated as age 30, and a "mountainer."[2]

All biographical sketches of Morin, including those written during his lifetime, say that he arrived at Cottonwood Springs, Nebraska, later the site of Fort McPherson, in 1853, where he established a road ranch in 1855. It seems more likely, however, that the date should be 1863, though he may have traded in the region earlier. The first known establishment in the region was in 1858, and many of the

---

[1] J. Sterling Morton and Albert Watkins, *Illustrated History of Nebraska* (Lincoln, 1907), II, p. 169; I. A. Fort, "Edward Morin," in Nebraska State Historical Society, *Proceedings and Collections,* ser. II, vol. II (Lincoln, 1898), 48-52.

[2] U.S. Census, 1850, St. Louis, Mo., Ward Two, 187.

early ranchers lived to be interviewed by historians. None mentioned Morin as being the earliest trader.[3]

From the birthplaces of his children, as shown in the 1870 census for Lincoln County, Nebraska, it would appear that Morin moved from Missouri to Kansas about 1856, returning to Missouri in 1860, then to Nebraska about 1863. The marriage license of his second daughter, Mary, states she was born at St. Joseph, Missouri, in 1861. This does not attempt to prove that Morin was living continually with his family during these years, of course.[4]

Military troops were stationed at Cottonwood Springs in 1863, laying the foundation for the later Fort McPherson. During the following decade, Morin worked as an independent trader in the Platte and Republican valleys, occasionally serving the military as guide and interpreter, though in the census of 1870 he was listed as a farmer with personal property valued at $1,000. Known by the Indians as "Iron Legs," supposedly for his great walking ability, at least one contemporary spoke of his great influence with the Brule and Cut-off Oglala Sioux. During the early seventies, he traded in partnership with his son-in-law, Leon Francois Pallardie, who as a youth in 1849 had come west from St. Charles.[5]

Mrs. Morin was shot accidentally by an emigrant hunting antelope and died September 28, 1875, at North Platte.[6]

[3] Morton and Watkins, op. cit., 169; Fort, op. cit., 51.

[4] U.S. Census, 1870, Lincoln County, Nebr., Cottonwood Springs, 11; *Marriage Records*. Lincoln County, Nebr., Book 1, p. 91. Mary Morin married Sylvester Friend, December 1, 1872.

[5] 1870 Census, *ibid;* "Fort McPherson" letter, in Omaha *Daily Herald,* May 15, 1873, reprinted in Paul D. Riley, "Dr. David Franklin Powell and Fort McPherson," in *Nebraska History,* vol. 51, no. 2 (Summer 1970), 160, 161.

[6] *North Platte Republican,* October 2, 1875. The Morin family were going "graping" and an emigrant wagon ahead of their wagon stopped to shoot at some nearby antelope. Morin stopped his wagon directly behind the other. In getting out of his wagon, the emigrant let a gun fall. It went off and Mrs. Morin was fatally injured, dying the following day.

During the following years Morin was employed around Fort Robinson and the Sioux agencies. In January 1881, Valentine McGillycuddy, Indian agent at Pine Ridge, complained that Morin was "about to open a whiskey ranch, liquor to stock the same is now in Sidney." He also claimed Morin had "more or less" connections with the Doc Middleton horse thief gang then active in northern Nebraska, though, when he dislaked a person, McGillycuddy was not above false accusation.[7]

Morin's exact whereabouts for the following fifteen years are not known, though it is likely he was living with his sons in the Black Hills. He returned to North Platte, where his daughters lived, about 1896, and he died June 16, 1902. Six of his eight children survived him.[8]

A portrait of Morin appears in this volume at page 18.

---

[7] National Archives (microfilm), RG 75, Series 14, Reel 3: Records of Bureau of Indian Affairs, Special Case No. 96.

[8] Morton and Watkins, *op. cit.,* 169.

John B. Didier

by PAUL D. RILEY
Nebraska State Historical Society

John B. Didier was born in France, December 25, 1827, the son of Professor John B. and Anna Didier. He came to the United States in 1847, finding work as a clerk in a store in Cincinnati, Ohio, where he was joined by his parents the following year. With a letter of introduction to the firm of P. Chouteau. Jr. & Company, he moved to St. Louis in 1849, while his parents moved to New Orleans, later returning to France.[1]

In 1852 Didier was sent as clerk to the Chouteau trading post, Fort John, located about five miles below Fort Laramie. Managed by J. P. B. Gratiot, the post was known locally as Gratiot Houses. Little is known of his life as clerk at the post, though it appears that he was often in charge of affairs, as he is sometimes referred to as the manager. On August 19, 1854, Lieut. John L. Grattan and his small force were killed by the Sioux Indians in their camp just south of Gratiot Houses. Didier was one of those who tried to stop Grattan from entering the village. The following day the Sioux broke into one of the Chouteau buildings and took their annuity goods which were stored there. On the 21st, they again returned, this time stealing the company's trading stores.[2]

Didier, having had enough of the West, returned almost immediately to St. Louis, where he gave a statement of

---

[1] Lewis C. Edwards, *History of Richardson County, Nebraska* (Indianapolis, 1917), 665-68, 976, 977.

[2] *Ibid.,* 665; Lloyd E. McCann, "The Grattan Massacre," in *Nebraska History,* vol. 37, no. 1 (March 1956), 5, 11-23.

affairs to the company,[3] and he then severed relations with Chouteau. That same fall, he moved to Barada Precinct, Richardson County, Nebraska Territory, where he lived the rest of his life. In 1855 at Brownville, Nebraska Territory, he was married to Marie Pineau, a half-blood daughter of a Louis Pineau. Her father was said to have been a trader in the vicinity of Fort Laramie and had recently died, after which she came east to Brownville with other unidentified relatives. John and Marie Didier were the parents of eight children. Mrs. Didier died in 1908, and John B. Didier died September 26, 1918.[4]

Didier's portrait appears in this volume at page 19.

[3] Didier's deposition is found in McCann, 22.
[4] Edwards, *op. cit.,* 666; *Falls City* (Neb.) *News,* October 4, 1918.

James Douglas

by KENNETH L. HOLMES
Oregon College of Education, Monmouth

On a family monument over his grave in Ross Bay Cemetery in Victoria, British Columbia, the date of the birth of James Douglas is inscribed: August 15, 1803. However, in an old account book written in Douglas' own hand, he once recorded his natal day as June 5, 1803. This discrepancy is indicative of the problems faced by any biographer of the "Father of British Columbia" in assessing the events of the fur trader's early life. In the words of the most perceptive student of the subject, W. Kaye Lamb, "James Douglas kept his own counsel all his days, and even the men who worked with him for many years in the service of the Hudson's Bay Company knew only bits and pieces of his story." [1]

Although there have been those who told of Douglas' birth in Scotland,[2] it can be stated with certainty now that he was a native of Demerara, in present Guyana, where he was born to a "Miss Ritchie," his father being John Douglas, a Glasgow merchant.[3] At some time during James' early boyhood his father took him to Scotland. He grew up in the home of a step-mother, the former Miss Jessie Hamilton; however, much of his time seems to have been spent in boarding schools, a common custom even today in Britain. He attended school at Lanarck, Scotland, and at Chester, in England. At the latter place he acquired a "polished French accent" under an *émigré* French tutor.[4] This would stand

---

[1] W. Kaye Lamb, "Some Notes on the Douglas Family," in *British Columbia Historical Quarterly,* XVII (1953), p. 41.

[2] Walter N. Sage, *Sir James Douglas and British Columbia,* University of Toronto Studies, History and Economics, vol. VI, no. 1 (Toronto, 1930), 14.

[3] Lamb, *op. cit.,* 44.   [4] Sage, *op. cit.,* 16.

him in good stead through all his years in the fur trade, as ability to communicate with French Canadians was a real asset.

At what seems to us to be a very early age, James Douglas signed on with the North West Company and sailed from Liverpool to enter the service of that vigorous fur establishment on May 7, 1819, a few weeks before his sixteenth birthday. He embarked on a life in the West after reaching Quebec City on May 25 and did not return to Scotland until forty-five years later in 1864. An account book which he kept throughout the years following contains the entry, "August 6, arrived at Fort William."[5] This was the North West Company post at the northwestern extremity of Lake Superior, the gateway to the Canadian West.

A tantalizing problem about Douglas' background is the claim that he was a mulatto. He was described as a "West Indian" by Governor George Simpson in 1832,[6] and John Tod, a good friend, stated in later years that the mother in Demerara was a creole.[7] Now these statements in themselves do not necessarily mean that Douglas was a black man, for a creole in most of Latin America was a second generation European. A most intriguing reference is to be found in a letter of Letitia Hargrave, wife of a fur trader farther east, written in December, 1842: "Mr Douglass is a *mulatto* son of *the* renowned Mr Douglas of Glas^ow."[8] The problem here is that Letitia Hargrave, so far as is known, had no contact whatsoever with Douglas, although her reference probably reflects a tradition abroad in the fur country. There is circumstantial evidence as to Douglas' interest in the plight of non-whites in an entry in his account book

---

[5] *Ibid.*, 18.

[6] Governor George Simpson's "Character Book," Hudson's Bay Company Archives, A34/2.   [7] Lamb, *op. cit.*, 43.

[8] Margaret Arnett Macleod (ed.), *The Letters of Letitia Hargrave*, Champlain Society *Publications*, XXVIII (Toronto, 1947), 132, letter of December 2-9, 1842.

made some time in 1849, "To goods to ransom a slave 14/." [9]
Was this an Indian slave, as was so prevalent among northwest coast tribes, or was it a black man? When Douglas was
governor of British Columbia in the 1860s, he encouraged
several hundred black persons to migrate from California to
Victoria. He even had his own private regiment – three
officers and fifty men – which was called "Sir James Douglas' Colored Regiment." [10]

A few years later Douglas wrote his daughter Jane (Mrs.
Alexander Grant Dallas) : "We are one and all, longing to
know who baby resembles, is she like papa, mama, or does
she take after her remoter ancestry; is she stout or thin, dark
or fair – all these, and many other questions you are expect-
ing to answer." [11] Should we read into these words curiosity
as to whether Negro or Indian characteristics had shown
up in the new baby? Undoubtedly the latter would be a
factor, was the former as well? We cannot know on present
evidence.

The question has been raised by some as to why James
Douglas did not return to Scotland until 1864, a long forty-
five years after leaving. This was certainly in contrast to the
practice of other Scots in the fur trade. They periodically
returned to the homeland to visit relatives and friends during their furlough years. Did Douglas wait for this until

[9] B. A. McKelvie, "Sir James Douglas: A New Portrait," in *British Columbia Hist. Quar.,* VII (1943), 95.

[10] George Nicholson, "The Negro Rifle Brigade Was Victoria's Pioneer Militia," in *The Islander* (Victoria, B.C.), May 21, 1961, p. 11.

[11] James K. Nesbitt, "New Douglas Letters Give Insight Into Governor's Char-acter," in *The Islander,* May 14, 1961, p. 16. There is another quote of great interest given by Nesbitt (in *The Islander,* August 27, 1961, "Return to England after Many Years," p. 16) in which Douglas describes his interest in some of his fellow-passengers on ship-board on the "Shannon" among the West Indies en route home to Scotland in 1864: "A bevy of Creole ladies took possession of the seats at my cabin door, and for several hours carried on an animated conversation in a very peculiar, drawling style of English." What did Douglas mean here by "Creole"? In light of his early background it is easy to see how his curiosity must have been aroused by this trip through the region where he was born.

after being knighted, so that he might say to them in effect,
"You see, in spite of my background I made it on my own"?
But that too is speculation, not evidence.

After the arrival in Canada, Douglas spent the next years
working his way west, serving at Ile à la Crosse as a clerk
from 1820 to 1825. He changed over to the Hudson's Bay
Company when the two firms combined in 1821. From 1826
to 1830 he worked as assistant to Chief Factor William
Connolly at Fort St. James, at the southeastern tip of Stuart
Lake, north of the fifty-fourth parallel in present British
Columbia. In the region then called New Caledonia, this
was the chief trading post and center of the fur trade. This
was in the northern part of the great Columbia District,
made up of the Old Oregon Country, an area of 668,223
square miles, much larger than present Alaska, nearly three
times as large as Texas. At the northern post he worked
alongside another clerk, Pierre Pambrun, with whom he
would continue associations for many years to come.[12] During the summer of 1826 Douglas accompanied Connolly and
Pambrun on a trip to Fort Vancouver, taking with them the
furs from the northern region. This was Douglas' first visit
to the lower Columbia River where he would spend many
future years. The famous emporium of the fur trade was still
unfinished. There he met another of the Douglas clan,
David, the botanist, whom he got to know well.[13]

It was on April 27, 1828, that James Douglas was married
to Amelia Connolly, daughter of the chief factor at Stuart
Lake. The wedding was according to "the custom of the
country," the bride, whose mother, Suzanne, was of the Cree
tribe, being only sixteen years old. Amelia would later be·
come the toast of Victoria and be given the title, Lady
Douglas.[14]

In the Minutes of Council of the Northern Department

---

12 Kenneth L. Holmes, "Pierre Chrysologue Pambrun," this *Series,* III, pp. 239-247.
13 *Journal Kept by David Douglas* (London, 1914), 180.
14 Walter O'Meara, *Daughters of the Country* (New York, 1968), 160, 184.

for July, 1828, there is a notation "That the undermentioned Clerks whose engagements expire be re-engaged on the following terms subject to the approval of the Governor and Committee . . . Jas. Douglas 3 Years from 1st June 1828 @ 100." [15] The minutes a year later listed under "Winter Arrangements," "Columbia Fort Vancouver . . . Jas. Douglas." [16] So would begin a period of service during which James Douglas would work under the tutelage of John McLoughlin in what would later become part of the United States. [17] He would be assistant to the big doctor for fifteen years and would then move up to the top position with the settlement of the Oregon Question.

An insight into Douglas' personality about this time is recorded in Governor George Simpson's notorious "Character Book," in which he noted down his private opinions, for his own use only, of servants under his command: [18]

A stout powerful active man of good conduct and respectable abilities: — tolerably well Educated, expresses himself clearly on paper, understands our Counting House business and is an excellent Trader. — Well qualified for any service requiring bodily exertion, firmness of mind and the exercise of sound judgment, but furiously violent when roused. — Has enough reason to look forward to early promotion and is a likely man to fill a place on our Council board in course of time.

[15] The amount of pay was in pounds sterling. R. Harvey Fleming (ed.), *Minutes of Council Northern Department of Rupert Land, 1821-1831* (London, 1940), 216.

[16] *Ibid.*, 243.

[17] The highest praise for both men is expressed by Hubert Howe Bancroft, *History of British Columbia* (San Francisco, 1887), of the Pacific States set. In fact, Bancroft went completely overboard in the pæons of praise he heaped upon McLoughlin and Douglas: "The world unites in according the highest praise to Douglas as well as to McLoughlin" (p. 296); "Douglas was the stronger; McLoughlin the purer. McLoughlin was weakened by his good qualities; Douglas was strengthened by his bad ones" (p. 300). However, McLoughlin is the paragon of the two: "Douglas was possessed of a cold, proud, formal egoism, wholly apart from the warm and generous sympathies of McLoughlin. His sluggish impulses were in the right direction, but they must all be made to play within the hard, passionless limits of conventionalism and aristocratic tradition" (p. 300).

[18] Governor George Simpson's "Character Book," Hudson's Bay Company Archives, A34/2. Quoted by permission of the Governor and Committee, Hudson's Bay Company, London.

Douglas fulfilled all of Simpson's expectations, becoming a chief trader in 1834, chief factor in 1839.

The news of his new appointment did not reach Douglas until the end of January 1830, and on January 30 he and his family left for Fort Vancouver. Over the following years he became the trusted co-worker with John McLoughlin, taking charge of the fort when the doctor was away, and acting as the chief factor's key representative on missions to establish relations with the representatives of Imperial Russia to the north in Alaska as well as with the Mexican government to the south in California.

While filling in for McLoughlin during the latter's furlough year of 1838-1839, Douglas wrote several key letters that reveal facets of his character. Written in a vigorous, memorable style, the letters show a man capable of thinking in depth about many problems.

Long before that philosopher of the fur trade, Harold A. Innis, made his simplistic statement, "The history of the fur trade in North America has been shown as a retreat in the face of settlement,"[19] McLoughlin and Douglas evidently talked at length about this problem at Fort Vancouver. As they saw the American settlers moving into the Willamette Valley, with the trapper-entrepreneur, Ewing Young, as the central figure, McLoughlin wrote to the company headquarters in London in 1836: "Every One Knows, who is acquainted with the Fur trade that as the country becomes settled the Fur Trade must diminish."[20] Two years later Douglas was even more explicit as he penned the following words to the Governor and Committee:

> The interest of the Colony, and the Fur Trade will never harmonize, the former can flourish, only, through the protection of equal

---

[19] Harold A. Innis, *The Fur Trade in Canada* (New Haven, 1962), 386.

[20] E. E. Rich, *McLoughlin's Fort Vancouver Letters, First Series, 1825-38* (London, 1941), Hudson's Bay Record Society *Publications,* IV, letter of November 16, 1836, p. 173. For a discussion of this matter see Kenneth L. Holmes, *Ewing Young, Master Trapper* (Portland, Oreg., 1967), 112.

laws, the influence of free trade, the accession of respectable inhabitants; in short by establishing a new order of things, while the fur
Trade, must suffer by each innovation.[21]

In the same letter he described the activities of Young and
the Willamette settlers aptly: "The restless Americans are
brooding over a thousand projects." [22]

With trenchant words and Scotch Calvinistic fervor
Douglas described in 1838 the type of religious leaders
needed on the frontier:

> A Clergyman in this Country must quit the closet & live a life of
> beneficient activity, devoted to the support of principles, rather than of
> forms: he must shun discord, avoid uncharitable feelings, temper zeal
> with discretion, illustrate precept by example, and the obdurate rock
> upon which we have been so long hammering in vain will soon be
> broken into fragments.[23]

Fort Vancouver, the Hudson's Bay Company Columbia
District headquarters, was on the north shore of the great
river, just opposite the mouth of the Willamette. A picture
of the *mélange* of racial and tribal representatives making
up the population of the fur depot is painted in the following word picture by Governor George Simpson, as he tells
of the crew and the passengers in a boat under James Douglas' command in 1839:

> Our bateau carried as curious a muster of races and languages as
> perhaps had ever been congregated within the same compass in any
> part of the world. Our crew of ten men contained Iroquois, who spoke
> their own tongue; a Cree, half-breed of French origin, who appeared
> to have borrowed his dialect from both his parents; a north Briton who
> understood only the Gaelic of his native hills; Canadians who of course,
> knew French; the Sandwich Islanders, who jabbered a medley of
> Chinook, English, &c., and their own vernacular jargon. Add to all
> this, that the passengers were natives of England, Scotland, Russia,

---

21 *Ibid.,* letter of October 18, 1838, p. 242.　　22 *Ibid.,* 241.
23 W. Kaye Lamb, "The James Douglas Report on the 'Beaver Affair,'" in *Oregon
Historical Quarterly,* XLVII (1946), letter from Fort Vancouver, October 2, 1838, p.
28.

Canada, and the Hudson's Bay Company's territories: and you have the prettiest congress of nations, the nicest confusion of tongues, that has ever taken place since the days of the Tower of Babel.[24]

The settlement of the Oregon Question in 1846 marked a year of decision for the men of the fur trade in the Columbia Valley. They were given a choice between remaining south of the line between British and American territories and declaring their allegiance to the United States – as McLoughlin did to the surprise of many – or of moving to the north to retain their British connection – as Douglas did to the surprise of nobody. Douglas, in fact, became the key figure in the northward movement. He was sent by the company to establish a new fort at the southern tip of Vancouver Island in 1843, and, although he was not made governor of the new crown colony established there in 1849, after the short term of the first governor, Richard Blanchard, Douglas was appointed to the office in 1851. With the gold rush into the valleys of the mainland in 1858 Douglas was made governor of the new colony of British Columbia. His fame really rests more upon his political career in western Canada than upon his fur-trading experiences earlier, when he had always played second fiddle to some other leader. This "Father of British Columbia" was knighted by Queen Victoria in 1863 and passed the rest of his life quietly in the city he had founded, Victoria. He died on August 2, 1877.

Douglas' portrait appears in this volume at page 19.

---

[24] George Simpson, *Narrative of a Journey Round the World* (London, 1847), I, p. 176.

Lewis Dutton

by REX W. STRICKLAND
University of Texas at El Paso

In addition to the great figures in the fur trade, there were many obscure trappers and *engagés* whose names flicker uncertainly in the annals of the mountains. Especially is this true in the history of the Southwestern trade that centered at Taos and Santa Fe. In recent years, however, some of the hitherto unknown men have been partially rescued from anonymity through the application of extant, though fragmentary, data in the archives of New Mexico and Chihuahua. A scrap here and a tag there used within the bounds of probability, a generous allowance for Peg-leg Smith's tall tales as related by George Yount, and a tongue in cheek use of James Ohio Pattie's confused narrative enables the biographer to arrive at some sort of credible synthesis. Such is this effort to place Lewis Dutton within the context of time and place.

Dutton was born in New Hampshire in 1802[1] or 1804.[2] He entered recorded history February 28, 1824, when in company with the legendary Hugh Glass and three other companions, E. More (Moore), A. Chapman and one Marsh, he left Henry's Fort near the juncture of the Yellowstone and the Bighorn to carry dispatches directed to William Ashley *via* Fort Atkinson. Dale Morgan's account of their misadventure is predicated in the main upon Dutton's story which he subsequently related to George Yount;

[1] Census of El Paso County, Texas, 1860, 114. He gave his age as 58, a native of New Hampshire. He was a merchant and well-to-do by frontier standards; he owned $1000 worth of personal property and $8000 of real property.

[2] Habitantes de Barranca Colorada, Partido de Galeana, Distrito del Paso del Norte, April 23, 1841, *Docs. de Ciudad Juarez* (Microfilm Reel 58/0145, University of Texas at El Paso Library Archives) renders his age as 36.

since we are placing Dutton central in our narrative, it seems only fair that we should let him tell of the escapade as he remembered it. Hugh Glass supplied a few details about their departure: "At the opening of the following Spring (1824) he accompanied this party (Major Henry's) to trap again on the Plat River;" actually of course they were working out of the fort on the Bighorn. Then Yount continues:

> It then became necessary to send an Express, . . . down the Plat River, & thence to Ashly at St. Louis – Glass and four others volunteered for this hazardous enterprize – One of the four was Dutton, the individual who gave to Yount the balance of Glass' adventurous life, . . . – Up to the *present date* Glass told to Yount all which we have here written & Allen confirmed the truth of it all.[3]

On the North Platte they built bullboats "made of Buffalo skins" and took advantage of the spring rise to float downstream. Near the confluence of the Platte and Laramie they discovered a sizeable village of Indians which they assumed to be Pawnees who spoke nearly the same language as the Arikaras, "& were often mistaken one for the other." With a strange lack of caution for men who should have known Indians, they accepted the chief's cordial invitation to come ashore for a feast. All except Dutton left their rifles in the boats. They sat down to a sumptuous meal and all went well until Glass, more alert than his companions, detected a chance remark which revealed that their hosts were not friendly Pawnees but Arikaras, deadly foes. "He said to one near him – 'these are Pickarees' " to which Elk's Tongue, the chief, who understood a little English, replied, "No, Pawnees we." The frightened whites bolted from the tipi and ran for the river where they found that their rifles had been filched from the boats. They shoved out into the current and paddled for their lives with the Indians swimming like so many retrievers in pursuit. Reaching the opposite shore, they ran into the covert of trees and rocky ledges that

---

[3] *George C. Yount and his Chronicles of the West,* Charles L. Camp, ed., (Denver, 1966), 203.

fringed the stream. Chapman and Moore were overtaken and killed; the Arikaras did not follow Dutton who had retained his rifle, nor overtake Marsh who outran his pursuers. The two succeeded in joining forces and went together to Fort Atkinson (Council Bluffs) which they reached in May to report their three companions dead. In truth, we know, as Dutton and Marsh learned in June, that Glass had lived through another incredible journey; though without gun, he had his knife, flint and steel. He lived on buffalo calves until a party of Sioux found him and carried him to Fort Kiowa whence he went down the Missouri to Council Bluffs.[4]

Dutton's association with Glass apparently continued for the next two or three years; thus we may track Dutton's activities as he traveled from Council Bluffs to New Mexico. He told Yount that Glass was given a purse of three hundred dollars at Fort Atkinson and "with this money he traveled to the extremely western settlements on the Missouri & became a partner in an enterprize for trading in New Mexico." A year later found Glass in Taos[5] (this would make the date of his arrival in the late summer of 1825); Dutton was probably with him, certainly he and Glass were in the vicinity of Taos in 1826. Quite probably the two went separate ways thereafter. Glass took service with Etienne Provost and trapped the streams of central and northern Utah.[6] No available evidence associates Glass with the Gila whereas Dutton spent almost a quarter century in the area of the Gila and Janos.

The great names in the beaver hunt *(caza de nutria)* poured into New Mexico in 1826 lured by the friendliness of Antonio Narbona *(padre)*, governor of the territory in

[4] For particulars not found in Dutton's story see Dale L. Morgan, *Jedediah Smith and the Opening of the West* (Lincoln, 1965), 105-108.   [5] *Yount*, 205.

[6] Glass left New Mexico in 1827 in a party under the leadership of Sylvestre Pratte who obtained a *guia*, January 1827, that authorized them to trap outside the Mexican territory. David J. Weber, *Los Extranjeros* (Santa Fe, N.Mex., 1967), 37.

1826-1827.[7] During the spring and summer of 1826 he issued a large number of *guias* and *pasaportes* to American trappers and traders authorizing their activities in the Gila and Sonora areas. The echoes of their adventures in Apachería can be found in the *Documentos de Ciudad Juarez* and the custom house archives of New Mexico.

In addition to individual permits, group passports were granted to S. W. and/or J. Williams (almost certainly Old Bill Williams since in New Mexico the Christian name William was transliterated Julian instead of Guillermo) and Ceran St. Vrain, August 29, 1826, allowing them to proceed to Sonora, i.e., the Gila, with thirty-five men for private trade; at the same time Narbona gave passports to Michel Robidoux and Sylvestre Pratte with 30-plus men; John Rowland and eighteen hired men; and Ewing Young with a like number. James Baird, on the eve of his departure to trap the Gila, wrote to Alejandro Ramirez, October 26, 1826, saying there were over a hundred Americans on the river, which simple addition will prove rather accurate.[8]

Besides the group leaders some four men received passports as individual traders: E. Bure (Dubreuil?), Alexander Branch, S. Stone and "Louis Dolton," so Marshall read his Spanish documents but in other data the name is Hispanicized "Dotton." Anyone who has pored over Spanish frontier paleography can readily forgive Marshall for his *erratum*.

Dutton's exact role in the fur trade escapes history; that he trapped the Gila in company with men of note in the beaver hunt is clear, but our meager sources do not disclose his comings and goings. Obviously at one time or the other he was a member of a party that included George Yount –

7 Francisco Almada, *Diccionario de Historia, Geografía y Biografía Sonorenses* (Chihuahua, n.d.), 500. This work is absolutely indispensible for the study of the north Mexican states.

8 Thomas M. Marshall, "St. Vrain's Expedition to the Gila in 1826," *Southwestern Historical Quarterly*, (January 1916), XIX, pp. 253-54.

his relating of the scrape at the mouth of the Laramie is evidence of this association. Our data simply refuse to reveal the liason between Yount, Young, the Patties and Robidoux in 1826 and 1827, but it must have been in the time of Yount's residence in New Mexico (1826 to 1830) since there is no evidence that Dutton ever went to California nor did Yount leave California after his arrival there in 1831.

After 1826 Dutton faded from the annals of the fur trade although there is no reason to surmise that he left the southwest. Perhaps he associated with St. Vrain and others of the Taos-based trappers and hunters. Some of his old companions emigrated to California; others, notably Glass, lost their lives in Indian affrays. A new breed of men, merchants, mule traders and miners, moved into New Mexico and there was no lack of work for a man of courage acquainted with long and arduous trails. It has been said that at one time Dutton was one of James Kirker's scalp hunters and he may well have been.[9] An informed guess would place him with Robert McKnight at the copper mine at Santa Rita del Cobre during the late 1820s and the early 1830s.[10] In 1840 McKnight and Stephen Courcier, a native of Philadelphia and former associate of McKnight in the Santa Rita del Cobre, obtained a concession to work the mine at Barranca Colorado, five miles southeast of Corralitos.[11] In April 1841, Dutton was listed in the census as a resident of the Barranca Colorado, the only inhabitant other than Robert McKnight who bore an English surname. In the census he is described as a single man *(soltero)* living with Donacinda Villegas, a single woman *(soltera)*. By occupation he was

---

[9] Personal conversation with Bill McGaw.

[10] Fayette Alexander Jones, *New Mexico Mines and Minerals* (Santa Fe, 1904), 37, contains a fairly accurate summary of McKnight's operations at Santa Rita del Cobre; H. A. Thorne, *Mining Practices at the Chino Mines,* Nevada Consolidated Copper Co., Santa Rita, N.M., Dept. of Commerce, Bureau of Mines I.C. 6412 (March 1931), furnishes additional information even though nothing concerning Dutton. It does show that Kit Carson was one of McKnight's teamsters at one time.

[11] *Docs. de Ciudad Juarez,* Reel 58/0178. UTEP Microforms.

listed as an *alquilado* which comes out in English as a renter or leaser. As previously stated he rendered his age as 36.[12] His daughter, Maria Simona, was born in the first half of the year of 1842. Though subsequent censuses for Barranca Colorado, Corralitos and Janos have been consulted, they do not reveal his presence; this lack, however, does not argue that he was not a resident of the area where he probably continued to reside until 1848 and the end of the Mexican War.

Apparently he moved to El Paso del Norte where he was seen by H. W. C. Whiting, April 13, 1849, who wrote in his journal

> Here I fell in with an old man named Dutton, one of the few remaining Rocky mountain trappers of the old school. He knows, as it is said, the Gila country very thoroughly, and I mention his name here as a memorandum.[13]

Not long after his meeting with Whiting, Dutton took up residence at San Elizario, where he moved in the common current of life until his death in 1875. He is listed in the census of 1860 and 1870 and appeared year after year on the tax rolls of El Paso County. These records reveal that he was a man of substance measured by the frontier standards.

When he removed from the Barranca Colorado to the El Paso area, he brought his daughter, Simona, with him; September 6, 1851, he claimed her as his legal heir.[14] She was then nine years of age.

Dutton died March 29, 1875, at San Elizario.[15]

---

12 *Ibid.,* Reel 58/0145.

13 Journal of H. W. C. Whiting, *Exploring Southwestern Trails* (ed. R. P. Bieber), *Southwest Historical Series,* VII (Glendale, Calif., 1938), pp. 310-11; 31 Cong., 1 sess., *Sen. Ex. Doc. 64,* XIV, pp. 235-50.

14 Liber A, El Paso County, Texas, 208. In the Census of El Paso County, 1860, she is listed as 18 years of age, the wife of Horace Stephenson and the mother of a ten month old son, Lewis. Incidentally, living in her house was Leonicio Dutton, a four year old boy whose relationship is enigmatic.

15 Jose Maria Flores, "Libro," entry for March 29, 1875, "Murio Dn Luis Dutton." Xerox copy supplied by the Flores family.

Russel Farnham

by HARVEY L. CARTER
Colorado College

Three of the Astorian clerks, Gabriel Franchère, Ross Cox and Alexander Ross, wrote accounts of the great venture in the Oregon Country in which they were involved. Russel Farnham, in some respects the most remarkable man among a group of able, observant, and active recruits, left no account of his part in the enterprise and, in consequence, is much less well known than he deserves to be.

He was a native of Massachusetts, born in 1784, the son of John and Susan Chapin Farnham.[1] He was among those recruited for the Astorian enterprise in Montreal and this fact, together with the fact that he knew French well enough to write letters in that language, is an indication that he may have been in Montreal for some years before 1810 and already engaged in some connection with the fur trade.[2] But of this we have no certain knowledge.

He was one of the thirty-three Astorians who sailed for Oregon aboard the "Tonquin," on September 6, 1810, and one of the six whom Captain Thorn attempted to abandon on the Falkland Islands. Among his activities in the Oregon Country, the following may be mentioned. He formed one of the party that pursued and recaptured the three deserters in November 1811. He was chosen to head a party with the purpose of recovering the goods cached at Caldron Linn on

---

[1] Stella M. Drumm, "More about Astorians," in *Oregon Historical Quarterly* (1933), XXXIV, p. 344. This information was derived by Miss Drumm from Farnham's marriage record in St. Louis. Apparently Washington Irving was wrong when he described Farnham as "a Green Mountain Boy" from Vermont.

[2] Alexander Ross, "Adventures . . ." in *Early Western Travels,* ed. by R. G. Thwaites (Cleveland, 1904), VII, p. 41.

Snake River but was forced to give up the task by the Indian attack on the larger party, headed by John Reed, at the Dalles, in March 1812, in which encounter he participated. He was the executioner of the Indian who was ordered by John Clarke to be hanged for stealing, June 1, 1813, at Fort Okanogan. Whether he volunteered for this duty or was ordered to it we do not know. He helped to build the post erected near Spokane and subsequently spent the winter of 1812-13 among the Flatheads. He traveled with them all the way to the headwaters of the Missouri River and was thus the first to open the fur trade in what is now western Montana. All these activities justify the characterization made of him by Alexander Ross as "a bustling, active, and enterprising fellow."[3]

Some months after Astoria was sold to the North West Company for $58,000 on November 12, 1813, Farnham, together with Wilson Price Hunt, Alfred Seton, and J. C. Halsey, boarded the brig "Pedlar," which sailed for Sitka, April 3, 1814. At Sitka, Farnham transferred to the "Forester," an English brig, commanded by W. J. Pigot, and it was this British vessel which set him ashore at Kamchatka by his own request. Farnham carried important dispatches for John Jacob Astor and $40,000 in bills of exchange upon London merchants.[4] He now proceeded to cross Siberia, being forced to walk most of the way. We only know that, at one stage of his journey, he was forced to eat the tops of his boots to keep from starving. He reached Copenhagen and procured a passport, dated October 16, 1816, which enabled him to sail to Baltimore.[5] Thus, his crossing of Asia and Europe consumed more than two years. As an Astorian, he had accomplished what John Ledyard had attempted unsuc-

[3] *Ibid.,* 186, 210-211; also Gabriel Franchère, "Narrative . . ." in *ibid.,* VI, pp. 261-64.

[4] Kenneth W. Porter, "The Cruise of Astor's Brig Pedler, 1813-1816," in *Oregon Historical Quarterly* (1930), XXXI, pp. 227-28.   [5] Drumm, *op. cit.,* 338-40.

cessfully some twenty years earlier, but in a reverse direction, and he had circumnavigated and circumambulated the globe. Had he kept a record or even written a reminiscent account, he would be regarded as one of the most renowned of world travelers. The War of 1812, which had seemed to necessitate his effort to bring news to Astor, had been ended for nearly two years by the time he reached New York.

His loyalty to the company was rewarded by his being placed in charge of operations on the Mississippi and Missouri rivers. At the instigation of his competitor, Manuel Lisa, he was arrested for employing Canadian aliens but won a suit for $5000, and continued to operate on the Missouri until 1821, when he was transferred back to the Mississippi.[6] During this period he had charge of what was known as the Lower Mississippi Division of the American Fur Company, which included that portion of the river bordering Illinois, on the one hand, and Missouri and Iowa, on the other. He owned land and a fine home at Portage Des Sioux in St. Charles County, Missouri. On October 27, 1829, he was married to Susan Bosseron of St. Louis.[7] Competition with George Davenport was resolved by his successful merging of Davenport's interests with his own. Davenport's headquarters were in the Iowa town that still bears his name and those of Farnham were across the river at Rock Island, Illinois, then known as Farnhamsville. The traders advanced credit to the Sac and Fox Indians to the extent of $40,000, for which the United States government assumed responsibility, according to the treaty of September 12, 1832, with those Indians.[8]

Farnham made a trip to New York in 1832, returning to St. Louis in October of that year. Cholera was epidemic in the area at the time and Farnham died suddenly, October

---

[6] David Lavender, *The Fist in the Wilderness* (New York, 1964), 270, 273-74, 275-76, 278.   [7] Drumm, *op. cit.,* 343-44.   [8] Lavender, *op. cit.,* 338-39, 404.

23, 1832, two hours after the onset of the cramps which signalled his contraction of the dread disease. He was buried in Catholic Cemetery in St. Louis. His wife survived him only to the following year and their only son, Charles Russel Farnham lived only to the age of eighteen.[9]

Upon hearing of Farnham's death, his friend and associate Ramsay Crooks wrote, "He underwent greater privations than any half dozen of us. He was one of the best meaning, but the most sanguine, man I almost ever met with." Farnham was of medium stature but strongly built, with light curly hair and brown eyes. A sociable man, fond of playing jokes, he was energetic in business but humane in his treatment of the Indians.[10]

A portrait of Farnham appears in this volume at page 20.

---

[9] Drumm, *op. cit.,* 344.   [10] *Ibid.,* 343-44.

William Gordon

by CHARLES E. HANSON, JR.
Chadron, Nebraska

William Gordon was apparently something of an adventurer, with an intellectual curiosity and ability that distinguished him from the average trader or trapper. He was by turns a surveyor, a clerk, a trader, a trapper, and an Indian affairs officer.

There was, however, no overriding drive in his nature to be a great business success. In fact, Frank Triplett claimed to be repeating the stories told by many of Gordon's former companions when he characterized him as "the laughing philosopher of the trappers" who took life easy and never crossed a bridge until he got there.[1]

In 1858, Menra Hopewell wrote the only known connected account of Gordon's early life. According to Hopewell, Gordon was the son of a wealthy Virginia family. After graduating from the University of Virginia he went to Europe and his parents died before his return. He was married a few months later but his bride died six months after the wedding. He fought under Jackson at New Orleans and was later wounded and captured in the first Seminole War.[2]

Just how he got to St. Louis is not clear, but he described himself in 1828 as "of St. Louis, Missouri (formerly of Tennessee)."[3] His birthdate is unknown but Pilcher still spoke of him as a "young gentleman" in 1823.[4]

[4] Dale Morgan, ed., *The West of William H. Ashley* (Denver, 1964), 48.

---

[1] Frank Triplett, *Conquering the Wilderness* (New York & St. Louis, 1883), 401.

[2] Stella Drumm, ed., "More Reports of the Fur Trade and Inland Trade to Mexico," in *Glimpses of the Past*, IX, no. 3, (Missouri Hist. Soc., St. Louis, 1942), 54.

[3] Dale Morgan and Eleanor Harris, eds., *The Rocky Mountain Journals of William Marshall Anderson* (San Marino, Calif., 1967), 320.

Stella Drumm said that Gordon was in St. Louis in 1818 and joined John C. Sullivan in surveying the northern Indian boundary in Illinois. She also said that Gordon and two others were involved in an affray with a night watchman that November.[5] He soon gravitated to the western fur trade and his activities for a decade were summarized in a letter written to Lewis Cass, Secretary of War, on October 3, 1831:

> I first went to the Rocky Mountains to engage in the Fur Trade in 1822, and have been every year since engaged, or connected with the business of the trade, either on the Upper Missouri River, or in the region of the Mountains. I have twice been beyond the mountains, and have seen all the variety of operations to which our trade and intercourse with the Indians is there subject. In the year 1822 I was clerk in an expedition conducted by Immel & Jones for the Missouri Fur Company, and was one of those who escaped the Massacre of that party when it was attacked, defeated & robbed by the Black Feet Indians on the Yellow Stone river.[6]

At the time of this massacre, the Missouri Fur Company, under the leadership of Joshua Pilcher, was making a determined bid for a stake in the Rocky Mountain fur trade. Gordon was a member of a large expedition under Robert Jones and Michel Immel which established a post on the Yellowstone for the Crow trade and then trapped on the headwaters of the Missouri in Blackfoot country.

That fact alone made it a precarious undertaking, but the party made twenty packs by the middle of May 1823, and started back to their Yellowstone post. On the way they met a party of about thirty-five Blackfeet warriors who gave every evidence of friendship and camped with the Americans that night. They left next morning with a few presents, apparently in a good mood. Immel and Jones mistrusted the evidences of Blackfoot friendship and hurried

[5] Stella Drumm, *op. cit.*, 54.
[6] Reproduced in Annie Heloise Abel, ed., *Chardon's Journal at Fort Clark, 1834-1839* (Pierre, South Dakota, 1932), 343-49

the party forward. Twelve days later, on May 31, 1823, the Americans were ambushed by a large party of Blackfeet on a narrow trail along a steep hill above the Yellowstone River. Immel was one of the first to fall and Jones was killed soon after trying to charge through the enemy blocking the narrow part of the trail.

The party was strung out single file when attacked and Gordon was cut off from the action around his leaders. He ran seven miles to escape and returned that night to find the Blackfeet encamped at the scene of the battle. Making off again in the darkness he finally reached a party of friendly Crows the next night and was soon reunited with the survivors of the party. Charles Keemle, another clerk, had assumed command in crossing the Yellowstone to reach the Crows. The party then proceeded to raise a cache of thirty-two packs from the fall hunt and bring them down in skin boats while Gordon went on to Fort Vanderburgh, the company post for the Mandans. There he sent a report of the disaster to Pilcher, listing casualties of seven killed and four wounded, with the loss of all the horses, traps and twenty packs of beaver skins.[7]

Pilcher came up soon after with sixty men, overtaking Colonel Leavenworth's boats going up to attack the Arikaras. When they arrived near the Arikara village, Pilcher was assigned command of the Indian auxiliaries and his men were formed into one company. The orders gave William Gordon the nominal rank of second lieutenant.[8]

Already exasperated by an Indian defeat, Gordon was thoroughly disgusted with Leavenworth's conciliatory attitude after the indecisive action against the Arikara villages. In his hastily drafted "treaty" the colonel promised to leave the now-deserted villages intact, but he was mortified to see them going up in smoke before his boats were out of sight.

[7] Letter from Gordon to Pilcher, June 15, 1823, reproduced in Dale Morgan, *op. cit.*, 48-49.　　[8] *Ibid.*, 52.

Gordon and Angus McDonald had blithely set fire to nearly every Arikara lodge amid the bursting of many unexploded shells lodged in the dirt roofs during Leavenworth's cannonade. During this operation they half-expected an attack by returning Arikaras and put off into the river as soon as the job was done. Leavenworth was furious, but McDonald made no secret of their deed and later wrote a justification in the *Washington Gazette*.[9]

With the upper Missouri closed off, Ashley outfitted a party under Jedediah Smith to go overland to the Crows. Having no better plan, Pilcher sent a small party under Keemle and Gordon to follow Smith. The two parties met on the west side of the Black Hills and went on to the Wind River, where they wintered with the Crows. Smith's party moved on in February, Keemle and Gordon lingered a while to trade and then started back by way of the Yellowstone River. Here again they met disaster. Benjamin O'Fallon, in charge of the Upper Missouri Indian Agency, wrote Superintendent Clark on July 9, 1824, that William Gordon had been robbed by a Crow war party on the Yellowstone. The Crows also took an Indian woman, wife of an Iroquois engagé, that Gordon had ransomed from another band of Crows.[10]

In 1825 Gordon assisted with the Yellowstone Expedition of Atkinson and O'Fallon. His name appeared as a witness to the treaties with the Poncas on June 9, 1825, and with the Teton, Yankton, and Yanktonai on June 22, 1825.[11] In his journal, Colonel Atkinson mentions Gordon at the mouth of the Yellowstone on August 17, and wrote at Fort Kiowa on September 9 that Gordon intended to stay there.[12]

He was still with Pilcher in 1826 and James Kennerly at Fort Atkinson mentions his going down to St. Louis in

[9] *Ibid.,* 57. [10] *Ibid.,* 82.
[11] Charles Kappler, ed., *Indian Affairs – Laws and Treaties* (Washington, 1904), II, pp. 227, 230. [12] Dale Morgan, *op. cit.,* 131, 135.

March 1826. In October of that same year Benjamin O'Fallon unsuccessfully recommended Gordon as sub-agent for the Sioux on the Missouri after George H. Kennerly resigned.[13]

Pilcher's plans to stay in the trade were rapidly thwarted and several of his trusted men eventually went to work for the American Fur Company. In his highly colored recordings of interviews with Thomas Eddie, Colonel Frank Triplett described a desperate fight that Eddie and Gordon had with an Arapaho war party which appears to have occurred about 1827 or early 1828.[14] If this is true Gordon may have put in a campaign with Smith, Jackson and Sublette, trapping in the mountains. In any event he is believed to have been with the American Fur Company in 1829.

On May 5, 1830, McKenzie at Fort Union wrote to Fort Tecumseh: "Gordon with four or five men is trapping on Powder River."[15] Instead of the dull tedium of the trade room, Gordon always seemed to prefer the expeditions, whether they were to trap, council with the Indians, or make a survey in some new place.

The Fort Tecumseh Journal records on August 23 that "Gordon, Chardon, Holiday, Campbell and several other clerks of the company" were there.[16] He spent the next few months assisting the Indian agents. On September 4 he was one of the witnesses to a new treaty with the Yankton and Santee Sioux at Fort Tecumseh.[17] On September 8 he left for St. Louis with sub-agent Jonathan L. Bean and twenty-one Sioux, most of them Yanktons.[18]

During this period Gordon had taken a Yankton wife[19] and she accompanied the party to St. Louis. The Fort Te-

---

[13] Morgan and Harris, *op. cit.*, 320. [14] Triplett, *op. cit.*, 392-94.

[15] Chouteau-Papin Collection, Missouri Hist. Soc., St. Louis.

[16] *Fort Tecumseh Journals*, Mo. Hist. Soc.

[17] Kappler, *op. cit.*, II, p. 310. [18] Morgan and Harris, *op. cit.*, 320.

[19] *Fort Tecumseh Journals* have this note on March 1, 1831: "Gordon's father-in-law (Yancton) arrived with a few robes."

cumseh Journal records the arrival of "Mr. Gordon and lady" from St. Louis on January 18, 1831, and the departure of "Mr. and Mrs. Gordon" for Laidlaw's post at the Grand Cheyenne River on February 10.

Vanderburgh, the veteran brigade leader, was wintering in the Rocky Mountains with a party of trappers[20] and Etienne Provost undertook to supply him with forty or fifty fresh horses. Gordon came down to Fort Tecumseh on March 26 and left on April 2 to conduct a party with some of the horses to Cherry River, where they would rendezvous with Provost.

Back in his beloved mountains again, Gordon was at the Green River on July 9, 1831, where Henry Fraeb gave him an order for $32.25.[21] Leaving that area on July 18, he arrived in St. Louis late in August, very possibly still in the company of Etienne Provost.[22]

At this point Gordon took some serious interest in trading and secured a two-year license from William Clark on October 29, 1831, to trade on the Missouri and its tributaries from the Niobrara to Cherry River. According to the license he had twenty employees and capital of $1,145.61.[23]

The extent of his activities under this license is not known. Trouble with the Sacs and Foxes erupted the next spring and General Atkinson, with whom Gordon had traveled in 1825, appointed him captain of a "company of spies" on June 22, 1832. This company of the mounted volunteers of Illinois militia, was organized as a company of spies by order of General Atkinson and served from June 22 to August 14 inclusive. In the company roster we note that Gordon's address is listed as St. Louis and that the great majority of the men came from Kaskaskia.[24]

---

[20] *Fort Tecumseh Journals,* February 22, 1831.

[21] Sublette Papers, Mo. Hist. Soc.

[22] Morgan and Harris, *op. cit.,* 321.   [23] *Ibid.,* 321.

[24] Ellen M. Whitney, ed. "The Black Hawk War 1831-1832," in Illinois State Historical Library, *Collections,* xxxv (1970), I, pp. 546-48.

Sometime in 1832 he bought an interest in Leclerc's trading venture in opposition to the American Fur Company on the Missouri.[25] Leclerc had completed a post near Fort Lookout and built a small trading house on the Bad River. In the spring of 1832 John P. Cabanné seized Leclerc's goods above Bellevue on the pretext that they included illegal liquor. Gordon and the rest of the partners bitterly protested the outrage. It was finally settled by a payment of $9,200 from the American Fur Company.

As flexible and optimistic as ever, Gordon again deserted trading for a government job. In the spring of 1833 he accepted an appointment as special Indian sub-agent that had just been declined by Joshua Pilcher. His responsibilities were chiefly concerned with supplies and equipment for the tribes just being settled in eastern Kansas.[26] Superintendent Clark evidently appreciated Gordon's ability and good disposition for the latter was retained in 1835 to survey the Sac and Fox lands under the treaty of 1832. In the spring of 1836 "Major Gordon" declined an appointment as sub-agent for the Chippewas but accepted the job of surveying the land reserved for Sac and Fox halfbreeds in the treaty of 1824. In May 1836, Clark granted a license to W. R. McPherson to trade with the Sacs and Foxes on the Des Moines River. Gordon was obviously interested in this venture since he signed as surety for McPherson.[27]

Gordon soon went back to the mountains. In February 1844, "Mrs. Gordon, the wife of Captain William Gordon," asked the Superintendent of Indian Affairs at St. Louis to help find information about her husband who had left on a

25 Morgan and Harris, op. cit., 321. Here Morgan and Harris identify the firm as J. B. D. Valois and P. N. Leclerc. See also notes by Doane Robinson in South Dakota Historical Collections Vol. IX (1918), 158. He identifies the trader simply as Narcisse Leclerc, outfitted by Henry Shaw, a young St. Louis businessman who made some investments in the Indian trade. Robinson also states that the firm styled itself "The Northwest Fur Company."

26 John E. Sunder, Joshua Pilcher (Norman, 1968), 98.

27 Morgan and Harris, op. cit., 321.

trapping trip to the Upper Missouri eighteen months before.[28] The identity of this wife, possibly a white woman, is not known.

Gordon was mentioned periodically in the accounts of Pierre Chouteau, Jr. & Company as late as 1846. In 1847 he was noted as guiding a party of emigrants to Oregon.[29] Colonel Frank Triplett wrote that Gordon went on many daring trapping expeditions and sometimes guided emigrant trains. He usually commanded respect from the Indians, who knew him as "White Wolf." Triplett said that Gordon continued hunting and trapping until the day he was struck by lightning while recklessly swimming his horse across the Yellowstone during a violent storm.[30]

Doane Robinson wrote in 1918 that one of Gordon's mixed blood grandsons, Joseph Gordon, was then a respected citizen of Burke, South Dakota.[31]

[28] *Ibid.,* 322. [29] Stella Drumm, *op. cit.,* 54.

[30] Triplett, *op. cit.,* 413-14. Two chapters in Triplett's book are devoted to "Bill Gordon" and other information about him is given in the summary of interviews with the aging Thomas Eddie, an early trapper under Ashley.

[31] Footnote by Doane Robinson, *op. cit.,* 133.

Richard Grant

by MERLE WELLS
Idaho State Historical Society

An aristocrat in the wilderness, Richard Grant (January 20, 1794-June 21, 1862) capably represented British interests in the Rocky Mountain fur trade after most of the Mountain Men had retired from trapping. In his native Montreal, he grew up in a family well established in that major fur trade center. His grandfather had been an officer with General James Wolfe at the capture of Quebec in 1759; two uncles preceded him in positions of leadership in the northwest fur trade.[1] His artisocratic background, coupled with positions of authority in the Hudson's Bay Company, made him anything but an ordinary Mountain Man. Yet he eventually chose to settle down in the mountains of the Pacific Northwest where he lived with his part Indian family in the best Mountain Man tradition. His career in the Rockies spanned the final years of the fur trade, the early decades of the Oregon and California trails, and the gold rushes to California as well as to his homeland in

---

[1] Frederick John Shaw's unpublished biography of Richard Grant, prepared for T. C. Elliott, June 27, 1934, in ms 249, Oregon Historical Society, p. 7. One of Richard Grant's uncles, Peter Grant (1764-1848), managed fur trade posts in the Rainy River District and on Red River; he became a North West Company partner and in about 1804 published an important work on the Saulteux Indians. L. R. Masson, *Les Bourgeois de la Compagnie du Nord-Ouest* (Quebec, 1889), II, p. 307. Richard Grants' first cousin (son of his other uncle who was a North West Company partner) figured prominently as the North West Company's métis Captain General (in which position he led the métis forces in the fight at Seven Oaks, June 19, 1816, and later captured Colin Robertson at Grand Portage, Minnesota, June 29, 1820) and, after the union of the North West and Hudson's Bay companies, became the Hudson's Bay Company Warden of the Plains. In that capacity, Cuthbert Grant controlled the métis of the Red River country and held many important offices in the government of Assiniboia. E. E. Rich, ed., *Journal of Occurences in the Athabasca Department by George Simpson, 1820 and 1821, and Report* (Toronto, 1938), 440.

the interior Northwest. In those years, he made a significant contribution in the transition from fur trade to settlement.

Of Scottish and French descent, Richard Grant had genuine promise for success when he entered the fur trade at the close of the War of 1812. Six years of service with the North West Company prepared him for a position as clerk in the Hudson's Bay Company when the firms merged in 1821. At that time, he was on the upper Saskatchewan at Rocky Mountain House. Assigned to continue in the Saskatchewan district, he was stationed at Edmonton House following the merger.[2] After a long trip from York Factory (on Hudson's Bay) to Carlton House (near the forks of the Saskatchewan), and another hike overland — partly on horseback — to Edmonton, he reached his new post, November 2, 1822.[3] There some Blackfoot Indians came to tell him of plans of a band of Mountain Men from St. Louis to build a fur trade post on the upper South Saskatchewan. Grant discounted the prospects of any such imaginative extension of the upper Missouri fur trade north into Hudson's Bay Company territory.[4] In any event, Blackfoot resistance the next season kept the Mountain Men a great distance to the south, far removed from any threat of competition with Edmonton.

At the end of a winter at Edmonton House, Grant left with two boats, May 19, 1823, for York factory where he spent the next four years.[5] In his initial service with the

[2] R. Harvey Fleming, ed., *Minutes of Council, Northern Department of Rupert Land, 1821-31* (Toronto, 1940), 442. In correspondence with the Montana Historical Society, August 18, 1935, F. J. Shaw indicated that Richard Grant entered the service of the North West Company in 1816. His grandmother was a French baroness; his father's ancestors prominent leaders in Banff, Scotland.

[3] Edmonton House Journal, 1822-23, p. 6, Hudson's Bay Company Archives.

[4] *Ibid.*, 13. The journal entry is for November 25, 1822.

[5] *Ibid.*, 25. Although Grant was assigned by the York Factory Council, July 5, 1823, as a clerk at Swan River the next winter, he evidently served at York Factory. On June 26, 1826, he received a three-year appointment as clerk at £100 per year. Fleming, *op. cit.*, 54, 83, 114, 152, 173.

Hudson's Bay Company, he had made a good impression on Colin Robertson, who identified him as

> an interested young man attentive to his duty, extremely anxious to please, and excellent store keeper, and [who] can make himself very useful in Land where we have an extensive establishment; in particular if the servants are Canadians, this is owing to his perfect knowledge of their language habits and manners.[6]

Concluding his assignment at York Factory, he took charge of Oxford House, October 6, 1827. According to custom, he had handed out rum and tobacco to the Indians, and "advised them to be thrifty & industrious in exerting themselves to make good Winter Hunts . . . they then withdrew to go and enjoy themselves."[7] While the Indians were out hunting, Grant and his men at Oxford House spent a lot of the winter fishing for subsistence. He also had to face the usual problems of dealing with Indians during an exceptionally severe winter in which ordinary hunting proved unproductive. To make matters worse, a cough epidemic took a toll that included Grant's infant daughter.[8] When spring finally came, he had to complete the season's trade with the Indians. His report of his dealings for June 1-2, 1828, show something of life there prior to his departure after he closed his journal on June 4:

> 1st SUNDAY – Weather and Wind same as yesterday Lake all broken and Ice drifting down the narrows in great quant[it]ies – Indians Drinking & fighting. In the Afternoon 8 Indians in 3 Canoes arrived these formerly were traders of Split Lake but have since a couple of Years abandoned that quarter and become traders at this Post received from above the weight of a pack in mixed Furs all of them have paid their debt except a couple who have suffered so much from starvation as to disable them from attending their traps and other hunting excurtions – Men employed about the Fort – Caught in 4 of our Nets 40

---

[6] Colin Robertson's District Report, June 20, 1823, B 60/e/5, H.B.C. Archives, quoted by permission of the Governor and Committee of the Hudson's Bay Company.

[7] Oxford House Journal, 1827-1828, B 156/a/10, p. 1, quoted by permission of the Governor and Committee of the Hudson's Bay Company.   [8] *Ibid.,* 11.

white 8 Trout & 88 Suckers two of the nets were not visited owing to
the quantity of Ice over them. –

2nd MONDAY   Weather Cold Wind North – Indians still Drinking
and continually asking for more Liquor They have made good hunts
I am under the necessity of indulging them more than I otherwise
would do they are now nearly ending their third Keg of mixed Liquor
finding the bouse nearly drawing to an End they now begin to trade a
few articles such as quill, Furs, &c &c which is over their debt. – 37
White fish 13 Trouts & 44 Suckers from the Nets. –[9]

From Oxford House, he returned to Edmonton House for
a couple of seasons.[10] As much as he disliked the task, he
kept the post journal. Among his other responsibilities there,
he examined incoming fur and dispensed supplies to freemen and other trappers.[11] Then from 1830-1832, he was
assigned to Fort Assiniboine, farther north.[12] During his
stay at Fort Assiniboine and Edmonton, Grant gained the
support of many of the company's chief factors for a promotion to chief trader, and had great confidence that this ad-
vancement would soon come to him. George Simpson
noticed him as active and bustling and "scampishly inclined;" in 1832, he regarded Grant as competent to manage
a small post, but not prepared as yet to become a chief
trader. Grant wrote well enough, but still was "deficient in
Education."[13] That spring, Grant took command of a

---

[9] *Ibid.*, 28.

[10] Grant came up from York Factory in a party with nine boats which arrived at
Carlton House September 5, 1828, and left for Edmonton two days later. Carlton
House Journal, 1828-1829, p. 28. H.B.C. Archives. At the York Factory Council, July
2, 1828, he had been assigned to Fort Assiniboine, but he kept the Edmonton House
Journal for 1828-1829 after his arrival in September, and the Norway House Council, June 22, 1829, designated him to continue at Edmonton for another year. Fleming, *op. cit.*, 207, 237.

[11] Edmonton House Journal, December 13, 1828, p. 24. B 60/a/26 1828-29, H.B.C.
Archives.

[12] Isaac Cowie, *Minutes of the Council of the Northern Department of Rupert's
Land, 1830 to 1834,* in Historical Society of North Dakota, *Collections,* IV, pp. 653,
668. For at least some of this time, Richard Grant may have been at Edmonton
House; in any event, his son, John Francis Grant, was born at Edmonton, January 7,
1831.

brigade of ten boats bound for York Factory with the season's return from Edmonton and Rocky Mountain House, May 24, 1832. He had four passengers from the Columbia, including William Kittson.[14] His trip back, lengthened by a hazardous crossing of Lake Winnipeg and delays from low water, took until September 20. Although he had been appointed to serve another season at Edmonton, on October 28 he left to take charge of Fort Assiniboine.[15]

Back at Edmonton in 1834, he had to meet an unfortunate situation. Following the death of his wife (Mary Ann Berland, whom he had married in 1821), he had to arrange for the care of three young sons and a daughter. He decided to send them back to live with some relatives in Canada "where they may pick up some learning and be brought up in Christian faith." [16] Then in 1835 he was assigned still farther north to a post on Lesser Slave lake. At this point, his long anticipated promotion materialized: he was commissioned as chief trader, March 2, 1836. He attended the annual council of the northern department at Norway House, June 21, 1836, where he belatedly obtained permission for a year's furlough to attend to his urgent personal and family business in Montreal.[17]

Grant spent his initial four years as chief trader in the York Factory region: his 1838 assignment took him back to

---

[13] George Simpson, "Servants Characters and Histories of Service, 1832," pp. 30-31, H.B.C. Archives, A 34/2, 1832.

[14] Edmonton House Journal, May 24, 1832, H.B.C. Archives, B 10/a/27, 1832-1833. This trip provided Grant with a good opportunity to learn a lot about the Snake country, where he eventually took over Fort Hall. There he later married William Kittson's widow.

[15] Ibid., September 20, 1832, p. 15; Cowie, op. cit., 683, 693, 699. At the Red River Council, July 9, 1832, Grant's appointment as clerk was renewed at the same rate for three more years.

[16] Richard Grant to George Simpson, January 14, 1835, H.B.C. Archives, D 4/127, fo. 48. In addition to making appropriate company records concerning Richard Grant available for consultation, Mrs. J. Craig, Hudson's Bay Company Archivist, has been helpful in identifying errors in need of correction in this account and in supplying this letter which clarifies a confusing point.

[17] Cowie, op. cit., 717, 726-28.

Oxford House where he managed the Island Lake District.[18]
By now he had reached the age of forty-five and had learned
not to push quite so fast, so his men would be in condition to
go trapping when they reached Oxford House at the end of
a twelve day trip, September 28, 1838. Although he did not
have staff there, he preferred his isolated post to York Factory. He disliked keeping a journal and doing paper work:
"the Office to me is a dungeon . . . put me admist Furs
and when the Yardstick is to be used I am then in my
element but do the writing yourself." [19] Regardless of his
preference, as late as 1840 he had to spend his summer tending to the sales shop at York Factory.[20] In the fall of 1840,
he got back to Oxford House, where his staff had grown to
four men: two to fish, one to cook and herd cattle, and one to
haul wood.[21]

After a number of years of managing his own posts, Richard Grant retained his gift for getting into unlikely situations. Concluding a Christmas trip down to York Factory at
the end of 1840, he had a long walk back to Oxford House.
The way he described it, he arrived at his post, January 13,
"not altogether in the best of humour, having had to walk at
least the three-fourth of the distance, our dogs from weakness and severe sore feet being hardly able to crawl . . .
by the Bee that stung Adam . . . I shall never again
be persuaded to take in tow half-naked *Ladies* at such a
cold season of the year as when I came up. . ." The only
way he could get his charges through the wilderness in a

18 *Ibid.*, 753, 769.

19 Richard Grant to James Hargrave, Oxford House, January 3, 1839, in G. P. de
T. Glazebrook, ed., *The Hargrave Correspondence, 1821-1843* (Toronto, 1938), 277-
81. This letter reveals a great deal about Richard Grant and his life in the fur trade.
In his new position as chief trader, Grant felt affluent enough to make a substantial
contribution toward a gift for George Simpson: George Gladman and Richard
Grant to Donald Ross, July 22, 1839, British Columbia Provincial Archives, M819.

20 Minutes of a Council held at Norway House, Northern Department of Rupert's
Land, June 18, 1840, pp. 237, 248, in the Public Archives of Canada, Ottawa.

21 Richard Grant to James Hargrave, Oxford House, February 1, 1841, in Glazebrook, *op. cit.*, 336.

real hurry was to load them into his own dog sled to do the driving himself. He left the rest of the party to come along behind at their own pace – twenty days compared to his eight.[22]

Completing four years as chief trader in the York Factory-Island Lake-Oxford House region to the west of Hudson's Bay, Richard Grant finally embarked on a very different career in the Rocky Mountains and the Pacific Northwest. Transferred to the Columbia in the summer of 1841, he was designated to accompany the Saskatchewan Brigade as far as Edmonton, after which he went on to Vancouver to await whatever assignment Chief Factor John McLoughlin might provide.[23] McLoughlin had an opening in the Snake country: Francis Ermatinger, determined to return to Canada, had McLoughlin's promise that a replacement would be found for him by 1842, and Richard Grant took over the management of the Snake country from Ermatinger.[24]

Two Hudson's Bay Company posts – Fort Hall and Fort Boise – were "maintained in the Snake country with a view of watching any trapping parties that might present themselves from the United States and of encouraging the Snake Nations to direct their attention (which formerly was principally occupied in the Buffalo chase) to fur hunting in both of which objects they have been successful."[25] George Simpson (who had over-all charge of Hudson's Bay Company North American operations) hoped that by 1842, when Grant would take over, an arrangement could be worked out with Jim Bridger for the Hudson's Bay Company to supply

[22] Ibid., 334-35.

[23] Minutes of a Council held at Red River Settlement, Northern Department of Rupert's Land, June 14, 1841, pp. 263, 275-76, in the Public Archives of Canada.

[24] John McLoughlin to George Simpson, Fort Vancouver, March 20, 1841, in E. E. Rich, ed., The Letters of John McLoughlin from Fort Vancouver to the Governor and Committee, Second Series, 1839-1844 (Toronto, 1943), 246-47.

[25] Certain Correspondence of the Foreign Office and of the Hudson's Bay Company Copied from Original Documents, London 1898 (Ottawa, 1899), II, p. 59.

what was left of the northern Rocky Mountain fur trade from Fort Hall.[26] In any event, competition with the Mountain Men posed a problem in the Snake country.

Shortly before Grant arrived at his new post, the Hudson's Bay Company had to revise its Pacific Northwest fur trade policy. Unlike Rupert's Land (the area draining into Hudson's Bay) the company had no fur trade monopoly over the Columbia. Neither Great Britain nor the United States owned the Oregon country. But ever since 1818, citizens of either country could occupy the area: Britain and the United States had agreed not to exclude any one of either country from old Oregon. Eventual settlement – presumably by farmers – was expected to lead to division of territory between the two powers. Fur traders generally didn't want farm communities around their trapping lands, yet in the case of the Pacific Northwest, the Hudson's Bay Company concluded by 1840 that British settlement was needed on the north side of the lower Columbia.[27] Otherwise the whole area was likely to wind up part of the United States. Willamette Valley and the rest of Oregon south of the Columbia appeared to be destined to go to the United States anyway, so the company refrained from encouraging British settlement there. At the same time, organized immigration from the United States to Oregon – directed toward Willamette Valley – was getting under way. In 1841, half of a sixty-four member California immigrant party was diverted at Soda Springs to Oregon. That same season, a substantially larger Hudson's Bay Company immigrant party came overland from Red River up the Saskatchewan and across the Canadian Rockies to the lower Columbia. They were supposed to settle north of the Columbia and join in the Puget's Sound Agricultural Company enterprise, but they tried

---

26 *Ibid.*

27 E. E. Rich, *The History of the Hudson's Bay Company, 1670-1870* (London, 1959), II, pp. 690-94; John S. Galbraith, *The Hudson's Bay Company as an Imperial Factor, 1821-1869* (Berkeley, 1957), 202-06.

Willamette Valley instead.[28] British preponderance in the actual settlement of Oregon was retained for another two years, but the Hudson's Bay Company concluded that sending more immigrants from Red River to Puget Sound would be useless. Having written off Willamette Valley long ago, the company felt it pointless to build up farm settlements there. Hudson's Bay Company efforts to encourage immigrants to move directly from Britain to Puget Sound also failed: colonization from Britain had lapsed into a considerable decline, and New Zealand attracted most of British attention right after 1840.[29]

Arriving in Fort Vancouver in November, shortly after the Red River settlers had come in, Grant set out to examine the Snake country at the end of only a week's rest. Getting to Fort Hall took most of a month. But after a short stay (December 19-30, 1841) he headed right back to Fort Vancouver to pack his outfit for the next season's trade. By the time he got back, he felt like a worn-out fur trader and shopkeeper.[30] But in the middle of April he set out again for Fort Hall. Reaching there June 16, 1842, he entered into what turned out to be a ten-year assignment as manager of the Hudson's Bay Company Snake country fur trade.[31] He had a force of sixty Canadians and métis "who served the company as traders, herdsmen and domestic servants."[32] A corral with high walls protected his horses and cattle each night. Since Fort Hall was in the center of one of the main Indian

[28] D. G. Lent, *West of the Mountains: James Sinclair and the Hudson's Bay Company* (Seattle, 1963), 100-108, 154-58; Rich, II, pp. 696-98; Galbraith, *op. cit.*, 208-16; George R. Stewart, *The California Trail* (New York, 1962), 18-19; David Lavender, *Westward Vision: the Story of the Oregon Trail* (New York, 1963), 350-52. [29] Rich, *Hudson's Bay Co.*, II, p. 696.

[30] Richard Grant to James Hargrave, Fort Vancouver, April 6, 1842, Glazebrook, *op. cit.*, 390.

[31] Dugald McTavish to James Hargrave, Fort Vancouver, April 2, 1842, *ibid.*; LeRoy R. Hafen, ed., *To the Rockies and Oregon, 1839-1842* (Glendale, 1955), 266-67.

[32] Lansford W. Hastings, *The Emigrants' Guide to Oregon and California* (Cincinnati, 1845), 49.

wintering grounds in the Snake country, Grant's community actually was a lot bigger than if there had been only a company post there.

Aside from the fur trade, he had the beginning of a major business supplying emigrant traffic. In August 1842, Elijah White stopped for a week with an emigrant party headed from the United States for Willamette Valley. White's guide, Thomas Fitzpatrick, had warned the emigrants that they could not take their wagons much beyond Fort Hall, and Grant concurred. As an accommodation to the settlers, Grant bought some of their wagons, trading for supplies. Mountain prices – reflecting the high cost of provisions at Fort Hall – proved to be pretty steep for the emigrants, but flour at Fort Hall still cost only half as much as at Fort Laramie.[33] White and his party appreciated the welcome they received from Richard Grant at Fort Hall. Both White and Lansford W. Hastings gave Grant some highly favorable publicity. In his emigrant guide, Hastings reported that "upon arriving at this fort, we were received in the kindest manner, by Mr. Grant, who was in charge; and we received every aid and attention from the gentlemen of that fort, during our stay in their vicinity."[34]

Even though emigrant trade held more future promise than fur hunting, Grant did pretty well in his first season at Fort Hall. A good fur return reached Fort Vancouver October 31, 1842.[35] And altogether in 1842, Grant sent out fur worth £3916 18s 6d, good for a profit of £2405 12s 8d and helpful in recovering losses elsewhere in the Columbia region.[36] Grant's Snake country (Fort Hall, Fort Boise, and

---

[33] Elijah White, *Ten Years in Oregon* (Ithaca, 1850), 164; F. N. Howay, W. N. Sage, and H. F. Angus, *British Columbia and the United States* (Toronto, 1942), 103-04; Louis Seymour Grant, "Fort Hall on the Oregon Trail" (M.A. thesis, Univ. of British Columbia, 1938), 62. This study, by a descendant of Richard Grant, makes good use of the Hudson's Bay Company archives.

[34] Hastings, *op. cit.*, 20.

[35] John McLoughlin to the Governor and Committee, Fort Vancouver, October 31, 1842, Rich, *Letters of McLoughlin*, 92.

a trapping party) altogether were responsible for about 2500 beaver.[37] This proved to be a considerable gain, showing that the Snake country fur trade had not come to an end, as James Douglas had feared four years before.

Emigrant traffic on the Oregon and California trails in 1843 reached Fort Hall in hundreds of wagons. Here a major crisis arose. Grant again assured the emigrants that they could not get their wagons over the fur trade trail to Fort Vancouver. He felt, though, that they might find a way to push through if they searched for an alternate route where the regular trail was impassable. Even though his advice was not quite as pessimistic as the forecast that the emigrants had received at Fort Laramie, his recommendations did not encourage anyone bound for Oregon. Grant had heard a lot about the wonders of California as soon as he had reached Fort Vancouver; because of the bad trail to Willamette Valley, he suggested that the California Trail had great superiority as a wagon road, and that California had great superiority as a destination.[38]

---

[36] John McLoughlin to George Simpson, March 20, 1844, *Oregon Historical Quarterly* (Sept. 1916), XVII, p. 223.   [37] Grant, *op. cit.*, 92.

[38] Peter H. Burnett, "Recollections and Opinions of an Old Pioneer," *Oregon Hist. Quar.* (March 1904), V, pp. 76-77; C. M. Drury, *Marcus Whitman, M.D.* (Caldwell, 1937), 337-38. Rufus B. Sage, who had spent most of two weeks with Grant ("a gentleman distinguished for his kindness and urbanity") November 9-20, 1842, reported that the road from "Fort Hall to Vancouver is generally considered impassible for other than pack-animals. It is said, however, that a new route has recently been discovered, by which waggons may be taken, without much difficulty, the entire distance. Should this report prove true, the emigrant may convey everything needed for his comfort during the long journey before him." Rufus B. Sage, *Scenes in the Rocky Mountains,* reprinted in LeRoy R. Hafen and Ann W. Hafen, *Far West and the Rockies,* V (Glendale, 1956), pp. 141, 174. Morton M. McCarver, who had the foresight to "leave his wagon to a teamster to drive from Fort Hall" on, and who came through on horseback, informed the *Iowa Gazette,* September 11, 1844, that the 1843 emigrants "had fewer obstacles . . . than we had a right to expect, as it was generally understood previously that the distance from Fort Hall . . . was impassable with wagons. Great credit is due to Dr. Whitman, who accompanied us out." Jennie Broughton Brown, *Fort Hall on the Oregon Trail* (Caldwell, 1934), 301. Grant's endorsement of California over Oregon grew naturally enough out of alluring reports from Hudson's Bay Company expeditions to California. Glazebrook, *Hargrave Correspondence,* 390.

Many of the immigrants followed his advice, either choosing to go to California, or leaving their wagons and packing on to Oregon, as White and Hastings had done in 1842. Most of the wagons went on to Willamette Valley. Marcus Whitman, who accompanied the emigrants on his way back to his Walla Walla Mission, assured the party that Grant was correct in admitting that a wagon road could be found. Some of the others who took their wagons the rest of the way wound up wishing they hadn't, and those who did found the mountain road just as bad as Grant said it would be.[39] But most of them had no real choice if they wanted to go to Willamette Valley instead of to California. From that year on, large numbers of emigrant wagons continued to roll west of Fort Hall on the Oregon and California trails. Grant developed a lucrative commerce, dealing in provisions as well as in livestock.[40] By trading for worn out oxen and

---

[39] John Minto, "Reminiscences of Life and Experiences on the Oregon Trail in 1844," *Oregon Hist. Quar.* (Sept. 1901), II, pp. 217-18; Grant, *op. cit.*, 64-65. When John Minto was ready to push on from Fort Hall, September 16, 1844, Grant was able to tell him that, in spite of the obstacles to traffic, wagons had got through in 1843. They had, of course, in some places to find an alternate route for the pack trail Grant used. A large immigration to Oregon came by in 1845, and William Henry Rector, who found Richard Grant to be "a very clever and obliging gentleman," appreciated the valuable information Grant provided him on the route of the Oregon Trail. Both Richard Grant at Fort Hall and James Craigie at Fort Boise advised emigrants on the Oregon Trail in 1845 not to risk following Stephen H. L. Meek through central Oregon west of Fort Boise over Meek's cutoff, but many of them did, with disastrous results that Grant and Craigie had anticipated.

[40] With heavy traffic on the Oregon and California trails in 1843, Grant did more business in trading with the emigrants than he really needed in spite of high mountain prices. Even John C. Fremont had to send Kit Carson ahead, August 19, to Fort Hall for supplies after running short because hunters for the thousand or so emigrants on the trail had wiped out all the game that was handy. Finally Grant stopped trading altogether, but some of the desperate California bound settlers, backed by Fremont's military expedition, forced him to sell them supplies anyway. Writing George Simpson, March 15, 1844, Grant reported profitable dealings in staples such as coffee, sugar, flour, and rice. Galbraith, *op. cit.*, 108; James W. Nesmith, "Diary of the Emigration of 1843," *Oregon Hist. Quar.* (Dec. 1906), VII, pp. 349-50; Charles H. Carey, ed., *The Journals of Theodore Talbot* (Portland, 1931), 48-49; John C. Fremont, *Report of the Exploring Expedition to the Rocky Mountains in the Year 1842, and to Oregon and North California in the Years 1843-44* (Washington, 1845), 131, 162-63; Overton Johnson and William H. Winter, "Route across the Rocky Mountains with a Description of Oregon and California . . . 1843," *Oregon*

cattle one season, and selling them in first-class condition to new immigrants the next, he managed to build up a flourishing business without having to make too substantial an investment in stock. By the time Joel Palmer came by, August 8, 1845, Grant (whom Palmer described as having "the bearing of a gentleman") had his system worked out:

> The garrison was supplied with flour, which had been procured from the settlements in Oregon, and brought here on pack horses. They sold it to the emigrants for twenty dollars per cwt., taking cattle in exchange; and as many of the emigrants were nearly out of flour, and had a few lame cattle, a brisk trade was carried on between them and the inhabitants of the fort. In the exchange of cattle for flour, an allowance was made of from five to twelve dollars per head. They also had horses which they readily exchanged for cattle or sold for cash. The price demanded for horses was from fifteen to twenty-five dollars. They could not be prevailed upon to receive anything in exchange for their goods or provisions, excepting cattle or money.[41]

Altogether in 1845, 456 wagons (in addition to several parties of packers) came by Fort Hall. About fifteen were California bound, although a California agent at Fort Hall – Caleb Greenwood – managed to divert a total of fifty that way. Grant managed to make a few hundred dollars in his trade that year with the emigrants. His main business,

Hist. Quar. (Sept. 1906), VII, p. 316. Some of Fremont's men expressed nationalistic displeasure with Grant and the British at Fort Hall, and Fremont recommended a United States post there to assist emigrants on the westbound trail.

[41] Joel Palmer, *Journal of Travels over the Rocky Mountains* (Cleveland, 1906), 86. J. M. Shively's guide, *Route and Distances to Oregon and California* (Washington, 1846), on the basis of a visit to Fort Hall, June 17, 1845, also gave Grant a good notice: "Here you will have an opportunity of buying provisions, swapping cattle for horses, and will receive many acts of kindness from Captain Grant, the superintendent of the Fort." Dale Morgan, ed., *Overland in 1846: Diaries and Letters of the California-Oregon Trail* (Georgetown, California, 1963), 749. These endorsements may have led some later emigrants to expect too much: for example, E. D. Smith complained, August 28, 1848, that Grant "is not that charitable gentleman that we expected to see, but a boasting, burlesquing, unfeeling man." *Transactions of the Oregon Pioneer Association, 1907,* 163. Unpleasant reactions such as this were not common among the emigrants, and generally reflected a nationalistic reaction against a British post, rather than any discourtesy of Richard Grant. Anyone who came to Fort Hall could expect to see that Grant was a genuine British aristocrat, and many of the travelers on the emigrant trails (including some of Fremont's men) found aristocratic habits offensive.

though, still was the fur trade, which totaled 1600 beaver that year. These were valued at $15,000.[42] That raised the total Hudson's Bay Company Snake country fur take to $150,000 in the period from 1824 on, when Mountain Men from the United States began to compete with the British in the region.[43]

Not long before the 1846 emigrants reached Fort Hall, the indefinite status of the country changed. Oregon was divided in such a way that the Snake country became part of the United States, which agreed to pay for all Hudson's Bay Company posts in the part of Oregon which Britain did not acquire. Fort Hall had to be maintained until this financial settlement was concluded, so Grant and his staff continued to help travelers on the emigrant trails. In 1846, John R. McBride (later a congressman from Oregon and Chief Justice of Idaho) found the British at Fort Hall very accommodating indeed:

> Captain Grant was now in charge [of Fort Hall], and his man of affairs was one [Angus] McDonald. Both were Scotchmen and gentlemen. They treated our party with great courtesy, and we visited the post without any restrictions. They furnished us with a written guide for the journey westward, with all the camping places specified; and the distance from each to the next, with information as to wood, water, and grass, good and bad roads, which was of exceeding value. Captain Grant had an Indian wife,[44] and two of his children appeared in his

---

[42] Richard Grant to George Simpson, January 2, 1846, in Grant, *op. cit.*, 55-56. A fur trade decline at Fort Hall came in 1844 with failure of a trapping expedition Richard Grant had sent out to Salt Lake that year, only to be scared off by hostile Indians. Richard Grant to George Simpson, March 20, 1845, in *ibid.*, 52; James Douglas to George Simpson, Fort Vancouver, March 5, 1845, in Rich, *Letters of McLoughlin*, III, p. 183.

[43] John McLoughlin to George Simpson, March 20, 1846, in E. E. Rich, ed., *Part of a Dispatch from George Simpson . . . 1829* (Toronto, 1947), xliv.

[44] On March 29, 1845, Grant married Eleanor MacDonald Kittson (known by then as Helene Kittson) at Fort Vancouver. The widow of William Kittson, Grant's second wife was the daughter of Finnan MacDonald. Except for an education in an Ontario convent, she spent her entire career, June 19, 1811-August 7, 1863, in the Pacific Northwest. She presumably married William Kittson while he was east in 1832. Biographical material is available in T. C. Elliott collection, Oreg. Hist. Soc.

office. The older was a daughter of fifteen. She wore the Indian frock of dressed deer skin, but it was scrupulously clean and neat, and she was strikingly beautiful, with her long dark hair falling around her bare neck and shoulders. She had sewing materials at the time in her hands, and seemed to be engaged in embroidering some garment made of deer skin. The boy was evidently the pride of the Captain. He was about ten years old, spoke good English, and took me all over the quarters and was full of fire and energy as live boys are.[45]

When Jesse Applegate arrived at Fort Hall, August 8, 1846, to induce Oregon traffic to take the California Trail to the Humboldt in order to reach his Applegate Trail leading into southern Willamette Valley, Richard Grant endorsed his new route.[46] For another two seasons, traffic on the regular Oregon Trail, the California Trail, and the Applegate Trail continued to come by Fort Hall. In 1847, Grant counted 901 wagons (and several pack trains as well) that reached his post between July 11 and September 2. Moses Harris diverted eighty of these at Raft River to the Applegate Trail.[47] The Mormon settlement at Salt Lake also gave him an expanded market. While the Mormon Trail ran no where near Fort Hall, Grant visited Salt Lake not long after the Mormons arrived there. Later that season, he furnished them with supplies.[48] Then in 1848, about

---

[45] This quotation, from the manuscript files of the Oregon Historical Society, was provided by Priscilla Knuth, managing editor of the *Oregon Historical Quarterly*.

[46] *Oregon Spectator* (Oregon City), June 25, 1846, p. 2, c. 3-4; Hastings, *op. cit.*, 137-38; Morgan, *op. cit.*, 634-36. Unable to stay at Fort Hall until all the season's emigrants had come by, Jesse Applegate left a letter with Grant, August 10, 1846, advising those who came later to head for the Applegate route along the Humboldt and into Southern Oregon. He also wrote his brother, Lisbon Applegate, that "the emigrants [at Fort Hall] have almost annoyed me out of my senses – and Capt. Grant who is proof against all kinds of annoyances, has out of charity undertook to put those behind upon the right track." The Applegate brothers also arranged to have Richard Grant's children (who now had completed their education in the east) come out from Three Rivers, Quebec, with the next year's emigration.

[47] Richard Grant to George Simpson, September 2, 1847, in Grant, *op. cit.*, 91.

[48] *Ibid.* Although Hudson's Bay Company trade at Fort Hall with the Mormons proved profitable, the "Company declined the Mormons' proposals for permanent trade and the latter eventually set up their own stores in rivalry . . ." Rich, *Hudson's Bay Co.*, II, p. 738.

three thousand emigrant wagons lined the road past Fort
Hall, and the Mormon trade continued.[49] That turned out
to be only a modest prelude to the deluge in 1849. By the
beginning of the California gold rush, vast herds of cattle,
horses, and mules had built up at Fort Hall. That was exactly what Grant needed to help accommodate the multitude
who came by. Grant figured that around 20,000 people, and
between 5000 and 10,000 wagons, tried the Fort Hall route
in 1849.[50] With the gold rush, Grant's emigrant trade
reached a climax.

An abrupt decline in the Fort Hall emigrant trade set in
just at the height of the gold rush. For years, a search had
been under way for a more direct route to California: Fort
Hall seemed pretty far north to travelers trying to go south
west. Part of the California traffic went through Salt Lake
over an alternate route opened by Mormons headed from
California to Salt Lake in 1848. Salt Lake, however, offered
no solution for those in search of a direct route, because those
who went that way still had to come back north into present-
day Idaho to pick up the regular California Trail. Finally
a large train of gold-seekers led by B. M. Hudspeth and
J. J. Myers (who had explored the country in 1848) struck
out to make a new track directly west of Soda Springs, July
19, 1849. Finding their way across the ridges south of Fort
Hall, they saved around twenty-five miles by establishing a
difficult route.[51] For the energetic, though, the cutoff was

---

[49] P. S. Ogden and James Douglas to the Governor and Committee, October 1,
1848, in Grant, *op. cit.*, 91.

[50] Eden Colvile to J. H. Pelly, Victoria, October 26, 1849, in E. E. Rich, ed., *London Correspondence Inward from Eden Colville, 1849-1852* (London, 1956), 6-7;
Richard Grant to George Simpson, February 22, 1850 in Grant, *op. cit.*, 92; Dale
Morgan, ed., *The Overland Diary of James Pritchard from Kentucky to California
in 1849* (Denver, 1959), 105.

[51] T. L. Campbell, "Benoni Morgan Hudspeth," in *Idaho Yesterdays* (Fall 1968),
9-13. Hudspeth's cutoff seemed like a better idea than it actually proved to be, and
the possibility for it had been anticipated in the spring of 1846, when E. A. Farwell
suggested to the New Orleans *Picayune* that John C. Fremont should go out and
discover such a route. Morgan, *op. cit.*, 19-20.

slightly faster. Speed on the road meant a lot to gold seekers on the California Trail, and Hudspeth's cutoff diverted most of the gold rush which followed. Richard Grant's trade at Fort Hall fell off rapidly. He sent one of his sons off to look for the new cutoff, but the search did not extend far enough. Unable to ascertain exactly where Hudspeth's cutoff ran, Grant concluded that the new "trail must be a very rugged one, and cannot abreviate the distance much." [52] This estimate proved correct. But when subsequent Oregon as well as California traffic preferred the Hudspeth route, Fort Hall did not recover its trading potential. Grant's trade with the Mormons also fell off rapidly. Not only did the new settlements around Salt Lake become self sufficient; by 1849 some of the Mormons came up to Fort Hall with dairy cattle and supplies for the emigrant trade. [53] Aside from this competition, Grant was greatly disturbed by having to pay around a thousand dollars in customs duty, an unexpected result of having Fort Hall located after 1846 in the United States. As a result, J. Goldsborough Bruff, a California forty-niner, found that the "old captain is very English, and anti-Yankee. . ." In spite of his disaffection for the United States, Grant continued to extend the hospitality of his fort to those who came by. Bruff reached the fort on August 24,

> entered the Great Portal, walked across the open square, and up a pair of stairs, to a balcony, and at a door of an upper apartment met Capt Grant, the former Hudson Bay commander. Grant is a Scotchman, from Canada, a fine looking portly old man, and quite courteous, for an old mountaineer. His wife is an Iriquois woman, [54] good looking,

---

[52] G. W. Read and Ruth Gaines, eds., *Gold Rush: the Journals, Drawings, and Other Papers of J. Goldsborough Bruff* (New York, 1949), 105.

[53] Morgan, *Pritchard*, 105, 160-61; Richard Grant to George Simpson, February 22, 1850, in Grant, *op. cit.,* 92. With the end of the Mormon trade with Grant at Fort Hall, and with competition between Grant and the Mormons for emigrant trade there, the Mormons concluded that Grant and the other fur traders in the region wanted "to stir up the natives" against them. Isaac Morley to Brigham Young, April 21, 1850, in Gustive O. Larson, "Walkara, Ute Chief," in this *Series,* II, p. 350.

very neat, and polite. She is, of course dark skin. – Her handywork, – of bead embroidered articles are very ingenious and beautiful: – pouches, sashes, mocasins, &c. &c. adorn the apartment, or office of her husband. I enquired if he had any of them to dispose of, but he said no, all spare things of that kind, had been sold, and those I saw were his own reservation. Mrs. G. made a pitcher of fine lemonade, and I found it very refreshing. He said that his whisky was out, and apologized for the deficiency.[55]

Another forty-niner described Grant as

a most remarkable looking man. He is 6 ft., 2 or 3 inches, high & made in proportion, with a handsome figure. His face is perfectly English, fat round, chubby, & red. His hair is now getting in the sere & yellow leaf & his whiskers are also turning grey.[56]

---

[54] Richard Grant's second wife was not Iroquois at all, but was the daughter of Finnan MacDonald and Peggy Ponderay MacDonald, the latter a daughter of a prominent Pend d'Oreille Indian leader whose band traveled in the Pend d'Oreille Lake area when David Thompson and Finnan MacDonald built a North West Company fur trade post there in 1809.

[55] Read and Gaines, *Gold Rush*, 102-06.

[56] David M. Potter, ed., *Trail to California: the Overland Journal of Vincent Geiger and Wakeman Bryarly* (New Haven, 1945), 152. The next year, Henry J. Coke, an Englishman, rode by Fort Hall and described Richard Grant's hospitality: "When I reached the Fort . . . Mr. Grant, the commander, was basking on the shafts of a wagon in front of his portals. His grey head and beard, portly frame and jovial dignity were a ready-made representation of Falstaff, and would have done justice to that character on the boards of any theatre . . . A more satisfactory specimen of the "old country" could not be wished for. He shook my hand as if he had known me half a century, and conducted me to the sanctum of his castle. Here we met a family party, consisting of Mrs. Grant, apparently a most serviceable woman, two grown sons and two or three very pretty little daughters. At supper I imagined that my prairie appetite would alarm the domestic circle, for I ate new-laid eggs and drank new milk until I almost astonished even myself; but when the second course appeared, and I was expected to keep pace with my worthy host in demolishing hot rolls and duck-pies, I felt quite ashamed of my own incapacity, and could only applaud with veneration an example I could not imitate. When the repast was over, and we had chatted and smoked to a latish hour, I took my leave, sighing at the remembrance of my hospitable reception, and walked back to my camp." *A Ride over the Rocky Mountains to Oregon and California* (London, 1852), 218, as quoted in T. C. Elliott, "Richard ("Captain Johnny") Grant," in *Oregon Hist. Quar.* (March 1935), XXXVI, p. 4. The name "Captain Johnny" Grant, as Elliott points out in his article, is an absurd mistake, confusing Richard Grant with his well-known son, John Grant. Elliott indicates that this error derives from O. W. Nixon's lamentable work, *How Marcus Whitman Saved Oregon* (Chicago, 1895), noting that he had found no earlier example of that mixup.

At the same time his post was losing its favored position in the emigrant trade, Grant found the Snake country fur trade to be hopelessly depressed. At the end of the gold rush, Grant offered the Indians one blanket for four beaver. Declining world prices had made his price far too high, so that the Snake country fur trade had become "more than unprofitable." [57] With beaver prices reduced, the Indians responded by hunting large animals for subsistance and for trade with emigrants.

Grant reported, February 22, 1850, that his fur trade practically ceased to exist: "the Indians have become careless, and still more indolent than they ever were in hunting furs . . . some old ones no doubt might yet be enticed to hunt Beaver. . ." [58] But with prices so low, prospects of revival of beaver trapping in the Snake country seemed hopelessly unflattering. An unexpected price revival at Fort Vancouver, from a dollar a pound in 1848 to $1.50 in 1850 and $2.50 in 1851, gave a temporary false hope for recovery.[59] Grant, however, decided to retire from the fur trade. Poor health and rheumatism made it hard for him to discharge his responsibilities at Fort Hall. Sir George Simpson suggested in 1850 that, after some time off to recover, he transfer to a less demanding post far to the north – Fort Dunvegan in the Peace River district.[60] Grant, though, preferred to settle near Fort Hall. Exercising an option for early retirement in 1851, he took over an abandoned United States military post – Cantonment Loring – only four miles away. There he continued in the emigrant cattle and provision trade, managing to move about the country in order to serve a long stretch of the Oregon Trail. In the summer of 1853, for example, he got down to Salt Lake to pick up supplies to sell to emigrants on Malad River more than a

---

[57] George Simpson to Richard Grant, June 30, 1849, in Grant, *op. cit.*, 57.

[58] Richard Grant to George Simpson, February 22, 1850, in *ibid.*, 92.

[59] William S. Lewis and Paul C. Phillips, eds., *The Journal of John Work* (Cleveland, 1923), 48.   [60] Grant, *op. cit.*, 74.

hundred miles west of Fort Hall.[61] Then, as usual, he spent the winter in his home at Camp Loring. When John Mullan visited Grant, December 13, 1853, he found a welcome bit of civilization isolated in a vast wilderness:

> Arriving at Cantonment Loring, we were most kindly received by Captain Grant, formerly of the Hudson's Bay Company at Fort Hall, who, inviting us into his house, spread before us all the comforts and many of the luxuries of life, and gave us a comfortable bed under his hospitable roof – all of which none more than ourselves could appreciate; and we thus passed the night once more near the abodes of civilization. Here Captain Grant is comfortably situated, surrounded by a happy family, and, with all the comforts and many of the luxuries of life, lives as happily and contentedly as he so well deserves.[62]

With his son-in-law, William Sinclair, in charge of Fort Hall from 1854-1856, Grant and his family were well situated in their new home.

In the summer of 1856, when Indian trouble farther west forced the Hudson's Bay Company to close Fort Hall, Grant had to move his winter base north across the continental divide to the Beaverhead. There he maintained a cabin and ranch from which he set out each summer to trade stock in good condition for worn out cattle on the emigrant roads in the Snake country. A number of other ranchers joined in this kind of enterprise which Grant pioneered.[63] He also kept a notable supply of Indian trade goods. As a help to

[61] "Diary of Celinda E. Hines," *Transactions of the Oregon Pioneer Association, June 20, 1918* (Portland, 1921), 111.

[62] *Reports of Explorations and Surveys, to Ascertain the Most Practicable and Economical Route for a Railroad from the Mississippi to the Pacific Ocean, 1853-4,* 33 Cong., 2 sess., H. Exec. Doc. 91, I, p. 335.

[63] Granville Stuart, *Forty Years on the Frontier* (Cleveland, 1925), I, p. 126, II, p. 97. Stuart reports that Richard Grant had "a good three room log house for his family to live in, but the others occupied Indian lodges made of dressed elk skins." As the leading resident of that part of the country, Grant was given the best color (a ten cent value) of gold found by some Deer Lodge prospectors in 1856, and he used to show it to everyone who came by. Grant lived to see the gold rush to nearby north Idaho after discoveries there in 1860, but expansion of the gold mining region into Montana came a few weeks after he died. Montana Historical Society, *Contributions* (Helena, 1896), II, p. 121.

the Indian trade, his son, John Francis Grant, had both Bannock and Shoshoni wives. Richard Grant had encouraged the arrangement because important bands of Snake Indians came in regularly to visit these relatives. Richard Grant's Flathead relatives also came down that way. His quarters thus continued to be the social center for Indians as well as whites.[64] For Christmas in 1857, he invited Granville Stuart and a number of other cattlemen to an elegant celebration: "The menu consisted of buffalo meat, boiled smoked tongue, bread, dried fruit, a preserve made of chokecherries, and coffee. This was an elaborate dinner for those days. Supplies were hard to get, and most of us were living on meat straight."[65]

Right after Christmas, however, Louis R. Maillet turned up on his way back from Fort Bridger with truly alarming reports of Mormon opposition to A. S. Johnston's army during the Utah war. His story of the conflict, and of Mormon intentions to expand to the Beaverhead, sounded frightening enough that Grant decided to leave for a more remote Bitterroot Valley location. In spite of poor health, Grant got Maillet to help him load all his possessions into three wagons for a hard trip early in January 1858 to Hell Gate, near later Missoula.[66] There his health improved.

---

[64] Grant had chosen a good part of the country for Indian trade because bands of Shoshoni and Bannock Indians from the south and Flatheads from the northwest often came that way. His second wife, half Pend d'Oreille, had close connections with a band closely related to the Flatheads, and his son had wives prominent in Shoshoni-Bannock circles. John Grant was a brother-in-law of Tendoy, noted until 1907 as a leader of the Lemhi band; his wife, in fact, also was a relative of Sacajawea. Difficulties between the Flathead and Shoshoni-Bannock bands of his relatives (Victor of the Flatheads objected to losses by horse stealing to bands of Shoshoni and Bannock visiting John Grant in the spring of 1862) complicated this already complex family situation at a time when Richard Grant was away and his son John had to adjust matters. F. W. Lander, writing A. B. Greenwood, August 16, 1859, strongly recommended Richard Grant as a man who "understands these western Indians perfectly." 36 Cong., 1 sess., Sen. Exec. Doc. 42, p. 138.

[65] Stuart, *op. cit.*, I, p. 179.

[66] "Historical Sketch of Louis R. Maillet," in Montana Hist. Soc., *Contributions* (Helena, 1903), IV, pp. 210-11; Stuart, *op. cit.*, I, p. 130; George F. Weisel, *Men and*

He continued his cattle ranching for four more years, until an extremely severe winter – the worst in more than a century – reduced his herd from two hundred to forty early in 1862.[67] After that disaster, he went out to The Dalles on a spring supply trip that proved to be too much of a strain. On his way back to his Bitterroot ranch, he got as far as Walla Walla, where serious illness made it impossible for him to continue to travel. So his party camped there until his death, June 21.[68] In the interior cattle ranching community of the upper Missouri and Clark's Fork news of this misfortune "cast a gloom over the entire settlement. Captain Grant was a jovial kind-hearted gentleman and very popular with the mountaineers."[69] His portrait appears in this volume at page 20.

Trade on the Northwest Frontier as shown by the Fort Owen Ledger (Missoula, 1955), 80, 147-48. On the trip, Maillet reported, "Captain Grant rode in the little spring wagon, where he had a bed of robes and blankets, Maillet driving and going ahead to look out the road. The spring wagon and the horses driven by Mrs. Grant and the girls could travel much faster than the ox teams. They therefore would go into camp, and Maillet would then mount a horse, meet the rest of the train and escort it to camp. These wagons are the first that ever crossed the Deer Lodge divide and passed down Hell Gate canyon. They had to cross Hell Gate river twenty-three times, and the crossings had to be chopped, as they were very slippery with melting snow. Many times the wagons were unloaded in the middle of the stream, and altogether it was the hardest trip Maillet ever made. The drivers were poor and unclad. Cold, wet, disheartened, the language sometimes used would have discouraged a salvation army."

[67] *Weekly Mountaineer* (The Dalles), June 4, 1862, in the *Oregonian* (Portland), June 5, 1862, p. 2, c. 3; Stuart, *op. cit.*, I, pp. 185, 200.

[68] *Washington Statesman* (Walla Walla), June 28, 1862, p. 2, c. 5; Stuart, *op. cit.*, I, p. 211. Upon hearing of their father's illness, both of Richard Grant's sons left for Walla Walla, and brought the survivors of the trip back. John F. Grant retained his Deer Lodge ranch for several years; in December 1866, he sold out to Conrad Kohrs for $19,500, and left the country sometime after his wife Cora died at Deer Lodge, February 24, 1867. He moved to St. Boniface, Manitoba, and finally to his native Edmonton, where he survived until May 1, 1907. *Montana Post* (Virginia City), December 29, 1866, p. 2, c. 1, March 16, 1867, p. 2, c. 2; biographical information in T. C. Elliott collection, of the Oreg. Hist. Soc.

[69] Stuart, *op. cit.*, I, p. 211.

Caleb Greenwood

by HARVEY L. CARTER
Colorado College

In 1846, Caleb Greenwood told Edwin Bryant, who encountered him in California, that he was eighty-three years old. If this statement concerning his age is correct, he was born in 1763. He was undoubtedly an old man in 1846 and, though he may have exaggerated by a few years, we may accept his statement as at least an approximation. As to the place of his birth, one of his sons gave it as eastern Tennessee and another gave it as Virginia. So we have only an approximate area as well as an approximate time for his birth. The widow of one of his sons told the story that he had killed a sheriff in Virginia, when he was eighteen, and had fled to the West as a consequence of his act.[1] Something like this may have occurred but the details of this traditional account contain obvious inaccuracies.

In a statement made by Caleb Greenwood to the missionary Moses Merrill, at Fort Bellevue in 1834, he claimed to have spent twenty-six years among the Mandan and Crow Indians. Again, the statement is not wholly consistent with known facts, except in the most general way, but it may be that the year 1808 marks the beginning of his life as a trapper or, at least, his arrival in St. Louis.[2]

The first indisputable record of Greenwood as a trapper occurs in the account books of Wilson Price Hunt's overland Astorian party during the time when the party was camped

---

[1] Charles Kelly and Dale L. Morgan, *Old Greenwood: The Story of Caleb Greenwood, Trapper, Pathfinder, and Early Pioneer* (Georgetown, Calif., 1965), 13-14. This biography contains all that is known of Greenwood but it also contains so much extraneous material that it is somewhat difficult to sort out the known facts. I have cited additional published sources wherever possible.   [2] *Ibid.,* 14, 88-89.

at the mouth of the Nodaway River in the winter of 1810-
1811. Eight entries, from December 3, 1810, to January 27,
1811, indicate Greenwood's presence among them at this
time, but for some unknown reason he did not continue with
them when they broke camp and embarked on their historic
journey to the Pacific.[3]

Greenwood next turns up, in company with Daniel Larrison, as a member of Manuel Lisa's expedition up the Missouri River in 1812. His name appears in Lisa's account
books several times during the summer of 1812. After the
founding of Fort Manuel, Greenwood was outfitted to go
trapping along with Reuben Lewis, Edward Rose, Antoine
and Abraham Ledoux and eight others. They returned to
Fort Manuel at the end of March 1813, after an absence of
more than six months. As a free trapper, Greenwood was
indebted to Lisa's company on April 13, 1813, for $211.45.[4]

We next hear of him in an entirely different location. He
was encountered, with a single companion, by the Chouteau-
DeMun expedition on the Arkansas River near the mouth
of the Huerfano, on November 27, 1815. Greenwood and
three companions had left St. Louis on September 7 to trap
on the Arkansas but had been forced into virtual hiding by
their fear of a Pawnee war party. Apparently they remained
in the vicinity of the Huerfano while the Chouteau-DeMun
party went on to Santa Fe and were picked up by them on
their return, remaining with them for protection from February 27 to March 27, 1816. They then separated from the
larger party and returned to St. Louis by a route of their
own.[5]

---

[3] *Ibid.,* 21-23; Kenneth W. Porter, "Roll Call of Overland Astorians, 1810-1812,"
in *Oregon Historical Society Quarterly* (June 1933), XXXIV, p. 107.

[4] Kelly and Morgan, *op. cit.,* 44-45; John C. Luttig, *Journal of A Fur Trading
Expedition on the Upper Missouri, 1812-1813,* Stella M. Drumm, ed., (St. Louis,
1920), 35, 61, 65, 157.

[5] Jules De Mun, *"Journals,"* Thomas M. Marshall, ed., in *Missouri Historical
Society Collections* (February and June 1928), V, pp. 207-08; 311-15.

For several years there is no clue as to his whereabouts but, in 1820-1821, he seems to have been once more on the upper Missouri but this time, illegally, having gone there despite the fact that he had for some reason been blacklisted by Benjamin O'Fallon, the Indian agent. He seems at this time to have been with a party of only six men, including himself. They must have ranged widely for its members had been reported, though falsely as it turned out, to have been killed by the Cheyennes.[6]

In 1824 his name appears in the account books of William H. Ashley, where he is credited with 202 pounds of beaver at $3 per pound.[7] It has been conjectured that he was with the Ashley men commanded by Captain Weber but no other details of his connection have been found and we next hear of him at Fort Atkinson on November 26, 1825.[8] Thus, he has returned to the upper Missouri River, where scattered references place him at intervals during the next several years.

However, family tradition places him among the Crows during this period and there is confirmation of a kind from James Beckwourth, who credits Greenwood with having persuaded the Crows that he (Beckwourth) was a Crow boy who had been lost and thus having paved the way for the acceptance of Beckwourth as a chief among the Crows.[9] It is certain that Greenwood married Batchicka Youngcault, half French and half Crow, and that she bore him a number of children. We may conclude that he did indeed spend some time in residence among the Crows but that this was not continuous. It is probable that his stay with them was broken by periodic trips to the upper Missouri River, with

---

[6] Kelly and Morgan, *op. cit.*, 62-64.

[7] Dale L. Morgan, *The West of William H. Ashley* (Denver, 1964), 4, 14, 119, 230, 290.

[8] James Kennerly, *"Diary,"* Edgar I. Wesley, ed., in *Missouri Historical Society Collections* (October, 1928), VI, pp. 88-91.

[9] T. D. Bonner, *The Life and Adventures of James P. Beckwourth* (New York, 1856), 139-41.

or without his wife and growing family. His marriage occurred probably about 1827. The children, in order of their birth, were John (1827?), Britton Bailey (1830?), Governor Boggs (1836?), William Sublette (1838), James Case (1841), Angeline (?), and Sarah Mojave (1843). In 1843, he is thought to have taken his family to St. Louis, where his wife died in that year.[10] From 1834, when he talked to Moses Merrill at Bellevue to 1844, when he joined an emigrant train going west, we have no certain knowledge of him.

In May 1844, a party of some twenty-seven wagons captained by Elisha Stephens left Holt County, Missouri, bound for Oregon. With them, as a guide, was Caleb Greenwood and with him were his two older sons, John and Britton. Upon reaching Green River, the party traveled directly to Fort Hall over what became known, for a few years, as the Greenwood cutoff, although it is by no means certain that Caleb Greenwood was responsible for choosing this route. It soon had its name changed to the Sublette cutoff by the author of *Ware's Emigrant Guide*. At Fort Hall the party split, with Stephens and thirteen wagons going to California, while the rest continued to Oregon. Greenwood and his sons accompanied the California group. They reached Sutter's Fort via the Truckee River route early in December, having been forced to leave most of their number on the Yuba River to be rescued later. Caleb Greenwood is credited with having ascertained the route over the Sierra Nevada from the Paiute Indian Chief Truckee, father of Chief Winnemucca.[11]

In 1845 the three Greenwoods returned to Fort Hall where Caleb constituted himself and his sons into a booster committee for the California land and climate and persuaded a number of Oregon bound emigrants to go thither with himself as their guide. The Greenwood sons were able

[10] Kelly and Morgan, *op. cit.*, 84-85.   [11] *Ibid.*, 112-31.

to scout out a better variation of the route across the Sierra Nevada by way of the Little Truckee River.[12]

Caleb continued this work in 1846, when he may have gone as far east as the Sweetwater River to meet the rest of his children and fetch them to California. Edwin Bryant encountered him in the California mountains on a hunting party with three of his sons and John Turner, a Mountain Man who had been with Jedediah Smith and who had come to California from Oregon, where he had remained after the Umpqua Massacre. Caleb gave Bryant a short summary of his life, mingled with some tall talk. Bryant described him as "about six feet in height, raw-boned and spare in flesh, but muscular, and not withstanding his old age, walks with the erectness and elasticity of youth."[13]

In March 1847, Old Greenwood, as he was usually called, and his son Britton, participated in the Donner relief party organized by naval Lieutenant Selim Woodworth. Later that year he and his sons may have returned to Missouri to bring out the younger children, if they were not already in California. Commodore Stockton, returning east by the overland route, described for a biographer a trapper who was one of his party. The description, complete with reference to his Crow wife, fits Caleb Greenwood.[14] If this trip was actually made they were back in California, living in Coloma by April 1849, where he seems to have precipitated a gold rush by stories of a lake full of gold.[15] Soon after this, the Greenwoods moved to a valley in El Dorado County, California, which had been settled by another former Mountain Man, Lewis B. Meyers. Despite the prior settlement by Meyers, the valley soon became known as Greenwood Valley, and his name was later given to the town. Caleb Greenwood died sometime in 1850, at the probable age of eighty-

12 *Ibid.*, 132-81; Dale L. Morgan, *Overland in 1846* (Georgetown, Calif., 1963, 2 vols.), I, p. 146; Charles Camp, *James Clyman, Frontiersman* (Portland, 1960), 228.
13 Kelly and Morgan, *op. cit.*, 219-26.   14 *Ibid.*, 259-66.   15 *Ibid.*, 278-306.

seven, reportedly somewhere between Bear and Yuba rivers, in the open and threatening to shoot anyone who tried to move him indoors.[16]

Greenwood is interesting because the references to him in his old age describe him as a rough-spoken character, dressed in dirty buckskin, roistering and drinking and living the legendary life of the Mountain Men, as it is popularly conceived, to the very last. If more were known of his earlier life, he might possibly appear to have greater historical importance. As it is, he looms as an authentic but shadowy character, who in his old age managed to impress some of his younger contemporaries as a crusty relic of a more primitive time that had already vanished.

---

16 *Ibid.,* 307-10.

Zacharias Ham

by JOHN E. BAUR
Los Angeles, California

There is no known record of the birthplace or birth date of Zacharias Ham. He remains one of the most obscure of William H. Ashley's important trappers. In 1825, when Ashley's great expedition to the Rockies set forth for the first important rendezvous, Ham was put in charge of five to seven other men, and ordered in late April to go directly west from the Green River.[1] Doing so with considerable rapidity, he discovered Ham's Fork, a major tributary of Black's Fork of the Green River in today's southwestern Wyoming, and crossed the mountain divide, probably to Bear River. By late May, Ham had fallen in with Jedediah S. Smith and joined Johnson Gardner and Etienne Provost, on their way to meet Peter Skene Ogden.[2]

Dale L. Morgan, prime student of Smith, concludes that although little is known of Ham, his efficiency and the high responsibility placed in him by Ashley mark him as an exceptionally able man, probably considered by Ashley as of equal caliber in this pioneering enterprise with his other lieutenants, Thomas L. Fitzpatrick and James Clyman.[3]

Five years later, Ham became a member of another fa-

---

[1] Dale L. Morgan, ed., "The Diary of William H. Ashley, March 25-June 27, 1825; A Record of Exploration West Across the Continental Divide, Down the Green River and Into the Great Basin," *Bulletin* of the Missouri Historical Society, XI (October 1954), 30.

[2] J. Cecil Alter, *Jim Bridger* (Norman, 1962), 64.

[3] Morgan, *op. cit.,* 30. Due to an error in Ashley's diary, Robert Glass Cleland mistakenly referred to the subject as "William Ham." See Cleland's *This Reckless Breed of Men* (New York, 1952), 19-20. For Morgan's high estimation of Ham, consult Dale L. Morgan, *Jedediah Smith and the Opening of the West* (Lincoln, 1953), 156.

mous trapping expedition, that of William Wolfskill, who followed the Old Spanish Trail to Los Angeles in 1830-31.[4] Like several other members of this group, Ham remained in Los Angeles for some time, and was mentioned by Governor Manuel Victoria in a provincial report of April 9, 1831.[5] His fate remains almost as clouded as his far western activities. It was reported as late as 1866 by the Los Angeles pioneer-historian, Henry Dwight Barrows, that Ham had drowned in the turbulent Colorado River in 1832 or 1833, presumably while engaged in the fur trade.[6] This unfortunate accident, however, could not have occurred until at least 1836, for Ham sold a brass swivel to the prosperous Los Angeles merchant, Abel Stearns, in that pueblo on June 2 of that year.[7]

[4] Hubert Howe Bancroft, *History of California* (San Francisco, 1886), III, p. 387; and LeRoy R. and Ann W. Hafen, *Old Spanish Trail, Santa Fe to Los Angeles* (Glendale, Calif., 1954), 139-54.

[5] Governor Manuel Victoria to the alcalde of Los Angeles, Archives of California, Departmental Records, IX, 95-96, as referred to in Iris Higbie Wilson, *William Wolfskill, 1798-1866* (Glendale, 1965), 67.

[6] Henry D. Barrows, "The Story of an Old Pioneer," Wilmington (Calif.) *Journal,* October 20, 1866, p. 1.

[7] Ms dated June 2, 1836, Abel Stearns Papers, Box 71, Huntington Library, San Marino, Calif.

William T. Hamilton

by L. CUSTER KEIM
Victor, Montana

In Mountain View cemetery at Columbus, Montana, is the grave of William T. Hamilton.[1] It is more than four thousand miles from the place of his birth in the Cheviot Hills district along the English-Scottish border. His birth date was December 6, 1822.[2] His death date was May 24, 1908, in Billings, Montana.[3] In those eighty-five years William Hamilton had much adventure and attained some fame.

His parents, Alexander and Margaret Hamilton [4] brought him to America in late 1825, landing in New Orleans in a boat built by his father and some friends. After some traveling the Hamiltons settled in St. Louis.[5] There young "Bill" lived until 1842, during which time he attended school five years. An asthmatic condition he developed prevented more attendance. With a view to improving his health, in early 1842 his father purchased for him a partnership in a fur-trading and trapping expedition to the Rocky Mountains.

His partners were William ("Old Bill") Williams and George Perkins, both experienced "Mountain Men." Five other men (four later identified as Docket, Evans, Noble and Russell) were members of the party.[6]

---

[1] J. T. Annin, *They Gazed on the Beartooths* (Billings, Mont., 1964), II, p. 61. Photo of grave marker.

[2] A. J. Craven, "Sketch of Hamilton's Life," in Montana Historical Society, *Contributions,* III (1900), 33.

[3] *River Press* (Fort Benton, Mont.), May 27, 1908, p. 1, col. 6.

[4] A. H. Favour, *Old Bill Williams, Mountain Man* (Norman, Okla., 1962), 140.

[5] W. T. Hamilton, *My Sixty Years on the Plains* (New York, 1905), 17. Actually, only thirty-four years of Hamilton's eighty-five years are given in much detail. Most material in this sketch, unless otherwise noted, is from this book. Some items are noted by page number.   [6] *Ibid.,* 232, and many other pages.

They left Independence, Missouri, March 15, 1842, with their pack outfit and trading supplies. Thus, "Bill" Hamilton began his career as a "Mountain Man." Although starting late in the fur trade, he was to become one of the best men in the vocation.

"Old Bill" Williams had had about thirty-five years on the plains and in the mountains at that time and was a "master trapper." He was also an effective teacher and he found in young Hamilton an apt pupil. Their travels together in the next three years are reported by F. E. Voelker in his sketch of Williams in vol. VIII of this *Series,* pages 365-94. Hamilton, himself, provides many additional details of those years.[7]

During this period Williams went twice to Taos, New Mexico, to spend the winters of 1842-43 and 1843-44. He rejoined the party each following spring. They finally disbanded in the summer of 1845 at Fort Laramie, when Williams and Perkins went to Santa Fe.[8] Hamilton said "It was the only sad parting I have ever experienced,"[9] thus expressing his high regard for both men. It was perhaps at this time that Williams gave Hamilton a manuscript history he had written of his life among the Pueblo, Navaho and Apache Indians. Unfortunately it was destroyed in 1872 in a fire at the Crow Agency on the Yellowstone River.[10]

However, Hamilton continued with the four of his original party already identified. They were immediately engaged by a North West Fur Company (Canadian) party to accompany it and explore the Big Horn Mountains to the north. They quickly met with trouble with Blackfeet Indians and the North West leader decided to return to Laramie. Hamilton and his partners were paid off and were glad to be "free trappers" again. They went to Green River, purchased $1000 in trade goods, and proceeded with Sho-

---

[7] See also Favour, *op. cit.,* 140.　　[8] Hamilton, *op. cit.,* 177.
[9] *Ibid.,* 177.　　[10] *Ibid.,* 102; Favour, *op. cit.,* 82.

shone Indians back to the Big Horns. In December they sold their furs at Green River and went southeast to the Arkansas River.

The next two years of Hamilton's life appear to be lost to us. He said they had "no bearing on prairie life." [11] He went to St. Louis in early 1848 to visit his parents, both of whom died within a year. In late July 1848 he left St. Louis to return to the West and his companions whom he had promised to meet at Green River that fall. En route he encountered an emigrant train and was hired to pilot it to Green River. He not only took it there, but beyond to Fort Hall, where they arrived October 1, 1848. He then returned to Fort Bridger and Brown's Hole where he met his four friends – "as well as fifteen of our old companions." [12] They planned to winter there.

The next day two wagons with trade goods arrived from Missouri and brought news of the gold discoveries in California. The trappers became excited and decided to go mining the next spring. With the wagons were three eastern sportsmen who desired to hunt in the Big Horn Mountains. With modern salesmenship methods the trappers warned them of the dangers of such a hunt but assured them that ten trappers could ensure their safety. The sportsmen offered $100 per month, per man – each trapper to keep his furs. During these negotiations Perkins arrived from Las Vegas with a letter to Hamilton from Williams inviting "Young Bill" to become his partner in a trading venture in the south country. Hamilton would have accepted had he not already decided on the California trip. He was never to see "Old Bill" again. Williams was killed, supposedly by Indians, March 21, 1849. [13]

Hamilton, Perkins and others accepted the sportsmen's

---

[11] Hamilton, *op. cit.,* 187-88. He may have gone to the Mexican War. He said "almost all the trappers joined General Price's forces."   [12] *Ibid.,* 195.
[13] Frederic E. Voelker, "William S. Williams," in this *Series,* VIII, p. 391.

offer and went on the hunt to the Big Horns. They met Chief Washakie and his Shoshones who accompanied them. They encountered some Pend d'Oreille Indians who tried to raid them but in a running fight they killed fifteen of the raiders and scalped them. Some scalps were given to the sportsmen. They hunted buffalo, bear, and other game and then returned to Green River. The trappers moved to Henry's Fork of the Green for the winter.

About the middle of February 1849 they started for California via Humboldt River, taking their horses, traps, and trade goods. They did well trapping, crossed the desert easily, but had some difficulty in the Sierra Nevada because of deep snow. They reached Hangtown, California, July 4, 1849, and went to Sacramento five days later. There they sold their furs and purchased mining equipment.

Hamilton might have prospered in California had future events differed. He married an "estimable lady and engaged in mining and agriculture," [14] probably in 1850. However, his wife and child died at childbirth in 1851, and he rejoined his trapper friends. By this time they, also, were losing interest in mining. Indians were molesting the miners, even killing some. (Note: No Indian reports of the reverse appear – Author.) "Young Bill" and his partners were recruited at Nevada City to fight Indians. Perkins was chosen captain; Hamilton, first lieutenant; Evans, second lieutenant; and Russell, first sergeant. They were delegated by the miners and merchants to chastise the Indians and this they effectively did – killing the chief, many warriors, women and children. They then continued to assist the miners at Hangtown and Shasta City. They fought "Tarhead" and Rogue River Indians with much success and went into the first Modoc war (1856). They were under command of General Crosby, "a third rate lawyer." Hamil-

---

14 Craven, *op. cit.,* 34.

ton also fought Pitt River Indians after the Modoc fighting. In early 1858 all his partners, except Russell, concluded to go to New Mexico.[15] Hamilton and Russell were hired to guide two pack trains to The Dalles in Oregon. This they did and then proceeded to Fort Walla Walla (Washington), where they met Colonel George Wright. Due to Hamilton's display of his proficiency in Indian Sign Language, and Russell's as well, when they met some Nez Perce Indians there, Wright hired them for scouting purposes against the Spokane, Yakima, Colville, and other tribes.

Before they started their scouting trip Russell was killed when he rode an unbroken horse he had just purchased. The cinch broke and he was thrown on some rocks. Hamilton was now without any of his early companions. Shortly thereafter he met Alex McKay, a half-breed Indian, and they were sent together to the Umatilla River area forty miles west to trade and spy. They arrived at an Indian camp there at night and aroused some suspicion. They pretended to be Hudson's Bay men, however, and were accepted. They traded tobacco and ammunition and, while so doing, learned the war plans of the Indians. They also pretended to continue west but reversed their route and returned to Walla Walla to report.[16] Colonel Wright soon defeated the Indians on the Spokane River and captured some as hostages. He immediately had eleven of these convicted of murder and ordered them to be hanged. Hamilton states Wright's *order* "was happily executed in fifteen minutes after its issuance." (Italics by author.) This was in early September 1858.[17]

Wright moved rapidly in other ways. There were rumors that the Indians east of the Rockies around the Missouri River might have war-like intentions. "About the 20th of September 1858 – at 2 p.m.," Hamilton says he was ordered

---

[15] Hamilton, *op. cit.,* 232.　　　　　　　[16] *Ibid.,* 233-41.
[17] William T. Hamilton, "A Trading Expedition among the Indians in 1858," in Montana Historical Society, *Contributions,* III (1900), 33-34.

to report for further duty. He and McKay were then sent with a trading outfit to the Missouri area. It was actually another spying expedition. They found conditions generally peaceful but had some skirmishes with Blackfeet Indians when they were with Kootenai friends. McKay was wounded but recovered and they returned to Walla Walla.[18]

On their outward journey one morning they "crossed a rolling prairie, a beautiful country about 11 a.m. and arrived at a beautiful creek, now called Rattlesnake, where we camped." Hamilton told McKay the location was so favorable for trade that he would establish a post there if they returned from their expedition safely. This he did in late 1858 or early 1859.[19] "His post was the first white-man building where Missoula, Montana, now is. Here he stayed until 1864."[20] In the first election held in 1860, after other whites arrived, he was elected sheriff of Missoula County, Washington Territory.[21] For some reason he did not qualify. In 1864 he sold his post and moved to Fort Benton, by that time Montana Territory. There he set up trading again and was again elected sheriff, this time of Chouteau County. He served in this capacity and, in addition, became a U.S. Deputy Marshal.[22]

He sold out at Fort Benton in 1869 and moved to where the Stillwater River empties into the Yellowstone River, about forty miles west of present Billings, Montana. In 1874 he joined the "Yellowstone Expedition" from Bozeman,

[18] *Ibid.* This narrative, of ninety-one pages (33-123), contains almost complete details of this expedition. Lest Hamilton may be thought of as having at all times animosity toward Indians, the following is quoted from page 123: "Little Dog and his son, Fringe, [Piegan Indians] also paid me several visits and we remained fast friends until their death[s], which occurred in 1867. Little Dog was one of the most remarkable Indians on the plains."

[19] *Ibid.,* 46.

[20] Will Cave, feature article in *Sunday Missoulian,* June 29, 1924, pp. 1 and 7.

[21] Frank H. Woody, "Sketch of the Early History of Western Montana written in 1876 and 1877," in Montana Hist. Soc., *Contributions,* II (1896), 99.

[22] Hamilton, *Sixty Years,* 242.

Montana, which was organized to slow down Indian depredations. It accomplished nothing except a few Indian deaths and more murderous feelings within the tribes. Hamilton said, "This was the expedition which brought on the war of 1876, that was so disastrous to General Custer and his command." Hamilton, himself, joined General Crook's forces in the 1876 campaign and served as a scout until its completion, when he returned to Stillwater, now Columbus, Montana.[23]

Here, in his remaining twenty-nine years he became "Uncle Billy" to almost all who knew him. He continued to trap and trade and also guided hunting parties into the mountains. In 1882 he went to Washington, D.C., to attend a government postal hearing and talked to Captain W. P. Clark who, in 1885, wrote a book about the Indian sign language. Hamilton said in 1905, "I taught him [Clark] the first sign he ever knew in 1876." Bill was called "Master of the Signs." Therein lay his fame among trappers such as Jim Bridger, and among many Indian Tribes.[24]

In 1894 "Uncle Billy" was a witness in federal court in Billings. His citizenship was questioned and he learned he was not a U.S. citizen because his father had never become naturalized. The judge (Milburn) quickly made him a citizen. Billy said, "Damn fine thing. Hope they don't disqualify some of my actions as sheriff at Fort Benton, and a deputy in other law enforcement, to say nothing of throwing out an election because I wasn't eligible to vote, but, maybe, I should ask for a refund of the poll taxes I have paid."[25]

In 1905 Hamilton published his book *My Sixty Years on the Plains*. In the last paragraph he said, "At eighty-two years I am hale and hearty and always spend a part of each year in the mountains trapping."[26] In that year, also, he

[23] *Ibid.,* 242-44.

[24] Annin, *op. cit.,* 59. See also Hamilton, *Sixty Years,* 65, 97, 233.

[25] Annin, *op. cit.,* 60.   [26] Hamilton, *Sixty Years,* 244.

wrote thirteen lessons in "sign" for the Columbus school students.[27]

Billy survived for three more years. In early 1908 he entered a Billings hospital and died there May 24 of that year. He belonged to the Montana Society of Pioneers [28] and had certainly qualified as a "Mountain Man" since leaving St. Louis in March 1842. He, perhaps, was one of the last survivors of those Mountain Men-Fur Trade days.

Hamilton's portrait appears in this volume at page 21.

[27] Annin, *op. cit.,* 59.

[28] James N. Sanders, ed., *Society of Montana Pioneers: Constitution, Officers and Members* (Akron, Ohio, 1899), 246.

Valentine Johnson ("Rube") Herring

by JANET LECOMPTE
Colorado Springs, Colorado

George Frederick Ruxton, writer of the two most entertaining books about the Mountain Man's west, delighted in the strange, and outlandish people and places he observed on a visit in 1846 and 1847. A prize in his collection of oddities was Valentine Johnson Herring, universally known as "Old Rube," upon whom Ruxton lavished several pages of description. In his *Life in the Far West* Ruxton discovers Rube sitting by his campfire at Beer (Soda) Springs, gazing intently into the bubbling waters:

> Dressed from head to foot in buckskin, his face, neck, and hands appeared to be of the same leathery texture, so nearly did they assimilate in color to the materials of his dress. He was at least six feet two or three in his moccasins, straight-limbed and wiry, with long arms ending in hands of tremendous grasp, and a quantity of straight black hair hanging on his shoulders. His features, which were undeniably good, wore an expression of comical gravity, never relaxing into a smile. . . [He] sat sulky and silent, his huge form bending over his legs, which were crossed, Indian fashion, under him, and his long bony fingers spread over the fire. . .

Herring had lost two of his three horses and three of his six beaver traps to Indian thievery, and had sought out this magical spring to "make medicine," "invoking the fountain spirits, which, a perfect Indian in his simple heart, he implicitly believed to inhabit their mysterious waters."[1]

Old Rube was not as simple as Ruxton thought. Credulous he no doubt was, and his conversion to, and later apostasy from, Mormonism were from no very deep conviction. But his picturesque qualities entirely hid from

---

[1] George Frederick Ruxton, *Life in the Far West* (N.Y., 1848), 90-91.

Ruxton's view a man of intelligence, administrative talent and even wisdom. To Ruxton, Rube was undoubtedly a "perfect" Mountain Man – that is, ideally suited to this savage way of life. Yet when he left the mountains, he shed his buckskin, settled down in a more or less civilized community and became a civic leader – superintendent of schools, county assessor, county clerk, and justice.

Rube Herring was born in Illinois in 1812,[2] and, judging by his later career, he was given a fair education. In the spring of 1831 he was at St. Louis where he was hired by John Gantt for a trapping expedition to the Rocky Mountains.[3] The trappers ascended the Platte and trapped until misfortunes made Gantt abandon the northern territory and settle on the Arkansas near later Pueblo, Colorado, to trade with the Arapahos. Gantt built a post, then another, and finally gave up his trade altogether before the spring of 1835.[4]

How much of Gantt's experience was shared by Herring we cannot tell, but not all, for by 1833 Rube had joined William Sublette on the Upper Missouri. He was back in St. Louis by early 1834, wooing a girl named Selina Perkins who weighed 160 pounds and had a face like a full moon. They were to be married, and Rube was to run her daddy's farm nine miles from St. Louis. The day before the wedding, Rube went to town to buy a mule and met, as he said, some of his "old pards who war out to the Rockies with me the year afore, in Bill Subbett's company." They fell to drinking together and soon Rube began to feel like taking another trip. The next morning he bought the mule and

---

2 Los Angeles County (Calif.) Census, 1852, p. 49.

3 His name was listed on Gantt & Blackwell's passport, dated May 5, 1831, issued by William Clark, Superintendent of Indian Affairs at St. Louis, now in the Ritch Collection, Henry E. Huntington Library, San Marino, Calif.

4 Janet Lecompte, "Gantt's Fort and Bent's Picket Post," *Colorado Magazine* XLI, no. 2 (Spring 1964).

after running around with his old pards all day, he still hadn't made up his mind whether to marry or start for the Rockies. As he rode along toward his sweetheart's farm, he pondered the problem until he came to where the road forked – the right branch leading to the farm, the left away from it. Just then a happy thought struck him – he would let the mule decide! He dropped the bridle, stuck his hands in his pockets, and the mule wandered off to the left. Rube joined his comrades and wrote Selina to "hold out faithful fur two years" until he returned with pockets full of dollars, "an' we'd hitch sure an' certain." Poor Selina![5]

According to Isaac Rose, Herring and his friends were hired as trappers by Nathaniel Wyeth, and ended up on the Snake River building Fort Hall. In March, 1835, Herring left the fort for the spring hunt under Joseph Gale, returning in June with the best catch of any of his companions – 26 beaver and an otter, worth $134. Two weeks later the trappers went out again on the fall hunt, again under Joseph Gale who this time proved so fractious and tyrannical that Herring and four others deserted in July on a branch of the Gallatin.[6]

From then on Rube Herring was a free trapper, working for no man, selling his furs where he pleased and buying supplies at the nearest fort. From fragments of information, we gather that he spent some time on the South Platte, where four trading posts were clustered within a few miles. In April V. J. Herring gave Henry Fraeb, owner of Fort Jackson, a note for $32, due in September and still not paid

---

[5] James B. Marsh, *Four Years in the Rockies; or, the Adventures of Isaac P. Rose* (New Castle, Pa., 1884), 30-32. Rose does not identify his faithless lover further than "Rube," but there is no other "Rube" or V. J. Herring who worked for Wyeth at Fort Hall (see below), according to the Fort Hall account books (Oregon Historical Society, microfilm copy loaned me by Dr. Richard G. Beidleman).

[6] Fort Hall account books. Herring left with four beaver traps and a horse belonging to Wyeth, and he owed the company $182.42, but the horse appears to have been returned later. See also Osborne Russell, *Journal of a Trapper* (Boise, 1921), 33.

by April of next year.[7] And he was in charge of Fort Lancaster for a time during the winter of 1841-1842.[8]

Rube also spent some time in Taos where he attached to himself a Mexican woman named Nicolasa ("Colasa"), whose first name was doubtless Maria like that of every other woman of Taos. He did not marry her at Taos, or probably anywhere else, but their childless and stormy liason proved to be remarkably stable, if she was the Maria he later took to California with him.[9] Nicolasa was some sort of temptress, for when Herring was at Lock and Randolph's fort (Fort Vasquez) in the winter of 1841-1842, Henry Beer took a fancy to her and, backed by his friends, provoked a quarrel with Rube which resulted in a duel meant to wipe out Rube and leave the lady to Beer. Beer chose rifles at fifty yards, for Herring was known as a poor shot. They met at a grove of cottonwoods. Beer shot and missed; Herring shot and hit. Beer soon expired.[10]

---

[7] Letter of Abel Baker, Jr. to Messrs. Sarpy & Fraeb, Fort Lookout, April 1, 1839, in LeRoy R. Hafen, "Fort Jackson and the Early Fur Trade on the South Platte," *Colorado Magazine*, VI, no. 1 (Feb. 1928), 16.

[8] John Brown, *Mediumistic Experiences of John Brown, the Medium of the Rockies* (San Francisco, 1897), 188-89.

[9] No marriage is listed for Rube in the Taos church marriage records; nor were any children of theirs baptized at Taos, nor mentioned in the 1852 Los Angeles County census, where both Rube and Maria are listed.

[10] Rufus B. Sage, *Scenes in the Rocky Mountains,* ed. LeRoy R. Hafen (Glendale, Calif., 1956), II, pp. 58-59. Tom Autobees, a poor source, indicates that Nicolasa was Beer's wife and that the duel was at Fort Lupton (Lancaster) on July 4, 1843 (F. W. Cragin's interview with Tom Autobees, Avondale, Colo., Nov. 8, 1907, Cragin Collection, Pioneers' Museum, Colorado Springs, Colo.), getting the event mixed up with the killing of Xervier at Fort Lancaster on July 4, 1843 (*The Journals of Theodore Talbot, 1843 and 1849-52,* ed. Charles H. Carey (Portland, 1931), 24). Tom added, surely in error, that the same woman caused the duel between John Brown and "Sissome" and between Jim Waters and Ed Tharp. Arthur Woodward, using F. W. Cragin's interviews as his source in his entertaining pamphlet "Trapper Jim Waters" (Publ. #23, Los Angeles Westerners) swallows Tom Autobees whole and gratuitously characterizes Nicolasa as a "little brown hell-cat" with "a certain wild beauty and animal magnetism" – probably just what she was – but he also assumes that she was the same as Jim Waters' Candelaria woman, which she was probably not. See F. W. Cragin's interview with Mrs. Felipe Ledoux, Las Vegas, Feb. 13, 1908, Cragin Collection; and December 1845 entry in Alexander Barclay's diary (soon to be published).

Rube's trapping days were over by at least 1845, when he and Nicolasa settled down, quarreling incessantly, at Hardscrabble, a farming settlement of ex-trappers on the upper Arkansas River.[11] He was frequently at Pueblo, another town of ex-trappers, where, in the fall of 1846, a group of Mormons came to build a village nearby for wintering. Their best convert among their neighbors was Old Rube, whom they promised should guide them to their "promised land" in the spring. Rube, as Ruxton tells us, adopted a Mormon's cast-off brown cloth coat whose waist was a mere hand's span from the nape of his neck, and whose skirts flapped about his ankles. A slouching felt hat covered his head, from which his long straight black hair hung in flakes to his shoulders. His pantaloons were of buckskin shrunk to his calves, and his huge feet were encased in buffalo-cow skin moccasins. In this extraordinary outfit Rube could be seen night and day reading the *Book of Mormon* out loud in his sonorous voice. He stood the badgering of his friends in perfect good humor, saying there never was such a book before, and that the Mormons were the "biggest kind" of prophets. His faith was complete until the spring of 1847, when the Mormons announced they would not need him as guide after all. Furious, he threw the *Book of Mormon* into the Arkansas, exclaiming, "Cuss your darned Mummum and Thummum! thar's not one among you knows 'fat cow' from 'poor bull,' and you may go to h—— for me."[12]

The Mormons moved on, but it was not the last Rube Herring would see of them. In June 1849, Rube and his woman, John Brown and his family, Jim Waters and others from Pueblo and Hardscrabble, left for California, arriving

---

[11] Rube bought his supplies at John Brown's store at Greenhorn and later at Lupton's store at Hardscrabble, where records exist of his purchases (John Brown's account book, Beattie Collection, Huntington Library; and Lupton's account book, Colorado State Historical Society, Denver). Alexander Barclay's diary has many references to Herring's comings and goings.

[12] Ruxton, *Life in the Far West*, 216-17.

in Salt Lake City July 4, 1849, and Sutter's Fort in September. For a while, Herring probably mined, but after his hope of riches faded, he and his Maria settled at San Bernardino, a Mormon colony from 1852 until 1857.[13] He was still considered a Mormon and was elected to several local offices not open to gentiles. In January 1853, he became county superintendent of schools, supervising 206 pupils in two adobe school rooms. He proved to be "a man of energy and fine administrative force," and the literary style of his superintendent's report of November 1853, has been described as "quaint" and "pithy."[14]

At the same time he was superintendent of schools, he also served as justice of the peace and county assessor. It was the latter position which got him into trouble with the Mormons. Although he was "generally considered a strictly honest man," in the words of another old-timer,[15] Mormon leaders did not like the way he valued Mormon property, and he was not paid in full for his services as assessor in 1854. He did not seek reelection, and his apostasy from the Mormon Church dates from this time. In 1855 he joined other "independents" in defying Mormon leadership, even to the extent of "forting up" in a neighbor's house in expectation of trouble. Mormon sources reported that he was "an apostate, married to a Spanish woman [who] had for some time been trying to stir up Californians against the Mormons."[16] In 1857 the San Bernardino Mormons were re-

[13] The 1852 census of Los Angeles County, which then stretched from the ocean to the Colorado River and included San Bernardino, shows "Maria Herring," aged 30, white female born in New Mexico, and "Valentine Herring," aged 40, born in Illinois. They were not found at the same address, and neither was listed in the 1860 census of San Bernardino city or township.

[14] L. A. Ingersoll, *Ingersoll's Century Annals of San Bernardino County, 1769-1904* (Los Angeles, 1904), 293-95; *History of San Bernardino, California, with illustrations . . .* (San Francisco, 1883), 119.

[15] The old-timer was Judge Rolfe (George W. and Helen P. Beattie, *Heritage of the Valley; San Bernardino's First Century* (Pasadena, 1939), 119, 206, 231-32). My thanks to LeRoy Hafen for copying out these references for me.

[16] Beattie, *op. cit.*, 264.

called to Salt Lake City, and the friction in San Bernardino came to an end. Rube Herring became sheriff in 1859, county clerk at some other time, and justice in 1861. From 1866 to 1868 he served again as county assessor, and by 1883 he was dead,[17] having earned a place of distinction in each of two entirely dissimilar worlds.[18]

[17] *History of San Bernardino*, 141-42; *Ingersoll's, op. cit.*, 293, 295, 297, 349.

[18] Mr. I. M. Templeton, Superintendent of the Pioneer Memorial Cemetery of San Bernardino, reports that he has no record of the death or burial of Valentine J. Herring; but their records go back only to 1886, when a fire destroyed the cemetery records. – Letter of Sept. 3, 1971, from Mr. Templeton to LeRoy R. Hafen.

John Hoback, Jacob Reznor and Edward Robinson

by HARVEY L. CARTER
Colorado College

The names of these three men are inseparably linked in connection with important events of the earliest years of the Rocky Mountain fur trade and because almost nothing is known concerning the origins of any of them they will be treated as a group. Such treatment seems appropriate, as well as a virtual necessity, for the reason that they lived and died together and shared all their wide wanderings and adventurous misfortunes.

The oldest of the three was Edward Robinson, who is said to have been sixty-six years of age in 1811. He was an early settler of Kentucky and, during the period of the Indian raids upon the Kentucky settlements, he had had the bad luck to lose his scalp, after which he always wore a handkerchief tied over his head.[1] Robinson is known to have been one of the original employees of Manuel Lisa in his first venture up the Missouri River to engage in the fur trade in 1807.[2] In 1809, the Missouri Fur Company, organized by Lisa, Menard, and others, got together a large expedition to penetrate to the Three Forks of the Missouri. Andrew Henry was field captain and the three Kentuckians, Hoback, Reznor, and Robinson were among the hunters.

---

[1] Washington Irving, *Astoria,* ed. by Edgeley W. Todd (Norman, 1964), 176. Irving says that all three men were Kentuckians but gives no particulars on the background of the other two.

[2] Richard E. Oglesby, *Manuel Lisa and the Opening of the Missouri Fur Trade* (Norman, 1963), 45. However, his name appears in the Menard Family Papers with those of John Potts and Peter Wiser, so it is not clear whether his association with Jacob Reznor and John Hoback had begun at this time or not. Probably it had, since all three were definitely employed by Lisa and Menard in 1809.

Plagued by constant trouble with the Blackfeet, they finally reached the Three Forks, guided by John Colter, whom they had met on the Missouri, returning from his solitary explorations, and persuaded to go once more into the wilderness.[3] Here they built a fort, but, constantly harrassed by Blackfeet, the bulk of the expedition returned to St. Louis in the summer of 1810. Henry, with sixty hardy men, including Hoback, Reznor, and Robinson, crossed the continental divide and built several cabins on Henry's Fork of the Snake River, where they continued to trap until the spring of 1811, when they broke up into smaller parties and made their way by varying routes toward home.[4]

The trio of Kentucky hunters was encountered near the confluence of the Niobrara with the Missouri by Wilson Price Hunt and his overland Astorians on May 26, 1811.[5] It was a momentous meeting for it altered the route of the Astorians and the lives of the three hunters. The trio told Hunt of the constant danger from Blackfeet along the upper Missouri and offered to guide his party to Henry's Fork of Snake River by the route which they themselves had recently traversed.[6] Soon after arrival at Henry's Fort, the

---

[3] The fullest account of this expedition is in Thomas James, *Three Years Among the Indians and Mexicans,* ed. by Milo M. Quaife (Chicago, 1953), 3-99. However, James does not mention the three Kentuckians who are the subject of this sketch.

[4] Irving, *op. cit.,* 140. Near Drummond, Idaho, certain stones have been found, one bearing the inscription "Camp Henry Sept. 1810," another which is carved with "A. Henry, J. Hoback," and three other names. Professor Edgeley Todd gives it as his opinion that these stones are genuine evidence.

[5] John Bradbury, *Travels . . .,* in *Early Western Travels,* ed. by R. G. Thwaites (Cleveland, 1904), v, p. 98. It was from Bradbury that Irving took the details concerning Robinson's age and appearance already given. Robinson's name first appears in Hunt's records May 28, 1811, at 1st Cedar Island; Hoback and Reznor's names appear June 13, 1811, at Arickaree Village. These dates and places indicate when and where the men first drew supplies or were advanced money on credit. See Kenneth W. Porter, "Roll of Overland Astorians, 1810-1812," in *Oregon Historical Quarterly,* XXXIV (1933), 103-12.

[6] The only variation seems to have been that they crossed the continental divide by Union Pass on their return whereas they had crossed by Twogwotee Pass on their earlier eastward journey. See Philip Ashton Rollins, *The Discovery of the Oregon Trail: Robert Stuart's Narratives* (New York, 1935), p. cii, where the route is traced in detail.

three guides detached themselves from the Astorians on October 9, 1811. Their desire was to trap for beaver and in this they were joined by Joseph Miller, a partner in the Astorian enterprise, and Martin L. Cass.[7]

The next we hear of them is over a year later, when they were encountered on Snake River, where they were fishing, by Robert Stuart and his returning overland party from Astoria, October 20, 1812. From what they told Stuart it appears that they had trapped as far south as Bear River, then eastward in northern Colorado and southern Wyoming at least as far as the Medicine Bow Mountains, that they had been robbed of all their furs and other possessions by some wandering Arapahoes, and had been deserted by Cass, who was no longer with them.[8] They traveled with Stuart and his party to Caldron Linn, where three of nine caches of goods were found undisturbed. Miller stayed with Stuart's party but Hoback, Reznor, and Robinson decided that, freshly outfitted, they would rather make a fresh hunt than to return home empty handed. Accordingly they seem to have trapped the Snake River and its tributaries until they at last met John Reed's party of trappers from Astoria on September 13, 1813, near Boise River and joined forces with him. Once again they had been robbed of most of their possessions, but they set to work with others of Reed's party to trap more beaver.

In January 1814, their trapping career came to an end when an Indian attack wiped out all of Reed's party except Marie Dorion and her two children, including her husband, Pierre Dorion, who was in company with Reznor when both were killed.[9]

---

[7] Rollins, *op. cit.*, 290.

[8] Rollins, *op. cit.*, 86, 104-05, 140. However, they later told a somewhat different story concerning Cass. Rollins is of the opinion that they did not find South Pass while on their wanderings.

[9] Gabriel Franchère, *Narrative* . . ., in *Early Western Travels,* ed. by R. G. Thwaites (Cleveland, 1904), VI, pp. 342-44; Alexander Ross, *Adventures* . . ., in *ibid.,* VII, pp. 265-69; also Irving, *op. cit.,* 498-500.

The three Kentuckians were undoubtedly of a hardy and independent type, capable of maintaining themselves under most difficult conditions, until their luck at last ran out. They were the earliest to feel the attraction of the beaver paradise wherein the rendezvous was to become an established institution for many years. Of the three, Hoback's name is perpetuated by the Hoback River and Hoback Mountain in western Wyoming.[10] Much of what they could have told of the Western Slope was rediscovered by later Mountain Men.

---

[10] Hoback's name is also recorded as Hobaugh, Hobough, Hubbough, and Hauberk. Variations of Reznor's name are Rezner, Rizner, Reesner, Regnier, Reasoner, and Reesoner.

David E. Jackson

by CARL D. W. HAYS
Columbus, New Mexico

One of the men who signed up with William H. Ashley to go along on his fur trading and trapping venture up the Missouri River in April 1822, was David E. Jackson.[1] Jackson was not, however, one of Ashley's "enterprising young men" as far as age went among that group of adventurers. He was already well into his thirties and was a settled family man with a wife and four growing children.

He had just recently decided to settle permanently near his brother, George E. Jackson, in what was then Ste. Genevieve County, Missouri.[2] George had already settled on a homestead in what later became Jackson Township, Ste. Genevieve County. Like most Jacksons anywhere in the United States in pioneer times, George was also the proprietor of a mill, on the Fourche de Clout [Fourche a du Clos] branch of Establishment Creek near his home. His was a saw mill.

---

[1] This outline sketch of David E. Jackson is extracted from a work in progress covering the complete story of Jackson and other members of his family who took part in the major westward movements.

A portrait of David E. Jackson, owned by family descendants, will appear in the above-mentioned work by the author of this sketch.

The main authorities relied on for this sketch for the period 1822-1830 can be found in Dale Morgan, whose research in the original documents has paralleled that of this writer every step of the way. Those works to which the reader is referred are: Dale L. Morgan, *Jedediah Smith and the Opening of the West* (Indianapolis, 1953), Dale L. Morgan, ed., *The West of William H. Ashley, 1822-1838* (Denver, 1964), and Dale L. Morgan and Carl I. Wheat, *Jedediah Smith and his Maps of the American West* (San Francisco, 1954).

It is believed that the above references are so well known that it will be unnecessary to repeat them in each instance here.

[2] All references to the Jackson family or the personal business of David E. Jackson, including court records, are from what I shall call the *Hays Family Papers,* the originals or copies of which are in the possession of this writer. That citation also will not be repeated in this paper.

David was not the first member of his family to enter or engage in the Indian trade. George had already been up the Mississippi River as early as 1810-11 trading with the Sauk and Fox Indians for the firm of James Gamble & Co. of Ste. Genevieve.

According to some members of the family, David Jackson is said to have fought in the Battle of New Orleans under Andrew Jackson, or at least to have been present at that battle. That tradition remains unverified. It is certain, however, that Jackson did visit New Orleans at least once in his career. If it was before his entrance into the fur trade, the two most likely times were in the winter of 1814-15 or in the spring of 1820. Some of the Jackson relatives were engaged seasonally in flatboating produce to the New Orleans market and David could have accompanied them on one of those trips.

It is not known whether David Jackson made arrangements to become a member of Ashley's party as a result of the much discussed advertisement in the Missouri papers or whether it was arranged through personal contact with Ashley or Henry. He and his brother George were living in the region adjacent to the lead mines of Missouri and George had known Ashley at least since 1810. It was not far from George's home to present Potosi in Washington County where Andrew Henry resided. George had clerked in Ste. Genevieve in at least one store which was engaged in furnishing supplies to the lead mines and could have known Henry also. At any rate David Jackson's plans for settling down as a farmer were altered abruptly in that spring of 1822.

A far greater number of men were recruited by Ashley from the Ste. Genevieve and Washington county areas of Missouri than has generally been supposed. Many employees so far unidentified by writers had settled in those areas. Several were known to the Jacksons personally.

Not much is known of David Jackson's movements during his first season in the Rocky Mountains. He made all preparations to start up the Missouri in early April and I have seen no evidence that he did not do so. In that case he would have been a member of Andrew Henry's group which started to leave St. Louis by April 3, 1822.

Jackson must have been employed to serve in a clerical capacity rather than as an expedition leader as he assumed the function early of maintaining a sort of temporary headquarters in the field. He became a steadying influence among the more boisterous spirits of the younger men in the group.

The first published information which has come to light in all these years on Jackson's presence with Ashley's men is William Waldo's account of Jackson's participation in the fight with the Arikara Indians when Ashley's men were attacked at the Arikara villages on June 2, 1823, while ascending the Missouri.

Waldo in his "Recollections of a Septuagenarian," says:

> . . . Sublette and Jackson after fighting bravely around the animals, until all were either killed or dispersed, fought their way through the crowded ranks of Indians, leaped into the river, and under a hail storm of arrows and balls, swam to the boats.[3]

William Waldo was an employee of David Jackson over a period of two years and should have known whereof he spoke. In addition the two families had known of each other for many years and David Jackson was associated with David, William, Lawrence L. and Daniel Waldo at various times or engaged in enterprises at the same places.

If Jackson had not returned to Missouri with Ashley from the 1822 expedition, he must have been accompanied by Jedediah Smith down the Missouri in 1823 in order to have been present at the fight, as Dale Morgan pointed out to me in a private letter.

---

[3] William Waldo, "Recollections of a Septuagenarian," in *Glimpses of the Past,* Missouri Historical Society (St. Louis, 1938), 82.

The next reference which can be applied to David Jackson is from Hiram Martin Chittenden.[4] After the first battle with the Arikara, Ashley and his men dropped down the river a safe distance and sent for reinforcements. In answer they were joined by Colonel Leavenworth with a contingent of men and Joshua Pilcher with a group of men of the Missouri Fur Company. Ashley's men were formed into a semi-military organization consisting of two groups. A man named as George C. Jackson was appointed a lieutenant in one group. The combined forces of Leavenworth, Ashley and Pilcher attacked the two villages on August 9-10, 1823, and the Arikara sued for peace.

The identity of the above George C. Jackson has given rise to several conjectures. My own personal opinion is that the name was meant for George E. Jackson, David's brother. I have several specimens of his signature and in them the "E" can easily be mistaken for a "C." That was the usual way in which he signed his name.

However, from what I know of the movements of the two brothers at that particular time, it is more likely that David was the one at the battle and that Ashley, having known George for a longer period of time and being familiar with his signature, was thinking of him when he submitted the names of his officers to Colonel Leavenworth.

George E. Jackson was busy raising a family at home along about that time, but he could have joined a relief group sent up the Missouri to help Ashley after the first battle and then returned home after their mission was accomplished. Such a group is said to have been formed and several names cannot be accounted for otherwise.

Family tradition places David Jackson in a fight with Indians along the Missouri during his fur trade experience and it is assumed that it was in the engagements with the Arikara.

---

[4] Hiram Martin Chittenden, *The American Fur Trade of the Far West* (New York, 1935 edition), 586.

The first written report that indicated Jackson's presence in the mountains with any reasonable degree of certainty was at the first annual rendezvous, held on Henry's Fork of Green River, present Utah, in July 1825.

General Ashley says in his letter to General Henry Atkinson, dated "Saint Louis, dec. 1, 1825":

> On the 1st day of july, *all the men in my employ or with whom I had any concern in the country,* together with twenty-nine, who had recently withdrawn from the Hudson Bay Company, making in all 120 men, were assembled in two camps near each other about 20 miles distant from the place appointed by me as a general rendezvous . . .[5]
> (Italics mine.)

If *all* of Ashley's men were present at the rendezvous that year, David Jackson was present, as he was one of them.

The first positive identification of Jackson in the fur trade which has been published, is his presence on Bear River in 1826 right after the summer rendezvous in Cache Valley that year. There William H. Ashley sold out his interest in the fur trade to J. S. Smith, D. E. Jackson and Wm. L. Sublette who began business as partners in a new firm to be known as Smith, Jackson & Sublette. On July 18, 1826, an agreement was entered into between General Ashley and the new partners "concerning goods to be brought to the mountains" the next year. That is the first preserved record of David E. Jackson's signature in the fur trade business.

That new partnership marked the beginning of the second era in the history of Ashley men in the Rocky Mountain fur trade.

From the moment the new partnership was formed the functions of the three partners became more specialized. Jedediah Smith became the explorer; David Jackson became the field manager, trying to keep a more or less settled

---

[5] Harrison Clifford Dale, "The Ashley Narrative," in *The Ashley-Smith Explorations and the Discovery of a Central Route to the Pacific, 1822-1829* (Glendale, Calif., 1941 edition), 152.

headquarters from which to direct the operations of the men in the field and to which the men could report; and to Bill Sublette fell the task of making the annual trip back to Missouri to deliver the year's catch of furs and bring back supplies.

Perhaps to Jackson fell the task of holding the men and business together because of his being somewhat older than the average employee, and partly because he had already apparently spent some time in that capacity under Ashley.

Certain it is that a guiding hand was necessary in the field in order to keep the business going and the men contented and satisfied. Without Jackson's personal supervision Jedediah Smith would not have been free to make his explorations, and Sublette would not have been wise to abandon the business in the mountains in order to bring in supplies. The importance of Jackson's contribution in this matter has been almost entirely overlooked by historians. Without a central location of some kind with someone in charge neither Smith nor Sublette would have had any place to report back to, nor would their business have lasted very long. So it became "the regular practice for Jackson to spend almost all his time in the mountains." [6]

During the winter of 1826-27, Jackson is said to have stayed in Cache Valley. Sublette left there on January 1, 1827, and started for St. Louis for the purpose of confirming the order with Ashley for a new outfit for the following season.

The annual rendezvous for 1827 was held at the south end of Bear Lake in present Utah. General Ashley had sent out supplies for that year. His caravan was accompanied by a small cannon on a carriage which was drawn by two mules. That was the first wheeled vehicle to cross South Pass. The trappers were practically all assembled by July 1 and the rendezvous broke up on July 13, 1827. Jedediah Smith ar-

6 Chittenden, *op. cit.,* 310.

rived from California on July 3 and planned another trip there. On his arrival he was met by a salute fired from Ashley's cannon. He planned to meet his partners again in one or two years at the head of the Snake River.

In the four years between July 1826 and August 1830, Jackson, according to family tradition, is said to have been back to Missouri at least once. Morgan states that Jackson accompanied Bill Sublette down to the States in the late summer of 1827, and that they returned to the mountains that fall.[7] If so, that would account for the tradition.

In this connection it may be noted that on October 5, 1827, Governor John Miller of Missouri issued a commission appointing George E. Jackson as justice of the peace of the newly created township of Jackson in the County of Ste. Genevieve. David may have had something to do with it.

Under date of October 1, 1827, Wm. H. Ashley issued a quitclaim to the firm of Smith, Jackson & Sublette for the sum of a note in his favor in the amount of $7,821, which he says has since been paid. So, Jackson and Sublette had reached the settlements by that date. Their party had been encamped near Lexington about the first of October, 1827.[8]

The rendezvous of 1828 was again held at Bear Lake in July and Jackson presumably was there. Smith had not yet returned from California.

After that rendezvous Jackson accompanied or led a party north and northwest into the Flathead and Kutenai lands of present western Montana and northern Idaho. Jackson and his men probably wintered near Flathead Lake, Montana. He was still in that area in the spring of 1829 when he was joined by Jedediah Smith back via Fort Vancouver from his second disastrous trip to California.

Smith met Jackson along the Flathead River north of

---

[7] Morgan, *West of Ashley*, 169.

[8] Sublette Papers, Mo. Hist. Soc.; and Morgan, "James B. Bruffee, Statement, October 1, 1827," in *West of Ashley*, 171.

Flathead Lake. The two worked their way down to Pierre's Hole on the west side of the Tetons in present Idaho and met Sublette there about the 5th of August, 1829. A general rendezvous was held that month. The gathering seems to have lasted two weeks or more.

Jackson's movements have not been definitely worked out for the remainder of that year of 1829, but when he cannot be accounted for otherwise he was almost always somewhere in the Snake Indian country along the Snake River or in Jackson Hole. The Snake country seems to have been his favorite grounds. It was also a more central location for use as a vantage point in overseeing the work of the various parties in the field and expediting the business. Jackson joined his partners at winter quarters on Wind River, present Wyoming, just before Christmas 1829.

Immediately after January 1, 1830, Sublette set out for St. Louis while Smith and Jackson decided to spend the rest of the winter on the Powder River to the northeast of their location on Wind River. They remained in that place until the first of April. Jackson then returned to the Snake country while Smith and party trapped farther to the northwest.

Sublette reached Missouri safely and set about making preparations at once for the return journey. His party left St. Louis in April, 1830. It consisted of eighty-one men mounted on mules. He also took along ten wagons, drawn by five mules each, and two dearborns, drawn by one mule each. This was the first time that wagons were ever taken to the Rocky Mountains by way of the overland route, thus demonstrating the practicability of that mode of travel. The caravan reached the meeting place in the Wind River Valley on July 16, 1830.

Jackson arrived at the rendezvous with a good catch of beaver.

At this rendezvous the firm of Smith, Jackson & Sublette

sold out to a new group called The Rocky Mountain Fur Company. It was made up of Thomas Fitzpatrick, Milton G. Sublette, Henry Fraeb, Jean Baptiste Gervais and James Bridger. The transfer was concluded August 4, 1830.

Various reasons have been advanced for this rather sudden action on the part of the three partners. The theory has been advanced that the death of Jedediah Smith's mother may have caused him to decide that he was needed at home and that the remaining partners were more or less forced to accede to his wishes. However, Jackson had lost four immediate relatives while in the mountains. Perhaps they all wanted to go home and mail which had been brought out by Sublette influenced their decision. Judging by their subsequent plans it seems more reasonable that the controlling factor in their decision was the fact that they would now be out of debt and financially able to set themselves up as landed proprietors.

Whatever the reason, the partners set out for Missouri the same day that the final transfer of the business was made. The ten wagons were brought back with them but the two dearborns were left behind. The return trip was uneventful and the route followed was good for wheeled vehicles. The last of the caravan arrived in St. Louis on October 11, 1830.

The value of the furs brought back by this last caravan of Smith, Jackson & Sublette netted the partners $84,499.14.[9] This was their best season financially in the mountains.

The partners set about almost at once drafting a letter to the Secretary of War, the Honorable John H. Eaton, detailing the significance of their accomplishments in the mountains. This was a five page letter dated St. Louis, October 29, 1830. The letter went to some length outlining the extent of their explorations in the West, the ease with which transportation could be accomplished to the Rocky Mountains and beyond, a description of the country, and

---

[9] Morgan, *Jedediah Smith,* 323.

suggested methods for dealing with the British in the Oregon country. Its contents were deemed of such importance that it was immediately printed as a Senate Executive Document and made available to the Congress and to the public.[10]

The authorship of this letter is still in doubt. The original has not been located. It obviously is a combination of the information and experience of all three partners and they may have availed themselves of the services of someone in St. Louis close to the government in its preparation or in its final form.

That winter of 1830-31 Jedediah Smith set about preparing a map of the western regions of the United States showing all the travels and geographical discoveries of the Ashley men. It was a landmark in mapping of the American West.

David Jackson contributed information and the results of his own explorations for that map. His greatest contribution is for the Snake River drainage basin. The originals of Smith's map have been lost, but the information from his was found superimposed on a base map of Fremont's in the files of the American Geographical Society of New York by Carl I. Wheat a few years ago. The transcription work has been ascribed to George Gibbs.[11]

That map bears a notation along the middle course of the Snake River across present southern Idaho reading as follows:

> Most of what is known of this section of country has been derived from Mr. Jackson and such Partisans as have travelled through it. Apply this note to the opposite waters of Lewis river and the Owyhee River. *Smith.*

After Smith's death a eulogy was printed in the *Illinois Magazine* for June 1832. It was by an unknown writer and signed "Alton, March, 1832." That writer said in part:

---

10 *Senate Exec. Doc. 39,* 21 Cong., 2 sess., 21-23.
11 See copy of that map in Morgan and Wheat, *op. cit.,* in back pocket.

. . . convinced as Smith was, of the inaccuracy of all the maps of that country, and of the little value they would be to hunters and travellers, he has, with the assistance of his partners, Sublitt [*sic*] and Jackson, and of Mr. S. Parkman, made a new, large and beautiful map; in which are embodied all that is correct of preceding maps, the known tracts of former travellers, his own extensive travels, the situation and number of various Indian tribes, and much other valuable information. This map is now probably the best extant, of the Rocky Mountains, and the country on both sides, from the States to the Pacific. . .[12]

Although David Jackson's contribution to the Smith map has been discounted, it might be but fair to point out that Jackson had learned the rudiments of surveying under his father while still a boy. He also, like most members of his branch of the Jackson family, possessed a true sense of direction and distance and the faculty of proper perspective.

Smith's map shows a "Sublette Lake" for what is now Yellowstone Lake and a "Jackson Lake" for the body of water in Jackson Hole which still bears that name, although those two lakes are not shown in their proper position with reference to each other and Jackson Lake is shown too large in proportion.

Smith's map is the first known time that David Jackson's name was applied on a map to a feature of the landscape.

In 1839, David H. Burr, geographer to the House of Representatives in Washington, published a map of the United States of North America which embodied all the features of Smith's map and showed his discoveries. Burr's map continued the use of the name "Jackson Lake."

"Jacksons L." is also shown on the "Map of the Oregon Territory, 1841" used by Commander Charles Wilkes, and from that time on David Jackson's name on the maps of that region was secure. The name "Yellowstone" was subsequently substituted for that of "Sublette Lake."

---

[12] " Captain Jedediah Strong Smith, A Eulogy . . .," in *Illinois Magazine,* June 1832, as reprinted in Edwin L. Sabin, *Kit Carson Days* (New York, 1935 edition), 823.

At some unspecified time during his career in the mountians the name "Jackson's Hole" had come to be applied by his comrades to the beautiful valley surrounding Jackson Lake. The first written record which has survived of that name being attributed to David Jackson is that by Warren Angus Ferris in the *Western Literary Messenger* of Buffalo, New York, in its issue dated July 29, 1843. Ferris published a series of articles in that magazine entitled "Life in the Rocky Mountains" relating his experiences in the fur trade in the Rocky Mountains. In that issue Ferris states:

> On the 4th [July 1832] we crossed the mountain, and descended into a large prairie valley, called Jackson's Big Hole. It lies due east of the Trois Tetons, and is watered by Lewis River. . . The Hole is surrounded by lofty mountains, and receives its name from one of the firm of Smith, Sublett and Jackson.[13]

Ferris also drafted a map in 1835 or 1836, apparently for publication with his narrative of "Life in the Rocky Mountains." On that map the name "Yellowstone L." appears on a map for the first time and the name is substituted for that of "Sublette Lake." "Teton L." is substituted for the name "Jackson Lake," but the name "Jacksons Hole" and "Little Hole" for Jacksons Little Hole appear for the first time on any map anywhere. Unfortunately the Ferris map was not published at that time, so it escaped public attention.[14]

Jackson Hole is still known by the name first given it. The name embraces the whole valley along the eastern base of the Teton Mountains.

From that time onward the names Jackson's Big Hole (now Jackson Hole), Jackson's Little Hole, Jackson Lake, and eventually the town of Jackson, Wyoming, came into general usage. They are all memorials to David E. Jackson.

Both Jackson and Sublette must have left St. Louis imme-

---

13 Courtesy of The Grosvenor Library, Buffalo, New York.
14 See copy of the Ferris map in W. A. Ferris, *Life in the Rocky Mountains,* ed. by Paul C. Phillips (Denver, 1940), insert between xiv-xv.

diately after furnishing Smith whatever information they contributed for his map. They both had urgent business elsewhere.

Jackson was trying to establish a homestead near his brother in what is now St. Francois County, Missouri. It was directly on the old original road north from Farmington to the Valle lead mines in present Jefferson County. David's brother, George, was in active management of his affairs during his absence, but George was now seriously ill and unable to do anything. David had four or five slaves and it is assumed that they were working on this homestead part of the time. During his absence he had transferred the slaves to his brother to be in his custody and be put to whatever use he saw fit. It is probable that David's personal servant, Jim, accompanied him in the mountains the latter part of his stay there.

On March 26, 1831, George E. Jackson deeded all the real estate owned by him in Ste. Genevieve County to David E. Jackson. This consisted of a half interest in the Establishment Trace (an old Spanish Land Grant) and the homestead on which George lived. George Jackson was on his deathbed and the reason for the transfer was to be sure to save the property for the family and save costs and uncertainties of administration of his estate.

George E. Jackson died on that same day. David subsequently deeded these same properties back to George's children. Return of custody of the slaves to David had already been arranged for and was subsequently carried out.

David had been quite busy that winter arranging for a merchandising trip to Santa Fe, New Mexico, with his partners. By April 7th he was back in St. Louis and executed a power of attorney to Joseph D. Grafton of Ste. Genevieve to act in his stead in all matters pertaining to the estate of George E. Jackson. That paper was witnessed by a clerk, E. S. Minter.

By that time plans for the Santa Fe expedition must have
already been agreed upon and the merchandise purchased.
The last wagons of the partners left St. Louis on April 10,
1831. They assembled for two weeks at Lexington, Missouri,
to conclude their business and make final arrangements for
the trip.

Among the new personnel was a young man from Con-
necticut named Jonathan Trumbull Warner. He hired out
as clerk to Jedediah Smith. Smith's two brothers, Peter and
Austin, and his friend Samuel Parkman, were also along.
Mr. Minter went as clerk to Jackson and Sublette. Thomas
Fitzpatrick arrived from the mountains for his yearly supplies just as they were leaving the settlements. It was decided that he too should accompany them as far as Santa Fe
where he could be provisioned.

On setting out the caravan consisted of eighty-five men
and twenty-three mule drawn wagons. Ten of the wagons
belonged to Jackson and Sublette, eleven are credited to
Smith, one belonged to Samuel Flournoy of Independence,
and the last was the joint property of Smith, Jackson &
Sublette. It carried a small cannon which could be unlim-
bered and quickly made ready for use. Another wagon,
drawn by oxen, was the property of two men named Wells
[sometimes called Mills] and Chadwick.[15]

The caravan broke camp on May 4th, 1831, near the Big
Blue and headed out over the prairie for Santa Fe. Before
reaching the Pawnee Branch of the Arkansas a band of
several hundred Comanche and Gros Ventre Indians attempted to charge them but were driven off by the use of the
small cannon. Mr. Minter, the clerk, next fell slightly behind to hunt antelope and was surprised and killed by a
party of Pawnees on May 19th.

The leaders of the caravan decided to try what has since
become well known as the Cimarron cutoff in order to

---

[15] Morgan, *Jedediah Smith,* 326 and 434, note 42.

shorten the distance; however, that was usually a two day trip without water. Water had to be hauled in barrels for the men and mules. On this trip the wagons were heavily laden and the deep sand slowed them to a snail's pace.

On the third day the men were crazed with thirst and Smith and Fitzpatrick set out in search of water. Jackson and Sublette kept on with the wagons over what appeared to be the trail. On May 27th Smith and Fitzpatrick separated in their search. Smith reached a dry hole in the bed of the Cimarron and began to dig for water. He was surprised by a small band of hostile Comanches and killed.

That evening, the main caravan, which had kept on, encamped on the Cimarron at a place where they found some water. The next morning a large party of about fifteen hundred Blackfeet and Gros Ventres approached as if to attack them. Fortunately Sublette was able to negotiate with them and they passed on without further molestation.

The caravan continued along the Cimarron for that day and encamped. A band of Gros Ventres surrounded them before dawn, but were successfully frightened off.

The first signs of civilization were reached at the small village of San Miguel, New Mexico. The caravan continued on and entered Santa Fe, July 4, 1831.

Changes had to be made in the organization on account of the death of Smith. A new partnership was entered into by Jackson and Sublette to handle the business in the mountains formerly conducted by Smith, Jackson & Sublette. The latter duly entered their merchandise at the custom house in Santa Fe on July 8, 1831, and proceeded to dispose of it as rapidly as possible.[16]

David Waldo was living in New Mexico at the time and was engaged in the Santa Fe trade and purchasing furs. He was a long-standing acquaintance of David Jackson. Jack-

---

[16] Customs Manifest of Jackson and Sublette dated July 8, 1831, Mexican Archives of New Mexico No. 2878, State Records Center and Archives (Santa Fe),.

son learned of the lucrative possibilities of purchasing mules in California for the Missouri and southern market from one Henry Hook, a fellow member of the Masonic Order. Hook was from the same part of the country as Jackson, had just recently arrived in New Mexico from California via Guaymas, Sonora, and was convinced of the profits to be made from such a venture. Jackson had already been thinking of making a trip to California and, since this would furnish him with an opportunity, he was easily persuaded to do so.

In order to provide for the disposition of his remaining merchandise and in order to continue in business in the Santa Fe trade, which promised to be profitable, Jackson formed another partnership in which David Waldo was to attend to that part of the business.

By the latter part of August, Jackson, Sublette and Fitzpatrick had all been in Taos, New Mexico, which was the headquarters for American trappers in the Southwest. There Jackson met Ewing Young who had returned from California in April from a trapping and trading expedition the preceding year. Young had also become aware of the possibilities of the mule trade with California and, having met Captain Cooper of Monterey, had discussed it with him in San Jose during the previous year. Young must have convinced Jackson that his knowledge of the route and his fur trading experience in the Southwest would be indispensible to him. He was taken in as junior member of a temporary partnership known as Jackson, Waldo and Young for purposes of the trip. There is no evidence that Young invested any money in the partnership, but he had an interest in the outfits of some of the trappers. He was put in charge of one group of men to do the trapping along the way and meet Jackson later in California.

On August 18, 1831, in Santa Fe, Henry Hook wrote a letter of introduction for David Jackson to Captain Cooper in Monterey requesting his assistance in purchasing mules. Captain Cooper may also have belonged to the Masonic Order as Hook ends his letter "I remain yours Fraternally."[17]

On August 24, Ewing Young also wrote a letter to Captain Cooper from Taos requesting aid for Jackson in the mule buying venture.[18] The following day, August 25th, Jackson left Taos for Santa Fe, and on August 29th, he and a party of ten men planned to set out from Santa Fe for California. They did all finally get on the road by September 6th.

Jackson planned to reach California as expeditiously as possible without stopping to trap along the way. For that reason he chose the southern route by way of the Santa Rita del Cobre mines, Tucson and the Gila.

As finally composed, the party consisted of Mr. Jackson, his negro slave Jim, and nine men. One was Peter Smith, a younger brother of Jedediah, who had accompanied the caravan from Missouri. Another was probably William Waldo. It was about this time that William entered the employ of David Jackson which continued for a period of two years. He may have joined the caravan upon leaving Missouri or he could have been in New Mexico with his brother, David, and joined there. Another was Jonathan Trumbull Warner, the historian of the trip. After the death of Jedediah Smith and the arrival of the caravan in Santa Fe, Warner had found himself without employment and his health being improved he decided to continue on to California. Still another may have been Moses Carson. Job Dye lists Carson as a member of Young's group. However, in 1850 in California, Moses Carson told David Jackson's nephew that he and David "came together to this coast trapping and that (Jackson) took away 80 mule loads of furs and that he never heard from him after that." As will be

[17] The original of this letter is in the Vallejo Documents, Bancroft Library, Univ. of Calif., Berkeley.   [18] Original letter in Vallejo Documents, loc. cit.

explained later, another member may have been Antoine Leroux, at least for part of the way. At least two were said to be native guides from New Mexico. Leroux could have been classed as one of those. The remainder of the party is still anonymous.

The main authority for the overland trip to California is found in various versions of the "Reminiscences" of Jonathan Trumbull Warner.[19] These are rather confusing if read independently, but by combining them with an expert knowledge of the available routes it can be worked out satisfactorily.

The party started south down the Rio Grande by way of the old Spanish Camino Real as far as the vicinity of Valverde. Each man had a riding mule; there were seven pack mules, and what interested Warner most was the fact that five of the pack mules were loaded with Mexican silver dollars. From Valverde they took a newer route down the west side of the river. This route had been used for some time by American parties on their way to trap the Gila, to reach the Copper Mines, and even to go back and forth to the province of Sonora by way of the presidio town of Janos, Chihuahua.

Just south of Hot Springs the route left the river somewhat and bore southwest toward the Santa Rita Copper Mines. That route was later followed by General Kearny with the Army of the West in 1846.

The copper mines were still being worked by Robert McKnight and Stephen Courcier and it is probable that

---

[19] There are several versions of Warner's reminiscences in manuscript in the Bancroft Library; a printed version entitled "Reminiscences of Early California from 1831 to 1846," in *Annual Publications of the Historical Society of Southern California, 1907-1908* (Los Angeles, 1909), 176-93; and still another version, the original of which was consulted by this writer, in the Holliday Collection, Arizona Pioneers' Historical Society (Tucson). There are also some newspaper accounts.

I have also consulted Job F. Dye, "Recollections of a Pioneer of California," in the *Santa Cruz Sentinel* (California), May 1, May 8 and May 15, 1869. I have relied on Warner for the most part.

James Kirker and other former trapper friends and acquaintances were also there. The party should have reached the mines easily well before the end of September.

From there the route led southwest over the old Janos Trail as far as the Ojo de Vaca (Cow Springs) in the northwest corner of present Luna County, New Mexico. That part of the route was later followed by Colonel Philip St. George Cooke and the Mormon Battalion in 1846.

From Cow Springs to the abandoned mission of San Xavier del Bac, David Jackson's party was opening a new direct route between New Mexico and Arizona. Their route proceeded from water hole to water hole by way of Doubtful Canyon, Apache Pass, and Dragoon Wash to the San Pedro River just north of present St. David, Arizona. There they crossed the north end of the old San Pedro Ranch on the west side of the river and proceeded to the Cienega Creek and thence to the San Xavier Mission.[20] From there they reached the presidio and settlement of Tucson over the old Indian and Spanish trail from the south.

This direct route from Cow Springs to San Xavier had been traversed in sections over its complete length by various Spanish and Mexican military parties under military members of the Elias-Gonzalez family of the northern frontier of New Spain and Mexico, but it had not been traversed in its entirety on any one particular expedition on account of Indian hostility. After Jackson opened that route there is no record of its having been used again until the Frémont Association party, of which Robert Eccleston was a member with Colonel John C. "Jack" Hays as guide, passed over it

---

20 Warner is here speaking in general terms when he refers to the San Pedro Ranch. That ranch as originally constituted was a Spanish land grant which was never fully confirmed. It was first granted to Don Ygnacio Pérez of Sonora, Mexico, who also received the San Bernardino grant. Under Pérez the San Pedro Ranch extended from the plains of Cananea north along the San Pedro River to Tres Alamos.

In the period 1822-1834 under the new Mexican regime the San Pedro Ranch was broken up into several parcels and granted to various members of the Elías-Gonzalez family. One of those was a much smaller San Pedro ranch.

with minor deviations in October and early November, 1849.[21]

Jackson's party should have reached Tucson by early October, 1831. Jackson must have been one of the first American citizens to have ever seen the mission of San Xavier and the old walled pueblo of Tucson. He may have been the first.

In Tucson, Jackson made an attempt to procure a native guide from that place to the Colorado River and beyond. No one in Tucson could be found who had any knowledge of the route. A messenger was sent to the Altar district in present Sonora, as it was thought that would be a more likely place to procure a guide. None could be found there either.

It is supposed that Jackson sent some native person from Tucson to Altar to make inquiry, and it is likely that he would also have dispatched some Spanish speaking person from his own party to accompany him. In this connection it is noted that on July 22, 1852, in the vicinity of the abandoned ranch of Calabasa [Calabasas] [22] John Russell Bartlett, boundary commissioner, noted in his journal: "This Calabasa, I was told by Leroux, was a thriving establishment when he visited it twenty years ago." [23] That statement puts Antoine Leroux in that vicinity close enough to the time the Jackson party was in Tucson for Leroux to have been with him either going to or returning from California. Leroux could have remained on the Colorado or in Arizona while the rest of the party proceeded on to California. Leroux had gone up the Missouri with Ashley's men in 1822 and remained there for two years. He would certainly

---

[21] George P. Hammond and Edward H. Howes, eds., *Overland to California on the Southwestern Trail, 1849: Diary of Robert Eccleston* (Berkeley and Los Angeles, 1950).

[22] The old ranch of Calabasas here referred to was thirteen miles north of the international boundary at present Nogales, Arizona.

[23] John Russell Bartlett, *Personal Narrative of Explorations and Incidents in Texas, New Mexico, California, Sonora, and Chihuahua* (New York, 1854), Vol. II, p. 307.

have been recognized by Jackson when seeing him again in New Mexico.

It was found impossible to procure a guide while in Tucson so the party started out for the Pima Villages on the Gila. From Tucson to "the Red River of the West" [the Colorado] the route was the same as that followed in 1775 by Juan Bautista de Anza and his band of colonists en route to found the city of San Francisco.

Upon approaching the Gila River the party must have noticed off to their right what appeared to be the ruins of a large building on the horizon. Their curiosity may have been aroused enough that they detoured to visit it. This was the famed Casa Grande, visited by Father Kino and all early Spanish and Mexican explorers who traveled that route.[24]

The Gila River had been followed and trapped by bands of American trappers all the way to its junction with the Colorado, but it is unknown whether any who had been over that part of the route were along with Jackson.

The Colorado was crossed at the lower crossing six miles downstream from its junction with the Gila, and within sight of Pilot Knob. From that point onward Jackson's route deviates somewhat from that of Don Juan Bautista de Anza. The route Jackson opened was followed by Colonel Cooke with the Mormon Battalion and later by the Butterfield Overland Mail. On this section across the Colorado Desert and on to the Warner's Ranch area, Jackson was again a pathbreaker as far as Americans were involved.

---

[24] I have never noticed it pointed out in this connection, but "P. Weaver" scratched his name on the walls of Casa Grande with the date "1832." Job Dye in his *Recollections* (Los Angeles, 1951) lists a Powel Weaver as accompanying the same party as himself from Arkansas to New Mexico in 1830. Again, a Paulin de Jesus Guiver (Weaver) was baptized at Taos, New Mexico, Aug. 26, 1832, and married Maria Dolores Martin there on Sept. 10, 1832 – Fray Angélico Chávez, "New Names in New Mexico, 1820-1850," in *El Palacio* (Santa Fe), Nov., Dec., 1957, p. 379.

It is possible that Pauline Weaver was one of the members of Young's party and that on the return trip with Jackson he left his name on the walls of Casa Grande.

His party passed by way of First Wells (later Cooke's Wells), the water hole of Alamo Mocho, on past the site of Calexico, California, thence across to and up the Carrizo Creek to Vallecito and over the divide to the present Warner Valley.

Jonathan Warner was so impressed with the beautiful valley filled with majestic oaks and surrounded by lofty mountains and possessed of hot and cold running water that he remained in California; later, having procured a large grant of land including the entire valley, he came back to it and settled down. It is now the site of the famous resort of Warner's Hot Springs and of the giant size Warner Ranch.

The party continued on through the groves of oaks in the direction of Los Angeles as far as the Indian village of Temecula. There they decided to change their course for the Mission of San Luis Rey and San Diego. The Mormon Battalion later did the same.[25]

They paused at Mission San Luis Rey and proceeded on to San Diego which they reached in early November 1831. From there they retraced their steps to San Luis Rey, passed on by way of the Mission of San Juan Capistrano and reached the pueblo of Los Angeles on December 5, 1831.

Jackson was still in the Los Angeles-San Gabriel area when he dispatched a letter dated December 24, 1831, to Captain Cooper at Monterey requesting his aid in arranging up and down the coast to purchase up to one thousand mules at up to eight dollars a head, depending on quality.[26]

As soon as he could conveniently do so, Jackson started up the coast himself by way of the old Camino Real from mission site to mission site. He left Mr. Warner and one other

---

[25] The city of Temecula, California, now has a monument to the memory of "those who passed that way." Among others, the names of Cooke, Jackson and Warner are proudly inscribed. *They Passed This Way, Biographical Sketches, Tales of Historic Temecula Valley at the Crossroads of California's Southern Immigrant Trail* (Laguna House, Temecula, 1970), sponsored by Temecula Valley Chamber of Commerce. [26] Vallejo Documents, Bancroft Library.

man in Los Angeles to look after his property already acquired.

He traveled as far north "as the missions on the southern shores of the bay of San Francisco." The wording of Mr. Warner here is somewhat ambiguous. Except for that statement there is no definite evidence that Jackson actually reached as far north as San Francisco. He did visit the missions of Santa Clara and San Jose, both of which were opposite the extreme southern end of the bay. If his success in purchasing mules was only moderate, it is very likely that he proceeded on to San Francisco where he would have a double opportunity, that being the location of both a mission and a presidio. He undoubtedly stopped at Monterey on his way north to visit Captain Cooper and transact his business with him.

On the return journey the party was detained for fourteen days opposite the mission of Soledad on account of high water in the Salinas River. They were at the mission of San Miguel by February 22, 1832, and reached Los Angeles again in the latter part of March.

Here the Jackson party met up with the party of Ewing Young which had arrived in the pueblo about the same time. The combined forces rendezvoused at the Sierra Ranch on the Santa Ana river. They had about six hundred mules and one hundred horses out of the thousand or more that had been anticipated. They set out for the Colorado River in May and reached it in June over the same route used in going to California.

When they arrived at the Colorado they found the river in flood and nearly bank full. They experienced considerable difficulty and it took twelve days to get all the animals and men across the river at the lower crossing below Yuma.

Here Jackson gave Young three thousand dollars in cash to purchase additional mules and follow him later; Young also received a large outfit of arms, ammunition, tobacco, steel traps, etc. (said to be valued at around seven thousand dollars), belonging jointly to Jackson, Waldo and Young. Young and five men, including Jonathan Warner, Job F. Dye and Moses Carson, then returned to Los Angeles.

Six and one-half bales of skins were turned over to Jackson. With these Jackson and the remainder of the combined Jackson and Young parties set out on their return journey to New Mexico over the same route used by Jackson on the outward trip. It was during the month of June, the weather was hottest of the season and water was scarce. Several mules are said to have been lost on account of the heat. Lieutenant Colonel Philip St. George Cooke with the Mormon Battalion, writing in his journal fourteen and a half years later on the evening of December 20, 1846, at a point sixty-two miles from Tucson and ten from the Gila River said:

> . . . but on the other hand it is said to have been an extraordinary drought here for several years. A Mr. Jackson once lost many of a small drove of mules he took through in an imprudent manner in July.[27]

It should be noted that at least two men thought to have been with Jackson were with Cooke as guides, Antoine Leroux and Pauline Weaver. That may be one of the reasons Cooke was guided over the same identical route.

Jackson's party continued on in spite of the heat and lack of water and reached Santa Fe the first week of July, 1832, with a large part of their herd and the six and one-half bales of beaver skins. The mules were probably held in the vicinity of Santa Fe while the bales of beaver skins were said to have been concealed temporarily in a hiding place near there. Information to that effect was given to the authorities about July 12, 1832, by one Manuel Leal who seems to have been one of those who returned with Jackson.[28]

---

[27] Ralph P. Bieber, ed., "Cooke's Journal of the March of the Mormon Battalion, 1846-1847," in *Exploring Southwest Trails, 1846-1854* (Glendale, Calif., 1938), 166.

[28] Statement of Francisco Rascon(?), Santa Fe, July 12, 1832, Mexican Archives of New Mexico, 3209, State Records Center and Archives.

This action aroused suspicion on the part of the New Mexican authorities. As a result several very confidential statements were taken from various natives in regard to the movements of Yaqueson, Baldo & Juiaquin Yon [Jackson, Waldo and Young] and the extent and value of their cargo.[29] The trouble with the authorities was evidently worked out satisfactorily in some manner.

Jackson and Waldo had some commercial dealings with Alexander LeGrand in the summer of 1831. In the late fall of 1831 a newcomer had arrived in New Mexico. His name was Albert Pike, late from New England. He was still in New Mexico in July 1832, when Jackson's party arrived there. LeGrand seems to have exerted some influence on the immediate future destination of both Jackson and Pike.[30]

If he ever seriously entertained the idea in the first place, Jackson abandoned the plan of driving his mules through Texas to Louisiana. While it was still summer, Jackson apparently started back in the direction of Missouri with that part of his livestock which had not been disposed of in New Mexico. Young Ira G. Smith, Jedediah's younger brother, had arrived in Santa Fe in the summer to meet his brother Peter. Peter had forty-five mules left from his share in the California venture. Ira was delegated to conduct these mules to Missouri.[31] It is assumed that he was a member of the Jackson party.

Somewhere along the route, probably along the Arkansas, Jackson must have sent some of his mules on to Missouri and directed some to the Cherokee lands. He was at Fort Gibson by the fall of 1832, supposedly at the same time that

[29] Statements relating to the embargo of the furs of Juiaquin Yon (Ewing Young), Santa Fe, July 12-25, 1832, Mexican Archives of New Mexico, 3209. Courtesy of Dr. Myra Ellen Jenkins.

[30] Since both Jackson and Pike were headed for the same destination upon leaving New Mexico that summer, I have never been able to understand why Pike did not accompany Jackson's party.

[31] Stella D. Hare, "Jedediah Smith's Younger Brother, Ira," in *The Pacific Historian* (Stockton, Calif.), vol. 11, no. 3, Summer 1967, p. 44.

Washington Irving was there.[32] It is possible that some mules were being held elsewhere, or Jackson could have sent for more from New Mexico.

David Jackson's movements are difficult to reconstruct for the next year. On February 22, 1833, he was back in Ste. Genevieve where on that day he deeded the George E. Jackson homestead back to George's son, Edward G. Jackson. A month later, on March 20, 1833, Jackson was in St. Louis where he and William L. Sublette settled their old accounts.[33]

Jackson's health had been poor ever since he had left Santa Fe and he wanted to return there or to the mountains at the first opportunity. He always planned to return at least to the Santa Fe trade personally, and he nursed a secret desire to settle in California at some future time. He had money invested in the Santa Fe trade with David Waldo, and continued to do so up until the time of his death.

In the meantime William Waldo had been tending a great number of mules for Jackson somewhere in the area of the Cherokee lands. Jackson was somewhere in Tennessee and adjoining territory. In the fall of 1833 Jackson sent his son, W. P. Jackson, across from Memphis, Tennessee, to Fort Smith-Van Buren, Arkansas, area where Waldo had been holding about two hundred animals for him. The son crossed 133 mules to one hundred miles beyond Memphis and had sold some in Arkansas.[34]

For the next four years Jackson's movements were dictated more by the state of his health than his wishes. He had

[32] For Irving's visit to Fort Gibson see Washington Irving, "A Tour on the Prairies," in *The Crayon Miscellany* (New York, 1835, and subsequent editions).

[33] David E. Jackson's Receipt for Accounts Settled, March 20, 1833, Sublette Papers (Mo. Hist. Soc.).

[34] It must have been as a result of this employment with Jackson that William Waldo met his future wife. He married Elizabeth Ely Vaill, daughter of a missionary to the Osage, at Union Mission, about 25 miles from Fort Gibson, Jan. 23, 1834. See "Introduction," p. 60, in Waldo's *Recollections of a Septuagenarian* (1938 reprint).

money invested in Tennessee and the South, proved up on his homestead in Missouri, invested money in lead mines at Rundlettsville in the Virginia Mines district in Union County, Missouri, and was planning on active participation in the Santa Fe trade and another trip to California the moment his health permitted. In the spring of 1834 he had definitely expected to start for Santa Fe or the mountains again. In the late fall of 1835 he was planning to go to the California coast in the spring of 1836 and take one of his sons along. Poor health intervened in both projects. Jackson never saw or heard from Ewing Young again after leaving him on "the Red River of the West." One of the reasons for his interest in a California trip was probably to force a settlement with Young.

As a result of the order issued by President Jackson in the summer of 1836 forbidding the treasury to accept anything but gold or silver in payment for further sales of public lands, there was a tightening of credit already being felt in the western areas where David Jackson had his investments. The result was the financial panic of 1837 which swept the country.

In January 1837, Jackson went to the Paris, Tennessee, area to attempt to make some collections on outstanding investments which he had made with citizens there. He arrived at the home of one of his partners just at the time they were all down with typhoid fever. He contracted the disease himself and was forced to put up at a tavern in Paris. In the meantime Jackson's creditors in his mining ventures were being sued by their own creditors. They in turn instituted suits against Jackson in order to get money to pay off their own suits. However, Jackson was unable to attend to any business on account of his physical condition. His son, W. P. Jackson, was dying in Missouri that same year.

Due to his weakened condition and his chronic poor health Jackson was unable to throw off the typhoid fever.

He lingered for eleven months during which time he was unable to do anything. He died from the effects of that illness at Paris, Tennessee, on December 24, 1837.[35]

An attempt was made to settle Jackson's estate at various times in four different states without any apparent references to each other. The settlement of his affairs was also dragged over a period of several years in at least three different places in Missouri.

At the June 1846 ('45), term of the Clackamas County Court in Oregon, Daniel Waldo in behalf of his brother David Waldo, brought suit against the administrator of the estate of Ewing Young for a settlement of the amount owed by Young to Jackson and Waldo. That court found that the deceased was one of the partners of the plaintiff and that the estate was indebted to the plaintiff, but in an amount uncertain. The court then appointed the presiding judge of the court to examine the books and papers of the plaintiff and ascertain the amount due said plaintiff.[36]

At a subsequent meeting of the court (apparently in August, 1846) a report was submitted "stating that there appeared to be due from said estate to the plaintiff the sum of four thousand three hundred and Eighty dollars fifty Eight cents."

The Court proceeded to rule as follows:

> It is therefore considered by the Court that the said plaintiff recover of and from the Administrator of the Estate of Ewing Young the sum of four thousand three hundred and Eighty dollars and fifty Eight cents, together with his costs in this behalf laid out and expended.[37]

The Provisional Government of Oregon had been organized to take charge of Young's estate. They controlled

---

[35] I have been told by genealogists that there was no typhoid epidemic in that part of the South at the time and therefore Jackson could not have had that disease. Nevertheless, that was diagnosed as the cause of his death.

[36] Case of David Waldo vs. Administrator of the Estate of Ewing Young, Clackamas County Court Records, p. 17 (State Archives Center, Salem, Ore.).

[37] *Ibid.*, 20.

the money and property of the estate and had been instrumental in appointing the administrator. Daniel Waldo then petitioned the legislature of Oregon in behalf of his brother David and Thomas Jeffreys his attorney, for payment of the above judgment against the estate of Ewing Young.

The legislature failed to take any positive action even though suit was brought for settlement in the supreme court of the territory. The supreme court delayed a decision. The remaining money from the estate had been used to construct a jail and was no longer available. The court decided that the claim was not properly presented, or at least they were so advised. The Mexican War was now imminent and David Waldo had been appointed a captain in Colonel Doniphan's Missouri Regiment. As a result the claim was never brought to a definite conclusion in the Oregon courts.[38]

David E. Jackson's contributions have thus far gone unrecognized mostly because they were the result of joint efforts of his partners and partly because his individual accomplishments have been unknown and he has had no champion to plead his cause.

However, through the joint efforts of all, the Southern Pass through the Rockies was first identified correctly and crossed, a wheeled vehicle crossed the continental divide for the first time, wagons were first used on the Oregon Trail as far as the continental divide, Americans reached the Pacific coast overland, the whole country was explored from the Canadian to the present Mexican border throughout the Rocky Mountains, the first map was made which showed the correct drainage pattern in the Rocky Mountains, and the Oregon country was saved for the Union.

Individually, Jackson first opened the direct route from New Mexico to Arizona through the Apache country; he

---

[38] See F. G. Young, "Ewing Young and his Estate," in *Oregon Historical Society Quarterly*, XXI, no. 3, September 1920, and compare with original documents in Oregon State Archives (Salem).

laid out the best watered course across the Colorado desert which was later followed by the Army of the West, the Mormon Battalion, used by the Butterfield Overland Mail and by the '49ers who came that way. He took Jonathan Trumbull Warner to California and first showed him the Warner Ranch country and lastly he unwittingly provided the money to set up the first organized government in Oregon.

Of all the memorials to the Rocky Mountain fur traders, that to David E. Jackson is the most sublime. Jackson Hole, "the crossroads of the fur trade," and Jackson Lake, both lying at the eastern base of the Teton Range in Wyoming, have together been called one of the most beautiful areas in nature. (Along with the Vale of Kashmir, Jackson Hole has been listed as one of the seven most beautiful spots in the known world.) A great part of it is still in its primeval state. Jackson's passing went unnoticed except by members of his immediate family, but his memorial lives on.

William Kittson

by GLORIA GRIFFEN CLINE
Bray, Ireland

Like so many fur traders, little is known about the early life of William Kittson of North West and Hudson's Bay company fame. At an early age he was adopted by George Kittson of Sorel, Quebec, and as a young man served on the British side during the War of 1812.[1] When he was in his twenties,[2] in 1817, Kittson became an apprentice clerk to the North West Company and soon moved west of the mountains where he served in 1819 under Alexander Ross at Fort Nez Percés (Walla Walla). At this time Fort Nez Percés was the rendezvous center for the interior trade from which point Donald Mackenzie led a brigade each year south and westward. Mackenzie was short of men, horses and goods on his second Snake Country Expedition so Ross dispatched Kittson and a small party with supplies which intercepted Mackenzie on the Boise River. Then later Kittson collected Mackenzie's furs and returned with them to Fort Nez Percés on July 7, 1819.[3]

Unfortunately little is known about Kittson and Mackenzie as they explored virgin territory for, as Ross said, "Mackenzie detested spending five minutes scribbling in a journal. His traveling notes were often kept on a beaver skin written hieroglyphically with a pencil or a piece of coal;

---

[1] R. Harvey Fleming, ed., *Minutes of Council Northern Department of Rupert Land, 1821-31* (London, 1940), Appendix, 443.

[2] When Governor Simpson wrote in 1832 about Kittson in his Character Book, he placed his age at "about forty years. . ." However, Simpson had a tendency of making people older than they really were. A.34/2, Hudson's Bay Company's Archives, hereafter referred to as H.B.C.A.

[3] Burt Brown Barker's Introduction to *Ogden's Snake Country Journals, 1824-25* (London, 1950).

and he would often complain of the drudgery of keeping accounts." [4] However, it seems that Mackenzie realized the importance of what he was doing in the Columbia and Snake river regions for in a letter written July 30, 1822, he indicated that the height of his ambition was to end his "days in a snug cottage at some healthy situation with my book, my pen, my horse, my dog, my fishing rod and my gun and give the world a full narrative of the fur trade." [5] Unfortunately this priceless narrative never saw printer's ink for as Mackenzie labored over his work, his wife, feeling that his literary efforts were impairing his health, burned his manuscript. Perhaps it was this early experience that convinced Kittson that a journal was of great importance and turned him into an excellent diarist.

After this sojourn with Mackenzie which reached Nez Percés on June 22, 1820, Kittson was assigned to Spokane House, a pleasant posting for there were "no females in the land so fair to look upon as the nymphs of Spokane." [6] While Kittson was at Spokane, the life and death struggle between the North West and Hudson's Bay companies reached its peak and culminated in 1821 with the merger of the two organizations under the name of the Hudson's Bay Company. Kittson was more fortunate than Peter Skene Ogden, Samuel Black and Cuthbert Grant for he made the transition into the new company easily and his name appeared on the list of clerks compiled by Nicholas Garry in 1821.

With the development of the Columbia by the Hudson's Bay Company, the North West Company's Snake Country Expedition was retained and gained a position of importance. In 1824 the able Peter Skene Ogden was chosen as the leader of this brigade and Kittson who was assigned to assist

---

[4] Alexander Ross, *The Fur Hunters of the Far West: A Narrative of Adventures in the Oregon and Rocky Mountains,* 2 vols. (London, 1855), I, p. 283.

[5] T. C. Elliott Collection, Oregon Historical Society, Portland, Oregon.

[6] Ross, *op. cit.,* I, pp. 138-39.

him arrived at the Flathead Post (this year's outfitting center) from "Kootenais" on December 11, 1824.[7] The Snake Country Expedition of 1824-25 was considered "the most formidable party that has ever set out for the Snakes"[8] and was comprised of 58 men equipped with 61 guns, 268 horses, and 352 traps[9] in anticipation of a year's hunt. This, Ogden's first Snake country command, was one to tax even the most efficient leader in the field for with Governor Simpson's new organization of the Columbia Department, he was ordered to live "off the land" rather than to rely upon European goods. Therefore, he was not only to discover a route that would produce the necessities of life, but to find streams with rich preserves of beaver. This was not always easy, as Alexander Ross pointed out: "It is indeed Shameful that no Correct Journal of the Snake Country has ever yet appeared to point out where Beaver are and where beaver are not. Much time is lost in Wandering through these parts on that account."[10]

Ogden was instructed to proceed "direct for the heart of the Snake Country towards the Banks of the Spanish River or Rio Colorado pass the Winter & Spring there and hunt their way out by the Umpqua and the Wilhamet Rivers to Fort George next summer sufficiently early to send the returns home by the Ship."[11] These initial instructions to hunt toward the banks of the Rio Colorado were based upon an incorrect conjecture by earlier Snake country leaders that the Colorado was an extension of the Bear River, which had been explored only in its upper courses, and the instructions

---

[7] Alexander Ross, Flathead Post Journal, B.69/a/1, H.B.C.A.

[8] T. C. Elliott, ed., "Journal of Alexander Ross," in *Oregon Historical Quarterly*, XIV, p. 388.

[9] E. E. Rich, ed., *Peter Skene Ogden's Snake Country Journals, 1824-25 and 1826-26* (London, 1950), 2-3.

[10] Letter, Alexander Ross to Peter Skene Ogden, October 14, 1824, B.202/a/1, H.B.C.A.

[11] Frederick Merk, ed., "Snake Country Expedition, 1824-25," in *Oregon Historical Quarterly*, XXXV, p. 99.

for the homeward journey were based upon the assumption that the Umpqua and Willamette rivers had their sources not far to the west of Bear River Valley. This geographical conception is clearly depicted on the map that Kittson drew during the course of this expedition on which he stated: "Bear River with all its branches enters the Pacific about 1 mile of Fort George, South side. The lower part of the above river was never visited either by us or Americans, although the latter said it was known to be rich. Their informers are the Utaws." [12]

It is not difficult to understand why the members of the Snake Expedition which left Flathead Post on December 20, 1824, did not develop a more accurate picture of the terrain which they traversed for they traveled through the modern states of Montana, Idaho, and Utah, a region hydrographically complicated. Within a relatively small area, not clearly defined by mountain barriers, streams rise which flow into the Pacific by way of the Columbia, into the Gulf of Mexico by way of the Missouri, and into the Great Basin directly by the Weber River or circuitiously by way of the Bear River. [13]

Unfortunately Ogden's first Snake Country Expedition was not able to solve these geographical problems that caused active speculation in cartographic and fur trading circles, because of the Johnson Gardner incident [14] in which Ogden lost twenty-three of his men. With the desertion of these free trappers to Americans, Ogden's much curtailed party was forced to confine its exploration and on July 16, 1825, he sent Kittson ". . . homewards with Joseph Pin

[12] The Kittson map, B.202/a/3b, H.B.C.A. has been reprinted in Rich, ed., *Ogden's Journals, 1824-26.*

[13] Gloria Griffen Cline, *Exploring the Great Basin* (Norman, Okla., 1963), 148; C. Gregory Crampton & Gloria Griffen (Cline) "The San Buenaventura, Mythical River of the West," in *Pacific Historical Review*, XXV, pp. 163-71.

[14] See David E. Miller, "Peter Skene Ogden's Explorations in the Great Salt Lake Region: A Restudy based on Newly Published Journals," in *Western Humanities Review*, VIII, pp. 139-50.

and Joachim Hubert, having . . . the charge of 18 horses loaded with Furs." [15]

Although this first Ogden Snake Country Expedition wasn't considered a great financial success from the Hudson's Bay Company's point of view, from it came some of the most brilliant and important pieces of Western Americana. Both Ogden and William Kittson kept articulate diaries,[16] which were the first literary descriptions of much of the trans-Mississippi West. Each reflects its author. Ogden, writing as the leader of the brigade, wrote his journal with the knowledge that it would eventually be assimilated in official circles in Fenchurch Street, London; but even so, he couldn't refrain from adding philosophical speculations which were so much a part of his personality. Kittson, as an unofficial observer with a more pedestrian mind, could write a fuller and more detailed account about general camp life and every day activities on the trail. The results are that each diary complements the other greatly. Also, Kittson's interest in detail is very well portrayed on his remarkable map [17] which depicts very accurately the streams and mountains of what is now northern Utah.[18]

With the end of Ogden's first Snake Country Expedition at Fort Nez Percés in 1825, Kittson was now disassociated from this brigade and was assigned to the Kootenay Post, where he was to act as clerk from 1826-29 and then as manager from 1831-34. He was qualified for this posting which lasted almost nine years and was only interrupted by his 1830-31 service in charge of Flathead Post, for as Governor Simpson had said, he was ". . . a short, dapper little fellow of very limited Education, but exceedingly active

[15] E. E. Rich, ed., *McLoughlin's Fort Vancouver Letters, First Series, 1825-38* (London, 1941), 27, fn. 4.

[16] These diaries are published in Rich, ed., *Ogden's Journals, 1824-26:* Ogden's, 1-205; Kittson's Appendix A, 209-250.   [17] Included in *ibid.,* end pocket.

[18] David E. Miller, ed., "William Kittson's Journal Covering Peter Skene Ogden's 1824-25 Snake Country Expedition," in *Utah Historical Quarterly,* XXII, pp. 125-42.

and ambitious to signalize himself. Speaks Coutonais and has a smattering of several other Languages spoken of the West of the Mountains. Conducts the business of his Post very well. . ." [19]

With such laudatory praise in Governor Simpson's terse prose, in 1834 Kittson was given the difficult management of the farming, stock raising and fur trading operations at Fort Nisqually.[20] This enterprise became even more cumbersome in 1839 after the formation of the Hudson's Bay Company's satellite, the Puget's Sound Agricultural Company, the outgrowth of British, American, and Russion relations during the 1830s.[21] The "zealous co-operation" of Kittson at Nisqually attempting to induce the reluctant Indians to trade at his post as well as to fertilize his fields to develop agricultural production [22] was more than Kittson's weakening health could withstand, so in October 1840, he was forced to retire to Fort Vancouver, where he died on Christmas Day, 1841.[23] The capable man whom Governor Simpson said could face "anything in the shape of danger" [24] was survived by his widow, Helen,[25] three sons and a daughter. He must be remembered as one of the first articulate geographers in the field who bequeathed to North America an important map and journal of much of that region's previously unexplored areas.

---

[19] Governor Simpson's Character Book, A.34/2, H.B.C.A.

[20] Fort Nisqually Papers, Huntington Library, San Marino, California; "Fort Nisqually, Washington, Journal of Occurrences," May 30, 1833-1859, Lilly Library, Bloomington, Indiana.

[21] See John S. Galbraith, *The Hudson's Bay Company as an Imperial Factor, 1821-1869* (Berkeley & Los Angeles, 1957), 197-99.

[22] James Douglas to the Governor, Deputy Governor and Committee, Fort Vancouver, October 18, 1838, and *ibid.*, October 14, 1839, as quoted in Rich, ed., *McLoughlin's Fort Vancouver Letters, Second Series, 1839-44* (London, 1943), Appendix A, 263 and 277.

[23] "William Kittson," in Fleming, ed., *Minutes of Council, Northern Department,* 443.   [24] Governor Simpson's Character Book, A.34/2, H.B.C.A.

[25] She became the second wife of Richard Grant, see: "Richard Grant," in Fleming, ed., *Minutes of Council, Northern Department,* 442.

Charles McKay

by JOHN C. JACKSON
Portland, Oregon

Charles McKay came to the Rocky Mountain fur trade in the employ of the Hudson's Bay Company. For ten years he was one of that breed of Canadian fur traders who, predating the American Mountain Men, could reckon their participation in the great skin game not by years but by generations. Grown accustomed to life in the wilderness, skilled in that backwoods diplomacy that allowed a handful of men to dominate a hostile environment, they were traders and canoe men and found it difficult when the time came to make a transition to the rough business of trapping for beaver.

Charles McKay was born in either Fair or Dulvighouse, small villages on the north coast of Sutherlandshire, Scotland, about 1798, and entered the service of the Hudson's Bay Company in 1816 at the age of eighteen.[1] Highlanders were suffering cruel clearances that drove tenant crofters from their homes as large acreages were converted to more profitable sheep raising. Refugees crowded the coastal cities and dispossessed young men were ready subjects for the recruiting inducements of the fur companies' agents. The northerners made ideal servants, stolid and dependable and natural boatmen. Among the numerous Scots in the fur trade the Clan McKay is represented throughout the literature, and various men bearing that name participated in significant events of North American history.[2]

---

[1] H.B.C. Arch. B. 239/g/65; A. 32/41, fo. 125; A. 16/15, fo. 165. Published by permission of the Hudson's Bay Company.

[2] There was another Charles McKay, the third generation son of the fur trade who came to the Oregon country from the Red River in 1841 as a member of the

Coming through the shipping depot at York Factory on the western shore of Hudson's Bay, young Charles entered the trade at the height of the rivalry between the English based Hudson's Bay Company and the Canadian oriented North West Company. By 1822 he is listed in the Register of Persons Employed by the Hudson's Bay Company in North America in the company's northern department.[3] This service was far enough west for him to gain a command of the Blackfoot language and to qualify as an interpreter. In 1824 he was sent from Fort Edmonton on the Saskatchewan River to join the combined parties of Sir George Simpson, governor of the company's affairs, and John McLoughlin, newly appointed to head the Columbia Department. McKay met them on the Athabaska River and crossed the Rockies over a long portage to the Columbia.

He was entering into a new field of service and a method of acquiring furs unusual for his company. Horses replaced the canoe for transportation and the traders must learn to live off the country. Hudson's Bay men generally operated from more or less fixed posts depending upon the efforts of native trappers and hunters. Growing competition from

Puget Sound Agricultural Company emigrant party. He became active in early Oregon history and has often been confused with Charles McKay of Fair. There appears to be no direct connection between the two. Still another Charles McKay, an American, was involved in the Pig War controversy in the San Juan Islands of Washington.

    [3] Duplicate register of persons employed by the Hudson's Bay Company in North America, 1821-24, Archives MS, Provincial Archives, Victoria, B.C. Also H.B.C. Arch. B.125/a/1, passim; B.60/e/3, fo.4; B.60/a/17; A.16/15, fo.165; A.16/38, fo. 241. Published by permission of the Hudson's Bay Record Society. McKay wintered at Merry's Lake (present Sharpe Lake, Manitoba) in 1817-18 and from 1818 at Edmonton House, Saskatchewan River. In his Edmonton District Report for 1818-19 Francis Heron noted: ". . . Charles McKay is sober and obedient, and on account of his having a little education I have sent him out with the Slave Indians to learn their language, so that he may become an interpreter. . ." McKay continued to be employed in the Edmonton District until summer 1822 when he was attached to the Bow River Expedition, the company's early attempt to offset American pressure from the south. He entered into contract for a further two years service at the Forks of the Bow River and Red Deer's River on October 10, 1822.

American trappers in the jointly occupied Oregon country forced the western effort into actual trapping. Since the days of the Astorians and their successors, the North West Company, expeditions had been sent into the 109,000 square mile drainage of the Snake River. In spite of a wealth of furs available, these expeditions had never been profitable. Governor Simpson came west to put the operation on a sound basis. He proposed to do this by a combination of price fixing, economy of operation and aggressive leadership. Unfortunately he failed to see that success was dependent upon the dubious loyalties of the western freemen who were to do the trapping, a raffish collection of alienated half-breeds and dispossessed Iroquois caught in debt peonage to the company and ruthlessly exploited.

At the Jasper House rest stop of the mountain portage, Charles encountered another of the McKays, McLoughlin's step-son Tom, who had been in the west since the death of his father, Alexander McKay, on the "Tonquin." They traveled together by batteau down the roaring Columbia to the Colville post, and overland to famed Spokane House. Charles McKay went east to join the expedition gathering under Peter Skene Ogden at Flathead House on Clark's Fork near present Eddy, Montana. Alexander Ross only a few days returned from his own rather unsuccessful venture into the interior, mentions working with McKay to equip the new brigade. McKay and Francois Rivet, Ogden's step father-in-law, were to be the interpreters. Old hand William Kittson was second in command to Ogden and there were nine other employed servants. The rest would be freemen trapping under agreement to sell their catch to the company.

On the twelfth of December 1824, Ogden's first Snake Country Brigade left the meager facilities of the Flathead Post for the pleasures of a winter in the mountains. The company more resembled an Indian village on the move than a business venture. The forty-six freemen were accompanied by their Indian families, thirty women and thirty-five children. There were twenty-two lodges and a horse herd soon to evaporate. For the leader his command had all the advantages of a small community of misfits. His freemen were given to excusing empty traps with the explanation that "the beaver were very shy." [4] They were addicted to the sport of buffalo running, would kill thirty, bring back the meat of three after driving the rest out of the country, and become lost in the process. The brigade lost horses because the trappers would not watch their property. First it was the traditionally friendly Nez Perce but soon twenty-six animals disappeared into the Blackfoot appetite and later another twenty. One of the horse guards in an unaccustomed fit of alertness mistook one of the precious beasts remaining for a wolf and shot it. Marital differences in the lodge of Louis Kanitagen, an Iroquois, were resolved by the accidental discharge of his gun in the hands of his wife. A disinterested bystander testified it was all a regrettable accident, and then moved in with the widow. [5]

On the headwaters of the Salmon they felt the winter. McKay, scouting three days march ahead, found the snow four feet deep and no grass. They were trapped in the Lemhi valley for seven weeks before breaking out into the Snake drainage.

The brigade had been accompanied from Flathead Post by a party of seven Americans – Jedediah Smith, William Sublette and five companions – who had had the audacity to return to the center of Hudson's Bay Company operations with Ross. [6] They had observed the company acquiring 1,183 beaver, assorted other skins and 11,072 pounds of

---

[4] E. E. Rich and A. M. Johnson (eds.), *Peter Skene Ogden's Snake Country Journals, 1824-25 and 1825-26* (London, 1950). Ogden's Journal is the official daily record of the incidents related here and is supported by the matching personal journal of William Kittson. [5] *Ibid.*, 216 (Kittson's Journal).

[6] Dale L. Morgan, *Jedediah Smith and the Opening of the West* (Lincoln, Nebr., 1953), 130.

dried buffalo meat in winter trade with the northern tribes, all without risking a hair, noted company prices, and traveled with Ogden for mutual protection. They drifted off after trading furs for ammunition but the two parties were never completely out of contact.

By the 8th of April Ogden's tribe had crossed the Snake and scattered to trap. Two men out checking traps on a raft had to jump and swim for it when the Blackfeet struck. Payette limped in naked having abandoned all and swum the river. Gervais was still out and Benoit unaccounted for. Kittson and McKay mustering twenty reluctant freemen set out to collect the scattered brood. They saw forty or so Bloods top a rise and go into the bushes along the river. The interpreter went forward to parley. All narrowed eyes and rifle muzzles in the brush the Bloods were innocent of everything. They also held the cover and great tactical advantage. Encouraged by the apparent success of diplomacy the freemen grew courageous and started to cock their guns. Kittson and McKay were between the two parties, certain dead men. As Kittson rushed back to quiet the danger Charles McKay had a lonely moment to reflect on the rewards of being a fur hunter. They beat a careful retreat. Benoit was found the next day, shot, stabbed, mutilated and stripped. Poetically they buried him in a beaver dam.

As they descended the Bear River, McKay climbed a high mountain and looking to the west saw a large body of water. Kittson records this sighting of the Great Salt Lake on the 12th of May. Ogden mentions it in his letter of July 10, 1825, and again in a letter July 1, 1826. While possibly not the first sighting by white men, McKay's discovery is perhaps the first documented record of this major piece of geography.[7]

[7] Frederick Merk (ed.), "The Snake Country Expedition Correspondence," in *Mississippi Valley Historical Review*, xxi (June 1934); and Merk, "Snake Country Expedition, 1824-25, An Episode of Fur Trade and Empire," in *Quarterly, Oregon Historical Society*, xxxv (June 1934). Both of these essays have been collected in Merk's *The Oregon Question* (Cambridge, Mass., 1967).

In camp along the Weber River on the 22nd of May, the brigade encountered an early fourth of July in the person of Johnson Gardner and twenty-six Americans complete with flag, who rode in to demand the foreigners leave American soil and American beaver. Although both parties were unknowingly on Spanish domain well below the 42nd parallel, Johnson delivered a patriotic address for the day, touching on individual liberty, the forgiveness of debt and national sovereignty. He introduced the free enterprise system by offering several times the company price for beaver and goods low in proportion. Ogden's brigade dissolved in the time it took to fold up a lodge, as eleven freemen taking seven hundred furs deserted. He could only try to collect his debts before the motley crew escaped. There was a lot of verbal abuse as only rough men can deliver it and a bit of a scuffle. Kittson and McKay under the guns of the Americans stood fast among the descending tents. Once again in two months time McKay found himself looking down a hostile muzzle. That evening he was sent over to the American camp to recover a loaned horse. John Grey, a spokesman among the deserters, threatened to shoot him but lost his nerve in eye to eye confrontation. When the desertions were over Ogden had lost twenty-three of his trappers and most of their furs.

The Snake Brigade, cleaned out and humiliated, retreated north with Kittson and McKay as rear guards. With only twenty men left they were now too few in number to operate with any safety. They crawled north through country swarming with Piegans, Bloods, and Gros Ventres. News came in of a large party of Blackfeet approaching and McKay went out to confront 150 tribesmen. Happily the band was accompanied by three old Edmonton men, Hugh Monroe, Picard and James Bird Jr., and turned into something of a reunion. From this camp on "the East Fork of the Missouri" Ogden took the opportunity to send back a letter. Four months later Picard delivered it to the factor at Edmonton.

Still retreating north Ogden caught some horse thieves, gave them a drubbing and clipped their ears. Later he sent McKay to the Indian camp to bring back a stolen horse but, while the interpreter was negotiating among the chiefs, someone stole his horse. The thieves whom Ogden had punished came into camp vowing revenge in kind. Warned McKay slipped away in the night, his ears intact.

With Kittson sent back to Spokane House, McKay assumed a place of greater responsibility until the 26th of September, when Ogden turned south toward Fort Nez Perce on the Columbia. He dispatched McKay and Joachin Hubert with four horses, all he could spare, to take up cached furs and return to Flathead Post. John Work notes in his Flathead Journal that the two were coming in and he had sent them a little tobacco.[8] By the 14th of December the two had reached the post with seventeen packs of furs and the portions of two others. McKay had hired some freemen to help transport them.

He spent the first month and a half of 1826 at this miserable collection of six huts linked together under one cover. Food was a problem. On a meat trading expedition to the Flathead camps he found the Indians starving and little meat to bring home. However, the foraging party obtained the skin of a mountain ram, horns and all, for stuffing, under the theory that if you couldn't eat it at least you could see what you were missing. By the middle of February everyone was eager to get out. McKay scouted the frozen river but found it clogged with ice and closed to any boat traffic. It wasn't until the 24th of March that the Flathead furs could be brought out to meet the downriver canoe brigade. With the Flatheads and Blackfeet warring behind him McKay

---

8 T. C. Elliott (ed.), "The Journal of John Work, November and December 1825," *Washington Historical Quarterly,* III (July 1912), p. 189.

struggled through snow three feet deep to lead out a gaunt
pack string. He pottered around Spokane House until the
upriver express for the mountains arrived under the leadership of John McLeod and James Birnie. By now he had
enough of the Snake country and took this opportunity to get
out. He reflected the feelings of Finan McDonald who
wrote his often quoted analysis of the mountains in 1823:
"I got Safe home from the Snake Cuntre thank God and
when that Cuntre will see me agane the Beaver will have
Gould Skin." [9]

In one boat with eight men the express struggled up the
Columbia against floating ice.[10] From the Boat Encampment they pushed on snowshoes through deep snow to Jasper
House, picked up McLeod's family which had wintered
there, and traveled by horse down the east slope to Fort
Edmonton by the 17th of May. Accompanying the flotilla
of the spring brigade down the Saskatchewan, across the
northern end of Lake Winnipeg and the ladder of rivers
descending to the bay, Charles McKay reached York Factory in July. The company ship "Prince of Wales" arrived
on September 7. When it sailed thirteen days later McKay
was on it, his ten years in the wilderness at an end. He had
experienced two winters in the Snake country, had seen the
business end of other people's guns and learned the fallacy
of chasing beaver for a living. He passes from the records
of the great company to a highland hearthside, a peat fire
and yarns of the mountains.[11]

---

[9] E. E. Rich and R. Harvey Fleming (eds.), *Minutes of Council Northern Department of Rupert Land, 1821-31* (Toronto, Champlain Society, and London, Hudson's
Bay Record Society, 1940), p. 53n.

[10] Sanford Fleming, "Expeditions to the Pacific," in *Proceedings, Royal Society of
Canada,* VII (1889), p. 114.

[11] H.B.C. Arch. B. 239/g/65; C. 1/809. Published by permission of the Hudson's
Bay Company.

Robert McKnight

by REX W. STRICKLAND
University of Texas at El Paso

Although there is no data to show that Robert McKnight was associated directly with the fur trade, his long connection with the history of northern Mexico as a merchant and a miner in the area of the beaver hunt (*caza de nutria*) and his acquaintance with the great names in business, give him deservedly a place in its annals. He came to New Mexico with James Baird to whom belongs the credit for first trapping the Gila; he was a friend of the St. Vrains and Thomas James; among his employees were Lewis Dutton, James Kirker and Kit Carson. He spent a third of a century, 1812-1846, in Apachería, a tenure of adventure longer than that of any other of the *estranjeros*. His descendants, the Flottes, still reside in eastern Chihuahua.

Robert McKnight was born in 1790[1] in Augusta County, Virginia. He was one of a gaggle of six sons and six daughters born to Timothy and Eleanor Griffin McKnight, Irish immigrants who had settled in the Great Valley of Virginia in 1774. The older brothers in the order of their birth were John, Thomas, James, Robert and William. Fragmentary sources establish that John and Thomas merchandized in Nashville, Tennessee, for some years prior to 1809, when they moved to St. Louis. There they met with Robert and James who had arrived there by the way of Pittsburgh and the Ohio River. It seems reasonable to assume that the parents and the younger brother, William, reached Missouri

---

[1] Habitantes de Partido de Galeana, Documentos de Ciudad Juarez (Microform Collection, University of Texas at El Paso), Reel #58/0199, lists Roberto "Mainckgt" as a resident of the Barranca Colorado, April 30, 1841, age 51, unmarried; *ibid.*, Reel #60/024, dated 1844, gives his age as 55.

about the same time.[2] There the McKnight brothers formed
partnerships with Thomas and John Brady in a series of
combinations that only the ingenuity of William McGaw
has been able to unravel.[3] Retailers and wholesalers and
realtors, they were known as the "Irish Gang."[4]

In April 1812, Robert McKnight formed a partnership
with James Baird, Benjamin Shreve and Michael McDonogh with the design of making a trading trip to Santa Fe.
In default of information to the contrary, it may be assumed
that the company of McKnight and Brady furnished the
trade goods carried by the party, or, at least, the major portion; Baird's estate, as subsequently recorded in the archives
of El Paso del Norte, revealed him as a man of meager
means. Neither McDonogh nor Shreve was likely to have
furnished any sizeable amount of goods. Certainly the remainder of the party were hired men. The trip westward
was uneventful until they reached Taos, where they were
arrested by Jose Manrrique, governor of New Mexico, and
carried as prisoners to Santa Fe. There their goods were
sold at auction and the proceeds allocated to pay for their
bed and board – a sum of eighteen cents per day. After a
brief interval they were sent to Chihuahua and imprisoned
in the old military hospital.

The story of their misadventures need not be recounted in
detail here. I have told the particulars in my sketch of
James Baird, Volume III, pages 26-37, of the present Series;
only the latter part of their imprisonment so far as it con-
cerns McKnight needs revision. For in the identification of
Gueraseme[5] I suggested that McKnight was a resident of

---

[2] Thomas James, *Three Years among the Mexicans and Indians* (Chicago, 1962),
94n. This reprint is valuable because it has the annotations by W. B. Douglas.

[3] McGaw bases his information about the McKnights and their business enterprises on Item 40612, Biography of Thomas McKnight, published in Dubuque, Iowa,
following his death, Missouri Historical Society, St. Louis.

[4] Frederic L. Billon, *Annals of St. Louis in its Territorial Days from 1804 to 1821*
(St. Louis, 1888), 232.

Galeana; I should have said Guarasímas, a place in Sonora in the valley of the Yaqui River, quite possibly Guarasímas de Soporoa near modern Moctezuma (called Opasura until 1826),[6] though there is a Guarasímas near Guaymas. In fact, the Guarasímas in the district of Guaymas meets Baird's estimate that it was situated three hundred miles west of Chihuahua more logically than does the site near Moctezuma.

In 1820, Ferdinand VII of Spain, having granted a constitution to his subjects, issued an edict in May directing the liberation of all foreigners (*estranjeros*) then imprisoned in the viceroyalty of Mexico. Alejo Conde Garcia, commandant-general of the western provinces, received the order in September and gave the Americans their freedom. A party of nine set off immediately for Missouri and in January or February 1821, they reached Fort Smith on the Arkansas River.[7] The story of their release and the realization that trade with Mexico was no longer prohibited energized adventurous men into preparations for trips to Santa Fe to exploit the new opportunity. But of especial interest to the McKnight family was the news that Robert was alive and even prosperous at Guarasímas. Thomas James says that the first information John McKnight had received in ten years concerning Robert was that brought by the nine who had left him in the interior of Mexico.[8] Perhaps so, perhaps not; at any rate John McKnight attached himself to a small party led by James that left St. Louis, May 10, 1821, for the mouth of the Arkansas, which stream James

[5] In a letter from James Baird from Durango Mexico, Sept. 12, 1820, to his son in St. Louis, *St. Louis Inquirer,* March 31, 1821, Baird said that McKnight was living at Gueraseme, three hundred miles west of Chihuahua, where he was merchandizing and mining. Alfred Allen had been with him but was reputed to have gone to California.

[6] Francisco R. Almada, *Diccionario de Historia, Geografia y Biografia Sororense* (Chihuahua, 1952) 322, 481. This work is indispensable to the student of the Chihuahua-Sonora frontier.

[7] *St. Louis Inquirer,* March 31, 1821.   [8] James, *op. cit.,* 97.

rather naively expected to ascend to a point of disembarkation sixty miles from Taos.[9] The Arkansas and its tributaries, the Cimarron and the Canadian, did not prove to be navigable above the mouth of the Cimarron and James was obliged to exchange his barge for horses as the means of transportation. In the latter half of November, the party, after a narrow escape from the Comanche, struggled into San Miguel. Thence the little caravan rode to Santa Fe, which was reached December 1, 1821.

In mid-December, John McKnight left for "Durango, about sixteen hundred miles south, where his brother Robert was living after his enlargement from prison."[10] James knew little of the geography of northern Mexico and he could well have been mistaken about the place of Robert McKnight's residence. The brothers returned to Santa Fe in April 1822. Robert's stay there was relatively quiet except for the Finch affair, an affray which of itself was of little moment. But it illustrates a point.

Finch, so James says, was one of many American deserters from Natchitoches, who had lived in Santa Fe as long as sixteen years. Likely enough Finch and his fellows were men of little means and bad character. McKnight placed a sword in Finch's hands to sell; the deserter pawned the weapon for twelve dollars and then began to spend the money. James warned McKnight that he would never recover any of the sword's value but the latter said, "There is no danger; Finch will not trifle with me." McKnight confronted Finch on the first opportunity and demanded the sword or the money; he was given no satisfaction, whereupon he collared the miscreant and hurled him head first against a door. Not contented with breaking the rascal's head, McKnight took his case before the *alcalde* who not only returned the sword to its original owner but gave him the twelve dollars the bailee had paid Finch.

9 James, *op. cit.*, 63.   10 *Ibid.*, 136.

McKnight left Santa Fe, June 1, 1822, to return to the United States with James and Hugh Glenn. Since James' narrative centers largely around his own truculent self-esteem, little of McKnight's activities emerge. Indeed, except for a quotation cited by James as McKnight's reply to a missionary who asked if there was need of his service in Mexico ("They would convert you into the calaboose d-nd quick, if you were to go among them – you had better stay here,"), there is nothing to characterize him.[11] Robert McKnight, as a member of the group, reached St. Louis in July 1822. He had been absent for ten years and three months.

Robert and John McKnight and Thomas James formed a partnership in the fall of 1822 designed to open trade with the Comanche resident west of the Cross Timbers in present Oklahoma. The brothers conveyed their trade goods in a keelboat by the way of the Mississippi and Arkansas to the mouth of the Canadian, where they awaited the arrival of James who had led his party overland from St. Louis. The combined group ascended the Canadian as far as Eufala where shallow water checked the further voyage of the keel-boat; they cached their heavier commodities and transported the remainder by pirogues on the river and horses along the shore. They started building a trading house at a point on the North Canadian above the Cross Timbers; from this place John McKnight with three companions was sent toward the south to invite the Comanche to come in for trade. Meanwhile a freshet on the river encouraged James to ascend the river for another hundred miles where a trading post was erected in present Blaine County. After days of anxious waiting, James and Robert McKnight learned that John had been killed by the Indians.[12]

---

[11] *Ibid.*, 186.

[12] In addition to James' account of John McKnight's death, there is a contemporary account in the *Missouri Intelligencer,* August 12, 1823.

The news of his death was brought to the fort by Ben Potter and Jack Ivey. Robert went to the Comanche village and with courage that bordered on recklessness charged the Indians with his brother's death. James says of him, "His conduct among them was that of a mad man's, storming and raging with no regard to consequences." The Indians a bit awed perhaps, finally agreed to let him return to the fort. Negotiations resulted in his release. He then proposed that the party give up its objective, load the goods on the boats and retire down the river. James gratutiously pontificated:

. . . He was an impulsive, passionate man, with but little cool reflection. His courage in the midst of danger was of the highest order and perfectly unyielding, but he was unfit for a leader or guide in critical situations, requiring coolness and presence of mind.

The remainder of the story of the unfortunate enterprise omits any significant reference to Robert McKnight but it is logical to assume that he returned to St. Louis in the summer of 1823.[13] He had suffered not only the loss of his brother but a small fortune as well. He was unsuccessful in his efforts to recover by application to American officialdom the value of his property lost in 1812 to the Spanish government. James relates the denouement of the affair as follows:

. . . The case of Robert McKnight, who returned in April (1822) with John, his brother, from Durango, after an imprisonment of ten years, was a remarkable instance of the delinquency of our government in this particular. His goods had been confiscated and himself and his companions thrown into prison, where they remained ten years, and during the whole time the government was sleeping on their wrongs. No notice whatever was taken of them; and when McKnight returned to his country he was equally unsuccessful in seeking redress. "I will go back to Mexico," said he, "swear allegiance to their government and become a citizen. I have resided the prescribed term of years, and there

---

[13] Grant Foreman, *Pioneer Days in the Old Southwest* (Cleveland, 1926), 56, says "the summer of 1824." However, the account in the *Missouri Intelligencer*, August 12, 1823, quotes the St. Louis *Enquirer*, July 19, 1823, saying that the traders had already descended the river to the settlements. Thus they had ample time to reach St. Louis by the fall of 1823.

is a better chance of obtaining justice from the Mexicans, scoundrels as they are, than from my own government. I will go and recover as a citizen of Mexico what I lost as a citizen of the United States. My own government refuses to do me justice, and I will renounce it forever. I would not raise a straw in its defense." He accordingly returned to Mexico, where he probably received remuneration for his losses, and where he now lives a citizen of the country.[14]

McKnight kept his solemn vow: he returned to Mexico in 1824 (Camp says in 1825 when he left Missouri, May 16, with a party led by Augustus Storrs).[15] Whatever the year, we may be sure he did not linger long in Santa Fe but sought his old haunts below the Rio Grande. Once there, apparently he never returned to the United States. Sometime during his decade of exile he had married a woman of the country, Brigida Trigeros, and fathered a daughter, Refugio. The baptisimal record of McKnight's grandson, Roberto Flotte, October 20, 1838, fixes his parents' marriage about Christmas, 1837: Flotte was twenty-one at that time and Refugio McKnight could not have been more than fourteen or fifteen, nubile by the standards of the time and place. Thus McKnight married Brigida Trigeros sometime before he left Mexico in early 1822.[16] In passing it should be noted that Trigeros is a rare surname in Mexico although there was a Trigeros family in the city of Mexico in the 1820s.

It seems possible that McKnight went to Guarasimas in search of his wife and daughter in the summer of 1824 (or 1825). An entry in James O. Pattie's *Personal Narrative*

---

[14] James, *op. cit.*, 154-55.

[15] *George C. Yount and his Chronicles of the West,* ed. by Charles L. Camp (Denver, 1966), 7.

[16] Libro de bautismos que van en esta Parraquia de Nuestra Senora de Guadalupe de la Villa del Paso da principio a las cuartras dies de mes de Noviembre de 1834, 171. The entry of the date, October 20, 1838, records that Father Ramon Ortiz baptized the son of Louis Flotte and Refugio McKnight. The child's grand-parents were Louis Flotte and Enriquetta (Henrietta) Walker and Roberto McKnight and Brigida Trigeros. The god-parents were Hugo Estebinson (Hugh Stephenson) and Juana Ascarate.

may throw light upon this obscure period in his career. Pattie in relating incidents that occurred in his trip into Sonora says:

> . . . On the 7th of October [1826?], I arrived at a town called Oposard [i.e., Opasura]. . . I here became acquainted with one of my own countrymen, married to a Spanish woman. He informed me that he had been in this country thirty years [thirteen] years, eight of which he had spent in prison. . . He assured me that he should have met the same fate [the Inquisition], had he not become a member of the church. He afterwards married a lady who gained his affections by being kind to him in prison.[17]

In a year or two after his return to Mexico, McKnight became involved in the operation of the famous Santa Rita del Cobre mine near present day Silver City, New Mexico. His connection with the Cobre requires a word about the discovery and development of the diggings which today is the site of one of the world's great open pit operations. The outcroppings of copper were first called to the attention of Colonel Jose Manuel Carrasco by an Indian chief in 1803. Carrasco interested Manuel Francisco Elguea, merchant, banker and sub-delegate to the Spanish Cortes, in the project and they denounced the property. In 1804 Elguea purchased Carrasco's share in the partnership and began activities at Cobre. He built a crude roasting oven and the partially refined ore was transported to Chihuahua by mule trains. A small, triangular fort was erected to protect the miners against the Apaches. Elguea died in 1809, and the mine passed into the hands of his widow and his son, Francisco Pablo Elguea; they in turn leased it to Juan Onis who worked the property until 1827 when the Spaniards were exiled from Mexico.

---

[17] James O. Pattie, *The Personal Narrative* (Philadelphia and New York, 1962), 99. I offer the above reconstruction of Pattie's narrative as a possibility. Certainly McKnight had resided at Guarasímas de Soporoa near Moctezuma (called Opasura until 1826) in 1821. His period of residence in Mexico appears more plausibly to have been thirteen years instead of thirty since he says he was made a prisoner at the outbreak of the revolution.

About the first of 1828 McKnight and Stephen Courcier got possession of Santa Rita del Cobre and opened the works again. Courcier, of French descent, was a native of Philadelphia. It seems probable that the partners were residents of Chihuahua and the mine was actually superintended by a mayordomo, though McKnight visited the site from time to time. The data are confusing but the consensus agrees that Courcier and McKnight gave up the Cobre in 1834 to escape Apache depredations.[18] Among McKnight's employees in 1828 was young Kit Carson, who was hired in Chihuahua to go to the copper mines. He worked there for a few weeks and then returned to Taos.[19] James Kirker had a longer period of service with McKnight, working as the leader of the pack mules trains that transported the raw copper from Cobre to Chihuahua.

Most of the writers that deal with the desertion of Santa Rita ascribe it to Apache depredation stimulated by the so-called massacre of the Indians by John Johnson and his scalp-hunters. Actually the affair which took place April 22, 1837, was fought in the Animas Mountains in the present Hidalgo County, New Mexico; it was not a massacre but a sharply contested fire fight. Neither were Johnson and his men scalp-hunters in the true sense of the term.[20] Furthermore, McKnight and Courcier had abandoned their operation at Cobre before the Johnson campaign.

The duo, who exercised considerable influence in the bureaucracy of Chihuahua, obtained a concession to work a mine at Corralitos in 1838-39. The project flourished and in

---

[18] H. A. Thorne, "Mining Practices at the Chino Mines, Nevada Consolidated Copper Co., Santa Rita, New Mexico" (Dept. of Commerce, U.S. Bureau of Mines, I.C., 6412, March, 1921) ; Fayette Alexander Jones, *New Mexico Mines and Minerals* (Santa Fe, 1904), 37.

[19] F. T. Cheetham, "Kit Carson, Pathbreaker, Pioneer and Humanitarian," in *New Mexico Historical Review,* I, p. 376.

[20] John J. Johnson to the commandant-general of Chihuahua, Janos, April 24, 1837, *El Noticioso de Chihuahua,* May 5, 1837. This letter should squelch all the folderol written by Cremony *et al* about the Santa Rita "massacre."

May 1840, they enlarged their holdings by the acquisition
of a century-old property located in the Sierra de Escondida
south of Corralitos; once owned by Mariano Aguirre it was
known as the Veta Grande.[21] Actually it became the site of
the famous Barranca Colorada mine which later passed into
the hands of Lewis Flotte, McKnight's son-in-law. A number of *estranjeros* were employed at Corralitos during the
early 1840s – James Buchanan, George Winn, John Ewell,
Lucas Doane and Lewis Dutton.[22] Despite Apache attacks
and the political machinations of Luis Zuloaga, owner of an
adjacent mine, the "uncrowned king of this region,"[23] the
Corralitos and Barranca Colorada flourished.

Robert McKnight died at Corralitos in the first half of
1846.[24] During the last six years of his life, he was listed in
the census of the district of Janos as a single man (not *viudo*
but *soltero*) which leads us to believe that Brigida Trigeros
was dead. In addition to Refugio McKnight Flotte, he left
an illegitimate daughter, the wife of a man named Lyles.[25]

[21] Documentos de Ciudad Juarez, Reels 58/0178, 0179 and 0180.

[22] *Ibid.*, Reel 60/024.

[23] B. B. Harris, *The Gila Trail,* ed. and annotated by Richard H. Dillon (Norman, 1960), 64.

[24] James, *op. cit.,* 155n. Letters of administration on his estate were granted in St.
Louis, August 31, 1846. It is to be assumed that four or five months must have
elapsed between his death and the initiation of legal process.

[25] Mrs. F. F. Victor, "On the Mexican Border," in *Overland Monthly* (May
1871), VI, no. 5, pp. 460-69. This article contains considerable detail of Lyles' efforts
to prove the legitimacy of his wife so that she and he might share in McKnight's
estate. Flotte stymied the attempts.

Joseph McLoughlin

by RUTH STOLLER
Dayton, Oregon

Although Dr. John McLoughlin was one of the best known figures in the fur trade of the Far West, few people know that he had a son, Joseph, who was part of the fur trade era also. During the dozen or so years that Joseph worked for the Hudson's Bay Company at Fort Vancouver, he was, at one time or another, an apprentice, a trapper, a servant and storekeeper, and a clerk.[1]

Nothing is really known about Joseph's early life. Available information is so contradictory that one begins to feel that the real truth may have been buried with Dr. McLoughlin. The good doctor wrote freely to his family in Canada about his last four children, but he does not seem to have mentioned, even once, this boy Joseph.[2]

Joseph, himself, apparently did not know who his mother was. When he married at Fort Vancouver in 1839, while his father was on a leave of absence, a blank was left in the marriage record where his mother's name should have been.[3] Birthdates given for him vary from 1808 to 1810, and his birthplace does not seem to be known, either.

Then there is the matter of Joseph's education – or lack of it. No more than four (and possibly only two) years separated Joseph and John, Jr., who was born to Dr. McLoughlin and Marguerite Wadin McKay on August 18, 1812; yet, Joseph received no special education and his half-brothers

---

[1] E. E. Rich, ed., *Letters of Dr. John McLoughlin to the Governor and Committee, First Series* (Hudson's Bay Record Soc., London, 1941), 350.

[2] Burt Brown Barker, *The McLoughlin Empire and its Rulers* (Glendale, Calif., 1959), see index.

[3] St. James Catholic Church Register, photostat in Oregon Historical Society Library.

were given every available educational advantage, including study in Europe. To say that Joseph was uneducated is not right either. A note written by Joseph in 1844 shows a good, legible hand and good business form.[4] At some time, he must have had several years of schooling.

If Joseph's baptismal record could be found, it would probably answer some of the questions in regard to his early life. When the missionary priests arrived at Fort Vancouver, Joseph was in good standing with the church, acting as a witness and godfather at marriages and baptisms.[5] This should mean that sometime before young Joseph arrived at Fort Vancouver he had been baptized by a Catholic priest.

Two scraps of information, one from Joseph's wife, Victoire, and the other from his half-brother, David, may or may not shed some light on Joseph's early years. Both are from interviews given long after Joseph was dead. Victoire says: "I married Joseph McLoughlin in 1839. He was born at Sault San Marie on Lake Superior by Dr. McLoughlin's first wife. I first saw and recollect him at Old Fort Vancouver – 1826."[6] The other by David, and taken down by George Himes in 1901, reads: "Dr. John McL. married his first wife about 18 –, and was mixed blood. By her he had one son Joseph who was born about 1808. He came to Oregon in 1825, having been left at St. Mary's by his father in charge of Chief Factor Bathein."[7] (Bathein may refer to Angus Bethune.)

Dr. McLoughlin arrived at Fort George, at the mouth of the Columbia River, on November 8, 1824. He was to take over the management of the Columbia District for the Hudson's Bay Company. His first big job was to move his center of operation to the north shore of the river – the assumption

---

4 Original letter is among the Phillip Foster Papers, Oreg. Hist. Soc.

5 Catholic Church Registers, photostats, Oreg. Hist. Soc.

6 William C. McKay Papers on microfilm, Oregon State Library, Salem.

7 David McLoughlin Papers, in Oreg. Hist. Soc. Interview by George Himes in 1901.

being that when the boundary dispute between England and the United States was settled, the river would be the dividing line.[8]

The site of Fort Vancouver was located and developed in 1825, and even before it was finished Chief Factor McLoughlin had moved in. If Joseph came in 1825, he would have come directly to Fort Vancouver.

Joe, as he was known to the men at the fort, began his apprenticeship in the fur trade when he was about eighteen years old. His first year was with the Outfit of 1827-28, and he was attached to the Coasting Trade, working out of Fort Vancouver. His wages were £10 per annum.[9]

His first opportunity to go out as a trapper came the following year. He was with Alexander R. McLeod's Southern Expedition and was, no doubt, the youngest and most inexperienced trapper in the brigade. His step-brother, Thomas McKay, was second in command – a fact that may have helped bolster his morale when the going got rough, because his initiation into the life of a trapper proved to be a rugged one.[10]

The expedition was gone for two seasons instead of the usual one. On the return trip they started through the Siskiyous the latter part of November and were caught in the winter snows. The weather was so severe that the expedition lost all its horses, traps, and heavy equipment, and the men almost starved to death. The furs had to be abandoned in make-shift caches, and snow shoes and sleds improvised to get the party out of the mountains and into the valley where they were to spend the rest of the winter. The expedition finally returned to Fort Vancouver at the end of July 1830.

The rigors of that first trapping expedition may have changed Joe's mind about being a trapper, or his father may

[8] Frederick Merk, ed., *Fur Trade and Empire* (Cambridge, 1968), xxi.

[9] Rich, *Letters of McLoughlin, First Series,* 350.

[10] Doyce B. Nunis, Jr., ed., *First Fur Brigade to the Sacramento Valley: Alexander McLeod's 1829 Hunt* (Sacramento, 1968), 39-42.

have chosen to keep him at the fort. Whatever the reason, Joe changed jobs again; this time he was a servant and storekeeper at Fort Vancouver.

Also working at the fort as a storekeeper was a young apprentice named John Dunn, who had come from England. Although John regarded Joseph's part Indian blood with a slightly prejudiced eye, and thought that the chief factor's son enjoyed a few extra advantages, he thoroughly admired Joseph's horsemanship.

> The cleverest fellow of this school, I ever saw was Joseph M'Loughlin, a natural son of the present governor, by a half-breed woman. He was a person of some little distinction from the accident of his birth, independently of his astonishing equestarian capabilities. When managing a wild stallion that galloped and plunged in desperation, he clung to the animal as if he were an inseparable part of him, playfully tossing his barehead over the upreared head of the horse, while his breech clung to his back with the tenacity of wax; and his heels seemed glued to his ribs with his hands fastened in the mane.[11]

Joe remained as a storekeeper at Fort Vancouver until the fall of 1838. Part of that winter he spent at the Cowlitz "erecting buildings and making preparations to begin farming there."

The Hudson's Bay Company's hierarchy was beginning to take a very dim view of its ex-servants continuing to settle on the Willamette. They had mentally ceded the country south of the Columbia to the Americans, but were still making a strong claim to the area to the north. Therefore, they were urging the settlement of Cowlitz Prairie. James Douglas, acting head at Fort Vancouver in the absence of Dr. McLoughlin, who was gone on leave, had decided, in deference to company wishes, not to allow any more ex-servants to settle on the Willamette, although he had to admit that the Cowlitz Country had never been popular with the French Canadians.[12]

---

11 John Dunn, *History of the Oregon Territory* (London, 1846).
12 Rich, *Letters of McLoughlin, First Series,* 240.

The building that Joseph was doing on the Cowlitz was not for himself, but was a part of Douglas's plan of making the Cowlitz a more attractive place, in hopes that some of the French Canadians would leave their farms on French Prairie and move to the new colony on the north. Douglas was confident that the arrival of a priest and the erection of agricultural machinery would decide the point in favor of the Cowlitz.[13] He could have saved himself the trouble and the expense – nothing would induce the French Prairie settlers to leave their farms in the Willamette Valley.

For the Outfit of 1839-40 Joe signed up as clerk of the Southern Brigade, which had been under the leadership of Michel Laframboise for several years. As usual when the brigade from the south arrived at Fort Vancouver in the summer of 1839, it made quite a stir.[14] The party presented a most festive appearance as it came into the stockade in single file, Michel at the head and everyone, men and women alike, dressed in their best and fanciest attire.

Father Blanchet, the Catholic missionary to the Columbia, was at Fort Vancouver when the southern brigade arrived in June 1839. To him it was not the picturesque group that most people described, but "a hideous assemblage of persons of both sexes devoid of principle and morals."[15] The good Father immediately got busy saving souls and remedying "the awful situation." By the time the brigade was ready to leave again he had "the happiness of baptizing forty peoples" and "of solemnizing thirteen marriages." Among the latter was that of brigade leader Michel Laframboise to Emily Picard, and of Joseph McLoughlin to Victoire McMillan, step-daughter of Louis LaBonte.

M.61 – Joseph McLoughlin and Victoire McMillan, July 9, 1839. Joseph McLoughlin, clerk in the service of the Hon. Hudson's Bay

---

13 *Ibid.*   14 A. J. Allen, *Ten Years in Oregon* (New York, 1848), 119.
15 Carl Landerholm, transl., *Notices and Voyages of the Famed Quebec Mission to the Pacific Northwest* (Portland, 1956), 29.

Company at Fort Vancouver, son of Dr. McLoughlin Esquire, Chief Factor, and of ——— and on the other part, Victoire McMillan, living at the home of her step-father Louis Labonte at Walamette, daughter of James McMillan Esquire, Chief Factor, and of Marguerite of the Clatsop Tribe. Not having discovered any impediment of the first or second degree, of the relation of the spouses, we have accordingly dispensed with the banns. By the consent of the interested parties, we the undersigned priest have received their mutual consent of marriage and have given them the nuptial blessing. In the presence of James Douglas Esquire, Chief Trader and Commandant of Fort Vancouver, John McLeod Esquire, and many others who have signed with the spouses, Victoire (X) McMillan, Joseph McLoughlin, James Douglas, John McLeod, George T. Allan, Wm Fraser Tolmie, W. G. Rae, Thomas McKay.   F. N. Blanchet.[16]

The brigade left again on the 20th of July with Joe, "a young man of determined character" acting as clerk.[17] Victoire, openly proud of her status as the wife of the second in command, was probably along. The departure of the brigade was accompanied by the usual festivity and fanfare, but trouble was lurking in the shadows. They got only as far as the Rogue River country when Joseph had "a severe pulmonary attack, accompanied by a discharge of blood through the mouth."[18] Victoire and a weakened Joseph hurried back to Fort Vancouver to seek medical aid.

This is the first indication we have of the disease that within ten years would take Joseph's life. There must have been signs of it previous to this, and it may have been the reason Joseph had been given assignments that kept him close to his father at the fort.

As soon as Joseph had sufficiently recovered from this attack, he resigned from the Hudson's Bay Company and became a settler, not on the Cowlitz, but in the Willamette Valley. By this time Dr. McLoughlin had returned from his leave of absence and to him it was pure nonsense to colonize

16 Marie L. Nichols, *The Mantle of Elias* (Portland, 1941), 270.
17 Rich, *Letters of McLoughlin, Second Series* (H.B.R.S., London, 1943), 219.
18 *Ibid.*, 220.

the Cowlitz when no one wanted to go there. Anyway, who knew where the boundary was going to be! He was right, of course – in a few short years the Cowlitz was as much in American territory as was the Willamette.

Joseph's farm was directly across the Yamhill River from his in-laws, the LaBontes, and bordered the Willamette River as well.[19] It was only a couple of miles across the Willamette to the Catholic Mission of St. Paul. An ideal location as far as Joseph and Victoire were concerned.

Medorem Crawford, who arrived in Oregon in 1842, and knew both Joseph and Dr. McLoughlin, bought the farm in 1852. In later years, he referred to it as "an old French place that had been in cultivation perhaps twenty years at that time [1852]. I bought the place Dr. McLoughlin's own son lived and died on."[20] If Crawford was right, the farm would have been settled as early as 1832 and Joseph would have acquired it from one of the old French-Canadian settlers. Perhaps this is how Joseph was able to have "an extensive portion of prairie fenced in" within a year after he settled there.[21] Further more, it would establish it as the oldest farm on the west side of the Willamette!

Joseph now became "a respectable landowner and farmer."[22] In a remarkably short time he had an extensive farming operation underway. It is probable that his father was providing some financial backing (which would have been only fair in light of the amount of money the doctor had spent on his four younger children!), because, by the fall of 1842, he had eighteen horses, fifty head of cattle, and forty hogs. His grain crop for that summer included 500 bushels of wheat and 335 bushels of other grains.[23]

19 Provisional Land Claims Book III, p. 67, Oregon State Archives, Salem.

20 "Crawford's Missionaries," Bancroft Papers, microfilm in Oreg. State Library.

21 "Diary of Wilkes in the Northwest," in *Washington Historical Quarterly,* vol. 17 (1926), 53.

22 Lieut. Neil M. Howison, u.s.n., *Oregon, a Report* (Fairfield, 1967), 12. Howison was in the Oregon country in 1846, and made his report in 1848.

23 Dr. Elijah White's census of 1842, microfilm in Oreg. State Archives.

The only clue that we have as to how Joseph's health was during these years comes from an autobiography written by Margaret J. Bailey. She came as a teacher to Jason Lee's Mission in 1837, and in 1839 married Dr. William Bailey, who for a time after the mission doctors left was the only doctor in the valley. She has a journal entry for October 1, 1844, which reads, "Dr. McLoughlin sent a request for Dr. Binney (the name she gives Dr. Bailey in the book) to visit his son, sick with the consumption." [24]

Joseph stayed remarkably active, in spite of his health. He often acted as a witness or a godfather in the parish at St. Paul. He was a candidate for justice of the peace in Yamhill County in 1845.[25] He did not receive many votes, no doubt because he was a half-breed. The prejudice of the newly arrived American immigrants against the people with Indian blood was becoming more and more pronounced. The remarkable thing is that his name was on the ballot at all!

His farming operations continued to prosper. On the 1847 tax list for Yamhill County,[26] out of a total of 241 tax payers, only 15 of them paid more taxes than Joseph.

Toward the end of 1848 Joseph's health began to fail noticeably. On November 8, he made a trip to Champoeg to have his friend, Father Buldoc, write out a will for him. It was written in French in Father Buldoc's beautiful handwriting. Joseph signed it in his usual steady hand. The will reflected his devotion to his church and to his wife, Victoire. She was to be the sole heir and executrix of his estate. The will further stated, "It is my wish that my body be decently interred in the Cemetery of the Catholic Church situated in the County of Champoeg, O.T., according to the rites and ceremonies of the Catholic religion and with that solemnity

---

24 Margaret J. Bailey, *Grains, or Passages in the Life of Ruth Rover* (Portland, 1854). A copy is in the Oreg. State Library.

25 Provisional and Territorial Documents, no. 1704, Oregon State Archives.

26 *Ibid.*, no. 822.

which my means admit of. That a funeral service be performed for me, thirty days after my decease." [27]

By December 14 Joseph was dead — the church record says he was about thirty-eight years old. However, his burial did not take place until December 23.[28] The weather may have been a factor in the late burial. Four days after his death the weather began to turn cold and December 20 and 21 were extremely cold for the Willamette Valley. The temperature ranged from 12 to 3 degrees, the coldest weather for the valley that a good many settlers could remember. On the 22nd the weather began to moderate a little. More snow fell that night making two and a half inches on the ground. On the 23rd the weather was still moderating and the sky was clear.[29] That day Joseph was laid to rest in the hallowed ground of the church cemetery at St. Paul.

Victoire lived almost 50 years after the death of Joseph. She married twice again. The first time was in July of 1850 to Pierre LaCourse, Jr., who was at least eight years younger than she. Soon after their marriage they sold the farm and moved to the east side of the Willamette. Pierre died in 1861 and she remarried in 1862. This husband was Simon Etienne Gregoire who was about twelve years her junior. He was killed by a train at Gervais, Marion County, Oregon, in 1892.[30] Victoire did not die until February of 1898 at about the age of 76.[31]

---

[27] The original of Joseph McLoughlin's Will is filed under Estate no. 192 in the Yamhill County Courthouse, McMinnville, Oregon.

[28] St. Paul Catholic Church Register, photostat in Oreg. Hist. Soc.

[29] *Oregon Spectator,* Dec. 28, 1848, and Jan. 12, 1849, photostats in Oreg. Hist. Soc.

[30] Biographical Index, Oreg. Hist. Soc.

[31] St. Louis Catholic Church Register, photostat in Oreg. Hist. Soc.

Robert Meldrum

by JOHN E. WICKMAN
Eisenhower Library, Abilene, Kansas

It is reported by one of his contemporaries that Robert Meldrum was offered a chance, by Harpers, to publish his autobiography.[1] Characteristically, he refused to do this. Modern researchers might well wish that he had reconsidered that offer.

One matter which Meldrum could have settled was the date and place of his birth.[2] All accounts do agree that he entered the fur trade while still in his teens. Lewis Henry Morgan has added that it was poor health which prompted Meldrum to go west.[3]

As with most of the young, strong men who moved through the Rocky Mountain trade in the 1820s, Meldrum's countless journeys went unreported, save for a notation in a ledger about his pay, or chance references in someone else's letters. He was with William Ashley in 1827,[4] and went into the service of the American Fur Company sometime before

---

[1] [James A. Bradley], "Affairs at Fort Benton from 1831 to 1869, from Lieutenant Bradley's Journal," ed. by Arthur J. Cravens, in Mont. Hist. Soc., *Contributions*, III (Helena, 1900), 255.

[2] James A. Bradley gives Meldrum's birth year as 1802 and says he was born in Scotland, *loc. cit.*, 255-56. Anne MacDonell, in notes and references she compiled for "The Fort Benton Journal, 1854-56," in Mont. Hist. Soc., *Contributions*, X (1940), 284, says Meldrum was born in Shelby County, Kentucky in 1806. In *The Indian Journals 1859-62, of Lewis Henry Morgan*, ed. by Leslie A. White (Ann Arbor, 1959), Morgan, on page 191, is quoted as saying Meldrum was born in Scotland in 1804. His editor sticks with Bradley, and on page 226, gives 1802 as his birth year and Scotland as the place. Subsequent authors have chosen freely between the three dates. It is doubtful if the matter can be successfully resolved. Morgan apparently obtained all his information from his discussions with Meldrum, though that is not certain.   [3] Morgan, *Journals*, 191.

[4] *The West of William H. Ashley, 1822-38,* ed. by Dale L. Morgan (Denver, 1964), 172.

1830. His activities with the company took him into the Upper Missouri River country, and eventually even beyond the Rocky Mountains. As he developed his knowledge of the country, he also became expert in working with the Indians who provided his trading clientele. As a trader, his specialty was dealing with the Crow Indians. In time he intermarried with the tribe and was accepted as one of them.

Several of his contemporaries have commented on how completely Meldrum was integrated into the social structure of the Crows. Lewis Henry Morgan discovered that Meldrum could not only speak the Crow language, but also could write in it with a facility comparable to his native tongue.[5] His assimilation by the Indians, coupled with a high degree of personal courage, carried Meldrum to positions of responsibility with the American Fur Company. He held, successively, positions at Fort Union, Fort Alexander, and Fort Sarpy.

During the 1850s Meldrum was one of the American Fur Company's chief traders working with the Crows. He was engaged in this work when he met Captain William F. Raynolds who led the Yellowstone Expedition of 1859-1860 of the Topographic Engineers. Raynolds met Meldrum on August 23, 1859, and used the latter's knowledge of the country to fill in the gaps in his information on the terrain between the Yellowstone and the North Platte rivers.[6]

In the prime of his life, Meldrum has been described as of medium height, strongly built, with dark sandy hair and

---

[5] Lewis Henry Morgan, "Systems of Consanguinity and Affinity of the Human Family," *Smithsonian Institution Contributions to Knowledge,* XVII (Washington, 1887), 186 note.

[6] For comment on Meldrum's work with Raynolds the most easily available source is *Exploring the Northern Plains, 1804-76,* ed. by Lloyd McFarling (Caldwell, Idaho, 1955), 259. McFarling publishes Raynolds' "Report of the Exploration of the Yellowstone and Missouri Rivers, 1859-60," and the reader should see especially note 3, on page 263. The full report is William F. Raynolds' "Report on the Exploration of the Yellowstone and the Country Drained by that River," 40 Cong., 2 sess., *Sen. Exec. Doc.* 77 (1868).

gray eyes.[7] His portrait appears in this volume at page 21. Though his disposition seems to have been even with both whites and Indians, he made an exception in the case of Jim Beckwourth.

Meldrum's dislike for Beckwourth was well known to his contemporaries. As both were operating among the Crows at the same time, it is not surprising that they might cross purposes. In one of the more tantalizing bits of gossip to be passed around trader's campfires, George Simpson has related that Meldrum was responsible for Beckwourth's leaving the Crows.[8] Whether Simpson's tale is true or not, most of those who knew Meldrum, or "Round Iron," as the Crows called him because of his ability at frontier blacksmithing, felt he was capable of forcing Beckwourth out.

When the American Fur Company discontinued its Crow post, Meldrum moved on to Fort Union, where Father DeSmet married him to a Blackfoot woman on July 11, 1864. In almost one year to the day, July 10, 1865, Meldrum died of natural causes and was buried in the fort cemetery.[9]

No epithet for Meldrum survives, but like others of his generation and occupation, the respect of his adopted brothers, the success of his employers because of his skill, and a peaceful death speak eloquently about his abilities in coping with a risky business in a violent time and place.

---

[7] James A. Bradley, *loc. cit.,* 255.

[8] George Simpson, writing as "Senex," "Pah-u-tah," in the *Trinidad* (Colorado) *Daily News,* said that Bill Williams had told him Meldrum and Beckwourth were rivals with the Crow, and that Meldrum's greater influence gathered forces which caused Beckwourth to leave the tribe. *Trinidad Daily News,* June 18, 1882. Readers unfamiliar with Simpson are referred to the excellent article by Harvey L. Carter and Janet Lecompte, page 285, vol. III of this *Series.* It is the most authoritative article on this subject. The conversation with Williams probably took place in 1838-39, or 1839-40, when both Simpson and Williams were on the upper Humboldt River, and at which time they encountered Beckwourth.

Lewis Henry Morgan, in his *Indian Journals* (p. 192), has quoted Meldrum as saying "Beckwith" (sic) [Beckwourth], "was a humbug." Meldrum is also reported as making other disparaging remarks about Beckwourth's abilities.

[9] Anne MacDonell's notes, *loc. cit.,* 285.

David Meriwether

by GLORIA GRIFFEN CLINE
Bray, Ireland

Few individuals enjoyed a career comparable to that of David Meriwether. His life spanned almost the entire nineteenth century which allowed him to be inextricably involved in the burgeoning United States of the period. Born in Louisa County, Virginia, on October 30, 1800, David was bequeathed a frontier heritage by his father, Captain William Meriwether, who had served with the Virginia Light Dragoons, later with George Rogers Clark, and had participated in the capture of Kaskaskia and and Cahokia as well as the British garrison's surrender at Vincennes.[1] When David was a little over four years of age, in 1805, his father bought a farm on the Ohio River about eight miles below Louisville in Jefferson County, Kentucky, and it was here that he resided until his death in 1892, with the exception of his years on the plains and in New Mexico.

Although David Meriwether had little direct connection with the fur trade, he was part of the expansion of the Far West and could recall vividly some association with many individuals or events on the American scene – i.e., how a survivor of the Pigeon Roost Massacre, perpetrated by the followers of Tecumseh, took refuge at their Kentucky home and how he, at the age of ten or eleven, was despatched to alert the countryside. Later as a youth of fourteen, he rode 148 miles carrying dispatches which facilitated the move-

---

[1] Malcolm H. Harris, *History of Louisa County, Virginia* (Richmond, 1936), 62, 160, and 387; Louisa H. A. Minor, *The Meriwethers and Their Connections: A Family Record, Giving the Genealogy of the Meriwethers in America Together with Biographical Notes and Sketches* (Albany, N.Y., 1892), 108-10, 118-19, and 151-63.

ment of Kentucky troops to support Andrew Jackson at the
Battle of New Orleans.

Like so many frontiersmen, he had relatively little formal
education, for his chores on the farm and his dislike of
academic confinement brought his schooling to a halt at the
age of fourteen. However, his alert, sharp mind, keen appraisal of human character, and shrewd judgement more
than compensated for this loss and equipped him well for
his long, active life. In 1819 when renewing acquaintance
with an old family friend, Colonel John O'Fallon, nephew
of George Rogers Clark and William Clark of the Lewis
and Clark Expedition, O'Fallon was quick to perceive these
traits and invited young Meriwether to join him in his new
post as sutler of the Yellowstone Expedition which was
under the command of Colonel Henry Atkinson with the
scientific branch in charge of Major Stephen H. Long.[2] The
object, as announced by Secretary of War Calhoun, was to
proceed to the Mandan villages in present-day North
Dakota or to the mouth of the Yellowstone River, in order
to extend protection to the northern frontiers and to promote the expansion of the fur trade which had been curtailed on the Upper Missouri during the War of 1812.
David Meriwether joined Colonel O'Fallon at a salary of
$200 for the first year and $300 for the second and began his
first duties as supercargo on a keelboat carrying trade goods
to St. Louis.[3] Immediately thereafter he was busily engaged

[2] Hiram Martin Chittenden, *The American Fur Trade of the Far West,* 2 vols.
(New York, 1935), II, p. 570; Edwin James, *Account of an Expedition from Pitts-
burgh to the Rocky Mountains,* in R. G. Thwaites, *Early Western Travels,* vols.
XIV-XVII (Cleveland, 1905).

[3] At the age of 86 David Meriwether dictated his extremely articulate memoirs to
his granddaughter, Miss Belle Williams, covering his life to the year 1856. A copy
of this manuscript along with numerous other Meriwether papers descended to Mrs.
Betsy Graves O'Neill of Redwood City, California, who allowed my father, Robert
Arnold Griffen, and myself to analyze them; which resulted in *My Life in the
Mountains and on the Plains: The Newly Discovered Autobiography by David
Meriwether,* ed. and with introd. by Robert A. Griffen (Univ. of Okla. Press, 1965).
For information in this article, I am deeply indebted to this book and to conversa-
tions with Mrs. O'Neill and Mr. Griffen.

in aiding Captain Bissell,[4] the sutler for the troops at Belle-fontaine and an O'Fallon associate, and at Fort Missouri, later known as Fort Atkinson.

By the spring of 1820 he was carrying trade goods to the Pawnee villages about one hundred miles west of Council Bluffs. Here he wondered about the practicability of a wagon route between the Missouri and New Mexico, and Captain Bissell asked him to undertake such a reconnais-sance. So one year before William Becknell opened the Santa Fe Trail, Meriwether with a Negro boy, Alfred, joined a party of Pawnees and traveled southwestwardly. While on the headwaters of the Canadian River, which they referred to as "Rio Colorado," the Pawnees were killed by the Mexicans, and Meriwether and Alfred were captured and taken to Santa Fe where they were imprisoned in the jail in the western portion of the Palace of the Governors. Through the kindness of a priest and the Spanish governor, the two Americans were released with the promise that they would never again return to New Mexico.

Their return trip was made over much of their outgoing trail, but the freezing temperatures forced them to erect a winter camp near the Arkansas River where they spent two months before finally reaching Council Bluffs in March 1821. Meriwether's term of duty was about to expire, and he was now asked to become sutler to the troops at Fort Osage at the salary of $500 for the next year.[5] In March of 1822 when his engagement again terminated, Colonel O'Fal-lon offered to recommend him highly to William Ashley and Michael Immel thinking that they could use Meri-wether's skill in their far western plans. Although David wished to go up the Missouri with the Rocky Mountain Fur Company, he felt that his parents were becoming elderly

---

[4] Francis B. Heitman, *Historical Register of the United States Army* (Washington, 1893), I, p. 221.

[5] Fort Osage was located about forty miles below the mouth of the Kansas River near the present Sibley, Missouri. Griffen, *op. cit.,* 103.

and needed him so he had to forsake the frontier for the Kentucky plantation.

He soon settled down on the farm and in 1823 he married Sarah H. Leonard from which union thirteen children were born. Each fall he took the produce from the plantation by flatboat to New Orleans, where he would sell it for a small profit. One year his enterprising spirit took him to Cuba where he exchanged his Kentucky produce for sugar, coffee, and other exotic goods which he sold in Louisville.

David Meriwether became involved in Democratic politics on the local and state level and even ran for Congress, although unsuccessfully, in 1847 and 1851. However, his efforts were rewarded and upon Henry Clay's death in June 1852, Governor Powell appointed him Clay's successor as senator from Kentucky. Meriwether played an active role in Congress and was a member of the committee which investigated the dispute evolving from the surveying of the United States-Mexican boundary following the Treaty of Guadalupe Hidalgo which ended the Mexican War. Because Meriwether had drafted the committee's report, President Pierce felt that he would be an ideal governor of New Mexico Territory, that region that lay on the United States' southwestern boundary and now is encompassed by the states of New Mexico, Arizona, and southern Colorado; so, therefore, he appointed him to that post in 1853.

The Meriwether party arrived in Santa Fe on August 8, 1853, and was taken to the cathedral on the plaza where a Te Deum was sung in honor of his safe arrival. According to legend, the roof of the cell at the west end of the Palace of the Governors in which Meriwether had been confined as a prisoner in 1820 collapsed on that day, the day of the new governor's inaugural address as well; [6] this was considered by the Mexicans to be a good omen. Indeed it was a good

---

[6] *San Jose Mercury-Herald,* April 7, 1893. For the text of the inaugural address, see Griffen, 157-58.

omen for Meriwether proved to be an intelligent and practical governor in an area of strife and turmoil.

In February 1854 Meriwether took a leave of absence and returned to the East where he arrived on April 1st. He reported to the Secretary of State and had meetings with the Postmaster General and the Commissioner of Indian Affairs. Shortly thereafter the President asked him to return to New Mexico as soon as possible because of Indian depredations on the frontier. By the middle of May 1854 Meriwether was heading westward again to attempt to still the incursions of the Navajos on the west, the Utes and Jicarilla Apaches on the north, the Mescaleros on the east, and the Gila and Mogollon Apache on the south. Such depredations would continue to plague his four year New Mexican administration. Immediately upon his return to Santa Fe, Meriwether adopted a policy of force and called for a regiment of volunteers to which he appointed as colonel, the able Ceran St. Vrain, who had been prominent in the southwestern trade for the past decades.[7] Meriwether himself participated in attempting to quiet Indian disturbances [8] and through the years visited the various tribes, distributing food and trade goods among them, and negotiating treaties.[9]

Too, Meriwether was feeling the American expansionist attitudes and pressures. Many people were disgruntled about the southwestern boundary, particularly in the 1850s when the survey for transcontinental railroad routes showed that a small portion of land south of the Gila in Mexican territory was needed for a successful connection with the Pacific. Thus the United States minister to Mexico, James Gadsen,

[7] W. W. H. Davis, *El Gringo; or, New Mexico and Her People* (New York, 1857) ; L. Bradford Prince, *A Concise History of New Mexico* (Cedar Rapids, 1914), 193; Blanche C. Grant, *When Old Trails Were New* (New York, 1934), 156; Grant, ed., *Kit Carson's Own Story of His Life: As Dictated to Col. & Mrs. D. C. Peters about 1856-57, and Never Before Published* (Taos & Santa Fe., 1926).

[8] Griffen, *op. cit.,* 164-238.

[9] These treaties, which were never ratified by the Senate, form a considerable portion of the O'Neill Meriwether Collection.

was pressed to buy the necessary triangle of land which he did successfully in December 1853 for the price of $10,-000,000. Therefore, it fell to David Meriwether in 1854 to accept the Gadsen Purchase [10] and incorporate it into New Mexico Territory, giving the United States the continental boundaries that she knows today.

Late in the fall of 1855 Meriwether went East again in hopes of resigning his post. However, Washington officials encouraged him to remain in office since money had been appropriated by Congress for the building of a new state house and penitentiary, and they wanted an honest man to administer this project. This he did, but in May 1857, he left Santa Fe for the last time and with the expiration of his official term of office on October 30th, he was able to return to his home and family which he had missed greatly during the past four years.

It didn't take Meriwether long to regain his position as agriculturalist and state politician, and in 1858 he was elected to the Kentucky House of Representatives, where he was to serve intermittently for the next twenty-seven years, until he was eighty-five years of age. Then, until the spring of 1892, the man who had known Daniel Boone, the O'Fallon brothers, Henry Clay, Jefferson Davis, and Chief Justice Taney, enjoyed his friends and relatives on the banks of the Ohio River. Upon his death in the spring of 1892,[11] the old frontiersman was laid to rest in the family plot on the plantation, but some years later his body was exhumed and reinterred in the historic cemetery of Cave Hill, Louisville.[12]

Meriwether's portrait appears in this volume at page 22.

---

10 Paul Neff Garber, *The Gadsen Treaty* (Philadelphia, 1923).

11 Meriwether's obituary appeared in the *San Jose Mercury-Herald,* April 7, 1892.

12 Interview with Mrs. Betsy Graves O'Neill, September 28, 1963.

J. B. Moncravie

by CHARLES E. HANSON, JR.
Chadron, Nebraska

Unlike many of his compatriots, J. B. Moncravie was neither straight-laced nor savage. Instead, he was a refreshing mixture of intellectual and artistic attainments, skilled as a trader but also fond of girls and the bubbling cup.

His name has been spelled in various ways. He is often referred to as Jean Baptiste Moncrevie. American Fur Company correspondence generally used the name J. B. Moncrevie, and Larpenteur spelled it Moncravie. However, all of his personal papers use the name John B. Moncravie.

He was born in Bordeaux, France, about 1797. He and his brother were apparently among the French refugees who settled in Philadelphia. James Moncravie, a blacksmith listed in Philadelphia directories of the 1849-60 period, may have been his nephew.[1]

In March 1820, "Jhon Moncravie'" enlisted for five years in the Army of the United States at Philadelphia. He was described as twenty-three years old, five feet, three inches tall, light complexion, hazel eyes and light hair, by profession a musician.[2]

The army gave Moncravie his first view of the West. Assigned to the 5th Infantry he was at St. Peters and Fort St. Anthony the first year, becoming a corporal in October

---

[1] His birthplace is shown on his original enlistment papers. For a great deal of information about Moncravie's descendants, the writer is indebted to Mrs. Virginia Moran of Colorado Springs, Colorado, daughter of Charles Alexander Moncravie, and great-granddaughter of J. B. Moncravie; and to Mr. John Moncravie of Eureka Springs, Arkansas, son of Sylvester A. Moncravie and great-great grandson of J. B. Moncravie. Family traditions agree that two brothers came to America and some say that they accompanied their father.

[2] Original enlistment papers in the National Archives, Washington, D.C.

1820.[3] He had become a sergeant by the time his term of service expired in March 1825. Apparently Philadelphia had little to offer on his return, for he reenlisted at Fort Snelling in December 1825, and served until honorably discharged from Company C, 5th U.S. Infantry, on December 31, 1829.[4]

After nearly ten years of service on the Minnesota frontier, the diminutive Frenchman was thoroughly familiar with Indians and the fur trade. With his restless disposition it was only natural that he turned to the fur trade of the wilderness and secured an engagement with the American Fur Company.[5] He is next recorded as one of three clerks, "Messrs. Chardon, Brazeau, and Moncrevie," left with Hamilton at Fort Union in the summer of 1833.[6]

That fall Campbell and Sublette built an opposition post near Fort Union and Moncravie frequently carried letters over to Robert Campbell at the new post and often dined and visited with him. Campbell called Moncravie the "little doctor" and made some half-amused references to Moncravie's activities in his journal. The classic example is Campbell's notation of Moncravie's first divorce at Fort Union:

> Last night Joseph Dechamp seduced from the Bed and board of Doctor McCrevee his own lawfully purchased wife which he obtained from her father for the sum of 280$ in merchandise to him in hand paid . . . The little doctor was outrageous but today the fair damsel accompanied her paramour on a Buffalo hunt and thus left her late spouse time to forget her before they again meet.[7]

---

[3] Registers of Enlistments in the United States Army 1798-1914, vol. 32, National Archives.

[4] Returns From Regular Army Infantry Regiments – 5th Infantry, June 1821-Dec. 1831. Microcopy no. 665, Roll 53, National Archives.

[5] Moncravie's movements 1830-32 are not known. He may have been the "J. B. Moncreve" listed in the 1830 census at Green Bay Township, Wisconsin Territory. That name does not appear at Green Bay in the territorial census of 1836.

[6] Annie Heloise Abel, ed., *Chardon's Journal at Fort Clark 1834-39* (Pierre, S.D., 1932), xxx.

The American Fur Company bought out Campbell and Sublette that winter. When Charles Larpenteur was hired at Fort Union in the summer of 1834 he found a crew of workmen dismantling their Fort William and rebuilding it near the company buildings. "A clerk by the name of Moncravie, who was at the time a trader, and also in charge of the men, had this to attend to; but he was a little too fond of whiskey, and much too fond of the squaws, to do this or any other as it should be done." Characteristically, Larpenteur wrote with relish of Hamilton's anger one afternoon because the rebuilding was going badly and Moncravie was not on the job: ". . . it was an awful piece of work. The pickets were set in crooked, some too high, some too low . . ."[8]

Larpenteur wrote later that he was retained and Moncravie was discharged but the latter actually stayed at Fort Union for several years. There is every indication that Moncravie was trusted and respected at Fort Union and despite Larpenteur's statement, he was on the payroll there in 1835 and 1836. On May 5, 1835, Daniel Lamont wrote him an appointment to command Fort McKenzie if anything happened to Mr. Culbertson, placing him ahead of Harvey in succession to the position.[9]

In addition to his skill as a trader, Moncravie was able to contribute some artistic skill to the improvement of Fort Union. When Edwin Denig wrote a description of the fort for Audubon in 1843, he noted: "There are two large outside gates to the fort, one each in the middle of the front and rear, and upon the top of the front one is a painting of a

---

[7] George R. Brooks, ed., "The Private Journal of Robert Campbell," reprinted from *Bulletin, Missouri Historical Society,* Oct. 1963, and Jan. 1964, pp. 8, 16-17.

[8] Elliott Coues, ed., *Forty Years a Fur Trader, The Personal Narrative of Charles Larpenteur, 1833-1872* (New York, 1898), 72-74.

[9] Fort Union Letter Books, Missouri Historical Society, St. Louis.

treaty of peace between the Indians and whites executed by
J. B. Moncrevie, Esq." [10]

During their visit to Fort Union in 1843, Audubon and
his party often hunted with Moncravie and another clerk
named Pike. Audubon found Moncravie to be not only a
skilled hunter and fisherman but also an accomplished enter-
tainer. In his journal he noted on August 7, "a sort of show
by Moncrévier which was funny, and well performed; he
has much versatility, great powers of mimicry, and is a far
better actor than many who have made names for themselves
in that line." [11] Their friendship continued throughout Audubon's visit and Moncravie, an expert boatman, was one of
the frontier passengers in the Mackinaw boat "Union" when
it left Fort Union for St. Louis with the Audubon party. [12]

Moncravie's propensity to enjoy life and his desire to
share that enjoyment with others almost cost him his job on
the upper Missouri a short time later.

In June 1844, while going up from Fort Pierre with keel
boats of goods for the Blackfeet, he couldn't resist tapping
the whiskey kegs to the point of getting drunk several times.
Worse still, he gave the crews nearly twenty gallons to keep
them happy too. People being as they are, F. A. Chardon,
Alexander Harvey, Baptiste Champagne and Etienne Provost, all informed their superiors as soon as the opportunity
offered. Picotte was furious, because he had ordered Moncravie not to dispose of a single drop on the way. When
Picotte left Fort Pierre in June 1845, he left instructions
that Culbertson be requested to collect $400 from Moncravie
for the liquor consumed. This information was forwarded
to Culbertson by A. T. Bouis on October 9, 1845. [13] Picotte

---

[10] Reproduced in *North Dakota History,* vol. 29, nos. 1 and 2 (Bismarck, 1962),
206.

[11] Maria Audubon and Elliott Coues, eds., *Audubon and His Journals* (New York,
1897), II, p. 138.

[12] John Francis McDermott, ed., *Up the Missouri With Audubon – The Journal of
Edward Harris* (Norman, 1951), 176.

[13] Fort Pierre Letterbooks, Mo. Hist. Soc.

also decreed that Moncravie should be fired as soon as he
returned from his current expedition to the Kootenais.[14]

However, Moncravie still had many friends in the Upper
Missouri Outfit. Furthermore, Pierre Chouteau, Jr. & Company did not at this time relish having any disgruntled
employee down in St. Louis telling people about the liquor
trade on the upper river frontier. The account was settled
for cash and that was that. Soon after, however, Moncravie
disappeared from the annals of Fort Union and was noted in
the journals at Fort Pierre.

In January 1848, he delivered merchandise to the Yanktonai post. Later that year he helped with the trade to both
the Yanktonai and Yanktons and supervised transportation
to various posts dependent upon Fort Pierre.[15]

Things were changing rapidly on that part of the frontier.
In 1849 Fort John on the Laramie was sold to the U.S.
Government. On July 25, 1849, instructions were sent from
Fort Pierre to Bruce Husband, directing him to begin a
new fort some distance down the Platte and advising him
that "G. B. Moncrevie" was hired as "Clerk Trader &c .
. ." Moncravie would also assist him in building the fort.
With this move the rollicking trader and mountaineer left
the Missouri River for good.[16]

Andrew Drips took charge of the new post. It was located
first at Robidoux Pass and then moved soon after to a point
about eight miles south of Scotts Bluff. In the summer of
1850 Andrew Drips took leave for a visit and left James
McCluskey in charge. However, McCluskey also planned
to leave in the fall and Picotte wrote him on August 14,
1850: "In the event, however, of your resigning the charge
of the Post, I see no other person with you, better adapted
to take its charge than Mr. J. B. Moncrevie." Any service
under this directive was of short duration, for Drips was

[14] Abel, *op. cit.*, 238.
[15] See various references to "Moncrevie" in portions of Fort Pierre Letterbook
reproduced in *South Dakota Historical Collections* (Pierre, 1918), IX, pp. 220-31.
[16] Fort Pierre Letter Books, *loc. cit.*

back at the post in December, but it demonstrates the continued regard of the Upper Missouri Outfit for "Mr. Moncrevie."

Surviving accounts show that Moncravie was still there in 1851 and he may have stayed on for several years. Drips was reporting a good trade in buffalo robes in the spring of 1852.[17] At that time he moved the post to a new location closer to the Oregon Trail and continued its operation, probably for several years.[18]

It must have been evident to anyone at Fort John that the day of permanent settlement and development of the West was at hand. Moncravie was now in his fifties without any competence for his old age. Irrepressible as ever, he hit on an audacious scheme to make his own treaty with the Indians for a cession of land, just like the government.

It seemed logical to the relatives of his Sioux wife and so the treaty was formalized by two interpreters and none other that Superintendent Mitchell himself: [19]

To All Whom it May Concern

Before me came several Indian Chiefs of the Ogalala Band of Sioux Malo Ayocuni, Red Wing, Long Chin and Standing Elk to tell me by Charles Gueru & Joseph Bissonette (Interpreters) that they gave to John B. Moncravie a French man that has traded with them several years in the Employ of the Amr. Fur Co., a tract of Land S.W. of Fort Laramie Seven miles square more or less on the line of Laramie Pick to N.E. corner of said land and back to the praira of Laramie Plains, as a gift on account of his relation to them by their Sister, it includes both branches of Laramie River and heads at Labonte Creek.

(signed) D. D. Mitchell
General Superintendent of *Indns*
Treaty

Horse Shoe Creek Assembly, 1856

Joseph Bissonette ⎫
Charles Gueru ⎭ Interpreters

[17] T. L. Green, "Scotts Bluffs, Fort John," in *Nebraska History*, XIX, no. 3 (Lincoln, July-Sept. 1938), 175-88.

[18] Merrill J. Mattes, *The Great Platte River Road* (Lincoln, 1969), 463-71.

[19] Letters Received by Office of Indian Affairs from Whetstone Agency. National Archives.

This forty-nine square miles included some of the Laramie Plains and a bit of the Black Hills on the headwaters of the Laramie River. In later years he furnished the government a sketch of the land cession showing "Bissonette House" on the left bank of the Laramie opposite "Moncravie House" on the right bank, "12 miles (upriver) from Fort (Laramie)." It appears that he had left Fort John and built himself some kind of little trading house in the Fort Laramie vicinity.[20]

The continued business along the Oregon Trail and the obvious prospects for developing a farm in eastern Nebraska tolled him eastward. By 1858 Moncravie had a farm and stock ranch near Daniel's Ranch in the Blue River Valley. Unfortunately it lay in the path of Pawnee and Otoe hunting parties who were, at that time, still careless of any settler's property. In February 1858, a band of Otoes, which he estimated at three hundred, drove off "two horses worth $125.00, two cows worth $50.00, two calves worth $10.00 and one yoke, or two oxen, worth $75.00" making a total loss of $520. In July 1858, a band of Pawnees carried away or destroyed a hundred acres of growing corn, a field of potatoes estimated to be worth $400 and a garden of vegetables.[21]

In the 1860 Census we find J. B. Moncravie listed as living on his farm near Daniel's Ranch in Nebraska, aged 63, profession, "interpreter." He was living alone then but not all of his romances had turned out as badly as his first Indian marriage at Fort Union. A son, Alexander B. Moncravie, was born to an Indian mother at Fort Union about 1844 and his father had gone to some lengths to provide him an education. In August 1861, Alexander enlisted in Company A, 7th Regiment of Kansas Cavalry Volunteers and was dis-

20 *Ibid.*

21 Claim no. 6690 by J. H. Broady, adm. of John B. Moncravie, Records of U.S. Court of Claims, National Archives.

charged as a corporal from the same unit in September
1865.[22]

Aging, but still hopeful, J. B. Moncravie finally filed
claims in 1866 totaling $520 for the stock taken by the Otoes
and $2,462.50 for the crops destroyed by the Pawnees, but
no action was taken on them. On April 11, 1874, while living
at Brownville, Nebraska, he wrote the commissioner of the
General Land Office in a shaky hand, forwarding a copy of
his 1856 treaty and accompanying map, and asking the commissioner to recognize his claim to the land. Receiving no
answer, he wrote again on May 17, saying that he wished to
establish a settlement on the land. A quick denial of his
rights to the area in question was sent him on May 22, 1874.[23]

It was just as well; seventy-seven years had sapped the
fighting spirit of the jolly boatman. He apparently saw little
of his son but surviving correspondence indicates that he did
spend some time with the latter at Decatur, Nebraska, in
1874. However, Alexander died in 1876 from the effects of
war wounds, and the 1880 census lists the elder Moncravie
as living with a family named Carlson in Nemaha County,
Nebraska.[24] He died at his own residence in Brownville,
Nebraska, on July 18, 1885, at the age of eighty-eight.[25] In
his will he made no mention of relatives, leaving five hundred dollars each to the Brownville Chapter No. 4 of the
Royal Arch Masons and the rector of Christ Church Parish,
with the rest of his estate bequeathed to one Abigail Shadley
of Brownville.

The petition for settlement of the estate six years later

[22] Information on Alexander B. Moncravie's birthdate and Civil War record was
assembled by his granddaughter, Mrs. Virginia Moran, from military records and
made available through her courtesy. In annotating extracts from the Fort Pierre
Journals in *South Dakota Historical Collections* (Pierre, 1918), IX, p. 217, Doane
Robinson identifies an "Isidore Montouie (or Moncrenie)" as a half-breed son of
J. B. Moncrevie. No evidence for this identification is given.

[23] Letters Received by Office of Indian Affairs, *op. cit.*

[24] Information supplied by Mrs. Virginia Moran.   [25] Claim no. 6690, *op. cit.*

stated that he had no widow, children or "relation." However, the records show that Alexander's widow, then remarried and living in Kansas, did come forward and inform the court that she had been married to Alexander B. Moncravie, "the only son of J. B. Moncravie." She listed four sons from that marriage, "all in the Indian Territory." [26] The administrator of his estate made one last effort in 1892 to collect his old depredation claims, but it was found that most of the supporting papers had been lost through the years by lending them to members of Congress who had promised help.[27]

Moncravie's four grandsons, Charles Alexander, Fred A., Henry E., and John B. Moncravie, were original allotment holders on the Omaha reservation in the 1880s by virtue of a most interesting fur-trade heritage.[28] Their father was Alexander B. Moncravie, John's son born on the Yellowstone in 1844. Their mother was Elizabeth Paul Moncravie, the daughter of Mary Jane Barada. The latter was the daughter of Michael Barada, interpreter for the Omahas at Prairie du Chien in 1830, and an Omaha woman. She was first married to John P. Cabanné and bore him a son, Antoine.[29] She later married Edward Paul, also known as Edward Loise, a mixed blood Osage, and had several children including the wife of Alexander Moncravie.[30] Her

---

[26] Information supplied by the Clerk of the Court, Nemaha County, Nebraska.

[27] Claim no. 6690, *op. cit.*

[28] The list of allottees is reproduced in the *Twenty-seventh Annual Report,* Bureau of American Ethnology, (Washington, 1911), 643-54.

[29] See photograph and biographical sketch of Antoine Cabney in J. Sterling Morton, *Illustrated History of Nebraska* (Lincoln, 1906), II, pp. 145-46. There are some theories that Mary J. Barada married one or another of the sons of J. P. Cabanné, Sr., but Antoine was specific in referring to them as his half-brothers.

[30] Morton, *op. cit.,* says that Mary Jane Barada's second husband was Edward Loisell, a former clerk of John P. Cabanné. In the census records and Omaha allotment list Mary Jane is shown as Mary J. Paul. However, both Mrs. Virginia Moran and John Moncravie say that her grave marker in Cedar Vale, Kansas, gives her surname as "Loise." John Moncravie says that Edward Loise was the son of Paul Loise, interpreter at the treaties with the Osage in 1818 and 1825. He has a copy of

sister was the Indian wife of Joshua Pilcher at Council Bluffs.[31]

a baptismal record for Paul, Antoinette and Louisa, children of Paul Loise "and a savage Osage woman," November 1, 1801. Sponsors included Teresa Papin, Mary Felipe Le Duc, Sophia Labadie, Francis Chouteau, Antoinette Labadie and Auguste Chouteau. The half breed son Paul was the "Edward Paul" who married Mary Jane Barada. In the 1860 census Mary J. Paul is listed in Richardson County, Nebraska, as the head of a household with children: Teresa 21, Madeline 20, Elisabeth 16, Louisa 11 and William 18. Her son "Antonio Cabony" lived next door to her with his wife Anna.

[31] See sketch of her son John Pilcher in Morton, *op. cit.*, II, pp. 142-43.

John Newman

by CHARLES G. CLARKE
Beverly Hills, California

John Newman appears to be the great-great grandson of Walter Newman, born in England, who in 1683 emigrated to New Jersey.[1] Walter's son, also named Walter, had a son, John, who settled in Heidelberg Township, Lancaster County, Pennsylvania, where he founded the village of Newmanstown. This John was the father of Walter III, 1761-1851, who married Catherine Zimmerman. To them was born about 1785, John Newman. There were several other John Newmans by this time, mostly cousins, but it seems probable that the above is the ancestry of our man.

From Pennsylvania, Walter III and family migrated to Point Pleasant, Virginia, and from there to Licking County, Ohio, where Walter III died, April 15, 1851. As indicated above, the Newman family had been settlers in frontier America for over a hundred years.

Like many other young men of his time, John Newman found that the frontier and excitement had moved farther west. Joining the U.S. Army seemed the obvious way to see the action and participate in the fascination of forest life – and get paid for it.

By the fall of the year 1803, when Lewis and Clark were seeking active young men for their forthcoming expedition to the west, they found John Newman enlisted as a private in Captain Daniel Bissell's 1st Infantry Company then stationed at Fort Massac on the lower Ohio.[2] Liberal cash

---

[1] Genealogical data furnished me by Mr. Newman A. Hall of Washington, D.C. See also, Frederick A. Vircus, ed., *The Compendium of American Genealogy* (Chicago, 1942; reprinted, Baltimore, 1968, VII, p. 400.

[2] Donald Jackson, ed., *Letters of the Lewis and Clark Expedition and Related Documents, 1783-1854* (Urbana, 1962), 103, 370n, 425. (Hereafter cited as: Jackson).

inducements and the promise of additional adventure undoubtedly prompted Newman to volunteer for the Lewis
and Clark Expedition.

The new additions to the command were moved up to
Wood River, on the east side of the Mississippi, opposite the
mouth of the Missouri. Here a camp was established during
the winter of 1803-04, where the men were observed and
trained for the duties of the expedition. Although John
Newman was a large man, extremely powerful, strong
willed and of short temper, he seems to have avoided temp-
tation to violate the stern military rules of the camp, as some
of his companions did.[3] He was entrusted with letters to
deliver to Captain Lewis in St. Louis and others to be left
at the village of Cahokia.[4]

In the spring of 1804, the expedition started its voyage up
the muddy Missouri. En route, on June 29, 1804, Newman
was a member of the court martial which tried the case of
Hugh Hall for stealing whiskey.[5] Newman seems to have
been a model soldier and hunter until October 12, 1804,
when something happened to cause him to utter highly
criminal and mutinous remarks. Meriwether Lewis, in a
letter to Henry Dearborn, Secretary of War, dated January
15, 1807, gives the most lucid account. He writes, in part:[6]

> . . . John Newman was a private in the infantry of the United
> States Army, who joined me as a volunteer . . . and was mus-
> tered as one of the permanent party. . . shortly before we arrived
> at the Mandan village he committed himself by using certain mutinous
> expressions which caused me to arrest him and to have him tried by a
> court martial formed of his peers: they, finding him guilty, sentenced
> him to receive seventy-five lashes and to be discharged from the per-
> manent party. . . The conduct of this man, previous to this period,
> had been generally correct; and the zeal he afterwards displayed for

[3] Reuben G. Thwaites, ed., *Original Journals of the Lewis and Clark Expedition,
1804-1806* (New York, 1904), I, p. 9. (Hereafter cited as: Thwaites).

[4] Ernest S. Osgood, ed., *The Field notes of William Clark, 1803-1805* (New
Haven, 1964), 28.

[5] Thwaites, I, p. 61.   [6] Thwaites, VII, p. 356. See also, Jackson, 365-66.

the benefit of the service, was highly meritorious. In the course of the winter, while at Fort Mandan, from an ardent wish to atone for the crime which he had committed at an unguarded moment, he exerted himself, on every occasion, to become useful. This disposition induced him to expose himself too much to the cold of that climate, and on a hunting excursion, he had his hands and feet severely frozen with which he suffered extreme pain, for some weeks . . . he asked forgiveness for what had passed, and begged that I would permit him to continue with me through the voyage; . . . although he stood acquitted in my mind, I determined to send him back, which was accordingly done. Since my return I have been informed that he was extremely serviceable as a hunter, on the voyage to St. Louis, and that the boat, on several occasions, owed her safety, in a great measure, to his personal exertions, being a man of uncommon activity and bodily strength. If under these circumstances it should be thought proper to give Newman the remaining third which will be deducted from the gratuity awarded Baptiste Le Page, who occupied his station in the after part of the voyage, I should feel myself much gratified.

A few months later Lewis must have been gratified to learn that under the Land Compensation Act of March 1807, John Newman received a warrant for 320 acres of land and also the extra pay as awarded the regular members.[7] I have been unable to locate any record of Newman selling this land warrant, or otherwise disposing of his land. It is therefore possible that he received title to this land located in Franklin or Howard counties, Missouri, and may have lived there, or nearby, for some years thereafter.

He had returned from the expedition to St. Louis in June 1805, and may have then gone to Ohio to visit his parents and may have possibly married there. Unfortunately there are no records extant until July 5, 1832, when he was married by Reverend Lutz to Miss Olympia Dubreuil, born, Aug. 17, 1810, daughter of Antoine and Elisabeth (Paran) Dubreuil – all of St. Louis.[8] There is the possibility that this was a second marriage. This John Newman, according

---

[7] Jackson, 378, 380, 372n, 422.

[8] St. Louis Cathedral Marriage Records, and *Missouri Republican* for July 10, 1832. In this last newspaper account he is mentioned as John Newman, Esq.

to the old St. Louis Cathedral Register, was a son of Walter and Catherine (Zimmerman) Newman of Pennsylvania. There are no recorded children of the Newman-Dubreuil marriage. This John Newman had a brother, Jonas Newman, born in 1795 in Pennsylvania, but living with his family in St. Louis at this time.

Undoubtedly, the above John Newman is the same John Newman who attended a meeting at the Town Hall of St. Louis on September 10, 1832, in connection with the cholera epidemic then raging, in which Newman and eight other men were appointed a committee "to carry measures into effect" which included the prohibition of the sale of watermelons, green corn, cabbage and other foods; to examine the stalls in the public market and see that they were thoroughly cleaned every day; to proscribe the manner of erecting outhouses, the depth and the manner of constructing the same.[9]

The first record of John Newman's being in the fur trade is a reference in the Chouteau ledgers in the Missouri Historical Society, where an order is found, dated July 22, 1833, to pay Newman from the P. Chouteau, Jr. account. John Newman next appears in the journal of Francis A. Chardon,[10] for on November 2, 1834, while Chardon and William P. May were on the Missouri near the Knife River, close to the former site of Fort Mandan of Lewis and Clark, Chardon writes:

. . . Proceeding along the river to find a good camping place, we were hailed from the bushes "Hollow." "Hollow" was the answer, and out rushed one of the largest Kind of Americans, with a rifle in his hand, ready to drop one of us – however, We camped with him that night – his name was John Newman, a trapper, who had left the little Miss° [Chardon's name for the Teton River] in September last, with an associate, who left him on the Cheyenne river. – Newton [sic]

_____

[9] Kindly furnished me by Mrs. Frances H. Stadler, archivist, Mo. Hist. Soc., quoting article in Mo. Hist. Soc. Colls., III, no. 3 (March, 1936), 48.

[10] Annie Heloise Abel, ed., Chardon's Journal at Fort Clark, 1834-1839 (Pierre, S.D., 1932).

mistook the Knife river for Cherry river. [On which there was a Post of the American Fur Company which he was probably seeking.]

Tuesday (Nov. 4, 1834). Started for the Fort [Clark] with our horses loaded with Meat in company of Newton [sic] who had made up his mind to go down [to Fort Pierre] by way of the Miss° – in a canoe. [Which he did on November 6th] [11]

Chardon's Journal contains some twenty-five references to Newman in all, but many are terse notations of his starting out on a spring or fall hunt for beaver; returning from the hunts and like activities in the area surrounding Fort Clark. On July 2, 1836, Chardon writes:

Newmas [sic] wife [Mandan] run off, he went to the Village armed like a Don Quixotte, determined to bring her back dead or alive – brot her and the whole family down, had a talk when she concluded to stay at least one night more.

July 3 . . . Newmas [sic] wife has now left him positively he seems to think that marrying here is not the thing it is cracked up to be. only married 15 days and his wife deserted him. [12]

May 22, 1837. Newman arrived from Beaver hunting – he made a tolerable hunt, sixty-four skins, he was robed of his gun by a war party of Rees and Gros Ventres on the little Miss°. Out five days without eating. [13]

June 29, 1837. Newman and Benture started up to Fort Union, to proceed from thence to the Coquille [Musselshell River] to trap Beaver down as far as Fort Clark. [14]

March 25, 1838. Newman started Out Beaver hunting. The Rees started Out to Make dried Meat. . . [15]

July 1, 1838. The Indians reports the Death of John Newman who left here the 25th March to Make his spring hunt, he was Killed by the Yanctons. . . [16]

So ends the life of John Newman. If he was the same John Newman who was born about 1785, this would make him over fifty years old when he met his death. If this seems

---

[11] *Ibid.*, 13, and note 318, p. 290.

[12] *Ibid.*, 70-71. This suggests similar trouble with his Dubreuil marriage and the reason why Newman became a trapper.

[13] *Ibid.*, 113.   [14] *Ibid.*, 119.   [15] *Ibid.*, 154.   [16] *Ibid.*, 166.

rather old for a man to be exposed to the below zero weather of the upper Missouri, wading icy streams in quest of beaver, it may be recalled that at this very same time, one of his former companions of the Lewis and Clark-Fort Mandan days, Toussaint Charbonneau, was in this area, trading and trapping, aged some eighty years.[17]

While Newman's life as a trapper seems to comprise only the years 1833 to 1838, the pattern of his early life may in general apply to many others who became Mountain Men.

[17] *Ibid.,* various entries.

Pierre Didier Papin

by WILLIAM A. GOFF
Kansas City, Missouri

There are many names connected with the fur trade of the nineteenth century, quite a few of which have been rescued from oblivion since the inception of the *Mountain Men Series,* but of all these names, none has been so obscured by confusion and neglect as that of "Papin."

Spelled variously as "Pappan," "Papan," and "Pepin," it is one of the oldest and most respected French names in St. Louis, in these and other times. The Papins were one of the first families to take residence in St. Louis; Joseph Alexandre Papin was with the expedition of Pierre Laclede Liguest, when, in 1763 he founded St. Louis.[1]

Three generations of Papins had lived in Canada before St. Louis was established. The blood of knights, captains and governors flowed in the veins of the Pierre Papin who brought the name to the new world. Born in the Province of Maine, France, in 1631, at age twenty-two he was an officer in the expedition headed by M. de la Dauversier which founded Montreal (Ville-Marie). There had been Papins living in Anjou, Orleans, Picardy, Hainault and Bretagne; at least one authority has connected the family with royalty in the thirteenth century. The Brittany line produced Pierre Papin of Maine, and subsequently Pierre Didier Papin.[2]

He was born in St. Louis March 7, 1798, the sixth son of Joseph Marie and Marie Louise Bourgeois (Chouteau).

---

[1] John Thomas Scharf, *History of St. Louis City and County* (Philadelphia, 1883). Also, see Papin Papers, Missouri Historical Society, St. Louis, Mo. There is a Papin Street which parallels Chouteau Avenue on the north, extending, with interruptions, from 10th Street to Forest Park.

[2] Papin Papers, Mo. Hist. Soc.

The J. M. Papins were blessed with fourteen children, only the last of which did not reach maturity.[3] Pierre Didier's father had failed in the fur business in 1796,[4] so it is just barely possible that he may have been born somewhere in the confines of what is now Forest Park, instead of the two-story stone house which his father had built on Main Street in 1780.[5]

Lieutenant-Governor Zenon Trudeau upon hearing of Joseph M. Papin's financial difficulties had made him a concession of 3200 arpens (approximately 2000 acres), which embraced all of what is now Forest Park, except a narrow strip on the south. The grant extended north beyond what is now Olive Street. There is, however, no record that Joseph Papin and his family ever actually lived, or even built a home, on this site. Pierre Didier Papin was probably born in the original Papin house on Main Street.[6]

Nothing is known of Didier's childhood.[7] He was, except

---

[3] Baptismal Records, St. Louis Cathedral, Mercantile Library, St. Louis, Missouri.

[4] Scharf, *op. cit.,* 752. Also see Papin Papers, *loc. cit.*

[5] Scharf, *op. cit.,* 752. On Sept. 1, 1796, a concession was signed by Zenon Trudeau, a French colonel acting for the Spanish as Lieutenant-Governor of the western part of Illinois Territory, which invested the family of Joseph Marie Papin with the ownership of a tract of land measuring 3200 arpens, embracing all of present Forest Park except a narrow strip on the south and extending north quite a distance beyond what is now Olive Street. Title was invested in the wife, Mme. Marie Louise Chouteau Papin. Merc. Lib.

Also, see Papin Papers. A letter from Henri C. Berthe (son of Zoe Papin), dated Feb. 20, 1938, Hollywood, Calif., stating that he had found several land grants executed by Charles Gratiot in favor of his (Berthe's) great, great, grandmere, Mme. J. M. Papin (Gratiot was her brother-in-law). "These grants cover property which is now part of Forest Park." Mo. Hist. Soc.

[6] Scharf, *op. cit.,* 130-31. "Market Square was bounded by Main, Market, Walnut, and the River (Mississippi). As you came down Main Street there were the Sarpys, Brazeaus, Papins, Connors, Labbadies, etc.," Papin Papers. A letter from Mrs. Clementine Carriere to her brother, Theophile Papin, Sr., (no date) states that Joseph Marie Papin in 1780 purchased from M. Duralde the southeast corner of what is now Block 32. On this site he replaced an old standing-post house with a two-story stone house.

[7] It seemed to be a common practice for the French to use the middle name as often as the first name, a not too inconvenient custom, as he and Mellicourt had identical first names.

for Theodore D'artigny and Joseph who died in infancy, the baby of the family.[8] He was afforded at least an adequate education, for he was fluent in both English and French. In a time when many a contract was signed with an "X," all St. Louis Papins were literate in two languages. Regrettably, Pierre D. left no journals or diaries, which accounts, in good part, for the veil surrounding his activities among the Indians in the wilds of the Upper Missouri.

It is reasonable to accept the statement that "as a boy he spent much time with the American Fur Company."[9] Of his six living brothers, five were engaged in the fur trade at one time or another, as had been, to some extent, his father and grandfather.

An older brother, Alexander LaForce Papin, born 1782 and called sometimes "Alex" and sometimes "LaForce," was a trapper on the Upper Missouri for a good many years, later moving to the Osage trade.[10] Hippolyte Lebert Papin, born 1787, and Sylvestre Vilray (Villeray) Papin, born

[8] Baptismal Records, St. Louis Cathedral. Merc. Lib.

[9] H. L. Conard, *Encyclopedia of the History of St. Louis*, III, p. 1693.

[10] Edwin James, *Account of an Expedition . . . Stephen H. Long*, in R. G. Thwaites, ed., *Early Western Travels*, xv, p. 143, note 44. "*Comment by Ed*. Laforce Pappan (Papin, Papan) was probably the grandson of Joseph Pappan, a Canadian fur-trader who came to St. Louis about 1770, and was for many years a trader among the Pawnee. He died of cholera (1848) while on his way to St. Louis. Emily, his daughter by a Pawnee woman, married Henry, son of Lucien Fontenelle."

In the second generation of Papins in Canada, Gilles Papin married first Marie Bouchereau, in 1693. There were six children, one of whom was Joseph Alexandre, the first Papin in St. Louis, and the grandfather of Alexandre LaForce Papin, to whom reference is made above. Upon the death of Marie Bouchereau Papin, Gilles remarried and fathered several more children. This second family could well be the origin of the Papins who operated the ferry across the Kaw, and with whom the St. Louis Papins are so often confused.

Alex's grandfather, Joseph Alexandre Papin, died in 1772, presumably in St. Louis, of natural causes. Alex's father, Joseph Marie Papin, was engaged in the fur trade, but probably not as a trapper. He was out of the business by 1796, and died in 1811. The Papin Papers in the Missouri Historical Society embody an extensive and detailed genealogy of this branch of the family, and the Baptismal Records at the Mercantile Library contain the names and dates of birth of the fourteen children of Joseph and Marie Louise. The names of the daughters are: Margaret, Marie Therese, Pelagie, Sophi, and Emilie.

1794, were both artisans in metal, designing and manufacturing hatchets, axes, arrow-points, etc., for trade goods. Vilray died in 1827, and Lebert went into partnership with Theodore, a year younger than Didier, in the confectionery business. Theodore had previously spent some time in the Santa Fe trade.[11] Pierre Mellicourt (shown as "Mellicour" on Cathedral Records) Papin, born 1793, was certainly the most widely known of the Papin brothers. He was the American Fur Company agent to the Osage until his death from cholera in 1849. He had lived for many years in Indian Territory and had returned to St. Louis on business when he was stricken and died in a day or two.[12] Papinsville, Missouri, was named in his honor.[13] Joseph, the eldest child of Joseph Marie and Marie Louise Papin, operated a confectionery in the market square area of St. Louis until his death in 1850 at age 70.[14]

On August 10, 1826, a marriage contract was drawn up between Pierre Didier Papin and Catherine Louise Cerré, the only daughter of Leon Paschal and Therese Louise Lamy Cerre.[15] This union lasted for twenty-seven years and was blessed with four children: Leon J., Alfred D., Armentine, and Palmire. There were twenty-six grandchildren.[16]

Pierre Didier Papin's name first appears on the American Fur Company's books under the date of May, 1825.[17] In 1827 when the union between the Columbia Fur Company and the American Fur Company, which created the

---

[11] Papin Papers. Letter dated August 25, 1893, from Leon J. Papin to his cousin, Clementine Carriere at Selma, St. Louis County, Missouri.

[12] "Kansas Before 1854: A Revised Annals," ed. by Louise Barry, in *Kansas Historical Quarterly*, XXXI (1965), 324-25.

[13] *Missouri Historical Review*, X, p. 285.

[14] Joseph Papin was the only brother who did not engage in the fur trade; he operated a grocery and confectionery at 111 North First Street from before the time John A. Paxton published his 1821 *Directory of St. Louis*, until 1842 when he moved the business to another location.

[15] Church Records, St. Louis Cathedral, Merc. Lib.   [16] Papin Papers.

[17] Ledger "H," American Fur Co. Books, Mo. Hist. Soc.

Upper Missouri Outfit, had been arranged, Papin was sent up to Fort Tecumseh by Ramsey Crooks.[18] There he assisted Kenneth McKenzie, who had been the president of Columbia Fur Company, in taking inventory of Columbia Fur's property. This event took place in the fall of 1827.

We next read of Pierre D. Papin in the summer of 1829, when the new firm of P. D. Papin & Co. was formed with the intention of competing in the fur trade with the Upper Missouri Outfit which was under the impression that it had eliminated all competition. In the summer of 1829, Messrs. Papin, Chenie fils, Michel and Gabriel Cerré, Honore Picotte, Denis Guion, Delaurier (Antoine ?) and Louis Bonfort (Bompart), set out to slay the giant with a capital of $16,000.[19] In spite of reverses, such as the wreck of one of their barges and the loss of three of their trappers, they succeeded in annoying Kenneth McKenzie to such a degree that he bought them out.[20]

[18] H. M. Chittenden, *History of the American Fur Trade of the Far West* (Stanford, Calif. 1954), I, p. 326.

[19] Paul Chrisler Phillips, *The Fur Trade* (Norman, 1961), II, p. 423.

[20] *Ibid.* The Bompart File at the Missouri Historical Society contains a letter of Aug. 19, 1829, from M. Louis Bompart to Papin, Picotte and Guion discussing the wreck of their barge and the loss of merchandise, and outlining plans for an expedition "up the river as soon as navigation permits."

Also, see letter of July 28, 1830, from P. D. Papin to P. M. Papin in the Chouteau-Papin Collection at Mo. Hist. Soc:

You have doubtless heard of our misfortune and I thought after such an accident I would never be able to pay our creditors. We had $16,000 worth of debts payable the 1st of July and almost all our negotiable securities in the bank. Our opponents were not very glad when we paid and still less to see us outfit another barge. We have to thank Devins, Delaurier and Bompart who served for nothing. Chenie, Picotte, Pascal, Lemi and I are still together and will perhaps do better next year. . .

The Fort Tecumseh Letterbooks, as shown in the *South Dakota Historical Collections*, IX, p. 133, contain an entry of Tuesday, August 24, 1830, which says:

I have just heard that three white men have been killed by the Rees, viz. Pierre Bouchet, Jos. Paffiche (or Passiche) and another whose name I do not know. They were killed between the Rees Village and the Mandans by a war party of Rees. They had Merchandise and horses to the amount of $1,000.

The Western Monitor (Fayette, Mo.) Nov. 3, 1830, announced that Joseph Papiche was killed by the Arikaras, along with Pierre Bouchet and Baptiste Hebert, employees of P. D. Papin & Co.

During Papin's tenure as head of P. D. Papin & Co., the Fort Tecumseh journal records frequent exchanges of hospitality between the American Fur Company representatives, and Messrs. Papin, Picotte and others from Papin House;[21] this, in spite of the intense rivalry between the two posts. Loneliness was common to "The Company" and "Opposition," alike. Then, too, they could have been discussing the sale of Papin & Co. which took place soon after.

McKenzie put Papin and Honoré Picotte, one of his old partners in the Columbia Fur Company, to work for the Upper Missouri Outfit. Papin signed a contract to clerk and trade for three years at $1,000 per year. He traded with the Yanctonnais and Ogallala, on, and in the vicinity of, the White River of South Dakota.[22]

Evidently his work for the Upper Missouri Outfit was at least satisfactory, for on August 27, 1832, before his contract had run two years, he wrote his brother Pierre Mellicourt that he had made a new arrangement with the company for two more years at $1,500 per year.[23]

In the years 1830 to 1834 Papin continued to trade with the Sioux on the White River, under the somewhat jaundiced eye of William Laidlaw who headquartered first at Fort Tecumseh, and then at Fort Pierre, upon its completion in 1833.

---

[21] Ft. Tecumseh Letterbooks, *So. Dak. Hist. Collections,* IX, p. 95. "Mr. Papin's House refers to the post that was located a few rods south of Bad River (earlier called the Little Missouri) upon the site of the present city of Fort Pierre. It was known variously as Fort Teton, the French Post, and Papin's House. . . It was built in 1828."

Sunday, 11 (April 1830) Messrs. Papin, Cerre, and Noble dined with us.

Wednesday, 14 Messrs. Laidlaw, Papin, Cerre, Chardon and Laboue, with 6 men and 10 or 12 horses left here for Medicine Hill on a hunting excursion.

Tuesday April 20 . . . At 1 pm Messrs. Laidlaw, Chardon, Holliday, Laboue and myself rode down to Mr. Papin's house. We returned in the evening accompanied by Messrs. Papin, Cerre and Noble. . .

[22] Phillips, *Fur Trade,* 423. Also, see Chouteau-Maffitt Collection, Mo. Hist. Soc., agreement signed at Ft. Tecumseh, Oct. 16, 1830, Papin, trader and clerk for 3 years with Yanctonnais, at $1,000. High pay for this classification of work.

[23] Chouteau-Papin Collection, Mo. Hist. Soc.

The Fort Pierre Letterbook projects the image of Laidlaw as a rather carping fellow. Witness a letter to one of his traders, Colin Campbell:

> Mr. Colin Campbell: Yesterday I was much surprised by the arrival of your man with four horses and six carts all in the most passable order. . . You may judge of my surprise upon seeing that you had taken on that expensive equipment to the Ogallalah Post, when there was no earthly cause for it, and besides I took such pains in explaining to you that the equipment was to be left at the fork of the Cheyenne. .
>
> You have therefore thwarted my plan entirely. . . It was certainly a great want of forethought on your part . . . this is certainly very galling, I must say I feel ashamed of it (however you may feel).[24]

Trader Papin succeeded William Laidlaw as agent for the Upper Missouri Outfit at Fort Pierre in the summer of 1834.[25] The following spring, Laidlaw sent a letter to Pierre Chouteau, Jr., which, among other things, voiced sharp disappointment at "the arrangement entered into with Papin, Picotte and Chardon . . . I feel both my feelings and interest injured." Nevertheless, letters from Fort Pierre were signed by Halsey and Colin Campbell "for P. D. Papin." See note 24.

In contrast to Laidlaw's letter to Colin Campbell, shown above, is Papin's communication addressed to the same man:

> Friend Campbell: Starting for Saint Louis, I leave you in charge of Ft. Pierre, until our return. I have reason to believe that you will use your best endeavors in everything that will promote and interest the Company during our absence. I flatter myself to presume so, from the long knowledge I have of you. . .
>
> > I remain with confidence and consideration,
> > your truly and sincere friend   P. D. Papin [26]

24 Fort Pierre Letterbook. The Clay County Museum Association has copies of William Laidlaw's correspondence which were obtained from the Missouri Historical Society. The copies were kindly placed at the writer's disposal.

25 *Chardon's Journal at Fort Clark,* ed. by Annie Heloise Abel (Iowa City, Iowa, 1932), 371. McKenzie's letter to Pierre Chouteau & Co. June 30, 1834: "Mr. Papin (who is in charge there. . ." (Ft. Pierre).

26 Chouteau-Papin Collection, Mo. Hist. Soc.

Papin renewed this man's contract with the Upper Missouri Outfit as a clerk and trader on November 11, 1836.[27]

In 1836 Pratte, Chouteau & Co. became Pierre Chouteau Jr. & Co. with no apparent change in Papin's status; the last entry in F. A. Chardon's *Fort Clark Journal,* May 6, 1839, states:

> . . . off at daylight and arrived at Ft. Pierre the 10th – found Messrs. Papin and Halsey there. Mr. Picotte had left for St. Louis 2 days before.[28]

At this point there is a hiatus extending from 1839 to 1845, except for a brief mention of Papin in company with some of his men overtaking John Sibille, of Sibille and Adams, in September of 1842, on the way to Fort Laramie (Fort John). The two parties proceeded northwestward together, Sibille arriving at Fort Platte October 12, 1842.[29]

Papin had moved from Fort Pierre to Fort John in the period 1839 to 1842, as W. D. Hodgkiss wrote to Andrew Drips on March 25, that "Mr. Papin (at Fort Laramie) received an express from Bridger and Vasquez in the winter. They had not done much. The body of traders equipped by H. B. Coy was a strong opposition to them."[30]

The American Fur Company, per se, had ceased to exist in September of 1842. Although business was carried on by Pierre Chouteau Jr. & Co. (as it had been in 1838) the concern was generally known as the American Fur Co., and its policies remained the same as in the past. Pierre Chouteau, Jr. no longer ran the company from the office at 50 North Front, St. Louis, Missouri. By the middle 1840s he had banks, mines, coal interests and steel companies to take

---

[27] *Ibid.*   [28] *Chardon's Journal,* 194.

[29] "Kansas Before 1854," ed. by Louise Barry, in *Kansas Historical Quarterly,* XXIX, p. 443.

[30] William Marshall Anderson, *The Rocky Mountain Journals,* ed. by Dale L. Morgan and Eleanor Towles Harris (San Marino, Calif., 1967), 375.

CEDAR STUMP MARKING PIERRE DIDIER PAPIN'S GRAVE
AT THE MOUTH OF HELVAS CANYON, NEAR SCOTT'S BLUFFS NATIONAL MONUMENT
Courtesy of Scott's Bluffs National Monument, National Park Service.

up his time, more and more of which was spent in New York, and in the European financial centers.[31]

Alex Culbertson, a company "pillar," had been sent to Fort John in late 1843 to stem the business decline at that post.[32] In 1844 he was back at his old stand at Fort Union; Joseph Picotte (a relative of Honoré Picotte) had been sent to Ft. John to take over.[33] Joseph did not last long, and the reliable Papin was the bourgeois in the fall of 1845.[34]

The year 1846 was remarkable in that P. D. Papin received press notices in profusion. He was conspicuous by his absence at Fort John on June 15, when Francis Parkman arrived, but the young traveler had already met the affable Frenchman down the Platte, en route to St. Louis. Parkman reports:

> The boats, eleven in number, deep-laden with the skins, hugged close to the shore, to escape being borne down by the swift current. . . Papin sat in the middle of one of the boats, upon the canvas that protected the cargo. He was a stout, robust fellow, with a little gray eye, that had a peculiarly sly twinkle. . . I shook hands with the *bourgeois,* and delivered the letter: then the boats swung around into the stream and floated away. They had reason for haste, for already the voyage from Fort Laramie had occupied a full month, and the river was growing daily more shallow.[35]

A week or so later the *St. Louis Reveille* of July 27, reported the same party, as of June 12:

> The party from the Fort (John), numbering *thirteen* mackinaw boats, were in charge of Mr. Papin, who has long been the popular and efficient superintendent of affairs at the Fort. We saw eleven of the boats yesterday morning, on the western side of the river, with whom, as we are informed, is Mr. Papin. . .

---

31 Chouteau Papers, Mo. Hist. Soc.

32 Ray H. Mattison, "Alexander Culbertson," in this *Series,* I, p. 254.

33 *Chardon's Journal,* note 195.

34 Cash Book "HH," American Fur Co. Books, p. 203; also, *Chardon's Journal,* note 195.

35 LeRoy R. Hafen and F. M. Young, *Fort Laramie and the Pageant of the West* (Glendale, Cal., 1938), 114-15.

After tribulations and herculean labors the caravan, or flotilla, arrived in St. Louis, July 6, with eight boats containing 1100 packs of buffalo robes, 10 beaver packs, and 3 packs of bear and wolf skins. The journey had started May 7.[36]

Pierre had returned once more to his home at the southwest corner of 2nd and Pine; to Leon, Alfred, Armentine and Palmire, and, of course, his beloved "Catiche." It would be September before he would start the long trek back to Fort John and the long, cold nights and danger-fraught days. In the interim the "Company" bestowed upon him a partnership – just about the pinnacle of achievement for a fur man.[37]

"From the Riviere de Kansas" Papin wrote his wife Sept. 8, 1846, that the return journey was "thus far very fortunate." "10 miles de Westport" he wrote:

Chere Femme: I have been thinking of you and I am always angry at leaving you for so long a time. . . Embrace the children for me. . .[38]

About the middle of May 1847, "Arriving on Missouri's border (Westport?) from Fort Laramie by way of the Oregon Trail, were Pierre D. Papin, Charles Beaumont, and seven other traders with 3 wagons. . ." They had left Fort Laramie (Fort John) April 20, and had traveled at night to avoid Indians. Six of the traders arrived at St. Louis on May 24, but Papin arrived on July 8, aboard the steamboat "Martha" along with John Sarpy and Honoré Picotte, two other members of the company's hierarchy.[39]

The *St. Louis Reveille* and the *St. Louis Daily News* carried the information on July 9, 1847, that the "Martha," from the American Fur Company post at Fort Union, to St.

---

[36] "Kansas Before 1854," in *Kansas Historical Quarterly*, XXX, p. 374.
[37] *Chardon's Journal*, note 195.   [38] E. V. Papin Collection, Mo. Hist. Soc.
[39] "Kansas Before 1854," *loc. cit.*, p. 514.

Louis, passed Kawsmouth July 7. On board were John B. Sarpy, Honoré D. Picotte, and Pierre D. Papin; this would indicate that the party had terminated their overland journey at Leavenworth, rather than Westport.

On the return trip Papin and six men joined the party of Andrew Goodyear at Ketchum's Creek, September 18, and arrived at Fort John October 16, 1847, without trouble from the Indians.[40]

> Ma Chere Catiche: I wish to take advantage of every opportunity to assure you of my love and attachment. . . You must have received 2 letters from me before this by 2 Mormons descending the Platte on their return from California. . . I was much pleased with your letter and that of Leon. I hope that his noble sentiments will continue all his life. . .

This letter was written from Fort John, December 17.[41] The two Mormons to whom Papin refers are mentioned in the "Journal History," Mormon Church, Salt Lake City, Utah, under the date of October 6, 1847; the "Chief proprietor of Fort John" met the Mormons 160 miles east of Fort John.

Early in 1848, Joe Meek, having forsaken trapping for politics, was on his way to Washington City as an ambassador from the Oregon Territory:

> Following wagon tracks along the river, they made good time into Fort Laramie where a French trader, Pierre D. Papin, who was in charge, treated them most hospitably during their two day stay and sent them on their way with fresh mules and this warning advice: "there is a village of Sioux, of about six hundred lodges a hundred miles from here. Your course will bring you to it. Look out for yourself." [42]

The *St. Louis Daily Union,* July 20, 1848, contained the news that "Major Hamilton, Mr. Culbertson, Mr. Papin and 70 men connected with the American Fur Co. arrived here yesterday aboard the *Wyandotte.*" The gathering of

---

40 *Ibid.,* 543.　　　41 E. V. Papin Collection, Mo. Hist. Soc.
42 Harvey E. Tobie, *No Man Like Joe* (Portland, Oregon, 1949), 159.

such an impressive group of employees could only have been for the re-organization of the "Company" which took place that year.

The fall of 1848 did not find Papin departing for the trading post on Laramie River, or any other trading post; he remained in St. Louis. Andrew Drips, who had been in charge at Fort Pierre since 1846, received the following message from Pierre Chouteau Jr. & Co., dated August 18:

> Mr. P. D. Papin declining to return in the Missouri, as well as Mr. Picotte, we have decided you shall have the charge of Fort John. . .[43]

There was no reason given for Papin's refusal to return to his duties at Fort John. It could have been due to dissatisfaction with the company's new plans as they concerned him, or possibly an inclination to indulge himself with the company of his family and friends in St. Louis. He may even have entertained the idea of retiring altogether from the strenuous life of a fur man, although it is highly unlikely. Finances would have been no real obstacle to retirement – Papin's income from rental properties, during the period of 1849 to 1851, averaged over $300 per month.[44]

The Chouteau Papers for 1847 to 1853 make no reference to Pierre D. Papin, nor does the Papin Collection from 1847 to 1850, but in September, 1850, Theodore Papin wrote to his brother Pierre D. on the "Haut Mifsouri" (Upper Missouri). He apologized for not writing sooner, but gave no hint as to how long Pierre had been gone from St. Louis.[45] Whatever Pierre D.'s motivation to abandon the post on the Laramie and give up the fur trade, it was not strong enough to withstand for long the magnetism of a life which, once experienced, few men were ever able to renounce.

H. Renard wrote to Papin in February 1851, on the Forks of the Cheyenne:

[43] *Chardon's Journal,* note 247.
[44] Chouteau-Papin Collection, Rent Book of P. D. Papin, Mo. Hist Soc.
[45] E. V. Papin Collection, Mo. Hist. Soc.

Your country may be fine, but it does not have the advantages of communication. We hear from you so seldom we get worried about you,
knowing the risks you run. . . Your wife and children come to
dine with us, and all are well. . .[46]

After the purchase in 1849, of Fort Laramie by the
United States Army, Andrew Drips was instructed to establish a post in the neighborhood of Scotts Bluffs to catch the
Oregon Trail trade. The establishment had to be moved
twice, and never achieved the importance of the post on
the Laramie. Papin was there, doing his daily stint, in a
subordinate role.

The last entry for Pierre D. Papin, in Day Book SS of
the Upper Missouri Outfit records is dated Feb. 24, 1853:

> To Fort John Outfit, Papin, 1852
>   Balance of account transferred, due 12/31/1852 $19,277.32

Pierre Didier Papin died suddenly in May 1853, and is
buried in a lonely grave near a section of Scotts Bluffs called
Wildcat Hills. His resting place was discovered by Mr.
T. L. Green in the early 1930s. At that time a cedar stump
about three feet high was all that remained of a large cross
which had been the original grave marker. The few remaining old-timers could remember only the date, 1853; no day
or month.[47] The will was filed for probate on June 24, 1853.[48]

An attempt is alleged to have been made by Madame
Papin to have her husband's remains brought back to St.
Louis for burial, but due to a misapprehension regarding
the location of the new Fort John, the effort was a failure.

Catherine Cerré Papin died in 1884.

---

[46] *Ibid.*

[47] Letter of Sept. 30, 1970, from Mr. Paul C. Henderson, Bridgeport, Nebr.

[48] Letter from T. L. Green, Scottsbluff, Nebr., in Papin Collection, Mo. Hist. Soc:
"Miss (Stella) Drumm wrote 'The files of the *Mo. Republican* were carefully examined covering April 1st to September 1st, 1853, without finding any references to
the death of Pierre Didier Papin. *The St. Louis Intelligencer* for the same period
was also searched, although this file is not complete. I am at a loss to explain no
reference to Mr. Papin, as he was a wealthy and prominent citizen, and related by
blood and marriage to the most outstanding families here. . . His will filed for
probate, June 24, 1853.'"

This is a scanty accounting for nearly thirty years of deep involvement in one of the most exciting and challenging occupations which ever evolved upon this continent. As previously stated, Pierre D. Papin kept no private journal. The hardships he endured and the dangers he experienced can only be conjectured from the trials of his contemporaries who *have* left personal records. His portrait, and Parkman's description, indicate that he was a compact, well-built man of medium build. His letters reflect refinement, and his record of performance in positions of responsibility for the twenty years preceding his death prove his competency, but he "made no waves," attracted no undue attention, and is therefore unchronicled. It is somewhat of a surprise that Charles Larpenteur, while describing and discussing Papin's contemporaries, even his associates, never once mentions this sturdy countryman of his, even by implication.

As one enters the library of the Missouri Historical Society on the second floor of the Jefferson Memorial in St. Louis, he faces two large beautifully executed portraits. The one on the left is of Pierre Didier Papin, and the one on the right is of Catherine Cerré Papin, Pierre's beloved "Catiche." The portraits were presented to the Missouri Historical Society by Leon J. Papin, the eldest child of the couple.

A portrait of Papin appears in this volume at page 22.

Acknowledgements for help on "P. D. Papin":
  Missouri Historical Society, St. Louis, Missouri, Mrs. Stadler and Mrs. Dotzman
  Mercantile Library, St. Louis, Missouri, Mrs. Kirchner and Miss Mewes
  Clay County Museum Assn., Liberty, Missouri
  Nebraska State Historical Society, Omaha, Nebr., Mr. Paul Riley
  South Dakota State Historical Society, Pierre, So. Dakota, Mrs. Bonnie Gardner
  Missouri Valley Room, Kansas City Main Library, K.C., Missouri, Mrs. Smith and
    Miss Goldsmith
  Scott's Bluffs National Monument, Nat. Park Service, Mr. Homer L. Rouse
  Mr. Paul C. Henderson, Bridgeport, Nebr.

Simon Plamondon

by HARRIET D. MUNNICK
West Linn, Oregon

Few voyageurs in the employ of the great fur companies
were recorded for their individual deeds; they worked together as a team, and any discovery, exploration or success
was rightly credited to their leader. Simon Plamondon was
an exception. Although an engage, he traveled alone whenever possible, probing new routes in the way of a Daniel
Boone. The Northwest of 1820 was largely unexplored territory back of the main waterways, that is to say, the Columbia
River and its tributary Willamette and Snake rivers.

The state of Washington is half-bisected by the ramose
Puget Sound coming down from the north. The Cowlitz
River, a branch of the Columbia, reaches up from the south
as if to meet it, but in its upper reaches turns eastward, leaving a relatively low-lying region, sometimes known as "the
portage," between river and sound. The entire system –
river, portage and sound – lying between the Cascade
Mountains and the Coast Range, forms the geographic
"Puget Sound Trough."

In the heyday of the fur trade under the Hudson's Bay
Company the trough became the highway of travel to the
Fraser River in British Columbia, but in the earlier years of
the Pacific Fur Company and the North West Fur Company, it appears never to have been explored and only
vaguely known to exist. Neither Captain Robert Gray of
Boston nor Lieutenant Broughton of Great Britain had
noted the mouth of the Cowlitz on their voyages up the
lower Columbia in 1792. Gray probably did not ascend far
enough; Broughton missed it because the Cowlitz flows into

the great river through a swampy region of blind channels and overlapping islands densely grown up with cottonwood and willows.

In May of 1811 Duncan McDougall, then engaged in establishing Astoria at the mouth of the Columbia for the Pacific Fur Company, dispatched a party "to ascend the great river to spy out an establishment of white men" reported by the Indians "above certain rapids," which the Americans correctly suspected to be a rival post of the North West Fur Company.[1] Gabriel Franchère, a member of the party, left a clear account of the first recorded visit of white men to the Cowlitz River:

> . . . we procured a large canoe and a guide and set out on May 2 – Messrs. Alexander McKay, Robert Stuart, Ovide Montigny and I – with a sufficient number of men . . . The river narrows considerably about thirty miles from its mouth and is obstructed with islands covered with willows, poplars, alders and ash. Without exception, these islands are uninhabited and uninhabitable, for they are only swamps and are inundated during the months of June and July. So said our guide, Coalpo, who seemed to be an intelligent man.
>
> On the morning of the fourth we arrived at a large village of the same name as those we had passed the evening before, and we landed to obtain information about a little river that empties into the Columbia here. It comes from the north and is called Cowlitz by the natives. Mr. McKay embarked with Mr. Montigny and two Indians to examine the course of the river a certain distance upstream . . . after ascending the Cowlitz about a mile and a half, on rounding a bend of the stream they suddenly came in sight of about twenty canoes full of Indians, who made a rush upon them with the most frightful cries and screams.[2]

The party found to their dismay that they had pitched camp the evening before, to which McKay and his three companions returned, directly between two warring tribes.

---

[1] David Thompson, of the North West Fur Company, had come from Canada down the Columbia as far as Spokane Falls and there built a trading post in 1810-11.

[2] Gabriel Franchère, *Adventure at Astoria, 1810-14*, trans. and ed. by Hoyt Franchère (Univ. of Okla. Press, 1967), 48.

They spent a restless night trying to placate first one faction
and then the other as the two passed and repassed between
the villages, and were glad enough the following morning
to get back to the Columbia.

> . . . these savages who had never seen white men regarded us with
> astonishment and curiosity, lifting our trousers and opening our shirts
> to see if the skin of our bodies resembled that of our faces and hands.
> . . Then, giving them some looking-glasses, knives, tobacco and
> other trifles, we departed.[3]

It remained for Simon Plamondon to explore and open up
the Cowlitz route to the north ten years later.

Simon Plamondon had been born in 1800 to Jean Baptiste
Plamondon and Catherine Gill at St. François du Lac, a
village near the southern shore of the St. Lawrence and
about thirty miles above Three Rivers. He was the youngest
of seven children, and in youth became something of a lone
wolf. Although his father had a fair education, being Royal
Surveyor of his region and a sort of agent for the nearby
Abanaki tribe, Simon had little or none. Both his parents
and an older brother were drowned in the St. Lawrence
when the boy was ten years old. Henceforth, being large and
mature for his age, Simon seems to have wandered about
with his Indian friends very nearly at will. His grandfather
Gill had spent some years in Indian captivity following the
Revolutionary War, his father had been an Indian overseer,
and he himself had been reared in Indian country. He became fluent in various native languages, and ranged as freely
as if belonging to any tribe he happened to encounter.

At the age of fifteen he cut whatever home ties may have
remained and struck out for the Mississippi River. He
seems to have ranged the entire length of it before drifting
westward across the Great Plains. The three years he spent
as a nomad are unrecorded; it can only be surmised that he
spent them as a buffalo hunter with some Plains tribe or as a

---

[3] *Ibid.*, 49.

trapper in the Rocky Mountains, gone native as thoroughly as it is possible for any white man to do. All that has come down from those years are family traditions that he "could outrun and outwrestle any Indian buck," being lean, strong and well over six feet tall, even at eighteen, and that he had acquired several more Indian languages.[4]

By 1818 he had crossed the mountains and reached the Pacific Ocean at Fort George. Here he joined the North West Fur Company in its final years before its absorption by the Hudson's Bay Company. He worked about the fort as carpenter and jack-of-all-trades for a time, occupations that no doubt galled him. As soon as possible he qualified himself as voyageur and spent his time probing the unknown streams of western Washington for trapping and trade prospects.

By midwinter of 1818-1819 he was on the Cowlitz, the largest of the tributaries coming into the Columbia from the north, traveling alone. The Cowlitz was never an easy stream to follow, for despite the meandering and swampy debouche, the river above is swift and turbulent. A man alone and in winter must have made innumerable carries around obstructions. Twelve years later, when the route was well established and should have been in better shape, William Fraser Tolmie wrote of the trouble he and Archibald McDonald with "four Kanakas, stout fellows, who paddled lustily," had in ascending the river in May:

> The river was now a continued rapid & it was only by the most stren-uous efforts that the canoe could be urged on — on one occasion were obliged to disembark and tow up with ropes & again the channel being obstructed with trunks and branches of trees, I disembarked. Mac. con-tinued poling & the men were deep in the stream straining every nerve to get the canoe past the embarass, where there was an imminent risk of its being swung round by the current & dashed broadsides against the highest of the colossal trees which lay across the stream — their efforts

4 "The Plamondon Family," mimeo., 79 pages, by George Francis Plamondon, re-lates informally family recollections and legend, and has been the source of this writer's conjectures where exact documentary statement has not come to light.

being only sufficient to keep canoe in its position, without moving it upwards in the least. Mac. jumped out to assist and I who as yet was a spectator from one of the trunks forming embarass followed his example by leaping off the trunk nearest to stern of canoe . . . being hurried down against embarass, unable to obtain footing in three or four feet of water, by swimming strongly, at length caught hold of canoe by stern and by its support planted feet firmly on the bottom & lent my strength to push canoe upward, which by our united efforts was effected & we got into comparatively smooth water.[5]

Plamondon, whether or not he realized it, was under constant surveillance by the Indians. He saw a few and talked to them; owing perhaps to his custom of traveling unarmed as an indication of good faith, he met no unpleasantness from tribes usually hostile to intruders. He returned to Fort George with a report of good trade prospects and a beautiful country of wooded hills interspersed with fine level prairies. He had explored as far as the big bend to the east, and said he should like to go back for deeper penetration into such a promising region.

He had, in fact, covered the part of the river that was to furnish a main trade route to the north, since the upper reaches to the east lead only into canyons and formidable mountains. He was allowed to return to the Cowlitz the following year with two companions. This second expedition made side trips up neighboring streams and explored the region more thoroughly than Plamondon had been able to do alone. However, they proceeded very little farther upstream, for upon reaching approximately the place where he had turned back, they found themselves suddenly surrounded by natives and were taken as captives to the Cowlitz chieftain.

They made no resistance, which would have been useless in any case, and managed to convince Chief Scehaneewah that they came as guests rather than captives, and should be treated accordingly. The idea seemed reasonable to the

---

[5] William Fraser Tolmie, *Journal* (Vancouver, B.C., 1963), 187-88.

chief; after holding them several weeks in wary detention while he learned about their plans for trade, he released them to return to Fort George, and as a mark of special esteem, presented Simon with his daughter for a wife.

At this point Simon's wanderlust appears to have gone into temporary eclipse, for he became a routine middleman for the Hudson's Bay Company working out of Fort Vancouver. Along with regular brigade duty he was sent out on various construction jobs at new forts and on punitive expeditions against hostile tribes. His Indian marriage worked out well enough and produced one son, Simon, Jr., and three daughters between 1821 and 1827. At the birth of the last daughter, the mother died. Whether from grief or freedom from domesticity, Simon set out at once on another lone wandering which could hardly have been company business. He continued working his way northward, by what routes we do not know, but inasmuch as in old age he regaled his grandchildren with tales of what he had seen and done amongst the Eskimos, he seems to have reached northern Canada before drifting back to Fort Langley on the lower Fraser River, a year later.

There is some evidence that he had been given certain land rights in the "fine plain" he had visited on the Cowlitz, or had inherited the holdings of his father-in-law when the old chief was killed in 1826. Furthermore, the native population of the Northwest was rapidly fading under several years of an epidemic called ague by the whites but known only as "cole sick" by the Indians.

Plomodo says, [wrote Chief Factor James Douglas in 1840] that in 1830, the first ague summer, the living sufficed not to bury the dead, but fled in terror to the seacoast, abandoning the dead and dying to the birds and beasts of prey. Every village presented a scene harroeing to the feelings. The canoes were drawn up upon the beach, the nets extended on the willow boughs, the very dogs appeared as ever watchful, but there was not heard the cheerful sound of the human voice. . . Oh, God, wonderful and mysterious are Thy ways! [6]

The closing comment was probably that of Douglas. In spite of the wrathful visitation, Plamondon knew how to grasp an opportunity. He took up the occupation of his land along the Cowlitz, not far above the present Toledo, Washington, where he could hunt, farm, and be handily reached from Fort Vancouver at any time the need for a guide arose. He was at least semi-officially retired from the company.

At the same time he took another wife, Emelie Finlay, often spelled Fenlay. She was the métisse widow of an old Nor'wester, Pierre Bercier, and was the mother of seven children. Ten years later, Captain Charles Wilkes, who had engaged Simon as guide for the Washington leg of his exploratory tour, wrote that he "had seldom seen so pretty a woman as his [Plamondon's] wife, or a more cheerful and good housewife; before her marriage she was the belle of the country and celebrated for her feats of horsemanship." [7] For a woman of forty-five, with ten children of her own to date as well as four stepchildren, she must have been indeed remarkable. Of Simon himself Wilkes wrote, "A more useful person I have seldom met with, or one that could be so well depended on. He had been for several years in this territory, having left the Company's service, married an Indian wife, and was now living on a farm of about 50 acres at the Cowlitz, independent and contented." [8]

The Catholic Church reached the West with Fathers Blanchet and Demers in 1838, late in the year. Within three weeks the priests separated to look for suitable mission sites. The former selected Cowlitz Prairie for one such site, for although sparsely populated, it was on the trail to the north, and in addition, the Hudson's Bay Company was even then establishing an agricultural station known as Cowlitz Farm, which would employ many workmen and natives. On his

[6] James Douglas, "Diary," ed. by Herman A. Leader, in *Oregon Historical Quarterly,* XXXII (March 1931), 8.

[7] Charles Wilkes, *Narrative of the United States Exploring Expedition, 1838-42* (excerpts in *Oregon Historical Quarterly,* March 1931, p. 8). [8] *Ibid.*

first visit to the Cowlitz, Father Blanchet held mass in the Plamondon house, where, amongst other children, he baptized the three youngest of Simon's family. He then returned to Fort Vancouver, leaving his servant, Augustin Rochon, to construct a chapel of some sort against his next visit in the spring.

By April Rochon had got far enough along with the rough log and bark structure (which from its uncouth appearance, came to be known as the Wolf's Head Chapel, a title credited to Plamondon) that the priest was able to hold services there. Here he formally married Simon Plamondon and Emelie Finlay Bercier on April 6, 1839, and legitimatized their three sets of children – Marguerite, Francois, Pierre, Cecile, Louison, Elizabeth and Basile – Sophie, Simon, Jr., Therese and Marie Ann – Lina and Daniel. Three more children were to follow of this marriage, and one more of still a third.[9]

Although officially retired from service, Plamondon was still a vital link in the trade, since his bateau landing on the river became the port for Cowlitz Farm. "Sent down forty barrels (of salmon) to Plamondon's landing place, . . . twenty-seven packs furs sent Plamondon's landing, . . . a batteau with six Owyhees arrived at Plamondon's landing to resume their duty at the farm," ran the journal entries of Manager George Roberts in 1847-48. Roberts noted also how the farm work of his neighbor progressed: "Observe beyond the Mission Plamondon's wheat . . . It came up thick as it could stand & the plants have no room to litter. I am anxious to see this wheat in the fall ear," and, "Had a

---

9 His numerous recorded progeny, together with one or more dubiously recalled from more distant regions, have created for Plamondon a legendary character of rather excessive domestic prowess. His daughter, Marie Anne St. Germaine, last born of his Cowlitz wife, in her old age was interviewed by a reporter for the *Tacoma Daily News* for an account of her father. "He was a very pretty man," she recalled, but fairly shrieked at mention of the legend – "Soixante-dix-trois enfants! Et mon Pére!"

tough job to get a wild Steer home from Plamondon's little plain that had followed Mr. Wooley's cattle there." On August 31, 1847, he wrote, "Plamondon's new saw mill commenced operations." Thereafter, month by month, he entered lists of lumber the mill was supplying the company farm buildings, "planks, boards, braces, Clap Boards, rafters." [10]

At some time during the mid-eighteen forties Simon was again left a widower. In a third marriage, 1848, he seems to have over-reached himself, for despite his good looks and natural aplomb, he was still a middle-aged widower, illiterate, with a huge family, while his new wife was niece to Bishop Blanchet. Three Pelletier sisters, daughters of the bishop's deceased sister Rose, had come west in 1845 with a group of Catholic nuns to keep house for their uncle and hopefully to find husbands, for all were past thirty years old and still single. Three years after their arrival, Louise Henriette married Simon Plamondon, and in 1850 bore him a final son, Francois Norbert.[11]

The marriage was hardly ideal, for although the two remained on amicable terms, most of their wedded life was spent apart. Henriette seems to have been deeply concerned that her son should be well educated under the bishop's eye (in the Willamette Valley) and her occasional visits to the Cowlitz farm were brief.

Simon may have been well enough satisfied with the arrangement. He was prospering in the way of life he enjoyed; he may even have found relaxation in prowling the wild canyons of the Cowlitz streams. He added a brick kiln to his other ventures. His son Simon returned unharmed from the Indian Wars, his daughters had married well and were living nearby. Affable and experienced, he became guide

---

[10] George B. Roberts, "Cowlitz Farm Journal, 1847-51," in *Oregon Historical Quarterly,* LXIII (1962), p. 117 passim.

[11] Catholic Church Records, Vancouver, Wash., 1848.

and counsellor to the American immigrants that came to replace the withdrawing company personnel. He took an active part in forming Washington into a territory north of the Columbia, and lived to see many of his name bring credit to it as professional men of high standing.

Old Simon aged gracefully, handsome to the last, and as he had been born at the opening of the century, so he went out with it in 1900, aged one hundred years. He is buried in the cemetery of the St. Francis Xavier church at Cowlitz, the site of the original Wolf's Head Chapel. His portrait appears in this volume at page 23.

Antoine Reynal, Jr.

by CHARLES E. HANSON, JR.
Chadron, Nebraska

Antoine Reynal, Jr., didn't have to be a Mountain Man. At least he had more economic opportunities than the average young man in the French settlement of St. Charles, Missouri.

Antoine Reynal Senior was a physician who came to St. Louis about 1776 and was included in the list of inhabitants there in 1793.[1] In 1799 he moved to the village of St. Charles and lived there until his death in 1821.[2] Dr. Reynal built a fine home and was very active in community and church affairs. He represented the wealthy and intelligent class of French citizens in the new territory. Dr. Reynal's son, Antoine, married Marie Louise Saucier,[3] member of another prominent local family, and eventually inherited much of his father's property. One of this fortunate couple's sons was a third Antoine, born about 1809 or 1810[4] and the subject of this sketch.

In later life Reynal said that he became a wandering trader and trapper "at an early age" and claimed to have been captured by the Pawnees while accompanying a Sioux war party.[5] In 1842 he was one of the traders contacted by Indian agent Andrew Drips during the latter's war on the whiskey trade.[6]

---

[1] American Historical Association, *Annual Report, 1945* (Washington), IV, pt. III, p. 185. [2] Louis Houck, *History of Missouri* (Chicago, 1908), II, p. 86.

[3] *Index to St. Charles County, Missouri, Baptisims 1792-1863* (Missouri Historical Society, St. Louis), 94.

[4] From census records, Fort Laramie, 1860, and Fort Fetterman, 1870.

[5] Sir Richard Burton, *The Look of the West, 1860* (Lincoln, Nebr.), 103.

[6] Drips Papers, Mo. Hist. Soc.

Francis Parkman became well acquainted with Reynal at Fort Laramie in 1846 and characterized him as a "vagrant trader . . . the image of sleek and selfish complacency." He was apparently allied or at least on good terms with the old "opposition" traders like Richards and Bissonette, and liked to travel with the Indians. Parkman criticized him for adopting many Indian attitudes and ideas. At that time Reynal was living in an Indian camp with his plump Sioux wife Margot and two of her nephews.[7] Unlike the more conventional traders, his was almost an Indian economy. Parkman noted that Reynal had killed enough buffalo to make a new lodge and was then planning a trip to secure a set of poles. In the meantime he was living in a "wretched oven-shaped structure made of begrimed and tattered buffalo hides stretched over a frame of poles; one side was open, and at the side of the opening hung the powder-horn and bullet pouch of the owner, together with his long red pipe, and a rich quiver of otter-skin, with a bow and arrows; for Reynal, an Indian in most things but color, chose to hunt buffalo with these primitive weapons."[8]

In spite of these criticisms, it is apparent from other sources that Reynal was a competent trader. After Bruce Husband had negotiated the sale of Fort Laramie in 1849, he received directions for building and staffing a new fort some distance below the old fort. A letter to him from Fort Pierre on July 25, 1849, said in part, "If Raynald (sic) is about and you can hire him on reasonable terms, do so."[9] He must have accepted some kind of employment because the records of the new post include accounts for him as late as 1851.[10]

In 1854 Reynal was one of the persons who attested to the

---

[7] Francis Parkman, *The Oregon Trail* (Boston, 1892), 124.
[8] *Ibid.*, 124-25, 128, 271.   [9] Drips Papers, *loc. cit.*   [10] *Ibid.*

accuracy of James Bordeaux's account of the Grattan Massacre.[11] Sometime in this period he went "back East" for a time, returning to Horseshoe Creek in 1858.[12]

In the summer of 1860, Sir Richard Burton found Reynal operating the stage station near Horse Creek, east of Fort Laramie, "– a companionable man; but an extortionate." His household consisted of a wrinkled old squaw and a beautiful and fascinating half-breed daughter, about sixteen years old. Reynal had grown weary of a wandering life and had settled down but "was garrulous as a veteran soldier on the subject of his old friends the trappers."[13] He took up ranching in a small way, but the Cheyennes destroyed his ranch and store on the South Platte, taking sixteen horses and twenty head of cattle. During the next few years of desultory trading and ranching on the Platte, Reynal continued to lose some of his meager assets to the hostiles. At Cold Springs Ranch, ninety miles east of Fort Laramie, he lost four oxen in 1869. The Cheyennes killed a cow and bull at his camp on La Bonte Creek and then stole a mule while he was moving to Richard Creek in 1871. In 1872 the count was one mule on the Laramie River and four near Red Cloud Agency.[14]

From this time on, the trail grows dim. Reynal is not listed on the early Pine Ridge or Rosebud Agency census rolls where most of his contemporaries appear. In 1892, Louis Richard submitted depositions as administrator for Reynal's original Indian depredation claim prepared in 1872.[15] Louisa Reynal, who was listed with Reynal on the 1860 Fort Laramie census at the age of sixteen, was still living in the Medicine Root District of the Pine Ridge

[11] Nebraska State Historical Society, *Publications* (Lincoln, 1922), XX, p. 260.

[12] Deposition of Louis Richards, Claim no. 827, by Antoine Reynal, Records of the U.S. Court of Claims, National Archives.   [13] Burton, *op. cit.*, 99-103.

[14] Claim no. 827 by Antoine Reynal, Records of U.S. Court of Claims.   [15] *Ibid.*

Reservation in 1901.[16] She filed the last of the Reynal Indian depredation claims in 1894.[17]

A younger brother of Antoine's was Francis, born in 1812 at St. Charles, Missouri.[18] It does not appear that Francis was active in the fur trade but he was an early settler in Richardson County, Nebraska. He was listed there with his family in the 1860 census.

[16] *Indian Census, Pine Ridge Reservation 1900-1901*, National Archives.
[17] Claim no. 10588 by Louise Reynal, Records of U.S. Court of Claims.
[18] *Index to St. Charles County, Missouri, Baptisms*, 94.

by WILLIS BLENKINSOP
Long Beach, California

In a land where mere survival was sufficient evidence of success, Edward Rose lived in affluence.

During one of the great epochs of his life when he lived with the Crow Indians, he was almost literally the master of all he surveyed – and there was much to survey. Absaroka, the Crow domain, extended across the immense region comprising present-day Sheridan County, Wyoming; and Big Horn and Rosebud counties of Montana. As one of the principal chieftains of Absaroka, Rose had his choice of the best clothing, horses, weapons and women. He had power. And his fame was not confined to that abundant land south of the Yellowstone. It extended into the land of the Sioux, the Mandans, the Minetarees, Arikaras, Poncas and Omahas. He had an uncanny sense of presence and he knew precisely how to use it. With his powerful frame, sinister countenance and haughty bearing, he commanded both fear and respect.

One of Rose's peers, Jim Beckwourth, has said that it is difficult for an Indian to become a white man, but a white man easily learns to live like an Indian. Rose not only found it easy; he virtually became one. His was the dark hair and skin of an Indian. His whim was dress. He adopted the dress of his Indian friends, covering himself with native finery. And it was the best, for Crow-made clothes and personal adornment were preferred by all the Plains tribes. Plumes, beads and bells glistened and jingled when he moved. His children, as he came to regard his Crow consorts, stretched their arms upward when greeting him to signify that he was as high as it was possible for a man to be. He exchanged his favorite rifle for an Indian wife and became an expert with bow and arrow.[1] But in the role he was destined to play, his most potent weapon was his aptitude for language.

How did this notorious renegade, aside from his unique skill with language, achieve such popularity? Again, he found it easy. As a young man he had learned the simple expedient of stealing from one man to enhance his position with another. The only difficulty was that throughout his life he deserted one alliance after another until finally he was driven to honesty. It was too late. He had used up the best years of his life as well as the confidence of his friends, both white and Indian.

Yet, unscrupulous as this case-hardened rascal was, he did influence the course of western history in a very real way. Far-reaching decisions in critical situations were based upon his service as guide and interpreter. Many notable military officers, explorers and fur trade entrepreneurs relied upon his prodigious knowledge of a harsh land and its unpredictable natives. Surely no more colorful or reckless character ever roamed the trans-Mississippi wilderness.

Sullen, moody and often mysterious, Rose was an enigma. Even the exact dates of his birth and death are shrouded in uncertainty. The son of a white trader and a half-breed Cherokee-Negro woman, Rose grew up near Louisville, Kentucky. At about age eighteen he made his way to New Orleans as a deck hand on a keelboat. There his penchant for robbery and his savage readiness for a fight laid the cornerstone for his later reputation as a "celebrated outlaw."[2] Here, too, he may have received the severe cut across his nose that gave him the nickname of *Nez Coupé* or Cut Nose.

---

[1] Capt. Reuben Holmes, "The Five Scalps," in *Glimpses of the Past,* Missouri Historical Society, v, nos. 1-3, p. 27.

[2] Letter written by Joshua Pilcher in 1823, quoted in H. M. Chittenden, *History of the American Fur Trade of the Far West,* II, p. 685.

Returning upriver to St. Louis in 1806, the lure of complete freedom in a remote and lawless land drew him into the fur trade. In the spring of 1807 he joined Manuel Lisa's expedition to the Bighorn River where a fort and trading post were to be established. Rose's ability to extricate himself from any precarious situation as well as his all-round usefulness was soon evident and on this premise Lisa sent him to spend the winter trading among the Crow Indians, adequately supplied, of course, with trade goods and presents. Although it was Rose's first sojourn among the Crows, he soon realized the power a man could wield with a bolt or two of bright cloth, a few iron kettles, some trinkets and a small supply of tobacco. He exploited his realization to the fullest with Lisa's merchandise.

Upon his return to the fort, Lisa called upon him to account for the disposition of his trade goods and to produce the expected harvest of furs. Regardless of what Rose reported, it soon became the spark that touched off a violent meleé in which fifteen men finally subdued Rose while Lisa departed in haste for St. Louis. Gathering up what trade goods he could brow-beat out of the remaining employees, Rose returned to his friends, the Crows.

The squaws, young and old, welcomed him. The old men smiled knowingly. Most of the young braves sought his favor. Those who didn't were soon impressed by a demonstration of his ferocious abandon in a hand-to-hand fight. Captain Reuben Holmes describes it like this:

A war party of Minnetarees were forted up in a rocky outcrop well sheltered from Crow attack. Reluctant to charge such an impregnable position, the Crows hung back. Rose quickly took charge. "You are dogs," said he, "that dare not bite until the wolf shows his teeth. You would run from a dead badger in the prairie. Pull open your shirts!" continued he, "and let me see if you are not all squaws. Follow me . . ."

The Minnetarees answered with a volley of arrows and bullets. Five of the foremost Crows fell dead. The remainder retreated. With a scornful smile that branded his Crow companions as cowards, Rose turned away in apparent distain. Soon, instead of blaming Rose for his ill-considered bravado, they began bickering and reproaching each other. Rose stood aloof. He knew that at this juncture he could not afford to jeopardize his exalted position with them.

So, snatching two shields from one of his warriors and armed with only an ax and a knife, he leaped to the attack alone. Simultaneously, three bullets struck his shields. He appeared dead as he fell backward. Then, as though imbued with some magic power, he rose and vaulted over the rocky breastworks. Paralyzed by the shock of such audacity, the Minnetarees were easy prey for Rose, now enraged with the full heat of battle. Initially, three Minnetarees fell in as many blows from his battle ax, two more succumbed later. In their triumph, the Crows changed Rose's name from *Nez Coupé* to *Chee-ho-carte* (The Five Scalps).[3]

By this feat Rose attained even greater eminence than he had ever known, and while other Mountain Men waded hip-deep setting traps in icy streams or faced starvation in the grip of winter, the "ferocious character with steel nerves and nine lives"[4] enjoyed a warm tipi, plenty of food and admiring companions, both male and female. Many of them were sure he was some kind of diety or at least an apostle of the Great Spirit.

Precisely how long Rose remained with the Crows on this visit is not known, but apparently it was most of the time until the spring of 1809 when Andrew Henry found him living in one of the Arikara villages on the Missouri. Bound for the beaver-rich waters of the Northwest, Henry hired Rose as interpreter to the Crows, whose land he intended to cross. As usual, Rose made himself extremely useful for the sole purpose of gaining his employer's confidence. When he had, and when he had also accumulated a considerable supply of Henry's trade goods, he decided once more to remain with his Crow friends.

During these first years with Lisa and Henry, Rose ap-

---

3 Holmes, *op. cit.*, 12-18.
4 Bernard DeVoto, *Across the Wide Missouri* (Boston, 1947), 428.

pears to have set something of a life pattern for himself with similar performance, results and reaction in each case. For each of his employers he was apparently an excellent hunter, guide and interpreter, but before he finished applying his special blend of skullduggery and perfidy, they were invariably glad to be rid of him.

Whether by luck or sagacity, the notable Astorian, Wilson Price Hunt, found a way to eliminate Rose and at the same time keep everyone reasonably happy. In June 1811, Hunt had found Rose again at the Arikara villages. Lack of field experience and a full load of responsibility weighed heavily upon Hunt and early in his renowned westering he became suspicious of Rose. Rumors of robbery and desertion – all attributed to Rose – forced Hunt into his own best solution.

Fearing that Rose might desert with enough of his men seriously to cripple the expedition, Hunt suggested to Rose on September 2nd that he leave and join his Crow friends. Moreover he added a *douceur* in the form of half a year's pay, a horse, three beaver traps and other sundry supplies. Apparently stunned by such open-handed liberality on the part of his employer and utter lack of opposition, Rose's "brow cleared up and appeared more cheerful; he left off his sullen, sulking habits, and made no further attempts to tamper with the faith of his comrades."[5] In his diary Hunt further described Rose (How succinct can the exigencies of the wilderness force a diarist to be?) as "a very bad fellow full of daring." It is very probable, however, that before they parted company, Rose mapped Hunt's passage through the Big Horn Range where generations yet unborn would follow on the tide of western expansion.

A year later in 1812 Rose is listed with other Mountain Men in account with the Missouri Fur Company,[6] Lisa's expedition of that year.

[5] Robert Stuart, *Discovery of the Oregon Trail* (New York, 1935), 284-85.
[6] Books of the Missouri Fur Company, Kansas Historical Society.

By this time he had deceived and antagonized so many people that his former ties were wearing thin. Accordingly, he descended the Missouri to the Omaha village and there married a chief's daughter by whom he had two children. Using his customary generosity with the presents he had finagled from unsuspecting traders, he was soon established again in his exalted position with the best of everything the Omahas could provide. There was only one drawback: the village was near a trading post [7] where by his natural guile he could obtain whiskey. Strongly influenced by its availability and the lack of excitement in the village, he became a heavy drinker. Drunk, his innate violence and love of a fight for its own sake, plunged him deeper and deeper into trouble. Finally he became so troublesome to traders and Omahas alike that he was put in chains and sent to St. Louis. This, in all probability, is the basis for acid-tongued Joshua Pilcher's remark when in 1823 he referred to Rose as "a celebrated outlaw who left this country in chains some ten years ago." [8]

He was soon released, however, and after returning from a visit to the scenes of his youthful escapades in New Orleans, he lived with the Crows much of the time for the next eight or ten years. He could not have remained with them later than 1820, however, for it was then that he established his longest residence with the Arikaras on the Missouri.

Edward Rose not only lived for several years with the Arikaras; their two adjacent villages a few miles above the mouth of the Grand River in today's Corson County, South Dakota, were frequently the place where he made contact with traders and explorers coming up the Missouri. It was here in 1809, it will be recalled, that he met and joined Andrew Henry; Hunt in 1811. Here too, in 1823, he was one of the key figures in William H. Ashley's disastrous

---

[7] Holmes, *op. cit.*, 40.　　　　　　　　[8] See note 2 above.

defeat at the hands of the Arikaras and Colonel Leavenworth's punitive military campaign. Many other publications describe these two events in documented detail.

Suffice it to say, then, that as an old resident among the Arikaras and interpreter for Ashley, Rose suspected trouble. Ashley ignored Rose's advice and as a result was forced to retreat many miles downriver. Ashley apparently held no grudge against Rose. On the contrary, he recommended him for the rank of ensign in Leavenworth's military force when it moved in a month later.

Leavenworth's campaign was not without some comic overtones. At one juncture Rose told the colonel that the Arikara squaws were readying the villages for evacuation during the coming night. As had Ashley, Leavenworth rejected Rose's warning. The next morning there was no enemy to fight. Overall, the campaign was something less than satisfactory.[9] It incurred the bitter disappointment as well as the contempt of Leavenworth's Sioux allies, it lost the respect of all of the Upper Missouri tribes for white men and, along with Ashley's defeat, virtually closed the river route to fur country for some time.

In spite of, or perhaps because of, these depressing events, Leavenworth evidently held Rose's service in high esteem. Reporting to General Henry Atkinson, he said:

> I had not found any one willing to go into those villages except a man by the name of Rose, who had the nominal rank of ensign in General Ashley's volunteers. He appeared to be a brave and enterprising man, and was well acquainted with those Indians. He resided about three years with them; understood their language, and they were much attached to him. He was with General Ashley when he was attacked. The Indians at that time called to him to take care of himself, before they fired upon General Ashley's party. This was all I knew of the man. I have since heard that he was not of good character. Everything he told us, however, was fully corroborated. He was perfectly willing to go into their villages, and did go in several times.[10]

[9] Letter, Joshua Pilcher to Major O'Fallon, Aug. 23, 1823.
[10] Official Report of General Henry Atkinson, Oct. 23, 1823.

Abandoning the traditional water route, Ashley dispatched his trusted lieutenant and "confidential young man," Jedediah Strong Smith, to seek a land passage directly to the interior West. By this time Rose had beaten such a well-worn path between Absaroka (the Big Horn Basin) and the Arikara villages that he was the obvious choice as guide and interpreter for Smith's expedition. After a journey of agonizing hardship through the Black Hills and the badlands of present-day South Dakota, Smith sent Rose ahead to Absaroka for food and replacements for their broken-down horses. The Crows willingly provided lodging and food for Smith and his men during this winter of 1823-24 in their camp near today's Dubois, Wyoming. But Rose had to be consulted on all occasions; his word was law and he recited it in elevated tones upon the slightest provocation.[11] The Crows would do nothing without the approval of their mighty *Chee-ho-carte*. And as usual, since he was the only one who could speak the Crow language, the price of his approval raised hob with Jed Smith's supply of presents and trade goods.

Although this first Ashley brigade fared well in the Crow encampment, it was with profound relief that Smith saw the first signs of spring and the possibility of release from Rose's iron grip on the language barrier. In desperation, one of Smith's men, James Clyman, contrived a partial solution. His remarkable diary explains:

> . . . I spread out a buffalo robe and covered it with sand, and made it in heaps to represent the different mountains, (we were then encamped at the lower point of the Wind River Mountains) and from our sand map with the help of the Crows, finally got the idea that we could go to Green River called by them Seeds-ka-day.[12]

By this crude but effective means the Crows may have

---

11 Col. Charles Keemle, "Reminiscences," in *St. Louis Beacon* and *Weekly Reveille*, July 24 and 28, 1848.

12 Dale L. Morgan, *The West of William H. Ashley* (Denver, 1964), 79.

been telling Clyman and Smith of Union Pass as Rose probably did for Hunt in 1811. In any event, Smith left the Crow camp and began compressing a staggering amount of western history into the few remaining years of his life.

However liberal and exasperating he was with Smith's goods, and whatever his new motive, Rose at this point decided to gain some wealth by his own honest effort. Alone and with only two horses and a minimum of equipment, he undertook a trapping expedition of his own. All went well until his return trip. Then, as though in retribution for his past misdeeds, a band of Blackfeet raided his camp and took every one of his three packs of beaver. While following the thieves to recover his furs and equipment, he had the misfortune to be discovered by them before he could turn back. Assuming the vandals were some of the younger Crows who had become agitated with his high-handed conduct in their tribe, Rose called to them in Crow. One of them answered in kind.

During the next several day's travel Rose recognized his captors as Blackfeet. He began cracking jokes injuring his old friends to gain new ones. Not without good reason; his life hung in the balance. But as in all human relations, primitive or otherwise, perfidy is soon recognized for what it is. Accordingly, one day while Rose was lost in the thought that perhaps he might soon find as great favor among the Blackfeet as he had among the Crows, the Indian who had answered Rose's first greeting stood before him and slowly pronounced the name, *Chee-ho-carte!*

For once, Rose lost control of his nerves. He sprang to his feet in alarm, but he knew he had been caught in a snare of his own making. But as Blackfeet had been known to do on certain other occasions, they did not murder him on the spot. They gave him a chance to run for his life and after a life-and-death game of hide and seek, Rose finally eluded his enemies by hiding in a "raft" of driftwood floating in the river. When at last the Blackfeet gave him up as drowned, he swam to shore where he made a crude canoe. He survived the balance of his journey to the Mandan villages by floating stealthily past unfriendly camps at night (and now the unfriendlies were becoming quite numerous) and eating carrion from which he had chased the wolves away. It was a bitter lesson for the man who had known such high living at the expense of others and one which, in the light of subsequent events, confirmed his conviction that honesty is not the best policy.

At the termination of this only recorded attempt at honest living, Rose met General Henry Atkinson and Major O'Fallon at the Mandan villages. They had recently come up the river to effect peace among the tribes of the Upper Missouri and to promote better relations between Indians and traders. Rose again served as interpreter. Atkinson mentions him frequently, much of his comment to Rose's credit. But wherever Rose was, there was violence.

While the "big talk" was in progress, some of the more knowing Crows slipped away to the unguarded cannon and stopped up the touch holes with dirt. Shortly afterward, through some misunderstanding, Major O'Fallon snapped a pistol in the face of one of the braves and then knocked him down with the butt end. The Crows, confident that the cannon would be useless, rose to the occasion in a furious tumult. In an unexpected fit of sympathy as a white man, Rose broke the stock of his gun over the head of a Crow warrior and swung the barrel about with such savage pleasure that the whole throng dispersed. There was no further trouble and despite his stand against the Crows, Rose lived with them again.[13]

There is no record as to when or how long he lived with the Crows after Atkinson's peace expedition expired without adding anything of consequence to public relations in

---

[13] Holmes, *op. cit.,* 53-54.

Indian country. The last that is known of him is when
Zenas Leonard saw him with the Crows in 1832 and again
in 1834.

At the latter time, Leonard was an eye witness to a scene
of carnage similar to Rose's encounter with the Minnetarees
in 1807. This time the battle was between the Crows and
their traditional enemies, the Blackfeet. This time greater
numbers of both tribes were involved. This time the "old
Negro," as Leonard referred to him, was more violent than
ever in his exhortations and as quick as ever to lead the
charge. The final butchery was "enough to sicken the stout-
est heart." [14]

Violent, significant and veiled in uncertainty to his last
day, Edward Rose beat an opulent living from a reluctant
wilderness. The Crows say the Minnetarees killed him; the
Minnetarees say the Crows killed him. Zenas Leonard says
he saw him as late as 1834, but may have been incorrect in
his date. The most likely conclusion is that he died on the
frozen Yellowstone late in the winter of 1832. The authority
for this is a letter dated July 26, 1833, from John F. A.
Sanford to General William Clark stating that a war party
of Arikaras killed Rose and two other notable Mountain
Men.[15]

Mountain peaks and passes, forests and deserts, lakes and
rivers abound in the land that Rose and his contemporaries
mapped in their minds for future generations. Their names
virtually delineate the geography of the West. Ironically
the name of Edward Rose is preserved only in an obscure
notation on old Missouri steamboat itineraries directing the
attention of passengers as they pass the mouth of the Milk
River to "Rose's Grave."

[14] Zenas Leonard, *The Adventures of Zenas Leonard, Fur Trader,* ed. by John C.
Ewers (Norman, Okla., 1959), 145-49.
[15] National Archives.

Hubert Rouleau

by CHARLES E. HANSON, JR.
Chadron, Nebraska

"Your bones will dry on the prairie, Rouleau." Francis Parkman heard this malediction pronounced at Fort Laramie by a fellow trapper in the summer of 1846.

Parkman found this "Rouleau" to be a strong, square little man not much more than five feet tall, dressed in shiny worn buckskins and dancing around on the stumps of two feet once-frozen and now visibly shortened. Though his equipment was worn and dingy, Rouleau's round, ruddy face was gay and animated. At the moment he only wanted beaver enough to buy his squaw a pacing horse and some red ribbons. Then, he was going below and retire on a farm.[1]

Rouleau never got to his Missouri farm but his bones didn't bleach on the prairie either. His adventurous life had begun in Canada.[2] Work in the fur trade brought him to the West and when Parkman met him in 1846 he was a seasoned mountain trapper with many years of experience. Parkman noted that Rouleau talked, sang and frolicked through their camp even though he was still recovering from severe injuries received when he was thrown from his horse

---

[1] Francis Parkman, *The Oregon Trail* (Boston, 1892), 140-41.

[2] Information given on Whetstone Agency Employment Roll 1873, Letters Received by Commissioner of Indian Affairs from Whetstone Agency, National Archives. There were a number of Rouleaus in the Canadian trade, including Louis and Baptiste Rouleau, voyageurs for the Hudson's Bay Company in the 1821-24 period.

Parkman does not provide Rouleau's first name but several men who knew Hubert Rouleau in later life identified him as an early Fort Laramie figure. Albert Rouleau, born in the 1840s, and William Rouleau, killed in 1867 by the Cheyennes while working as a teamster for Joseph Bissonette, may have been his sons. In *The Indian War of 1864*, Captain Eugene Ware mentions William Reauleau, a trooper in an Ohio unit who was discharged at Denver in 1865. All evidence available now indicates that Hubert Rouleau was the man Parkman met in 1846.

and trampled. "Rouleau had an unlucky partiality for squaws. He always had one, whom he must needs bedizen with beads, ribbons and all the finery of an Indian wardrobe; and though he was obliged to leave her behind him during his expeditions, this hazardous necessity did not at all trouble him, for his disposition was the reverse of jealous."[3] Anything not spent on his feminine companion was generally used up in feasting his comrades.

The next year Rouleau apparently gave up beaver trapping, for Henry Chatillon wrote Parkman on May 13, 1847, that Rouleau was then stationed at Fort Laramie and still had his scalp.[4] He still appeared in the accounts of relocated Fort John (Laramie) in 1851.[5] The gradual breakup of the Laramie trade necessitated a move and in 1854 Rouleau was working as a clerk for Joseph Bissonette at Deer Creek. That summer, following the Grattan Massacre, the post was looted by angry Sioux warriors.[6]

Rouleau was a literate man and he made some effort to see that his children were educated. In 1862 he placed an eight-year old daughter and two younger sons in the Presbyterian Indian Mission School at Highland, Kansas.[7] In 1865 he was apparently one of the several guides attached to General Connor's Powder River Expedition.[8]

Rouleau joined the general exodus of Indians from Fort Laramie in 1868 and was one of the persons hired by General Harney to assist in the final councils and the subsequent

---

[3] Parkman, *op. cit.*, 261.

[4] Mrs. James L. O'Leary, "Henry Chatillon," in *Missouri Historical Society Bulletin* (St. Louis), XXII, no. 2, pt. 1, p. 131.

[5] Andrew Drips Papers, Missouri Historical Society, St. Louis.

[6] Claim No. 1442, Joseph Bissonette, Records of U.S. Court of Claims, National Archives.

[7] Letters Received, Commissioner of Indian Affairs, Whetstone Agency. In 1873 officials of the school wrote to see if annuities could be issued to these children since they depended upon the charity of the church. At that time the daughter had married W. R. Sears, "a reputable mechanic of good social standing." The boys were in Highland University Preparatory School and were "bright, forward scholars."

[8] J. Cecil Alter, *Jim Bridger* (Norman, 1962), 314.

move to Whetstone Agency on the Missouri.[9] In the accounts for 1869 at the new agency we find twenty dollars paid to H. Rouleau for building a cistern and a chimney.[10]

When the Brule Agency was moved far up the White River, many of the squaw men were dissatisfied at being transplanted to such a remote, barren and hostile region. Some thirty-two of them sent a joint letter to Washington asking that they be permitted to return to the Missouri River and draw rations from Fort Randall. Hubert Rouleau was one of the signers of that letter.[11]

The agency stayed on the upper White River and Rouleau was carried in the Report of Employees as a laborer there in 1873.[12] When Agent Howard took the first census of his Agency in 1875, Rouleau is listed with a son and daughter but no wife.[13] The son was probably Nicholas Rouleau, born in 1867 or 1868, who was still living on the Pine Ridge Reservation in 1900.[14]

Rouleau continued trapping and trading, living for several years in a log cabin overlooking Chadron Creek south of the site of present Chadron, Nebraska. The soldiers later accused him of spying for Red Cloud, whose camp they disarmed just north of Rouleau's cabin in October 1876. He then moved to Spotted Tail's Bordeaux Creek camp.[15]

The old trapper spent the rest of his life close to the Sioux and died about 1890 near Pine Ridge; his Brule wife, Eagle Woman, had passed away many years before.[16]

---

[9] Letters Received, Commissioner of Indian Affairs, Whetstone Agency.

[10] *Ibid.*

[11] *Ibid.*   [12] *Ibid.*   [13] *Ibid.*

[14] Indian Census, Pine Ridge Reservation 1900/1901, National Archives.

[15] Hudson Mead, *A History of Chadron State Park, the Pine Ridge and White River Valley,* undated MS, Museum of the Fur Trade Library, Chadron, Nebraska. Mead was the son of a reservation storekeeper and an early surveyor in the area. In a map dated 1923 he shows the Rouleau cabin on the west side of Chadron Creek just above Red Cloud camp site of 1876.

[16] Information in letter from Joseph Bissonette to Sanborn & King, attorneys, July 28, 1891, Claim 1443, Records of the U.S. Court of Claims, National Archives.

John F. A. Sanford

by JANET LECOMPTE
Colorado Springs, Colorado

John F. A. Sanford spent seven and a half years as Indian agent, much longer than average in this ill-paid and frustrating job, before taking service with Pierre Chouteau, Junior, in the western branch of the American Fur Company. During his years with the company, he became a highly respected and very wealthy businessman, but posterity has known him chiefly through two circumstances that had little to do with his life accomplishments. One was a blistering criticism of his term as Indian agent written seventy-five years after his death; the other was his temporary ownership of a famous slave named Dred Scott.

His early life is obscure. He was born in 1806 in Virginia, whence his ancestor, also named John Sanford, first came from England via Barbados in 1679.[1] He was one of seven children, five of them girls.[2] His father, Alexander Sanford, moved to St. Louis where, in 1825, young John became a clerk in the office of William Clark, Superintendent of Indian Affairs. The boy also served as "express" and "interpreter," and witnessed the treaty with the Kansas Indians at St. Louis on June 3, 1825.[3]

---

[1] Rev. Charles E. Snyder, "John Emerson, owner of Dred Scott," in *Annals of Iowa*, XXI, no. 6 (Oct. 1938), 451. Sanford is said to have come from Winchester, Va., but my own search of genealogical records – wills, gravestones, birth and marriage lists, militia rolls and the 1810 census of the town of Winchester – has failed to turn up any Sanfords there between 1785 and 1810.

[2] John A. Bryan, "The Blow Family and Their Slave Dred Scott," in *Bulletin*, Missouri Historical Society, VI, no. 4 (July 1950), 223-31. Eliza Irene married Dr. John Emerson, an army surgeon; Mary married Dr. Harry Bainbridge; and another sister married General James Barnes of Massachusetts.

[3] William Clark Papers, Kansas Hist. Soc., Topeka, cited by Annie H. Abel, ed., *Chardon's Journal at Fort Clark, 1834-1839* (Pierre, S.D., 1932), 252, n. 219. Abel

When the sub-agency of the upper Missouri fell vacant in the middle of 1826, Sanford, highly recommended by superiors and associates for his energy, integrity and intelligence, was appointed sub-agent on July 17, 1826, at a salary of $800 a year. He was twenty or twenty-one years old.[4] On September 21, 1826, he left St. Louis for the Mandan villages far up the Missouri. At this most remote of all the Indian agencies, he had two "temporary" houses built, one to live in and one to store presents for the Indians. He remained there for over two years among the Mandans, Minitarees (Hidatsa or Gros Ventres) and Crows, making talks and giving presents on behalf of the United States government. His talks and particularly his presents attracted the attention of other tribes, and before long he was visited by Arikaras, Assiniboines, Knisteneaux (Crees) and Yanctonais Sioux, who expressed their curiosity about the white man's country and their desire to visit its Great White Father. When Sanford returned to St. Louis in November, 1828, he was eager to bring a delegation of these wild Indians to Washington, but his suggestion was ignored. After a five-month furlough he again ascended the Missouri to the Mandan villages.[5]

Sanford returned to St. Louis in May 1830, having served as upper Missouri sub-agent for four difficult years. He had visited eight different tribes containing, by his estimate, 75,000 Indians scattered over a vast area, for whom he was provided only $1000 worth of presents. He felt he deserved

cites 7 *U.S. Statutes at Large,* 244-47, for Sanford signing as witness to the Kansas treaty, but Charles J. Kappler, *Indian Affairs: Laws and Treaties,* II (Wash., 1904), 248-50, does not show Sanford as witness.

[4] Letters Received at the Office of Indian Affairs from the St. Louis Superintendency, M 234, R 883, and Letters Received at the Office of Indian Affairs from the Upper Missouri Agency, M 234, R 883, both National Archives Microfilm Publications.

[5] Letter of William Clark to the Secretary of War, St. Louis, Feb. 25, 1828, St. Louis Superintendency, M 234, R 748; letter of John F. A. Sanford to William Clark, St. Louis, June 20, 1829, Upper Missouri Agency, M 234, R 883; Abel, *Chardon,* 252-53, n. 224, citing Clark's book of accounts, William Clark Papers.

a job with less risk of life and better pay, and William Clark agreed. In the summer of 1830, Sanford called upon Secretary of War J. H. Eaton at his home in Tennessee, begging for a better situation or a salary increase, or at least a chance to take a delegation of his Indians to Washington. To the delegation Eaton assented. Sanford's other requests, including his desire to report to Superintendent William Clark instead of Agent John Dougherty, were passed over. He continued to report to Clark anyway.[6]

Sanford persisted in his struggle for better conditions for himself and his agency. In late 1830 his estimate of next year's expenses included a $400 salary increase for himself, the cost of another interpreter since no single man could speak with eight different tribes; $750 to build an agency and make him independent of traders or Indians for shelter; and an additional $500 for Indian presents. The Indian department allowed none of his requests.[7]

In November 1830, Sanford left again for his agency, returning a year later with a deputation of Indians to visit Washington. There were only four of them – an Assiniboine, Yanctonais Sioux, Saulteur (Ojibwa) and Cree, for the others had turned back. At St. Louis expenses began to mount. The Indians fell ill and before they could travel, ice had closed navigation on the Mississippi. The party, now consisting of Sanford, his Indians, two interpreters and Indian Agent Joshua Pilcher, went east rather expensively by stage. On arrival at Washington, the Indians were presented with lavish outfits of clothing and weapons, hiking the estimate of expenses to $6450. It was, as William Ashley protested in his maiden address to the House of Repre-

---

[6] Letter of William Clark to Col. McKenney, St. Louis, June 22, 1830, St. Louis Superintendency, M 234, R 749; letter of Sanford to Spencer Pettis, Nov. 24, 1830; letter of Sanford to Hon. J. H. Eaton, Franklin, Mo., Dec. 1, 1830; and Sanford to Eaton, Upper Missouri, Dec. 24, 1830; all from Upper Missouri Agency, M 234, R 883.

[7] Sanford's estimate for 1831, St. Louis Superintendency, M 234, R 479.

sentatives, an "extravagant expenditure" for four Indians. Ashley was especially vehement against Sanford's request for $700 (really only $350) as extra allowance for collecting the Indians, which Ashley asserted was no more than Sanford's duty. Although Joshua Pilcher criticized Ashley's address – "Never did a speech covering only *one square in a newspaper,* contain so many errors," he wrote – the publicity hurt Sanford's career in the Indian service, and even more, his feelings and pride. Congress allowed the expenses of the delegation, but not Sanford's extra pay.[8]

Sanford and his Indians were back in St. Louis by March 26, 1832, when they boarded the American Fur Company steamboat "Yellow Stone," along with one of its owners, Pierre Chouteau, Junior, and the artist George Catlin, whose paintings and letters give a delightful picture of Sanford's Indians. On its way up the Missouri, the "Yellow Stone" stopped to deliver supplies and take on furs at the trading posts, where Sanford's injunctions against selling liquor to the Indians were in effect. At Fort Pierre, Sanford gave government presents and made speeches to the assembled Indians, and again at Fort Union where he saw the Blackfeet for the first time. At Fort Union, the "Yellow Stone," with Sanford aboard, turned around and by July was back in St. Louis.[9]

Sanford may have known Pierre Chouteau, Junior, and

---

[8] Sanford's estimate for 1832 of expenditures made on account of a deputation of Indians, dated Jan. 15, 1832, and Jan. 16, 1832; letter of Sanford to Gov. Lewis Cass, Sec. of War, Washington, Jan. 17, 1832; and letter of Joshua Pilcher to Mr. Heron, St. Louis, April 24, 1832; all in St. Louis Superintendency, M 234, R 750. See also John E. Sunder, *Joshua Pilcher, Fur Trader and Indian Agent* (Norman, 1968), 87-89; and John C. Ewers, "When the Light Shone in Washington," in *Montana, the Magazine of Western History,* VI, no. 4 (Autumn, 1956), 2-11, for details of Sanford's delegation.

[9] George Catlin, *Letters and Notes on the Manners, Customs and Condition of the North American Indians* (London, 1841), I, pp. 56-7, 67, 138, 227-30; letter of Sanford to William Clark, July 17, 1832, St. Louis Superintendency, M 234, R 750; letter of Kenneth McKenzie to P. Chouteau Jr., Fort Union, Feb. 14, 1832, Chouteau Collection, Missouri Historical Society, St. Louis.

his family in St. Louis, but it was probably not until after his voyage on the "Yellow Stone" that a closer relationship developed. On November 22, 1832, Sanford married Chouteau's daughter Emilie in the St. Louis Cathedral.[10] Four months later he again went up the Missouri on the American Fur Company steamboat "Assiniboine," in company with Prince Maximilian who gives us another account of Sanford stopping at Fort Pierre and Fort Union to see his Indians. At Fort Union on June 26, 1833, the "Assiniboine" turned around and bore Sanford back to his bride. The marriage was brief, for Emilie died on April 27, 1836, aboard the Mississippi River steamboat "George Collier" returning from New Orleans. She left a son, Benjamin Chouteau Sanford, who was reared chiefly by his Chouteau grandparents.[11]

Before 1832 Sanford had been an extraordinarily zealous Indian agent, as he himself was quick to point out, and as documents attest. But in 1832 and 1833, after his scolding in the House of Representatives and his marriage into the Chouteau family, his zeal waned and his complaints waxed. In several letters to William Clark, he wrote again of the necessity for agency buildings and of the inadequacy of one interpreter and $1000 worth of presents. Without these necessities, Sanford declared, his agency needed him no longer than the time it took the steamboat to make its round trip to Fort Union and back. And William Clark had to agree.[12]

---

[10] (St. Louis) *Missouri Republican,* Nov. 27, 1832. A civil ceremony probably preceded, as was the custom in St. Louis, for on Nov. 12, Emilie's cousin P. M. Papin wrote that "Cadet Chouteau has married his Emilie to Mr. Sanford." Chouteau Collection.

[11] Maximilian, Prince of Weid, *Travels in the Interior of North America* (1843), reprinted by R. G. Thwaites, ed., *Early Western Travels* (Cleveland, 1906), XXII, pp. 241, 276, 311, 328, 351; XXIII, p. 12; XXIV, p. 98; (St. Louis) *Missouri Republican,* April 28, 1836.

[12] Letter of Sanford to Hon. Lewis Cass, March 20, 1832; Sanford to William Clark, St. Louis July 21, 1833; Sanford to Clark, St. Louis Sept. 3, 1833; all from St. Louis Superintendency, M 234, R 750.

In the fall of 1833, Sanford stated flatly that his sub-agency was unnecessary, and that he had decided to resign after he made a visit he had promised the Blackfeet in the spring of 1834. Sanford's strongly worded letter reached Commissioner of Indian Affairs Elbert Herring who, pressed by William Ashley, demanded to know just how much time Sanford had spent with his Indians and why he felt the agency should be discontinued. Sanford answered that he had spent four years and nine months on the upper Missouri out of his seven years four months in office. To the commissioner's latter query, Sanford replied loftily that everything necessary at the agency had been accomplished, and declined further comment. On Sanford's behalf, William Clark explained to the commissioner that the continuance of the agency depended upon the agent's constant presence there, which in turn depended upon suitable buildings and sufficient presents for the Indians, for which funds had not been tendered Sanford. The explanation appears to have satisfied the commissioner. Sanford again went up the Missouri in the spring of 1834, presumably made his rendezvous with the Blackfeet, and on December 31, 1834, submitted his resignation. He promptly went to work for Pierre Chouteau, Junior, in whose service he spent the rest of his life.[13]

Sanford's years as Indian agent interested the late Annie H. Abel, editor of *Chardon's Journal at Fort Clark, 1834-1839*. She devoted nearly two pages of introduction and four of fine-print footnotes to Sanford, whose name appears not once in the work she was editing. Excellent researcher though she was, disinterested she was not. She hated the American Fur Company and all its leaders with a naked

---

[13] Letter of Sanford to Clark, Sept. 20, 1833; Clark to Sanford, Feb. 4, 1834; Sanford to Clark, Feb. 4, 1834; Clark to Herring, Feb. 10, 1834; all from St. Louis Superintendency, M 234, R 750. Herring to William Ashley, Feb. 23, 1834, in Abel, *Chardon*, p. 252, n. 223. Sanford to Clark, Dec. 31, 1834, Upper Missouri Agency, M 234, R 883.

fury she did not attempt to clothe in scholarly detachment. She summed up Sanford thus: "In the career of this man, Sanford, as sub-agent for the Mandans and other Indians of the upper Missouri, is to be seen most pointedly the subordination of a public trust and a public duty to personal convenience and aggrandizement. His was a most glaring case of the exploitation of the Indian service in the interest of the American Fur Company." [14] She accused Sanford of never really living with the Indians; of giving government presents to Indians for which he and the American Fur Company took full credit, in return for which he accepted gifts of transportation and buffalo tongues; and of collecting evidence for traders to obtain indemnity for alleged Indian depredations. Like every dedicated muckraker, her evidence was weaker than her accusations. For instance, Sanford *did* live with his Indians before 1832; transportation for the agent and his goods on company steamboats was by contract with the government and not a gift (the buffalo tongues were a gift but hardly a bribe); and the duty of any agent was to investigate depredations by and against the Indians, nor did Miss Abel present evidence that Sanford failed in this duty. If Sanford was in fact venal, Miss Abel did not come close to proving it. [15]

When Sanford entered the service of Pratte, Chouteau & Co. in 1835, he was twenty-nine years old. Within two years he had assumed a role of great importance to the company as lobbyist and trouble-shooter in Washington. In the fall of 1837 he accompanied a delegation of Sac and Fox Indians from St. Louis to Washington, never letting the Indians or their agent out of his sight, to ensure that the treaty they would make with the government would meet the views of his company. In 1838 he was made a partner in the firm, and for the next three years Sanford spent every winter in Washington, lobbying, buying goods, collecting debts, bid-

[14] Abel, *Chardon*, xxxix.   [15] *Ibid.*, xxxviii-xxxix, 252-55.

ding for government contracts in annuity goods and transportation. In 1841 he moved to New York to manage the
company's new office there.[16]

Pierre and Emilie Chouteau frequently brought Sanford's son, Ben, a boy of "endless vivacity," to New York for
long visits. Chouteau settled $5000 a year on Sanford as
Ben's guardian. Sanford became ever more important to
Chouteau. In 1853 he withdrew from the fur company to
attend to Chouteau's railroad and railroad iron interests.
He was listed as an incorporator of the Illinois Central
Railroad on February 10, 1851, and served as director from
1851 until March 18, 1857. After 1852, when Sanford married Isabella Davis, daughter of Thomas C. Davis of New
York, Chouteau and his wife took "Belle" Sanford and their
two little children, John A. and Emily, into the family
circle, for Sanford was truly like a son to them. By 1857
Sanford was said to have a fortune of not less than a million
and a half dollars, having made $600,000 in a single year
on the importation of British iron. He lived at 138 Fifth
Avenue, a prestigious address in the big city.[17]

In 1853, Sanford became defendant in one of America's
most important lawsuits – Scott v. Sandford (sic). Dred
Scott, a negro belonging to Sanford's sister Irene and her
husband, Dr. John Emerson, had been taken to live in
Illinois from 1833 until 1838, which Scott's supporters believed should cause him to be freed. His suit, instituted in
1843 against Mrs. Emerson, was lost in the lower courts and

---

[16] Sanford's business activities are indicated in Grace Lee Nute, *Calendar of the American Fur Company's Papers,* in American Historical Association, *Annual Report, 1944,* vols. II and III (see index), and his personal life in the letters of the Chouteau Collection. See "Pierre Chouteau, Junior," this volume.

[17] Chouteau Coll.; *Ballou's Pictorial Drawing-Room Companion,* XII, no. 25 (June 20, 1857), 391, quoting from the *New York Tribune,* with thanks to Frances H. Stadler; *Guide to the Illinois Central Archives in the Newberry Library, 1851-1906,* compiled by Carolyn Curtis Mohr (Chicago, 1951), 170. Emily Sanford married Count Sala, French minister to the U.S., and Ben Chouteau Sanford married Louisa Berthold in 1858 [Paul Beckwith, *Creoles of St. Louis* (St. Louis, 1893), 56].

appealed. In the meantime, Mrs. Emerson left Dred Scott in St. Louis and moved to Massachusetts where she married Dr. Calvin C. Chaffee. Because Dr. Chaffee was an ardent abolitionist, Dred Scott was transferred ("by fictitious sale") to John F. A. Sanford, who became defendant when Scott's case was filed in the Supreme Court of the United States on November 2, 1853. The famous decision was handed down on March 6, 1857, and immediately afterwards the slave was either emancipated or sold back to Mrs. Emerson – authorities differ.[18]

Disposing of Dred Scott was one of the last sane actions of John F. A. Sanford's life. He had had a busy year in 1856, traveling to Washington and Chicago, so preoccupied when he returned that Pierre Chouteau, Junior, then in New York, complained that Sanford rarely came to the office and then hardly had time to talk. Sometime in the early part of December, Sanford had a mental breakdown. During the next weeks he improved slowly; on February 21, 1857, Chouteau wrote that Sanford was perfectly well and leaving soon for Europe. But again his mind failed, and on May 5, 1857, he died insane in an asylum in New York.[19]

A portrait of Sanford appears in this volume at page 23.

---

[18] Rev. Charles E. Snyder, "John Emerson," *loc. cit.;* F. H. Hodder, "Some Phases of the Dred Scott Case," in *Mississippi Valley Historical Review,* XVI, no. 1 (June 1929); John A. Bryan, "The Blow Family and Their Slave Dred Scott," *loc. cit.;* Walter Ehrlich, "Was the Dred Scott Case Valid?," in *Missouri Historical Review,* LXIII, no. 3 (April 1969).

[19] *New York Herald,* May 6, 1857; (St. Louis) *Missouri Republican,* May 8, 1857; *Ballou's Pictorial, loc. cit.;* letters in the Chouteau Collection.

Robert Stuart

by HARVEY L. CARTER
Colorado College

Robert Stuart, son of John and Mary Buchanan Stuart, was born in the parish of Callander, Perthshire, Scotland, February 18, 1785. His father was a crofter or small farmer but also a schoolmaster. Robert migrated in 1807 to Canada, where his uncle, David Stuart, was an agent for the North West Company.[1] Through his uncle's influence, he became a clerk for that company in Montreal, where he also learned the French language.

In 1810, both David and Robert Stuart decided to participate in John Jacob Astor's Pacific Fur Company. Robert became a partner to the extent of two shares, probably through the generosity of his uncle, who is thought to have assigned to his nephew two of his five shares just prior to their sailing for the Pacific Coast from New York City, September 6, 1810. While the "Tonquin" was fitting for the voyage, Robert became attached to Elizabeth Sullivan, whom he later married.[2]

Captain Thorn, who commanded the "Tonquin," was a martinet of irascible temper and, at the Falkland Islands, sailed off leaving David Stuart and five others ashore, through some misunderstanding regarding the time of the ship's departure. When they followed for some hours in a rowboat, he refused to take them aboard until Robert Stuart drew a pistol and threatened to blow his brains out, from

---

[1] For a discussion of Stuart's birth, ancestry, and early life see Philip Ashton Rollins, *Discovery of the Oregon Trail:Robert Stuart's Narratives* (New York, 1935), xxxv-xxxvii. See also David Lavender, *The Fist in the Wilderness* (New York, 1964), 134-35. [2] Lavender, *op. cit.,* 135.

which it will be seen that young Stuart had a temper of his own.[3]

At Astoria, both Robert Stuart and his uncle performed their part in the enterprise in a way which did them much credit. David Stuart built Fort Okanogan and wintered there, gathering in a good harvest of furs for the company. Robert was sent up the Columbia and the Cowlitz rivers in charge of an expedition to investigate Indan rumors of competition, which turned out to be groundless. On another occasion, an Indian sub-chief, with whom he had become friendly, divulged a plot to him and saved the company from a surprise attack.[4] When John Reed's party was attacked in March 1812, at The Dalles, it was Stuart who took charge when Reed was wounded and who negotiated for the withdrawal of the Indians, enabling the party to complete its journey to Fort Okanogan and return. It is true that Ross blames Stuart's decision to pass the portage by stealth at night for bringing on the attack, but he describes him as "brave and prudent."[5] Franchère calls him "a self-possessed and fearless man" and says he refused to abandon Reed, as McClellan in his excitement urged him to do.[6] Stuart himself, in his account of the fight, praises McClellan's actions highly and says nothing of his having lost his head after his conspicuous bravery.[7]

On June 29, 1812, Robert Stuart was placed in command of a small party, which was commissioned to return overland with dispatches for Astor. The route and sufferings of this party are well known and need not be described here.[8] It was this party which made the discovery of South Pass,

---

[3] Gabriel Franchère, "Narrative . . ." in *Early Western Travels,* ed. by R. G. Thwaites (Cleveland, 1904), VI, pp. 204-07; Alexander Ross, "Adventures . . ." in *ibid.,* VII, pp. 50-53. Both Franchère and Ross were among the six men left behind.

[4] Franchère, *op. cit.,* 255.   [5] Ross, *op. cit.,* 187-88.

[6] Franchère, *op. cit.*   [7] Rollins, *op. cit.,* 54-59.

[8] Selected details of the journey are given in this *Series* in my sketches of Robert McClellan (vol. VIII), and in the present volume, of Ramsay Crooks, and Hoback, Reznor, and Robinson.

which resulted from Stuart's discussion of the route with an Indian whom they encountered. Stuart was firmly in charge all the way and his leadership made the difference between success and failure. He refused to abandon Crooks when he was dangerously ill and probably saved his life. He refused to countenance LeClerc's suggestion that they should determine by chance which one of the party should be killed and eaten to save the rest. He allowed McClellan to wander off on his own but kept a course parallel to his and took him back into the party without recrimination. They arrived in St. Louis on April 30, 1813, after a most remarkable journey.[9]

Within a month after his arrival in New York City, Stuart was married to Elizabeth Sullivan, on July 21, 1813.[10] By the close of the War of 1812, he had resumed his employment under Astor and traveled for him in New York and Canada. In 1817 he became second in command at Michilimackinac to Ramsay Crooks and, when Crooks was transferred to New York in 1822, Stuart was placed in charge of Astor's American Fur Company's Great Lakes division with headquarters at Michilimackinac. Here he had under his supervision over four hundred clerks and traders and two thousand voyageurs.[11] Under his management, which lasted till 1834, it was one of Astor's most profitable divisions.

Under these circumstances, Stuart was both surprised and disappointed when, in 1834, his old friend and associate, Ramsay Crooks, bought the company from Astor without reserving a place for him in the organization he had served long and well.[12] Although he had a strict Presbyterian upbringing, Stuart had never been a religious man until 1829,

---

[9] Rollins, *op. cit.*, contains Stuart's narratives of the journey, fully annotated. See also Kenneth A. Spaulding, *On the Oregon Trail: Robert Stuart's Journey of Discovery* (Norman, 1953). Washington Irving, *Astoria*, ed. by Edgeley W. Todd (Norman, 1964), is the best edition of the famous classic which, in 1836, made the world familiar with the adventures of the Astorians.

[10] Lavender, *op. cit.*, 199, 452.   [11] Rollins, *op. cit.*, xl.

[12] Lavender, *op. cit.*, 413-14.

when he was converted to that faith at a revival. His religious views helped him to reconcile himself to the thought of leaving Michilimackinac and the company. Observers had noted the change earlier in that he was more content merely to give verbal orders without reinforcing them with physical force. He was known always for his authoritarian ways and, although he doubtless made enemies, he commanded respect, especially among the Indians.

Stuart moved to Detroit in 1834 where he built the first brick house and engaged in real estate operations. An able and energetic man, he served as director of poor relief in Detroit in 1837 and in 1839, as state treasurer of Michigan, 1840-1841, as superintendent of Indian Affairs, 1841-1845. He became interested in the Illinois and Michigan Canal and it was while in Chicago on business as secretary of the canal company that he died, October 29, 1848.[13] His $78,000 estate had increased to a value of $161,000 by the time his wife died in 1866. Of their nine children, five grew to maturity and left descendants. One son, David, was a colonel under Sherman in the Civil War and later served in Congress.

Though reputed a severe man, Robert Stuart was good company and fond of anecdote. He was a man of high personal standards and a public spirited gentleman. Assuming great responsibility at an early age, he discharged it well from that time until his death.[14] His portrait appears in this volume at page 24.

---

[13] Rollins, *op. cit.,* xli-xlvi.

[14] *Ibid.* In his will, made in 1847, Robert Stuart described himself as being "of Chicago." However, he had not established a residence there and his body was returned to Detroit for burial in Elmwood Cemetery. His uncle David Stuart, who had resided with him in Detroit, survived his nephew, dying in 1853.

Joseph Thing

by JUDITH AUSTIN
Idaho State Historical Society

On the morning of [April] 28th we were all equipped and mounted hunter like: about forty men leading two loaded horses each were marched out in double file with joyous hearts enlivened by anticipated prospects: led by Mr. Wyeth a persevering adventurer and lover of Enterprise whilst the remainder of the party with twenty head of extra horses and as many cattle to supply emergencies brot. up the rear under the direction of Capt. Joseph Thing an eminent navigator and fearless son of Neptune who had been employed by the Company in Boston to accompany the party and measure the route across the Rocky Mountains by Astronomical observation.[1]

Thus did Joseph Thing – "captain" by virtue of his past employment as a sea captain rather than because of previous experience with westward expeditions, and the eventual superintendent of Fort Hall – appear on the western scene.

Thing's involvement with Nathaniel Wyeth's second expedition had begun about three months before the expedition set out. Wyeth started organizing the Columbia River Fishing and Trading Company in the fall of 1833, immediately after his return from his first trip west; his formal proposal to his backers, Henry Hall and Messrs. Tucker and Williams of Boston, was made in November.[2] He was prepared to fulfill the commitment he had made to Thomas Fitzpatrick, Milton Sublette and their Rocky Mountain Fur Company to have goods for them at Green River by

---

[1] Osborne Russell, *Journal of a Trapper*, ed. by Aubrey L. Haines (Lincoln, Neb., 1965 [1955]), 1. Russell was a member of the expedition.

[2] *The Correspondence and Journals of Captain Nathaniel J. Wyeth 1831-6*, ed. by F. G. Young, in *Sources of the History of Oregon*, I, parts 3-6 (Eugene, 1899), 82. The letter is unaddressed and undated, but time and addressee have been inferred from its location in the collection.

July 1, 1834. Wyeth's plans for the 1834 trip were in two parts: fitting out a vessel – the brig "May Dacre" – which would carry supplies to Vancouver for his men, and fitting out the land expedition.

Wyeth reported on February 4, 1834, that he had engaged "Capt. Thwing who is well versed in taking observations to accompany the expedition and [had] provided suitable implements." [3] The next day Wyeth wrote Thing, in Boston, listing a variety of purchases to be shipped to Baltimore and telling Thing to bring with him "a memorandum of all the bills Charged by Tucker & Williams to the overland expedition in order that I may have with me the means of knowing at any time the amt. invested in this part of the business." A letter of introduction to Wyeth's brother Charles, in Baltimore, was sent as well. Wyeth continued to move about the east coast for two months, sending letters to Thing telling him where to pick up merchandise that had to be gotten to Independence. Such varied items as tents, guns, beaver traps, cloth, India rubber boats, and rum were included in Thing's charge. On February 26 Wyeth wrote, "it has occurred to me that some medicines for the clap and pox may be wanted, the men often contract these disorders before they leave the settlements and unless there are some remedys the consequences are bad often inducing the men to desert in order to obtain relief." [4] So much for medical supplies en

The man who followed Wyeth about the countryside in the winter of 1834 was then about forty-four years old and probably a Southerner by birth.[5] He had been master of a

---

[3] *Ibid.*, Wyeth to Thomas Nuttall, 106.

[4] *Ibid.*, Wyeth to Thing, 107; Wyeth to Charles Wyeth, 107; Wyeth to Thing, 113, 114, 117.
route.

[5] Thing is listed as being forty years old when he arrived at New Haven as a passenger on the brig "Henrietta" on February 17, 1830; index to "Copies of Passenger Lists for Vessels arriving at Atlantic, Gulf, and Great Lake Ports (excluding New York), 1820-1873" (I am indebted to Mark G. Eckhoff, director of the Legisla-

vessel at least as late as 1831, and he had been living in Boston when Wyeth hired him.[6] Little else is known about his background, except that he had a family to which some of his salary was paid directly while he was in the West.[7] Thing seems to have been a rather abstemious soul; he bought very little liquor during his nearly three years at Fort Hall, and his reaction to the quantity of liquor consumed at the first rendezvous he attended (in 1834) was somewhat strait-laced.[8] The records of his purchases at Fort Hall also suggest that this Southerner-turned-Boston-sea-captain took considerable care of his personal appearance. Undoubtedly some of his purchases of good-quality clothing, decorative buttons, soap, and other accoutrements of a gentleman were intended as gifts for friendly (or potentially friendly) Indians; but his consistent purchases of new shirts, fancy soap, and fine cloth pants and jackets do imply that he cared to keep up appearances.[9]

The party that traveled west between Wyeth at the front and Thing at the rear was a mixed one. There were a total of seventy men in Wyeth's own party, experienced and

tive, Judicial and Diplomatic Records Division, National Archives, for supplying this information and that regarding Thing's ship command). Thing received a regular birthday ration of rum at Fort Hall on January 25, 1835, Fort Hall Journal, p. 82 (microfilm of original at Oregon Historical Society). For his birthplace, see Russell, *op. cit.,* 155n; Clifford M. Drury, ed., *First White Women Over the Rockies* (Glendale, Calif., 1963), 78.

[6] Card index of "Masters of Vessels," Records of Bureau of Customs, National Archives, lists Thing as master of the brig "Susan," which entered Boston, April 25, 1831; see also Richard G. Beidleman, "Nathaniel Wyeth's Fort Hall," in *Oregon Historical Quarterly* (Sept. 1957), vol. 58, p. 199n. Hiram Chittenden was somewhat confused by Thing's title and believed him to be captain of the "May Dacre" – a job held by Captain James L. Lambert; *History of the American Fur Trade of the Far West* (Stanford, Calif., 1954 [1902]), 452.

[7] Fort Hall Ledger, II, p. 157 (microfilm, Oreg. Hist. Soc.).

[8] Joseph Thing to Tucker and Williams, Ham's Fork, June 29, 1834, in Letter Book of Henry Hall, pp. 40-41; quoted in W. Clement Eaton, "Nathaniel Wyeth's Oregon Expedition," *Pacific Historical Review* (June, 1935) IV, pp. 107-08.

[9] Fort Hall Ledger, II, pp. 76, 156. Thing had also joined in the men's purchase of a violin, later stolen by one of those who accompanied him to Fort Vancouver in the summer of 1835; see Janet LeCompte, "Abel Baker, Jr.," in this *Series,* I, p. 201.

tough. Wyeth had also invited two naturalists, Thomas
Nuttall and John K. Townsend, to come along, and they
went as far west as Hawaii.[10] Jason and Daniel Lee, the first
American missionaries to Oregon, also traveled with the
company and recorded their impressions of the journey.

The good captain seemed to go largely unnoticed by his
fellow travelers. Osborne Russell's only mention of him on
the trip itself is at the very beginning. Daniel Lee suggests
that "Captain Thyng" *always* brought up the rear; Jason
Lee recorded on Sunday, May 11, that the day had been
"spent in a manner not at all congenial with [his] wishes" —
immediately after noting that the party had "gotten lost at
midmorning and the Captain had taken an observation with
his sextant in an attempt to get them back where they
belonged." [11]

On June 19, Wyeth recorded in his diary the refusal of
the Rocky Mountain Fur Company to live up to its contract
to buy his goods, and he proposed to establish a fort some
150 miles west of "Ham's Fork of the Colorado of the West"
to dispose of them. On July 14 Wyeth selected the site for
his fort, at the junction of the Portneuf and the Snake; on
August 6, "Having done as much as was requisite for safety
to the Fort [they] drank a bale of liquor and named it Fort
Hall in honor of the oldest partner in [their] concern. . ."
Some of the party stayed behind to work on the fort, but
Wyeth, Thing, and most of the rest continued on to the
Columbia.[12]

---

[10] John K. Townsend, *Narrative of a Journey across the Rocky Mountains, to the
Columbia River,* in R. G. Thwaites, ed., *Early Western Travels* (Cleveland, 1905),
XXI, pp. 107-369, is a detailed and delightful account of the trip, but unfortunately
Townsend does not mention Thing between April 28 and September 2.

[11] Daniel Lee and J. H. Frost, *Ten Years in Oregon* (New York, 1844), 115;
"Diary of the Rev. Jason Lee," in *Oregon Historical Quarterly* (June 1916), XVII, p.
120. Presumably Jason Lee's displeasure was more with general levity on the Sabbath
than with the party's getting lost. This is apparently the only reference by any of
the party to Thing's employing the skill for which he was hired.

[12] Wyeth, *op. cit.,* 225, 227.

Townsend reported on September 2, while trudging through the Blue Mountains, that Captain Wyeth had left the group and that Captain Thing was in charge for the day and a half that it took the party to reach Fort Walla Walla and rejoin Wyeth.[13] Townsend also reported, somewhat wryly, that at noon on the 2nd he came upon his fellow naturalist, Nuttall, and Captain Thing in the last stages of devouring an owl which Townsend had killed that morning and intended to preserve; "the bird of wisdom lost the immortality which he might otherwise have acquired."[14] On September 14 the party made its last difficult passage: Captain Thing was put in charge of working the heavy, wet canoes over the last cascades of the lower Columbia, in the rain. At least one of the canoes was lost in this thoroughly messy process, but two days later Wyeth's expedition made it safely to the Pacific.

At this point the two halves of the expedition joined, and Wyeth began to explore the Willamette area in company with Thing and Captain James Lambert of the "May Dacre."[15] On September 26 Wyeth sent Thing eastward with supplies for Fort Hall, "12 Kanackas and 6 whites and all the best Horses," but on October 10 Wyeth received word at Fort Walla Walla that the Kanakas had deserted, taking with them twelve horses and two bales of goods. Although one horse was recovered (by an Indian, who brought it in to Wyeth), there seemed little hope of recovering more horses, goods, or men. Therefore, on November 18 Thing was again dispatched with nineteen men of whom Wyeth said: "This is a picked up lot and I have great fears they will commit Robbery and desertion to a greater extent than the Kanacks

---

[13] Townsend, *op. cit.*, 276-79.   [14] *Ibid.*, 277.

[15] Jason Lee recorded in his diary for September 19 that "Capts. Lambert, Wyeth and Thing explored the vicinity in search of a place to suit their business, but they could find none to please them" in "Diary of Rev. Jason Lee," *Oregon Historical Quarterly* (Sept. 1916), XVII, p. 263. Wyeth eventually established Fort William on the Columbia.

have done." [16] Not a particularly choice group with which to try to cross the Blue Mountains in the snow!

Thing reached Fort Hall on Christmas Eve. Although Wyeth had left Robert Evans formally in charge of the fort, the twelve deserters from Jim Bridger's party who appeared there on January 20 went to Captain Thing to arrange to "form a party for hunting and trapping." [17] This party consisted of both ex-Bridger men and some of the original men at Fort Hall. In April, while they were gone, Thing took twelve men to establish a trading post on the Salmon River; unfortunately, he tangled with some Blackfeet and was lucky to return with his men to the fort alive.[18] Rumors of this skirmish made their way to Fort Vancouver not long afterward, but not until Thing himself traveled to Fort Vancouver in the summer of 1835 was the full story recorded.[19] The tiny party was attacked by some five hundred Blackfeet the day after it had set up camp; the captain made a temporary fort in a thicket with his bales of goods, but when the Indians charged head-on the men were forced to hide in the bushes. However, the Indians then informed the whites through an interpreter that they wished only the goods and that Thing's party would be allowed to return to Fort Hall in safety. It was a rough experience and apparently a rough winter in general; Townsend wrote of Thing on the latter's arrival at Fort Vancouver, "Poor man! he looks very much worn by fatigue and hardships, and seven years older than when I last saw him." [20]

Captain Thing and his party returned to Fort Hall from the coast with supplies on November 15.[21] Apparently the captain spent a good part of January and February of 1836 on a trapping expedition on the Portneuf; Wyeth was at the

---

16 Wyeth, *op. cit.*, 234, 235. The Kanakas, or Hawaiians, had been picked up by the "May Dacre" in Hawaii.

17 Russell, *op. cit.*, 9.   18 *Ibid.*, 13.   19 Townsend, *op. cit.*, 327-28.

20 *Ibid.*, 326. Friendly Indians helped supply the men on their return journey.

21 Russell, *op. cit.*, 38.

time paying his first visit to the fort since its establishment.
At some point in early March, Abel Baker, Jr., who had
served as clerk at Fort Hall for over a year, resigned his
position, and command of the fort was formally entrusted
to Thing.[22] Early in Thing's command one of the most unfortunate episodes in the fort's history occurred: the murder
of Antoine Godin in late May.[23]

In his first months as clerk of the fort, Captain Thing was
portrayed in a new role, that of host. W. H. Gray, who was
with the Whitman-Spalding party that summer, reported
that his group had met Wyeth at the annual rendezvous
between July 6 and July 18 (Wyeth was then heading east
to discuss his financial problems with his backers). Wyeth
gave the missionaries a letter of introduction "to Capt.
Thing the Superintendent at the Ft by whome [they] were
treated verry kindly."[24] Mrs. Whitman reported that they
were hospitably entertained by the captain; her greatest
pleasure – and Mrs. Spalding's – lay in the bread he gave
them with their dinner. After dinner, Mrs. Whitman visited
the captain's small garden, in which grew – with varying
degrees of success – corn, peas, turnips, and onions.[25] The
Whitman-Spalding stop was the beginning of Fort Hall's
role as a major way station on the Oregon Trail.

Wyeth had stopped at the fort in June on his way east,
and it may be that he talked with Thing at that time about
disposing of the fort. Wyeth's arrangements with the Hudson's Bay Company for some sort of trade relationship had
been uncertain at best, and a letter which Wyeth sent John
McLoughlin in May of 1836 suggesting a scheme that
would preserve Wyeth's interest in the fort was annotated

---

[22] LeCompte, *op. cit.,* 202. Evans had been demoted after a few months, partly
because he drank too much; Eaton, *op. cit.,* 108.

[23] Aubrey L. Haines, "Antoine Godin," in this *Series,* II, p. 178.

[24] T. C. Elliott, "From Rendezvous to the Columbia," in *Oregon Historical Quarterly* (Sept. 1937), XXXVIII, p. 362. This is an edited version of Gray's letter of September, 1836, to David Ambrose.   [25] Drury, *op. cit.,* 78, 79, 195.

by McLoughlin to suggest explicitly that Wyeth simply
sell the fort to the Honourable Company.[26] Wyeth never
came west again; he left in Thing's hands the whole problem of disposal. The captain, however much he may have
enjoyed the life itself, was hardly enthusiastic about the
problems of conducting business in the region; he wrote to
the chief sponsors of Wyeth's expedition in July of 1836:

> A man wants two or three years experience in this wild place to
> know how to do business in it, every one when first in the country
> knows nothing of the ways and means of the people, to defraud, cheat,
> and steal as is the custom of the Mountain Boys and they call a new
> hand a greenhorn and they will be able to make a raise out of him
> which is very apt to be the case, lying, stealing, and cheating is the
> mottos of the boys in this country, they are certainly a very uncooth
> [sic] set, honesty hardly dare show his head.[27]

Thing must have spent at least some of his time in the
winter of 1836-37 planning how to make the best possible
deal with the Hudson's Bay Company, for he appeared at
the 1837 rendezvous at Green River with a list of prices:
the fort itself to be sold for $1000, traps for $12 each, horses
for $40 each; and the remaining men to be hired by the
Hudson's Bay Company and their accounts, whether debit
or credit, to be transferred to the company. John McLeod,
who was in charge of the Hudson's Bay Company outfit at
the rendezvous, turned down the offer. Thing, anxious to
get the business over with, sold his traps and horses to
Lucien Fontenelle and Andrew Drips of the American Fur
Company for the price he had suggested to McLeod. He
then reentered negotiations with the Honourable Company
and sold the fort for $500, left-over beaver for $4.50 per
pound, and everything else the fort held for the going rate
of importation, the account to be payable on the company's

---

26 *Letters of John McLoughlin from Fort Vancouver to the Governor and Committee,* First Series, 1825-38 (London, 1941), 340-41.

27 Joseph Thing to Tucker and Williams, Fort Hall, July, 1836, in Letter Book of
Henry Hall, 76. Quoted in Eaton, *op. cit.,* 110-11.

agent in Hawaii. The total value of all goods sold to the Hudson's Bay Company was just over $8000.[28]

Captain Thing then began a lengthy journey home after closing out all the fort's business. Wyeth's organization paid his expenses, sending him first to Fort Vancouver, then to Oahu (possibly to complete financial arrangements with the Hudson's Bay Company), then back to Monterey. In October of 1838 he boarded the bark "Kent" at Santa Barbara to return to Boston, arriving home in the spring of 1839.[29]

Ten years later, the captain returned to the West. In March of 1849 two companies of men from Massachusetts and New Hampshire, the Granite State and California Mining and Trading Company and the Mount Washington Company, were organized in Boston to proceed across the country and search for gold in California. Both were joint stock companies; the president of the Mount Washington Company was one Joseph Thing, who, "having several years previous traveled across the country from Independence, Missouri, to Fort Hall and Oregon, in company with some of the men of the American Fur Company, agreed to pilot the Granite State Company through to California for five dollars each."[30] Once again Thing, now 59, was sent off on

[28] McLoughlin, *op. cit.*, 208-09; Fort Hall Ledger, II, p. 161. J. Goldsborough Bruff, in his diary entry for August 24, 1849, records a conversation with Captain Richard Grant(chief trader at Fort Hall) in which the latter gave a most peculiar (totally inaccurate) version of Thing's departure from Fort Hall. Thing had, according to Grant, warmly welcomed a group of Blackfeet into the fort and allowed them to stay within the walls overnight. The next morning the gates were found open and all the stock gone. Therefore the company ordered Grant to relieve Thing and to rebuild the fort in sturdier fashion; *Gold Rush: The Journals, Drawings, and Other Papers of J. Goldsborough Bruff* (New York, 1949), 102.

[29] Beidleman, *op. cit.*, 249; Hubert Howe Bancroft, *History of California* (San Francisco, 1886), IV, p. 104n. Thing had earned $3200 in his first four years with Wyeth's company, which also paid his expenses all the way back to Boston and salary through April 10, 1839. Balancing credits and debits (including the salary payments to his family), Thing wound up $434.84 to the good for more than five years' service; Fort Hall Ledger, II, p. 157.

[30] Kimball Webster, *The Gold Seekers of '49* (Manchester, N.H., 1912), 21.

quartermastering chores; the rest of the two companies (which became known jointly as the Boston Pack Company) gathered in Independence in early May after a rather sociable trip from Boston by train and boat. The group was behind the main stream of emigration at the outset; its first few days were marked by difficulty in using the mules, causing further delays. In common with other trains that year, they soon began losing people from cholera; they also lost some from sheer discouragement at the slow pace. Fairly early, Kimball Webster (the company's chief diarist) began to note some problems of organization: the mules seemed somewhat overburdened, and much of the equipment brought along (especially items like picks and shovels) seemed useless to transport across the country but owners were reluctant to leave them behind.[31]

When the party reached Fort Laramie on July 8, it was decided that the light leather trunks, "a sad oversight by Captain Thing who suggested them" and had had them specially made in Boston, two for each mule in which to carry provisions and clothing, were simply too heavy. The next day they were broken up and bags were made from the leather. It also appeared that the group was too large; between the number of stock (over three hundred head of cattle, horses, and mules) and the lateness in the year, grazing was becoming a problem.[32]

On August 1, Webster wrote:

> We left the road today with the intention of taking a straight course through the mountains to Fort Hall, thereby avoiding the circuitous route by way of Fort Bridges [sic].
>
> Captain Thing, our guide, states that he once traveled the route and in his opinion we shall find good grass and water, and that there is an Indian trail through which he thinks he can follow.[33]

The train was at this point several miles north of South

---

[31] Ibid., 23, 36-37, 39, 40, 49.   [32] Ibid., 57-58, 38, 63.   [33] Ibid., 65-66.

Pass, in land that is rather barren but not particularly rough. On August 9 they left a stream, climbed a peak, and headed down the other side. "Captain Thing says he was never before at this place and is at a loss to know what route to take to get out."[34] The next day, Thing and two or three others found a passage, and on the 11th they crossed into the Columbia drainage.[35]

On August 12, "we had a dispute, or difference of opinion . . . about starting. Captain Thing wished to remain here today and look out for a route tomorrow, and go straight through to Fort Hall. He thought we had come too far north for the route he had taken eleven [*sic*] years previous, and said that had caused our misfortune." However, a majority of the company wanted to follow the stream they were on in the hope that it would lead to the Bear River. It did, and on the night of the 12th they were back on the trail again. "This route has been christened 'Thing's Cutoff.' A majority of the company was in favor of trying it, relying on Captain Thing's knowledge of the country and experience."[36]

In view of Thing's having gone West in the first place as a navigator, the company's getting lost is rather ironic. Equally so is the fact that on August 16 the party, nearly a month behind the heart of the year's flow of travel, reached the point west of Soda Springs at which the Hudspeth Company had turned off the regular route in mid-July. Most of the following parties had taken Hudspeth's Cutoff, and Thing led his group down it too – despite the fact that in so doing he by-passed Fort Hall (which was suffering badly from the decreased travel along the old route) and turned away from the trail with which he had been familiar.[37]

---

[34] *Ibid.*, 68.   [35] *Ibid.*, 69.

[36] *Ibid.*, 70-71. Bruff suggests that Thing thought he was taking Sublette's Cutoff. The party was forced to get supplies from Cantonment Loring in order to continue, Bruff, *op. cit.*, 625, 101.   [37] Webster, *op. cit.*, 73.

The next month's travel was uneventful, but on September 14 the party turned away from the main route once again to take the "Cherokee cutoff," better known as Lassen's cutoff, from the Humboldt. Thing had never been in this part of the world, which may explain why his party firmly believed itself to be only a week from the mines. It took twenty-nine days to reach the Sacramento Valley, with some bitterness at the "very unreliable and untruthful" information the party had been given by other travelers; Captain Thing had not verbally misled his followers.[38]

The Granite State and California Mining Company – and presumably the Mount Washington Company as well – broke up on October 19, and Webster then noted two or three "gross errors" made on the trip. He believed that it should not have been a joint-stock company (benevolent dictatorship perhaps having its advantages in difficult circumstances) and that the group should have been much smaller, with older and better-broken mules. However, no personal criticisms were directed toward Captain Thing; in fact, Webster simply ignored the captain once the party had come safely through "Thing's Cutoff."[39]

This sea-and-land captain did not leave a very deep mark on the West. Although Wyeth theoretically hired him as a navigator, the captain apparently did not often employ whatever skills he may have had in this field on the trip west in 1834.[40] By 1849, his efforts off the beaten track were nearly disastrous. Richard Grant's story of Thing's allowing Blackfeet practically to carry off Fort Hall, while

[38] *Ibid.*, 82-83, 87, 94.

[39] *Ibid.*, 96-97. Presumably the captain arrived in California safely, since any other fate would probably have been noted by Webster, but no word is found regarding his activities in California. We do not know whether he died there or returned to Boston once again.

[40] Although Jason Lee's is the only specific mention made by any of the diarists of an observation, it may be that Thing was responsible for some of the rather inaccurate mileage figures Russell uses; Russell, *op. cit.,* 155n.

probably a confusion on Grant's part of the unhappy battle with the Blackfeet in the spring of 1835, certainly suggests that the captain's reputation for wisdom was limited.[41] And Wyeth commented in a letter to his backers that Thing's ability as a "scribe" or clerk was even more limited than his own.[42] Nonetheless, Wyeth provided Thing with the opportunity for his most lasting reknown: responsibility for the sale of Fort Hall to the Hudson's Bay Company.

[41] See above, note 28. [42] Wyeth, *op. cit.*, 139.

John H. Weber

by LeRoy R. Hafen
Brigham Young University

Most of the data about the early life of John H. Weber comes from material supplied by his son William. Although this biographical information was given to a local newspaper by the son when he was eighty-five years old, it is probably correct as to the place and date of his father's birth and also regarding the father's personal appearance and characteristics.[1] We quote from this original account on these matters:

> The subject of this sketch was born in the town of Altona, then a part of the kingdom of Denmark in 1779. The boy received a fairly good education, and grew to a vigorous and well developed manhood. While quite young he ran away to sea, and for years sailed the "Briny Deep." He was captain and commander of a passenger ship before he was 21 years old, and in very turbulent times owing to the wars then being waged between England and France on land and sea. He commanded sailing vessels for nearly six years.

Then he came to America and by July 1807, he was living at Ste. Genevieve, Missouri, where he became acquainted with William H. Ashley and Andrew Henry, with whom he would later enter the fur trade. He probably served in the War of 1812, was at Mine a Breton in 1814, and in 1817

---

[1] Mr. Stallo Vinton, while preparing his edition of H. M. Chittenden's *American Fur Trade of the Far West* (New York, 1935), received from W. A. Struble a copy of the clipping about Weber (see Vinton's note, *ibid.,* 788). Vinton later supplied a copy to Dr. Charles Camp, who reproduced it in his article, "The D.T.P. Letters," in *Essays for Henry R. Wagner* (San Francisco, 1947), 24-25. Vinton says the clipping probably was from the Jackson, Iowa, *Sentinel* "about 1906." This article is hereafter referred to as William Weber's statement.

signed a petition (also signed by Ashley and Henry) asking statehood for Missouri.[2]

Weber joined the Ashley-Henry fur trade venture. "The party left St. Louis in the spring of 1822 and slowly ascended the Missouri River. They were six months reaching the mouth of the Yellowstone River, where they halted and made a cache in which to store their supplies they could not take with them."[3]

General Ashley came up the Missouri in his second boat, which reached the mouth of the Yellowstone on October 1, 1822, and there he joined his partner Henry. With Ashley came Jedediah Smith, who in a part of his precious extant diary dates Ashley's arrival and writes:

> Gen[l] Ashley and Maj. Henry immediately commenced arrangements for business and after furnishing the mountain parties with their supplies of goods and receiving the furs of the last hunt Gen[l] Ashley started for St. Louis with a large Pirogue. . .
>
> In the meantime a party had gone up the Missouri in a Boat and canoes for the purpose of trapping under the immediate charge of Maj. Henry, and another in canoes up the Yellow Stone for the same purpose. When Maj. Henry left the fort it was his intention to ascend the Missouri as far as the mouth of Milk River and the party of the Yellow Stone were by instruction to ascend that river to the mouth of Powder River and up it as far as practicable.[4]

Jedediah does not name the leader of the party that ascended the Yellowstone, but it was undoubtedly John H. Weber.

---

[2] Dale L. Morgan's sketch of Weber in D. L. Morgan and Eleanor Towles Harris, eds., *The Rocky Mountain Journals of William Marshall Anderson* (San Marino, Calif., 1967), 387; and in Morgan's *Jedediah Smith* (Indianapolis, 1953), 378; and in his *The West of William H. Ashley* . . . (Denver, 1964), 283-84.

[3] William Weber's statement, 24. Contemporary records do not mention John H. Weber's name in relation to the Ashley-Henry undertaking, although William Weber asserts that his father was a partner in the venture. We have found no evidence to substantiate the claim of partnership, but he undoubtedly was with Henry up the Missouri in 1822.

[4] Maurice S. Sullivan, *The Travels of Jedediah Smith; a Documentary Outline, Including the Journal of the Great American Pathfinder* (Santa Ana, Calif., 1934), 8.

In the biographical sketch of John H. Weber by his son, the latter writes: "Captains Weber and Henry took command of thirteen men each, the others returning or remaining with the boats." [5] Another original sketch of Weber was written by his neighbor, J. C. Hughey and was published in the *Salt Lake Tribune* of July 4, 1897, p. 31. Because this is the first published biographical sketch of Weber and is rather difficult of access, it is reproduced in full at the end of the present sketch. Hughey writes:

> The boats returned to St. Louis [from the Yellowstone], while Capt. Weber and his partner [Henry] each with thirteen men, entered upon their work as trappers and traders. [6]

Contemporary records of 1823 and 1824 fail to report the doings of Weber for this period, but W. H. Ashley, in his diary of June 7, 1825, mentions Weber as having spent the previous winter west of the continental divide, in the Bear River region.[7] Daniel Potts, though he does not name his companions, was a member of the Weber party, and gives in his letters very good descriptions of the country visited and circumstantial evidence about Weber.[8]

Potts tells of his trapping on the Bighorn and Wind River area in the fall of 1823 and the spring of 1824. In the Weber party he then crossed over South Pass in the summer of 1824

---

[5] William Weber's statement.

[6] Hereafter referred to as Hughey's Sketch. There is such close similarity in the wording of certain parts of the two sketches that it is probable that William Weber had a copy of Hughey's sketch when he wrote his own. The present writer had some difficulty in locating the Hughey article in the *Salt Lake Tribune*. Dale Morgan, in his reference to it in *West of Ashley*, 283; and in his and Harris, *Journals of Anderson*, 387, gives the date as July 24, 1897, p. 31. Also Charles Camp in his "D.T.P. Letters," cited above, gives the same date and page. There is no page 31 in that issue of the paper, nor does the article appear on any of the twelve pages of the issue of July 24th. Finally I looked into Morgan's *Jedediah Smith* and found on page 378 the correct citation: "July 4, 1897, p. 31."

[7] Morgan, *West of Ashley,* 116.

[8] The five Potts letters are reproduced in Gerald C. Bagley, "Daniel T. Potts, Chronicler of the Fur Trade," unpublished M.A. thesis, Brigham Young University, 1964. See also the same author's sketch of Potts in this *Series*, III, pp. 249-62.

and into the Green River Valley. In his letter of July 16, 1826, he writes:

> After passing from this valley, in a S.W. direction we had very good travelling over an inconsiderable ridge, we fell on a considerable river, called Bear River, which rises to the S. in the Utaw Mountains, bears N. 80 or 90 miles, when it turns short to the S.W. and S. and after passing two mountains, discharges itself into Great Salt Lake. On this river and its tributary streams, and adjacent country, we have taken beaver with great success Since the autumn of 1824.[9]

The Weber party went to Bear Lake, which Potts describes as " a small sweet lake, about 120 miles in circumference, with beautiful clear water, and when the wind blows has a splendid appearance." They continued to "Willow Valley" [Cache Valley] which "has been our chief place of rendezvous and wintering ground.[10]

In his excellent description of the Great Salt Lake area Potts tells of the outlet from Utah Lake and also describes "Weber's river." [11] James Bridger said he was with the "Weaver's [Weber's] party" when it came to Salt Lake.[12] James P. Beckwourth, with the Ashley men in the Salt Lake area in 1825 and 1826, refers to "Weaver's [Weber's] Fort" and to "Weaver's Lake" [Bear Lake].[13]

How long Weber remained in the mountains we do not know positively, but his son William says he returned to his family in 1827.[14] The son says his father moved to Galena, Illinois, in 1832 and remained there until 1844. He then settled in Bellevue, Iowa, where he lived the rest of his life.[15] The federal census records have him living at Galena as head of his family in 1840; and in 1850 as 70 years old and living in his son William's household.[16] William Weber's

---

[9] Donald M. Frost, *Notes on General Ashley, the Overland Trail, and South Pass* (Worcester, Mass., 1945), 62.   [10] *Ibid.*, 62-63.   [11] *Ibid.*, 63.

[12] Bridger's report in the Denver *Rocky Mountain News* of May 15, 1861.

[13] *The Life and Adventures of James P. Beckwourth*, ed. by T. D. Bonner (New York, 1931), 60, 62, 66.

[14] William Weber's statement.   [15] *Ibid.*   [16] Morgan and Harris, *op. cit.*, 388.

description and appraisal of his father is worth quoting:

> Captain Weber was no ordinary man. Nature had done well by him, he was a man of large and powerful frame, of erect carriage and graceful manner, his face indicated the superior intelligence behind it, he had a nose like a Roman Emperor and an eye as regal and piercing as that of an American eagle, the courage of a hero, and the staying qualities of a martyr. Those who knew him say they do not believe he ever experienced the sensation of fear, but he was impetuous and peculiar in many ways and at times disagreeable and unhappy. His was mercurial nature that went up in hope and down with despair. He made about $20,000 by hunting, trapping and trading in the Rocky Mountains but was beaten out of what was then a fortune by dishonest partners. He never made or saved much wealth afterwards and died poor. He performed clerical work in the county offices and for Bellevue merchants for years before he died. He, at last, became a victim of neuralgia in the face and suffered all the torments which this dread malady is able to inflict. Life became a burden to him and he resolved to shuffle off the mortal coil that bound him to this world. He deliberately committed suicide in 1859 by cutting his throat, bleeding to death in a few minutes. His remains lie buried in the North Bellevue cemetery. No stone of any kind marks the grave of this remarkable man who was one of the first pioneers of our great west.[17]

As promised above, we reproduce here the J. C. Hughey report of his neighbor:

J. C. Hughey Writes of Captain John H. Weber
[In *Salt Lake Tribune,* July 4, 1897, p. 31]

J. C. Hughey of Bellevue, Iowa, takes an interest in The Tribune's "Fifty Years Ago Today" sketches, and sends the following interesting bit of history:

In the spring of 1852 I became acquainted with Capt. John H. Weber, one of the first white men to look upon Salt Lake. I had the privilege of many conversations with him, as we lived in the same boarding house. From his story I learned that in the spring of 1822 a company was formed at St. Louis consisting of Messrs. Ashley, Weber and Henry, known as the American Fur company.[18] Mr. Ashley fur-

---

[17] William Weber's statement.

[18] The statement is in error; the Ashley-Henry venture was not the American Fur Company; and we have found no other information supporting the statement that Weber was a partner.

nished the outfit, consisting of two keelboats loaded with provisions, firearms, tents, traps and such other articles as were considered necessary for successful prosecution of such an expedition in trapping and bartering with the Indians. The propelling force consisted of about fifty men, mostly Canadians.

In six months from the time of starting they arrived at the mouth of the Yellowstone river, where they made a "cache" of things not to be taken with them. The boats returned to St. Louis, while Capt. Weber and his partner each with thirteen men, entered upon their work as trappers and traders with the Indians, beaver being the furs mostly sought after and largely found in the vicinity of the Columbia river. The Captain told me more than once of his discovery of Salt Lake in 1823.[19] He called it a great boon to them, as salt was plentiful around the border of the lake and for some time before they had used gunpowder on their meat,[20] which was principally buffalo. He said meat was the staff of life, and but seldom ate any bread.

Capt. Weber was also the discoverer of Weber canyon and Weber river, both of which bear his name. The keel boats continued to make annual trips with supplies for the trappers and to secure the furs for the market. In the autumn of 1827 they returned to St. Louis; in 1832 he removed to Galena, Ill., then famed for its lead mines, a few years later he came to Bellevue, Ia., where he died in February, 1859.

By birth he was a Dane. For six years he sailed a Danish vessel as skipper, before coming to America. He was a large, well-formed man with an eye like an eagle and a voice like a trumpet. His son, William, lives within two miles of town, was born six months after his father left for the mountains. When I knew him he had forgotten his native language and spoke the English language freer from provincialism than most natives do.

---

[19] Of the Americans, Etienne Provost is now generally considered the first to have seen Great Salt Lake. It is entirely possible that the British traders under Donald Mackenzie in their wanderings on the Snake, Bear, and Green rivers, 1819-23, and Finnan McDonald in 1823 had seen Salt Lake before any Americans. See Alexander Ross, *The Fur Hunters of the Far West,* ed. by K. A. Spaulding (Norman, Okla., 1956), 135-38, and other sources on British traders in the Snake River country.

[20] This was commonly done by Mountain Men.

Peter M. Weiser

by CHARLES G. CLARKE
Beverly Hills, California

For Peter M. Weiser[1] we are fortunate in having an ancestral line which gives some understanding of the life and heritage necessary to become a successful Mountain Man. Probably many others whose biographies appear in this *Series* had similar roots, but for many of these, genealogical proof is frequently lacking.

Peter M. Weiser was born October 3, 1781, in Berks County, Pennsylvania. He probably was a son of John Philip Weiser, born, September 21, 1753, who was a son of Peter Weiser, born, February 27, 1730,[2] son of Conrad Weiser, born, November 2, 1696, in Wurtemburg, Germany, son of John Conrad Weiser of Germany, who led a party of Palatines to America. This party lived the first four years at Livingston Manor in New York. In 1714 the family moved to Schoharie, New York, where young Conrad came in close contact with the Mohawk Indians. He was adopted into their tribe and lived among them several years, becoming a master of their language.

In 1729, Conrad Weiser and his family, now consisting of his wife and five young children, removed to what became Berks County, Pennsylvania. The new homestead was a mile east of the present town of Womelsdorf, and it became the center of hospitality, both for the German settlers and visiting Indians.[3] Conrad Weiser became the famed Indian diplomat.

---

[1] The spelling of the name appears in various forms. John Wiser is most frequently found in the literature of the west. Other variants are Wyser and Wyzer. The last was used by the Virginia branch of the family.

[2] Rev. Frederick S. Weiser, ed., *The Weiser Family* (Penn., 1960), 706.

[3] Reuben G. Thwaites, ed., *Early Western Travels* (Cleveland, 1904), I, p. 15.

It was in such a backwoods environment that our Peter M. Weiser spent his boyhood – hunting and associating with friendly Indians. As a young man he enlisted in the U.S. Army, as that service provided new adventures at the posts then established on the western frontier. When Lewis and Clark were seeking, as Clark put it: "robust, helthy hardy young men" as possible members for the expedition, Peter Weiser was transferred, probably from Captain Russell Bissell's command of troops at Kaskaskia, located on the Mississippi above the mouth of the Ohio River.

Captain Clark took the recruits thus far enlisted and went on to Wood River, some twenty miles above St. Louis on the Illinois side of the Mississippi. On December 12, 1803, he located a camp where the men would winter and would be observed and trained. At some date during this time, Weiser became a part of the expedition.[4]

By reference to the journals kept by various members of the Lewis and Clark expedition, we learn of Weiser's activities:[5]

March 3, 1804, while at Camp Woods, Peter Weiser was punished for visiting a nearby whiskey shop under the pretense of "hunting." He, among others, are confined to camp for ten days for this infraction of military orders. However, the Captains obviously viewed this as a minor offense, for Weiser became one of the permanent members of the party who went to the Pacific and return.

---

[4] R. G. Thwaites, ed., *The Original Journals of the Lewis and Clark Expedition,* also containing the journal of Sgt. Charles Floyd and the journal of Pvt. Joseph Whitehouse. (7 vols., New York, 1904), I, p. 11. Hereafter cited as Thwaites.

[5] Charles G. Clarke, *The Men of the Lewis and Clark Expedition* (Glendale, Calif., 1970). Clarke has compiled a "diary" from the various authors of the Lewis and Clark journals, including Lewis, Clark, Ordway, Floyd, Gass and Whitehouse, concentrating on the activities of the members throughout the expedition. This material was digested from Thwaites; Milo M. Quaife, ed., *Journals of Meriwether Lewis and Sergeant John Ordway* (Madison, 1916); Elliott Coues, ed., *History of the Expedition Under the Command of Lewis and Clark* (4 vols., New York, 1893); Patrick Gass, *Journal of the Voyages and Travels of a Corps of Discovery Under the Command of Captain Lewis and Captain Clarke* (Pittsburgh, 1807); Ernest S. Osgood, ed., *The Field Notes of Captain William Clark, 1803-1805* (New Haven, 1964); and Donald Jackson, ed., *Letters of the Lewis and Clark Expedition and Related Documents* (Urbana, 1962), hereafter cited as Jackson.

May 14, 1804. Captain Clark and the members of the expedition now decided upon, left Camp Woods for St. Charles on the Missouri, where they were to rendezvous with Captain Lewis a few days later.

May 26, 1804. Peter Weiser is assigned to Sgt. Nathaniel Pryor's mess.

August 12, 1804. While enroute up the Missouri, Weiser is appointed cook for Sgt. John Ordway's mess.

From *October 26, 1804* to *April 7, 1805,* the party wintered among the Mandan Indians in a large fort which they had constructed and called Fort Mandan. Weiser was active most of the winter on hunting forays; procuring corn from the Mandans and other assignments.

May 18, 1805. Weiser was now with the party enroute to the Pacific. On the upper Missouri the Captains named a creek for Weiser. This creek is presently known as Fourchette's Creek.

August 24, 1805. On the upper Salmon River, the Captains had concluded their purchase of horses from the Shoshoni. Weiser became very ill from a stomach disorder. Lewis administered peppermint and laudanum, which relieved Weiser, but he still was so sick that he was placed upon Lewis' horse, as the party moved on. Later, more horses were obtained so all the command could be mounted.

December 27, 1805. While at Fort Clatsop near the Pacific, Weiser helped carry the kettles to the seaside where other members remained to begin boiling down sea-water to make salt.

March 23, 1806. The party left Fort Clatsop to begin their homeward journey.

April 16, 1806. Having passed the Cascades of the Columbia, the Captains decided to purchase horses to travel overland rather than row up the rivers. Weiser was one of a party under Captain Clark detailed to purchase horses from the river Indians.

May 19, 1806. Back in their old camp among the Nez Perce Indians, awaiting the snows to melt on the Lolo Trail in the Bitterroot Mountains, Weiser was sent to purchase roots from the Indians upon which the party subsisted.

May 27, 1806. Peter Weiser and Robert Frazier went with Sgt. Ordway on an excursion to the lower Salmon River to purchase salmon which were then running in that stream. They arrived at the junction of the Salmon with the Snake River on *May 29th;* went up the Salmon some twenty miles to a camp where they purchased salmon on the *30th.* They tried to dry the fish, but on the *31st* they started back to the main camp, arriving there on *June 2nd*. This party was undoubtedly the first white men on this portion of the Snake and Salmon rivers.

July 3, 1806. Again reaching Travelers' Rest on the Bitterroot River, the party was divided into two main groups so that more new country could be explored. Weiser went with Capt. Clark's group up the Bitterroot River; over Gibbon's Pass and back to the fork of the Jefferson (Beaverhead) River where they had, the previous Fall, cached their canoes and extra goods. Reaching that site on *July 10th,* Weiser was assigned to the party who were to take the canoes down the Jefferson and Missouri rivers to the Great Falls and beyond to the mouth of the Yellowstone.

July 23, 1806. While assisting in the portage down around the Great Falls, Weiser cut his hand severely, and had to be carried overland in one of the canoes.

Captain Lewis' and Captain Clark's respective groups rejoined on *August 10, 1806,* below the junction of the Yellowstone River. Now all was down stream and the expedition made a rapid trip to St. Louis, where they all arrived on *September 25, 1806*. The men helped sort and pack the materials which had been collected on the expedition, for shipment to Washington. On *October 10, 1806,* the men were discharged and were free to enter private life. Peter Weiser received his pay: January 1, 1804, to October 10, 1806, @ $5.00 per month = $166.66 2/3. Later, double extra pay was granted.[6] Unfortunately, of Weiser's subsequent life, the records are scant.

Weiser apparently remained in St. Louis the following fall and winter of 1806-07. Sometime during the spring of 1807, Weiser had signed up with Manuel Lisa to return to the Upper Missouri to trap and trade for beaver. On March 6, 1807, Congress passed an act alloting each of the members of the expedition 320 acres of land located west of the Mississippi. I have not been able to locate any references as to the disposition of Weiser's land for which he signed Warrant #27.

---

[6] Jackson, 378, 425.

Manuel Lisa's party of some fifty-two men, including Peter Weiser, George Drouillard, John Colter, and John Potts, all former Lewis and Clark men, set out from St. Louis April 19, 1807. By November 21st they had reached the mouth of the Bighorn River on the Yellowstone, too late for the fall hunt. Here Lisa built a post which he named Fort Raymond after his son, but it became usually known as Manuel's or Lisa's Fort. Lisa immediately sent out a few select men in different directions to notify the Indians of his arrival with goods to trade for furs. Colter and Drouillard went to the south and Colter crossed the Wind River Mountains and into the upper Yellowstone country to alert the Indians of the new trading post. As will be explained later, it would appear that at this same time, Peter Weiser went west over the Bozeman Pass to the Three Forks of the Missouri. William Clark and his group had traversed this route in 1806 on their homeward journey. Although Weiser was at the time with the canoe party on the Missouri, he could have later learned of the route from Clark or some of his companions.

From the Three Forks, it is conjectured that Weiser ascended the Madison River "to find an easy pass at its sources, and [as Weiser reported later] [7] a beaver-rich country on the Snake waters to the south" [8]— and an eligible place for a fort.

On July 6, 1808, he was back at the fort where, with John Potts and Forest Hancock, they executed a note to Manuel Lisa for $424.50, probably as the cost of traps and supplies. [9]

Lisa left the Fort after signing that note and by late August 1808, was back in St. Louis. That fall the Missouri

[7] Letter from Reuben Lewis, dated Three Forks of the Missouri, April 10, 1810, to his brother, in Meriwether Lewis Papers, Mo. Hist. Soc.

[8] Dale L. Morgan, *The West of William H. Ashley* (Denver, 1964), p. xxxiii. Hereafter cited as Morgan.

[9] Stella M. Drumm, ed., *Luttig's Journal of a Fur Trading Expedition on the Upper Missouri, 1812-1813* (St. Louis, 1920), 102n.

Fur Company was organized, of which Lisa was a partner.[10] In the spring of 1809, men of this new company left St. Louis and part of them spent the winter at Lisa's Fort. In the spring of 1810, Lisa sent a brigade of trappers to the Three Forks under the partners, Andrew Henry and Pierre Menard. The Blackfeet Indians routed this party and killed five of the Americans, including Drouillard. The records do not state that Peter Weiser was among this party, but it is quite possible. Perhaps he may have been the guide who conducted the remnants of Henry's brigade on their retreat up the Madison, over the "easy" pass and down onto the stream which became known as Henry's Fork of the Snake. Here Andrew Henry built the first of the several subsequent Henry's Forts, but this one was soon abandoned, for game was scarce and the party had to subsist on its horses. The brigade broke up, some to return to Lisa's Fort, while others, including Peter Weiser, may have explored lower down on the Snake. The year before, Drouillard had returned to St. Louis and had visited William Clark, to whom he gave a report and maps of his explorations. Clark added these details to the large map he was preparing, which was intended to appear with the Lewis and Clark Journals when they were published.[11]

On the basis of this map, whereon Clark had also laid down a tributary of the Snake River as "Wiser's R.," the reconnaissance of Peter Weiser, as outlined above, is conjectured.[12] It is not known that Weiser gave Clark this information in person, or if it came from Drouillard, Lisa, Colter, Reuben Lewis, Henry, or some other person. At any

---

[10] Walter B. Douglass, *Manuel Lisa*, in Mo. Hist. Soc. *Collections*, III, no. 3, p. 257.

[11] Three manuscript maps made by Clark are of interest here. One is in the Library of Congress; the second in the Clark Papers, Mo. Hist. Soc.; while the third is in the Coe Collection, Yale University. Wheat, *Mapping the Transmississippi West*, II (Menlo Park, Calif., 1958), pp. 55-56, reproduces Clark's ca. 1809 and 1814 maps – the last showing the Wiser R. and the new "Southern Pass."

[12] Morgan, xl.

rate, the river and route appear on Clark's map, and it most certainly refers to Peter M. Weiser.

Presumably Peter Weiser was killed in one of the several skirmishes with the Blackfeet about the year 1810. Much later, during 1825-1828, William Clark prepared a list of former expedition members [13] in which he added terse comment after some of their names. He notes: "Peter Wiser – Killed." History apparently has left unrecorded the date and details of the passing of this man who showed great promise as an explorer and one of the first of the Mountain Men.

Even his proper name is sometimes forgotten, for some local historians ascribe the name of the town of Weiser, Idaho, and the Weiser River nearby, to one "*Jacob* Wiser – a German trapper." [14]

[13] Jackson, 638.

[14] American Guide Series, *Idaho, a Guide in Word and Pictures* (New York, 1950), 179.

Ezekiel Williams*

by F<small>REDERIC</small> E. V<small>OELKER</small>
St. Louis Westerners

All indications are that Ezekiel Williams was born in Kentucky about 1775. He stated that he lived in Kentucky "from my cradle until I came to this country [Missouri]." Family tradition is that he was born in Kentucky; and certainly if not one of the first white persons born there, he was at least one of its first white infant immigrants. Beyond that, the known record and family tradition alike provide little information about his ancestry, parentage and early life.[1]

During his years in Kentucky Williams acquired some schooling, became a competent woodsman and hunter, and developed into a well favored specimen of the hardy frontiersman with great strength of character. He was said to have married Margaret Thornton in Cumberland County; and he had a son, Samuel, born in Kentucky about February 1797.[2]

It appears possible, though on admittedly flimsy evidence, that Williams, seeking an adventurous livelihood in the

---

*In addition to the acknowledgments extended in the writer's "Ezekiel Williams of Boon's Lick" (see note 1), thanks for material help are offered to: the late Mrs. Louise H. Murphy, esteemed collaborator; Mrs. Helen Traman, North Aurora, Ill., and the late Mrs. Hettie Williams Henry, descendants of Ezekiel Williams; and Mr. Norman ("Spon") Imbush, Cole Camp, Mo.

[1] Frederic E. Voelker, "Ezekiel Williams of Boon's Lick," in *Bulletin,* Mo. Hist. Soc. (St. Louis), VIII, no. 1 (Oct. 1951), 18-19; writer's notes of an interview with Mrs. Henry, Lincoln, Mo., May 31, 1952. The *Bulletin* article provides some details of Williams' life and activities in Missouri.

[2] J. C. Ludlow to Will, Nov. 20, 1818, *Franklin County Record* (Union, Mo.), Nov. 30, 1876, reprinted in *Missouri Historical Review,* vol. 54, no. 4 (July 1960), 413; Voelker, *op. cit.,* 37, 41; interview with Mrs. Henry; gravestone inscription in Union Cemetery, Benton Co., Mo.

West, arrived in St. Louis before 1807, and there is some uncertainty about his western activities until the summer of 1810. Thus he could have made his first trip up the Missouri River toward the northwestern fur country with any one of several more or less attached outfits that went out in the spring of 1807.[3]

We may be fairly sure that Williams always operated as a free trapper, occasionally joining organized outfits for mutual protection against Indian hostility and other hazards of the western trails, with some responsibility for the security and sustenance of his party. As an independent contractor he was free to dispose of his furs as he saw fit, to employ his own men, to enter into temporary partnerships with varying degrees of obligation, to become an employed leader with some right to choose his own men and his own course. (In view of the confusion and controversy regarding Williams' business practices, and later accusations against him, it is necessary to understand the conditions under which he worked in those early days.)[4]

The main sources (all unsatisfactory) for this 1807-1810 period of Ezekiel Williams' life and adventures are David H. Coyner's *The Lost Trappers* and Thomas James' *Three Years Among the Indians and Mexicans,* both written nearly forty years after the events; and Williams' letter of August 7, 1816, to Joseph Charless.[5]

Coyner's account, which he averred was largely based on

---

[3] Could Williams have been one of many (Virginians and Kentuckians) haunting the St. Louis area in the fall and winter, 1803-1804, seeking to join Lewis and Clark? The false rumor, still persisting in central Missouri, that Ezekiel Williams accompanied that expedition was given added currency by James H. Lay, *A Sketch of the History of Benton County* (Mo.), (Hannibal, 1876), 16. David H. Coyner, *The Lost Trappers* (Cincinnati, 1847), 19-20, gives the somehow persuasive 1807 as the year of Williams' first trip up the Missouri.

[4] Ezekiel Williams to Joseph Charless, Aug. 17, 1816, in *Missouri Gazette,* Sept. 14, 1816. (See notes 31 and 32 and the text they document.)

[5] Coyner, *op. cit.,* 19-143; Thomas James, *Three Years Among the Indians and Mexicans* (Waterloo, Ill., 1846; new ed., Milo M. Quaife, ed., N.Y., 1966), 8-28; Williams to Charless, *loc. cit.*

an "old musty mutilated journal, kept by Captain Williams," is full of blatant anachronisms, confusions of personalities, and geographical misplacements, and erroneously assigns to the heroic "Captain Williams" the sole leadership of an 1807-1810 expedition to the Far West. James' narrative, apparently written from memory, while covering a considerable portion of the same ground, nowhere mentions Ezekiel Williams. Williams' letter to Charless scrambles the dates, and is aggravatingly lacking in important details.[6]

However, from these and a scattering of other sources we may construct a pretension toward the truth which probably would withstand all but well documented evidence to the contrary.

Williams went up the Missouri with one of several parties which left St. Louis in the spring of 1807. Mounted, they followed the river at some distance south or west of it, through territories claimed, respectively, by the Osages, Kansas, Pawnees, Otos, Omahas, Sioux, Arikaras and Mandans, without meeting any hostility, and continued toward the northwestern plains controlled by the Gros Ventres and other tribes of the Blackfeet confederacy.[7]

Somewhere near the mouth of the Yellowstone they must have met, perhaps by prearrangement, the larger Manuel Lisa-George Drouillard party, which had come up the Missouri in barges, and made some sort of trade arrangement with these representatives of a St. Louis partnership. The combined parties turned up the Yellowstone and at its junction with the Bighorn constructed a post called Fort Raymond.[8]

They worked that region (Crow-Blackfeet war grounds), including the remote Three Forks country, during the 1807-

[6] *Ibids*. Coyner, x-xi, mentions some of his other sources.

[7] Richard E. Oglesby, *Manuel Lisa* (Norman, 1963), 40-41, 50-51; Hiram Martin Chittenden, *The American Fur Trade of the Far West* (N.Y., 1902; repr. Stanford, 1954), I, p. 120, front. map; Coyner, *op. cit.*, 19-20, 28-31, 38, 51, 53, 72, 81, 86.

[8] Oglesby, *op. cit.*, 40, 54; Coyner, *op. cit.*, 86-87.

1808 trapping season, and when Lisa and some of his men left for St. Louis about the late summer or early fall of 1808, Ezekiel Williams seems to have gone down with them. It probably was not long after their arrival in St. Louis, about November 1, that Williams went to Kentucky and brought his eleven-year-old son Samuel to Missouri, but he was back in time to join one of the outfits going up the Missouri the following spring.[9]

Fur trading activities on the Missouri in the spring of 1809 were a sort of repetition of those in the spring of 1807, but on a larger scale. Williams probably went out with the St. Louis Missouri Fur Company party under Colonel Pierre Chouteau, Sr., consisting of 120 Missouri militiamen, including forty "Americans and expert riflemen," which the company, under a government contract, furnished to escort the Mandan sub-chief Shahaka, his interpreter, and their families (all of whom had come east with Lewis and Clark in 1806) to the Mandan villages, about 1500 miles upriver.[10]

Upon the delivery of the Indians, the men of the escort were expected to join about two hundred company trappers and traders who had moved upriver under the command of Lisa and Pierre Menard, partners in the company. The Chouteau contingent left St. Louis on May 17, 1809. While most of the party performed as crewmen on the barges, others were detailed as hunters. Some of the hunters had started out mounted, some, at frequent intervals, left the boats to hunt afoot. Ezekiel Williams seems to have been one of the horsemen, and often traveled far out on the plains for buffalo and elk.[11]

9 Oglesby, *op. cit.,* 54-55, 63, 85; interview with Mrs. Henry, who said Samuel was ten when brought to Missouri; however, his gravestone (see note 2) indicates he would have been nearly twelve. Walter B. Douglas, "Manuel Lisa," in *Collections,* Mo. Hist. Soc., III, no. 3 (1911), 257, said "Lisa left for St. Louis in July [1808, and] reached home on the fifth day of August." He gives no source; and Chittenden, *op. cit.,* I, p. 137, generally agrees.

10 Oglesby, *op. cit.,* 74-76; Chittenden, *op. cit.,* 138-39.

11 Oglesby, *op. cit.,* 75-77; James, *op. cit.,* 10-11, 17, 22-23, 25; Coyner gives no hint of boat travel, and only incidentally mentions the Missouri.

Nothing of importance occurred until the Mandan travelers reached home on September 24. The fur brigade continued on to a point on the west bank of the Missouri, about eleven miles above the mouth of the Knife River and near a Gros Ventre village. There, in good beaver country, they built Fort Mandan, later an important post; and during the 1809-1810 trapping season Williams and others probably worked the surrounding area.[12]

Some time in August 1810, a mounted party of some twenty men, including Williams, Jean Baptiste Champlain, and one Porteau left Fort Mandan and headed southwest. The records do not disclose the names of all who left the fort with Williams, nor do they state a firm destination. Their purpose, said Williams, was "to hunt," but it has been established that besides being beaver hunters they formed a probing finger of the ambitious Lisa, who cherished plans to trade with the Spanish settlements of the Southwest. All but Champlain's two employees were free trappers.[13]

Although Williams said they "journeyed south forty or fifty days" their course, soon after starting, was definitely southwest, probably along the Little Missouri toward the head of the Belle Fourche. They passed west of the Black Hills, turned south and crossed the North Platte, keeping east of the Laramie Mountains and the Front Range, and finally struck the Arkansas. There, in Arapaho country, they trapped during the fall, and wintered, 1810-1811.[14]

In the spring of 1811, said Williams, "the indians commenced robbing and harrassing [sic] our company in every quarter," indicating that their trapping parties were scat-

---

[12] James, *op. cit.*, 25-28.

[13] Williams to Charless, *loc. cit:* "In 1810 I went with the Fur Company up the Missouri, near the head of the river, where I hunted two years." The year, of course, is incorrect, and there are indications that the error may have been deliberate (see note 38); however, he had trapped two *seasons*, 1807-1808 and 1809-1810 and he was on the upper Missouri in 1810. He gives the time the twenty men started from Fort Mandan as August, 1812; it was in 1810. This shift also appears deliberate (see note 38). The dates in our text are based on outside sources. Oglesby, *op. cit.*, 131-32, 135.   [14] Williams to Charless, *loc. cit.*

tered. In June they retreated north to a rendezvous near the junction of the North Platte and the Sweetwater.[15]

There they held a council and decided to break up the party, half going west seeking to cross the Rocky Mountains, half, including Williams and Champlain, going "southward along the mountain." By following up the Sweetwater the west-bound trappers would have struck the east end of South Pass; by going south the Williams group would have headed directly toward the Spanish settlements in New Mexico.[16]

Williams and Champlain and their people traveled to a crossing of the Arkansas, where they "were [erroneously] informed by indians that the fort on the Missouri was broke up." But the Indians, probably Arapahos, undoubtedly referred to Fort Raymond, not Fort Mandan. Nevertheless, said Williams, "We now thought it impossible to return to the Missouri, we concluded to part again. Four of our company determined to find the Spanish settlements, six remained; Champlain his two hired men, two other Frenchmen and myself." [17]

In October 1811, they resumed trapping "in a cove in the mountains" (probably at the head of the Arkansas between the Front Range and the Sangre de Cristos). About November 1 one of Champlain's men and the two French free trappers were found dead. The survivors, now only Williams, Champlain and Porteau, "took protection among the Arapahow nation of indians; there we found the horses and equipment of our three men just killed. The head chief advised us as the only means to save our lives was to stay with him, which we did, and passed a wretched winter [1811-1812], filled with despair of ever being able to return home." [18]

---

15 *Ibid.* 16 *Ibid.* Had they some knowledge of South Pass?
17 *Ibid.* Indian hostility had caused the abandonment of Fort Raymond in the summer of 1811. Chittenden, *op. cit.*, II, p. 964. 18 Williams to Charless, *loc. cit.*

These Arapahos confirmed the abandonment of "Manuel's fort" and advised against returning northward. "I determined," said Williams, "to find white people or some place of safety or lose my life in the attempt." Champlain and Porteau elected to remain and work the Arapaho country. After diligent inquiry among the Indians, Williams decided to descend the Arkansas to the Osage country, a thousand miles downriver. His companions helped him build a canoe, and on March 1, 1812, after caching his furs and saying a tearful farewell, Williams started down the Arkansas.[19]

Trapping as he went, he reached the mouth of the Fontaine qui Bouille (Fountain Creek), his closest point to Santa Fe, some three hundred trail miles south. It must have been near the junction that he cached his furs and met "a Spaniard" who told him something about affairs in New Mexico. As a free lance Lisa agent, Williams would have taken advantage of these circumstances; so it seems reasonable to suggest that he journeyed into New Mexico, where he apparently remained from the summer of 1812 until the spring of 1813. While there he must have learned something about trade with that province, or rather the difficulty of it.[20]

About June 1, 1813, back on the Arkansas, Williams lifted his cache, and worked downriver to a point on the Big Bend of the Arkansas. There, on June 23 he "was taken by the Kansas," bound and robbed of his furs. A party of Osages and whites, hunting in the vicinity, learned of his plight and sent Daniel Larrison and Joseph Larivee [Larivier] with ten Osages to demand the release of the prisoner, but were refused. Early in August the Kansas left the Arkansas with the captive and returned northward to their village, from

---

[19] *Ibid.*

[20] *Ibid.* Williams to some one in St. Louis (probably Lisa or possibly George C. Sibley), *Missouri Gazette,* Oct. 9, 1813. For an explanation of the suggested excursion to New Mexico see note 38. An old trail came down to the mouth of the Fontaine qui Bouille, ran south over Raton Pass, and southwest to Santa Fe. However, for fear of arrest, Williams may have stopped short of Santa Fe.

which Williams by unspecified means sent a letter to some one (probably Lisa) in St. Louis. A summary of the letter, published in the *Missouri Gazette* on October 9, gave no information about Williams visit to New Mexico or his captivity.[21]

About August 15 the Kansas Indians restored part of Williams' furs and sent him toward home under escort. He went through the Osage country, and some time early in the fall of 1813 arrived at Cooper's Fort, on the east bank of the Missouri in the Boon's Lick country, about 120 river miles below Fort Osage.[22]

From the Kansas, Williams had learned that they planned a trip to Arrow Rock, just across the river from Cooper's Fort, to claim their annuities from George C. Sibley, Indian agent at Fort Osage. When the Kansas appeared in November, Sibley demanded and got all but one of Williams' fur packs; and by December 15 Williams was in St. Louis reporting to and settling up with Lisa, and visiting Governor William Clark, with whom, as a fellow explorer of the West, he had much to discuss.[23]

Williams returned immediately to the Boon's Lick, then suffering Indian incursions spurred by British agents. During the early months of 1814 he served as a ranger in the troubled area along and north of the Missouri River, with headquarters at Cooper's Fort. Meantime on January 14, 1814, he married Nancy Jones, a widow with six children.[24]

On May 16, 1814, Williams, Morris May, Braxton Cooper and "Philleber's Company" [Joseph Philibert's] of eighteen trappers started west to trap and lift the furs Wil-

21 Williams to Charless, *loc. cit.*; George C. Sibley to William Clark, Nov. 30, 1813. Williams to some one in St. Louis (see note 20). See Coyner, *op. cit.*, 118-20, for his version of the robbery and captivity; stripped of verbiage, it is close to the facts.

22 Williams to Charless, *loc. cit.*; Sibley to Clark, *loc. cit.*

23 Williams to Charless, *loc. cit.*; Voelker, *op. cit.*, 22, 25.

24 Voelker, *op. cit.*, 25-26.

liams had cached in the Arapaho country in February, 1812. When they arrived at the Arapaho village Williams inquired about Champlain and Porteau, whom he had left there. As a result of the evasive answers he got Williams called a council of the head men to discover what had become of his companions.[25]

He was told that soon after he had left them the trappers had started with a pack train of furs (eleven horses in all) for "the fort on the Missouri" (Lisa's Fort Mandan). They were spotted "on the road" by two Arapaho hunting parties, and that was the last the Arapahos had seen of them. However, said Williams, the Crows had told the Arapahos they had "seen two white-men dead in their camp," in Crow country, "which they believed were my companions." Williams said he "despaired now of ever finding them," and gave up the search.[26]

Some time in July Williams lifted "part" of his cache and, with Cooper, May, and Michael La Clair [Francois LeClerc], one of Philibert's men, loaded it into canoes and started down the Arkansas for Arkansas Post, a fur market far down near the mouth of the river. About 500 miles downriver low water stopped them and, again caching the furs, they returned afoot to Boon's Lick.[27]

There, said Williams, "sometime in the winter [around Christmas, 1814], I had information that my man La Clair had told of my fur, and that a company were about to start to steal it, to be piloted by said La Clair." Williams recruited Joseph and William Cooper and, prepared to do battle, set off to anticipate "the plunderers," but they did not appear and the Williams party remained on the Arkansas until the spring rise of 1815 enabled them to proceed to Arkansas Post.[28]

His adversaries, said Williams, "were employed by *cer-*

---

[25] *Ibid.*, 26, 31-32. [26] *Ibid.*, 31-32. [27] *Ibid.*, 26-27. [28] *Ibid.*, 27.

tain men in St. Louis," and had orders, if Williams succeeded in lifting and carrying off the furs, to waylay and, if necessary to get the furs, kill him and his men. The scheme aborted when Indians hired to assist the LeClerc outfit learned its real purpose and promptly deserted.[29]

Williams and the Coopers returned to Boon's Lick during the summer of 1815 amid sinister rumors that they had plundered a cache belonging to others, sold the furs to "a trader on White River" for several thousand dollars, and thus avoided St. Louis, where they would have been "detected and punished."[30]

It now becomes necessary to inquire into the ownership of Williams' various fur caches. There are no known legal documents which specifically set forth the conditions under which he worked during his association with the St. Louis Missouri Fur Company and with Manuel Lisa.

The *Missouri Gazette* called Williams "a principal hunter belonging to the Missouri Fur Company;" and Sibley, in an official paper said Williams, "a hunter of the Missouri Fur Company was on his way from the Rocky mountains with a considerable quantity of *their* Furs" when robbed, but referred to the recovered furs as "*his* property." However, there is no reason to doubt Williams' own 1816 statement that during the 1810-1815 period he was "on his own footing." Further, he hired his own men and found his own market.[31]

Williams appears always to have bought equipment and supplies with no obligation to sell his catch to his supplier. All his work for Lisa or the company was as an independent contractor and not as an employee. He sold his furs at Arkansas Post because it was by far the nearest, most convenient market to his cache (most important when threatened with robbery), and not because he was evading appre-

---

[29] *Ibid.*, 27-28.   [30] *Ibid.*, 28.
[31] *Ibid.*, 20, 25-27; Sibley to Clark; Williams to Charless, *loc. cit.*   Italics supplied.

hension in St. Louis. If Williams had collected for company furs without accounting to Lisa he would have invited that gentleman's prompt, effective reprisal. Nothing of the kind occurred, and there is nowhere a hint of a difference with Lisa.[32]

Williams was at Boon's Lick in midsummer, 1816, when he learned that the *Western Intelligencer* of Kaskaskia, Illinois, on July 9 had, on information furnished by "a gentlemen of respectability," accused him of the murder of Jean Baptiste Champlain and the theft of his furs. "He cooly & premeditately committed" murder "for the sake of lucre," said the *Intelligencer*.[33]

Several obvious but extremely damaging circumstances surrounding the newspaper article itself are sufficient to destroy its credibility: the name of Williams' accuser was never revealed; the article was printed outside Missouri, where it would have been more difficult and costly for Williams to reach and maintain suit against libelers; the article was never picked up by the *Missouri Gazette,* the "big" newspaper of the area, to which it certainly must have been news. Further, no criminal charges were ever filed against Williams as a result of the accusations.[34]

Equally damaging to the accuser are the fantastic details concerning the discovery of "Champlain's" body: it occurred *either* "2 or 3 months since," at *either* "25 or 30 miles from Boon's Lick settlement" (no direction given); the ghouls who broke into the "tomb" were unidentified; they found a sitting body dressed in a "uniform" with "a nice pair of epaulettes" and "U.S. buttons on his coat," and with a sword cane between the legs, the initials on which were J.M.C. *or* J.B.C.; and there were other incongruities.[35]

---

[32] No authentic record has been found of Williams' employment by anyone. Lisa's way with "deviators" was well known.

[33] Voelker, *op. cit.,* 29-30. Why the editor of the *Western Intelligencer* ever published the charges is one of the great mysteries of the western fur trade.

[34] *Ibid.,* 31.   [35] *Ibid.,* 32-33.

Williams answered "the enormous charges" in a long letter, dated August 17, 1816, to Joseph Charless, editor of the *Gazette,* in which he recounted what little he had learned from the Arapahos about Champlain's supposed death.[36]

Apparently Williams' only important error was chronological, and for its correction and for verification of Williams' statement that Champlain was killed high up the Arkansas we have an impartial and trustworthy source: Robert Stuart, the leader of the returning Astorians, who said, in 1813, that he had learned from the Shoshonis that the Arapahos themselves had murdered Champlain on the Arkansas River in the spring of 1812.[37]

Further confirmation of Champlain's death at the hands of Indians comes from another competent source: Charles Sanguinet, one of Lisa's men who took the field to search for Champlain, and wrote "a Letter dated the 3d instant [December, 1812], in which he confirmed the sad News of the hunters, he found none and was informed by the Arepaos [who were talking to white men!] that 3 of them [the hunters] were killed by the Blackfeet, supposed Champlain and 2 others." Thus, that Champlain was killed by Indians on the upper Arkansas in 1812 can hardly be doubted.[38]

In July, Williams, who, since 1814 had been managing

---

36 *Ibid.,* 31.　　　　　　37 *Ibid.,* 32.

38 *Ibid.,* 32. The time of Champlain's death is critical in determining elapsed time between that event in the spring of 1812, and the fall of 1813: a year and a half. Williams accounts for only six months, leaving a one-year hiatus. Hence, the suggested trip to New Mexico (see note 20); hence also the seemingly contrived discrepancy in Williams' year dates. (After mentioning the erroneous 1812 as the year he left Fort Mandan, he mentions no years, only seasons, months, and sometimes specific days.) Williams wrote his account in the summer of 1816, not quite three years after the events. It seems incredible that, after so short a time, he had forgotten his years.

Apparently here was some attempted cover-up. The summary of Williams' letter to some one in St. Louis (see note 20) revealed little except some knowledge of Mexican-American affairs in New Mexico. The letter itself probably told much more. A valid guess could be that the cover-up was for the benefit of Lisa, who apparently sought no publicity for his schemes toward New Mexico. Lisa thrived on pre-emption.

the estate of James Jones, whose widow he had married, was confirmed as its administrator, and about a year later became legal guardian of the five minor Jones children. Administering the estate was proving a sore trial for Williams. On February 17, 1817, Williams bought 270 acres of farm land in "Boonslick Bottom" on the north bank of the Missouri, a few miles above the new town of Franklin, Howard County, and about the same time he acquired a lot in Franklin. The entire bottom was subject to periodic overflow.[39]

For the next four years all we know about Ezekiel Williams is that he lived the life of a frontier Missouri countryman, farming, hunting, laying out roads, establishing ferries, serving on juries, and racing horses. He is described in November 1818, by a sojourner in Boon's Lick as "a hunter . . . one of the noblest of the human family." [40]

Felix Renick of Ohio, probably a distant kinsman, visited Williams in 1819, and years later described "Old Zeke" and his situation:

> He was then one of the most advanced settlers of the far west. We stopped with him several days . . . He was then living very comfortably on a good farm of his own, well improved in good frontier style, plenty of negroes to do his farm-work, a wife (a fine old lady to all appearance, who, we understood, had been a widow when he married her). He was a man for whom nature had done a good part, both in mind and body.
>
> While there we were treated, both by himself and wife, with true pioneer hospitality, and, best of all, was entertained with a full detail of all his previous and early adventures in the far west, which was . . . truly astonishing. We could hardly have given credit to his story, had it not been corroborated by colonel [Benjamin] Cooper, his neighbor at that time . . .[41]

Late in June 1821, William Becknell of Franklin proposed that an expedition of seventy men "destined to the westward for the purpose of trading for Horses & Mules

[39] Voelker, *op. cit.,* 29, 33-35.
[40] *Ibid.,* 34-38; Ludlow to Will, *loc. cit.*   [41] Voelker, *op. cit.,* 36-37.

and catching Wild Animals of every description" should meet and organize at Ezekiel Williams' farm on the following August 4. The meeting was attended by seventeen men, Becknell was elected captain, and the date of departure set at September 1, when only four men showed up to commence the march. Williams may well have been among them, but proof is lacking. The party reached Santa Fe, traded successfully, and Becknell and one McLaughlin were back in Franklin on January 29, 1822.[42]

When the first expedition of the Rocky Mountain Fur Company, commanded by Andrew Henry, passed Franklin on April 25, 1822, Williams, "who spent several years on the head waters of the Missouri, Arkansas and Colorado, said with confidence that [the Blackfeet] Indians would attack, rob and kill his [Henry's] hunting parties whenever they had an opportunity. He spoke from experience. . ."[43]

In the early 1820s repeated devastating floods on the Missouri caused Williams to seek higher ground in neighboring Cooper County. In November 1822, he bought two lots in Boonville, just across the river, and about the same time acquired some 165 acres seventeen miles southwest of town. By the middle of 1823 he was settled in Cooper County.[44]

Again, in July 1823, some unknown accuser brought a serious charge against Williams. A Cooper County grand jury produced a true bill finding that on January 1, 1800, Williams had married Margaret Thornton in Cumberland County, Kentucky; that said Margaret was still alive; that, nevertheless, on January 1, 1810, Williams feloniously married Polly Jones, spinster, in St. Charles County, Missouri Territory; that Ezekiel and "Polly" continue to live together as man and wife"; all of which amounted to bigamy.[45]

Because it was easy for Williams to prove that the identical month and day for each alleged marriage rendered that

---

[42] *Ibid.*, 39. [43] *Ibid.*, 40. [44] *Ibid.*, 41. [45] *Ibid.*, 41-42.

charge spurious on its face; that he married no one in 1800
or 1810; that his present wife was not a spinster when he
married her in 1814; that her name was not Polly (a nickname for Mary); that many people in the Boon's Lick
country knew the truth and no doubt were ready to testify to
it; and that the said Margaret never appeared; Williams
had no trouble having the case dismissed at the March 1824
term of court.[46]

Perhaps presaging another move, Williams bought a lot
in the new, unsurveyed town of Rocheport, Boone County,
in November 1825, but apparently made no use of it. On
December 6, after twelve involved years, the Jones estate
was finally settled and Williams, as administrator, discharged.[47]

On May 15, 1827, a company of about 105 men met at the
previously appointed rendezvous, Blue Springs, immediately south of Independence, Missouri, to perfect the organization of a trading caravan of fifty-three wagons and
"pleasure carriages" bound for Santa Fe, New Mexico. The
train was "the largest which had traversed this route [the
Santa Fe Trail]." Ezekiel Williams was chosen captain and
doubled as a "commander of guards." That it was a most
successful enterprise was demonstrated when sixty men of
the party, with their wagons, returned to Missouri about
September 30 with 800 horses and mules worth about
$28,000; and the profits of the expedition were calculated
at about forty per cent, net.[48]

Williams' movements in 1828 and 1829 are difficult to
trace. Indications are that he was out on the trails most of
the time. It was a period of greatly increased activity in the
Santa Fe trade, and many of the traders were almost continually on the march. Court records indicate that Williams
was at home from October 1829, to February 1830. Before

[46] *Ibid.,* 42.   [47] *Ibid.,* 42.   [48] *Ibid.,* 43.

1831 arrived Williams, now in his middle fifties, had made some money from his western ventures, and about the latter part of 1830 decided to devote most of his time to farming; he also felt it time to change his location.[49]

Some time between the fall of 1830 and the spring of 1831 he moved his family, goods, and herds to a remote Ozark foothill wilderness in a corner of sprawling Cooper County, and finally settled on what naturally became Williams Creek, at a point centering about four miles southwest of Cole Camp. There he spent the rest of his life. An old trail called the "Old Road," soon to become the important Boonville-Springfield Road, ran past his cabin door, bringing travelers whom Williams sometimes entertained.[50]

In January 1833, Williams' corner of Cooper County became part of the new Pettis County; and early in 1835 the neighborhood became the northeast corner of the new Benton County, of which Williams was said to have been the first Anglo-Saxon settler. On February 16, 1835, the first act of the first county court was to grant Ezekiel Williams a "grocer's" (saloonkeeper's) license; and at the same court session the township of Williams was laid off, the court emphatically noting that "The Township of Williams is so called in honor of Ezekiel Williams Esqr resident therein"; Williams' house was designated as a polling place, and Williams named a judge for township elections. Soon after that Cole Camp postoffice was established at Williams' house, and he appears to have served for a while as postmaster.[51]

Late in 1839 Williams acquired title to the 320 acres previously entered and which he now cultivated and called his "prairie farm." He also owned the 120-acre home place on Williams Creek. In May 1842, he sold "a parcel of land" to the trustees of the local Methodist Episcopal Church. It became the site of a church and cemetery. At first the latter

49 *Ibid.*, 43-44.   50 *Ibid.*, 44-45.   51 *Ibid.*, 46-47.

was called "the Williams grave yard," but now is known as Union Cemetery.[52]

Williams was comfortably situated with many possessions lacking in most Benton County farm homes of his day. His farm was well stocked and equipped, his house was well furnished and had a bookcase with a small library of works on such serious subjects as history, geography, religion and the law. Somewhere around, too, were Zeke's "rifle gun," saddle and saddle bags, and, very likely, his "old musty mutilated journal" in which he had kept a record of sorts of his western adventures.[53]

Probably late in 1842, Felix Renick, Ezekiel Williams' 1819 Ohio visitor, thought of getting some of Zeke's stories put on paper, and amplifying them with what other relevant material he could get. But if Renick's long distance efforts appear fruitless, they actually may have provided the idea and the machinery that produced David H. Coyner's *The Lost Trappers*. Coyner, who knew some of Zeke's friends, almost certainly met Zeke during the early 1840s.[54]

On December 20, 1844, Ezekiel Williams was very ill, and feeling he was about to die, called in four of his neighbors and signed his will, bequeathing all his property to his wife Nancy and his son Samuel. On December 24 he died. He was buried in Union Cemetery. On June 30, 1963, a handsome monument, erected to his memory by his descendants, was dedicated at the grave site.[55]

[52] *Ibid.,* 47-48.   [53] *Ibid.,* 49-50.   [54] *Ibid.,* 50. (See also note 41).
[55] *Ibid.,* 50-51; *Sedalia* (Mo.) *Democrat,* June 26, 1963; *Lincoln* (Mo.) *New Era,* July 4, 1963. The writer was accorded the honor of delivering the memorial address, and formally dedicating the monument.

George C. Yount

by CHARLES L. CAMP
University of California, Berkeley

In the years after the close of the Revolution, emigrant backwoods families, as well as wandering hunters and adventurers poured across the Alleghanies seeking to expand their energies and fortunes in new lands. Most of them had just enough taste of frontier life to want more. So the great westward movement developed. The large Jacob Yount family was one unit in this throng of trans-Alleghany pioneers. They kept on moving west in 1804 until they became among the earliest of the trans-Mississippi settlers.

Jacob Yount's farm on Dowden Creek, Burke County, North Carolina, had been the home for himself, his wife, Amarilla, and their eleven children. Among these was George, a sturdy, blond boy of ten, born on the Carolina farm on May 4, 1794. Jacob's grandparents, Hans George and Anna Marie Jundt had come to Pennsylvania from Alsace in 1731 "to escape despotism and opression." Jacob's father, John, had changed the spelling of the family name to Yount and the descendants to this day maintain the original German pronunciation, though but few others do.

After crossing the Mississippi into Missouri, the migrant Yount family stayed for a time in the vicinity of Cape Girardeau. A few months later they packed up again and moved into unsettled country farther west, near White River in a dangerous frontier where it was necessary to post guards at the corners of the fields and set up constant vigilance against Indian raids. George grew up among these rugged surroundings, became expert with his rifle and the techniques of running a frontier farm. There was but little chance for schooling for anybody and none at all for George. He never learned to read and write, but he did train and improve a splendid memory which enabled him to repeat conversations he had heard years before. He did finally learn painfully to scratch out his signature, and to use it sometimes when he wished he hadn't. Unfortunately his lack of schooling accompanied an over-generous nature, too trusting of those who would try to fleece him.

George with an elder brother, Jacob, took an active part in the War of 1812 in the hinterland. He was twice called up, once to Cap-au-Gris, where a future trapping companion, Lt. Sylvester Pattie was also serving. After these stirring times he started a farm of his own, drove stock and found time to court and marry Eliza Wilds, a young girl from Kentucky. They prospered for several years until George foolishly placed his life savings into the hands of a neighbor for "safekeeping." These funds mysteriously disappeared. George's father-in-law became concerned over the competence of Eliza's husband. Ill feeling developed and George went off to engage himself as a teamster on the long road to Santa Fe. He arrived there in the autumn of 1826 evidently in the same caravan as the runaway boy, Kit Carson.

At Santa Fe the trading had slacked off. The Mexicans seem to have spent most of their savings on the goods brought in the previous season by the first cargo trains. The commerce of the prairies had hit an economic low, but beaver trapping had extended into the Gila and Colorado country (southwestern Arizona) the previous year. George joined a party of these trappers, fitted out by Ewing Young, a man of some experience in the region. The country they entered, along the headwaters of Gila and Salt rivers, was infested by Coyotero Apaches who had harassed, robbed and driven out a trapping party the previous season. In this early party were some men, the Patties, S. Stone, Alexander K.

Branch, Milton Sublette and Thomas L. Smith (later known as Peg-leg), most of whom joined Young and Yount at the copper mines of Santa Rita in this fall of 1826.

Still in the field was a party of French trappers under Michel (Miguel) Robidoux who had moved in with the Papago-Pima Indians at their village on the Gila. Unaccountably and foolishly, Robidoux had permitted liberties with these normally peaceful people. In consequence his party was exterminated in a horrible night massacre and Robidoux himself barely escaped. The Young-Yount party came on this scene a few days later, buried the remains of the poor Frenchmen, found their traps still in the river and set about giving the Pimas a royal thrashing. They have been pretty good Indians ever since.

From here, in the vicinity of present Avondale, Arizona, the trappers scattered in various directions, up the tributaries of the Gila and Salt rivers. Young and Yount worked their way down the Gila to the Colorado where they made dugout canoes of cottonwood logs and trapped up to the Mohave villages. They even visited the ancient salt mines along the lower Virgin River, needing the salt to preserve their beaver skins.

At the Mohave villages, the Pattie men and Tom Smith separated from Young-Yount, Milt Sublette and the rest. They didn't get along too well, and Tom Smith had an especial dislike for Ewing Young. At all events the Patties tried going out southeast, went down into Spencer Creek Canyon evidently and lost three men who had separated to trap there. The Indians killed them, cut the bodies to pieces and roasted them. Yount later said that the leader of this murdered party was one "Burr." Was this the "E. Bure" (Du Breuil?) of the Narbona documents?

Pattie and his associates tried to go on westward after this encounter but they didn't get far on account of the vertical cliffs of the lower Grand Canyon. Becoming disgusted with "those horrible mountains" they evidently turned back, crossed over the Colorado and went up the Virgin River Valley and as far as the Sevier, leaving the tracks observed by Jed Smith that summer (1827).

Young's party with Yount meanwhile had packed up their bundles of beaver fur and gone across a barren country to Zuñi Pueblo. They landed at Taos only to have their entire fur catch confiscated by the Mexican authorities. Yount found himself destitute again but this reinforced his determination eventually to succeed. Realizing what a wealth of beaver lay along the lower Colorado, he organized a party of twenty-four men for the fall (1827) hunt. His party again included the eight Pattie men although this doesn't seem to have been very sensible. William Workman is sometimes mentioned as the leader and (Hiram?) Allen, "of Mohave notoriety." This was the same Allen who had been with Ashley on the Missouri in 1823. He is also mentioned by Pattie along the Gila in 1826. And he is one of those who confirmed the Hugh Glass story when Glass told it to George Yount. Glass, Allen and Yount may have been together there in Arizona either in the spring or fall of 1827.

Pattie's men and dates have been questioned. There actually seems to be a fair record of both. His men were Nathaniel Pryor, Richard Laughlin, Jesse Ferguson, Isaac Slover, William Pope and Edmund Russell. All these evidently separated from Young, Workman and Allen on the Gila, went down to the Colorado and across Baja California to San Diego, California, where Sylvester Pattie died in a Mexican jail. Pattie mentions a "Dutchman" at this period, who could scarcely be anyone but George Yount, as there were no Germans in his detachment. Yet this Dutchman appears at a time in his story when George Yount was not present.

As to the accuracy of Pattie's dates, an article in the *St. Louis Times*, July 7, 1829, which gives the names of his

California party also says that they left Santa Fe on August 18, 1827, bound for the Gila, which agrees with the date given by Pattie except that his date is given erroneously as 1826. It seems that Pattie's editor must have had a memorandum of dates which may be accepted for the time he was with Yount where the dates are a year too early on nearly every count.

After the separation on the Gila, the Yount detachment went on down to the Colorado delta, thence up river again to Mohave land and further difficulty with that nation who had recently massacred Jed Smith's second party at its crossing of the Colorado. Something had turned these Indians against the whites. The Young party found themselves in overwhelming danger. The slick Mohaves were entreating them to come to their village and enjoy the charms of a "beautiful squaw" they had captured from Jed Smith's party. This was a little too obvious for Allen to swallow. He turned the men homeward as fast as possible out of the Circean clutches and temptations. On the way they followed the "trail" or tracks of the Patties the previous spring. This evidently led them into Spencer Canyon, scene of the Burr massacre. One man who had "been with Burr" was with them again this year. He wanted to raise some packs of fur he had cached in the canyon. But the steep cliffs along this route were just as difficult for the Younts as for the Patties. They tried all sorts of ways of boosting their animals along with ropes, and after nearly starving they finally went south to the uplands near San Francisco Peak, crossed the Little Colorado at Grand Falls, visited Hopi Land and eventually found their way back to Zuñi again in an exhausted state.

During a brief stay at Workman's (?) Taos distillery in the summer of 1828, George Yount managed by trickery or some sort of smuggling operation to keep his fur catch from confiscation. He made at least enough on it to pay his debts at Taos and organize another trapping venture for the vast

regions to the north, the middle branches of the great Colorado. In his dictated narrative he is not clear about the year
of this trip. It surely took place in the fall and winter of
1828. They met the Ceran St. Vrain ("Savery") party while
camped on the Green and they encountered one of the worst
winters on record (1828-29) in the region of the Great Salt
Lake. They holed up in Bear Valley when they found their
way blocked by ten-foot snow drifts. Yount froze his feet
and had many noteworthy adventures.

Perhaps they stayed over and spent the next winter also in
the same vicinity since it must have been here that Yount
met Jed Smith's man, Arthur Black, who had returned from
Oregon in the spring of 1830. From Yount's story, Black
was retailing stories of Jed Smith's discovery of gold in
California with other tales of the land which seem to have
set up an eternal fire in the adventurous soul of George
Yount. The gold stories were probably whole-cloth fakes
but the fact seems to be that Yount saw Black that spring
or summer (1830) and there is no evidence that Black ever
came down to Taos.

Yount's visit to California may have been encouraged too
by the divorce proceedings that were being advertised in the
Missouri papers in the winter of 1829-30. Communication
with his family was never vigorous, had now broken down
entirely and messages were being intercepted at the distaff
end of the line, or so thought George.

Making preparations for a long journey he returned to
Taos, or at least as far as Abiquiu, where he and members
of his party joined William Wolfskill's trappers westbound
along the Old Spanish Trail in the fall of 1830. This great
expedition to California, by a route largely untraveled, was
the most difficult, extended and important one of Yount's
ubiquitous career, a regular odyssey.

The route came to be known as the summer (or northern)
variant of the Old Spanish Trail. The southern (or winter)

variant of that trail had been traveled part-way by Esca-
lante, and was completely traversed by the Mexican trader,
Antonio Armijo who made a journey over it from Santa Fe
to Los Angeles in 1829-30. Jedediah Smith was the first to
travel along the westward extension of the trail through
central Utah into California in 1826 and again in 1827.

Smith must have left a barely traceable track followed
by Wolfskill and Yount until they reached Clear Creek
branch of the Sevier River. Here they failed to turn to the
right and instead went on up the main river toward where
Panguitch, Utah now lies. Here they found themselves on
one of the high plateaux, marooned in a violent mid-winter
storm and bitter cold at an elevation of some 10,000 feet.
They came down from these heights toward present Cedar
City and Little Salt Lake in a fairyland of plentiful game.
Reaching the Mohave villages they intimidated the Indians
by a clever show of force: a little brass cannon mounted on
a pack-saddle. Later expeditions avoided the river route
entirely and cut off through the desert where Las Vegas is
now.

They paid their respects to Father Sanchez at San Gabriel
Mission. He welcomed them cordially despite their rough,
battered appearance, just as he had welcomed Jedediah
Smith in years before. Yount was impressed with the size
and organization of the great missionary establishment, and
the missionaries were equally astonished at Yount's expert
marksmanship. This skill was put to good account some
weeks later when he took up sea-otter hunting at Santa
Barbara. The trick was to shoot the otters when they popped
their heads out of water to breathe; all this from a small
boat in rough water. Kanakas went along to dive over and
retrieve the otters before they sank.

Yount adapted the idea of the trappers' bull boat to this
work, using the hides of sea elephants. He coasted Santa
Cruz Island in one of these and used larger boats for trips

to the more southern islands, even far down off the coast of Baja California. Continuing the pursuit of otter and beaver in San Francisco Bay and the Sacramento delta, Yount and George Nidever rescued a tiny starving Indian child, abandoned during an epidemic of cholera. George Yount raised the little girl and she eventually married another Indian.

George Yount visited Sonoma, made himself useful to the missionaries and especially so to General Vallejo. He split out shakes ("shingles") and roofed one of Vallejo's new houses and he took charge of Sonoma Mission for a short time, thus ingratiating himself. Through the good offices of his new friends he secured a large grant of land near the head of Napa Valley. To obtain title legally he was required to become a Mexican citizen and to be baptized a Catholic. He then received the baptismal name of George de la Concepcion Yount, and he rarely, if ever, used this middle name. Incidentally, it was the only middle name he ever had although the name "Calvert" has been ascribed by error.

When he received his grant it was expected that he was to assist in defending the northern frontier against raids by wild Indians. Accordingly, he responded to early calls from Vallejo to join punitive expeditions to Russian River and into Lake County. While chasing the wild Hoter ("Jota") band in Pope Valley, Yount had two horses shot out from under him, his cap shot off and he barely escaped with his life.

At his famous Napa ranch, Yount had built a Kentucky style block house, a big log-adobe house the next year, a saw mill and a flour mill, the first of their kind to be found in the region. He raised stock, introduced grain and other crops, became famous as a vineyardist and pioneer fruit and berry farmer. He was the first white man to establish himself so far from civilization in California and the first white settler in Napa Valley.

In 1855, five years after the death of his divorced wife, he

married Mrs. Eliza Gashwiler, the widow of a minister
from New York State. She took over the management of
affairs that rapidly grew too complicated for him to handle
properly. Open-handed and liberal in offering help to
strange travelers, he was often imposed upon. Miscreant
squatters ("campers") took over and refused to be ousted.
Thieves stole stock and fruit. The primitive courts were
slow in giving relief. He had as many as seventeen court
cases against the squatters pending at one time.

The first overland emigrant families came with the Bid-
well-Bartleson party in 1841. Among those were old friends
and neighbors from Missouri, including Joseph B. Chiles
who planned to go back the next year. Yount asked him to
bring the Yount family out to California. Eliza would not
leave her new husband but the two daughters came, leaving
Robert, the son, behind. After Robert's early death, his
widow and her daughter came out and lived on the Yount
farm.

Yount took no part in the Bear Flag revolt, respecting the
rights of his hosts the Mexican authorities. At the same time
he held the respect of the American settlers, having gone
their bonds and done other favors. His home became a
famous center for trail-worn hunters, emigrants and settlers
in the days before the Gold Rush. He was blessed for his
hospitality and kindness to such waifs as the destitute child
survivors of the Donner Party who had special reason to
love and honor him.

Many were led to believe that Yount's dreams were influ-
ential in the rescue of the Donners. He no doubt had heard
of the plight of that party and his dreams may have stimulated him to speed assistance. His credence of dreams and
omens dated from his childhood associates in Missouri who
were superstitious about such things as comets and earth-
quakes. He also had some imaginary gold mines. His religious feelings were strong, influenced by the local Protestant

ministers. He became a prominent Mason, Bible bearer for the Yountville chapter. He donated the plot for the Yountville cemetery, in which he is buried, and he contributed to various churches. He died at his ranch on October 5, 1865, at the age of 71. His monument is carved to represent phases of his life as a hunter, trapper, farmer and pioneer. There were many famous pioneers at Napa and Sonoma and Yount was regarded as the most famous of them all. Yount's portrait appears in this volume at page 24.

George Yount was known under various names. Peg-leg Smith called him "Dutch George," James Pattie evidently referred to him as the "Dutchman" and quotes some alleged humorous remarks. In some of the Southwestern reminiscences he is identified as "Captain Youtz" and "Captain Buckskin." His uncompleted "Memoirs" cover the first thirty years of his life. A more complete story is the "narrative" dictated to the Rev. Orange Clark in 1855. This was edited by me under the title "The Chronicles of George C. Yount" from manuscripts now largely in the Huntington Library and published at Denver by Old West Publishing Co., 1966. References to other material on the life and times of this renowned pioneer may be found in my book.

*The tenth and final volume of this series will
provide an index to the biographies
and introductory materials in
all volumes of the work.*

The Series—

THE MOUNTAIN MEN AND THE FUR TRADE OF THE FAR WEST is a project comprising nine text volumes averaging over 400 pages each, containing carefully prepared biographies of some three hundred Mountain Men. The nine volumes have been issued during the years 1965-1972, and completion of the series is anticipated in 1972 with the publication of the index as volume 10.

Eighty-four scholars have cooperated in the project through their signed contributions of biographical sketches of participants in the fur trade drama. The biographies run from one to thirty-five pages each, depending on the importance of the subject and the available source materials. Each sketch gives not only the subject's experience as a fur man, but a brief account of his full life span, to the extent that dependable information can be found.

Illustrations in the set include portraits of 126 of the men who are subjects of biographical sketches, and forty-five other pertinent illustrations – many of which, the portraits in particular, are most difficult to find. Volume 1 includes a specially prepared two-color map of the fur-trade area.

The regions of exploration and activity include the present states of California, Oregon, Washington, Idaho, Montana, Wyoming, Nevada, Utah, Colorado, Arizona, New Mexico, the Dakotas, Kansas, Nebraska, Missouri, Oklahoma, and Iowa, as well as the Provinces of southwest Canada.

Subscription orders for the entire series may be placed, or individual volumes may be ordered as each is published. The publisher will furnish descriptive material or other detailed information on request.